Fodor's

BERKELEY

Critical acclaim for the Berkeley Guides

"[The Berkeley Guides are] brimming with useful information for the low-budget traveler—material delivered in a fresh, funny, and often irreverent way." —*The Philadelphia Inquirer*

"The [Berkeley Guides] are deservedly popular because of their extensive coverage, entertaining style of writing, and heavy emphasis on budget travel...If you are looking for tips on hostels, vegetarian food, and hitchhiking, there are no books finer." —*San Diego Union-Tribune*

"Straight dirt on everything from hostels to look for and beaches to avoid to museums least likely to attract your parents... they're fresher than Harvard's Let's Go series." —*Seventeen*

"The [Berkeley Guides] give a rare glimpse into the real cultures of Europe, Canada, Mexico, and the United States...with in-depth historical backgrounds on each place and a creative, often poetical style of prose." —*Eugene Weekly*

"More comprehensive, informative and witty than Let's Go." —*Glamour*

"The Berkeley Guides have more and better maps, and on average, the nuts and bolts descriptions of such things as hotels and restaurants tend to be more illuminating than the often terse and sometimes vague entries in the Let's Go guides." —*San Jose Mercury News*

"These well-organized guides list can't-miss sights, offbeat attractions and cheap thrills, such as festivals and walks. And they're fun to read." —*New York Newsday*

"Written for the young and young at heart...you'll find this thick, fact-filled guide makes entertaining reading." —*St. Louis Dispatch*

"Bright articulate guidebooks. The irreverent yet straight-forward prose is easy to read and offers a sense of the adventures awaiting travelers off the beaten path." —*Portland Oregonian*

budget guides

On the Loose
On the Cheap
Off the Beaten Path

THE BERKELEY GUIDES

Fodor's BERKELEY budget guides

london '97

On the Loose
On the Cheap
Off the Beaten Path

WRITTEN BY BERKELEY STUDENTS IN COOPERATION WITH
THE ASSOCIATED STUDENTS OF THE UNIVERSITY OF CALIFORNIA

THE BERKELEY GUIDE TO LONDON

Editor: Maureen Klier
Managing Editors: Tara Duggan, Kristina Malsberger, Sora Song
Executive Editor: Sharron Wood
Map Editor: Robert Blake
Creative Director: Fabrizio La Rocca
Cartographers: David Lindroth, Inc.; Eureka Cartography
Text Design: Tigist Getachew
Cover Design: Fabrizio La Rocca
Cover Art: Poul Lange (3-Dart), David Levenson/Black Star (photo in frame), Paul D'Innocenzo (still life)
Cover Photo: David Levenson/Blackstar

SPECIAL SALES

Contents

What the Berkeley Guides Are All About

Five years ago, a motley bunch of U.C. Berkeley students launched a new series of guidebooks—*The Berkeley Guides.* Since then, we've been busy writing and editing 13 books to destinations across the globe, from California, Mexico, and Central America to Europe and Eastern Europe. Along the way our writers have weathered bus plunges, rabies, and guerrilla attacks, landed bush planes above the Arctic Circle, gotten lost in the woods (proverbially and literally), and broken bread with all sorts of peculiar characters—from Mafia dons and Hell's Angel bikers to matronly B&B proprietors who insist you eat your stewed tomatoes. And don't forget about the train station sleep-ins, voodoo bus schedules, and gut-wrenching ferry trips across the English Channel.

Coordinating the efforts of 65 U.C. Berkeley writers back at the office is an equally daunting task (have you ever tried to track manuscript from Morocco?). But that's the whole point of *The Berkeley Guides*: to bring you the most up-to-date info on prices, the latest budget-travel trends, the newest hostels and clubs, tips on where to catch your next train—all written and edited by people who know what cheap travel is all about.

You see, it's one of life's weird truisms that the more cheaply you travel, the more you inevitably experience. If you're looking for five-star meals, air-conditioned tour buses, and reviews of the same old tourist traps, you're holding the wrong guidebook. Instead, *The Berkeley Guides* give you an in-depth look at local culture, detailed coverage of small towns and off-beat sights, bars and cafés where tourists rarely tread, plus no-nonsense practical info that deals with the real problems of real people (where to get aspirin at 3 AM, where to launder those dirty socks).

Coming from a community as diverse as Berkeley, we also wanted our guides to be useful to everyone, so we tell you if a place is wheelchair accessible, if it provides resources for gay and lesbian travelers, and if it's safe for women traveling solo. Many of us are Californians, which means most of us like trees and mountain trails. It also means we emphasize the outdoors in every *Berkeley Guide* and include lots of info about hiking and tips on protecting the environment.

Most important, these guides are for travelers who want to see more than just the main sights. We find out what local people do for fun, where they go to eat, drink, dance the night away, or just hang out. Most guidebooks lead you down the tourist trail, ignoring important local issues, events, and culture. In *The Berkeley Guides* we give you the information you need to understand what's going on around you, whether it's the latest on the redevelopment of the Docklands or another royal scandal.

We've done our best to make sure the information in *The Berkeley Guides* is accurate, but time doesn't stand still: Prices change, places go out of business, currencies get devalued. Call ahead when it's really important, and try not to get too stressed out.

Thanks to You

Putting together a guidebook that covers all of London is no easy task. From figuring out the British Museum to getting the lowdown on the clubbing scene, our writers and editor relied on helpful souls along the way. We'd like to thank the following people—as well as the hundreds of others whom our writers met briefly on the streets, on the Underground, in museums and pubs, and in strange unprintable places—for their advice and encouragement. We would like you to help us update this book and give us feedback. Drop us a line—a postcard, a note scrawled on a piece of toilet paper, whatever, and we'll be sure to pass on your tips to future writers. Our address is 515 Eshleman Hall, University of California, Berkeley, CA 94720.

Special thanks go to David Albarran at The Country Club (London), "Doy-Doy" Allan (Istanbul), Beth Ann (San Francisco), Maria Avino at Candid Arts Trust (Islington), Jay Bestmann (London), Clive and Merry Bolton (Lyme), Joan Bristow (Rye), Simon Brooks (Nottingham), Kate Caldwell (Oxford), Michael Copeman (Clapham), Thomas Day (San Francisco), An and Del Delaney (Edmonds), the Discover Islington Centre (Islington), Kathleen Dodge (Berkeley), Mr. and Mrs. Dorta at Arosfa Hotel (Bloomsbury), Karen Durham-Diggins at Cyberia (London), Toby Ellison (Sennen), Paul Evans (Cardiff), Lisa Fagan at Surrey County Cricket Club (London), Ed Fox at Tower of London (London), Natalie Gibson at the Sportsline (London), Mai Gray (London), Andrew Halstead (London), Richard Halstead and everyone else at Keildon Road (London), Sir Ronald Halstead (London), Hilary Hurt, Lynsey Gemmell, and Moriah Thomason (Berkeley), Ed Jones (Portsmouth), Mark Jones (Cirencester), Nick Jones (Birmingham), Matt Kumma (Seattle), Mrs. Marazzi at St. Margaret's Hotel (Bloomsbury), John McDonald (Portland), Ethel and Joanne McGrath (Buffalo), Laura McLachlan (Wimbledon), Scott McNeely (Istanbul), Lady McTaggart (Chelsea), David Munro (San Francisco), Irene Nexica (Berkeley), Michael Nosh (Chelsea), Claire Pack (Shrewsbury), Ros Price (Lyme), Jennifer Renk (San Francisco), Pat Riedman (Chicago), Graham Roden at London Zoo (London), Lindsey Schram (Berkeley), Christina Schwenkel (Irvine), Heather Siglin (London), Aria and Chris Smith (Berkeley), Natasha Smith (Henley), Suzanne Stein (San Francisco), Mr. and Mrs. Taafe (Salisbury), Maureen and David Turnbull (Bucks), Matt Vandenberg (San Francisco), Doll Vollmer (New York City), Kathie and Ed Vollmer (New Canaan, CT), Roger Walkden (Dover), Richard Wallen (New York City), Gene and Dean Ween (New Hope), Ania Wertz (Berkeley), everyone at the Westend Launderette (Pwllheli), Sharron Wood (San Francisco), Eddie Wu (Bath).

We'd also like to thank the Random House folks who helped us with cartography, page design, and production: Steven Amsterdam, Bob Blake, Judy Blumenberg, Denise DeGennaro, Tigist Getachew, Fabrizio La Rocca, and Linda Schmidt.

Berkeley Bios

Behind every restaurant blurb, write-up, lodging review, and introduction in this book lurks a student writer. You might recognize the type—perpetually short on time, money, and clean clothes. Two writers spent the summer in London researching and writing this book. Every two weeks they sent their manuscript back to Berkeley, where a frazzled editor whipped, squashed, and pummeled it into shape.

The Writers

Jennifer L. Brewer discovered the following categories in the London *Yellow Pages,* en route to looking up other things: Boring, Damp Proofing, Muno & Shoddy Mfrs., Mushroom Growers. So utterly foreign, this England! Undaunted, she trundled off to Hungary to write a chapter for *The Berkeley Guide to Europe,* before continuing onward to Turkey, Jordan, Pakistan, China, Uzbekistan, India, Nepal, and Tibet. She will perform the entire trip using only two pairs of pants, one "Teach Yourself Hindi" book, one pocket Nietzsche, and a single prescription of Ciprofloxacin.

After coediting the 1996 editions of *The Berkeley Guide to London* and *The Berkeley Guide to Great Britain and Ireland,* **Sunny Delaney** resolved not to spend another summer trapped inside the Berkeley Guides office in Eshleman Hall and leapt at the chance to write the 1997 London guide. She enjoyed herself at cricket matches, sang and chanted with her fellow England fans in Euro 96, drank countless pints of cider while researching pubs, lost countless hours of sleep while researching clubs, made herself ill by eating eels, and wore the soles off two pairs of shoes. In real life Sunny is working on a Ph.D. in British History at U.C. Berkeley and hoping for more funding to return to her favorite archive (and pub) in London.

After trekking halfway across the backroads of Asia, **Dino Asvaintra** thought genteel England would be a civilized excursion. He was quickly set right after being kidnapped by a band of renegade Cornish surfers, made to participate in a ritual Druidic sacrifice at Stonehenge, and hounded by packs of wild dogs in Dartmoor. Although these incidents were merely figments of an overactive literary imagination, he was, nevertheless, set back by the fact that pulse-dial phones are still all the rage.

Having spent most of her life traveling in search of sunnier climes, **Paula Turnbull** found it refreshing to explore her native Britain. Top moments involved a party in a launderette and a rather chilly midnight dip in the Irish Sea, while low moments presented more challenges to her sanity than a sizable serving of British beef. Paula is happy to retire the services of her trusty earplugs and backpack and would welcome any offers to review luxury hotels of the world.

The Editor

Editor **Maureen Klier** still doesn't understand the idea of royalty.

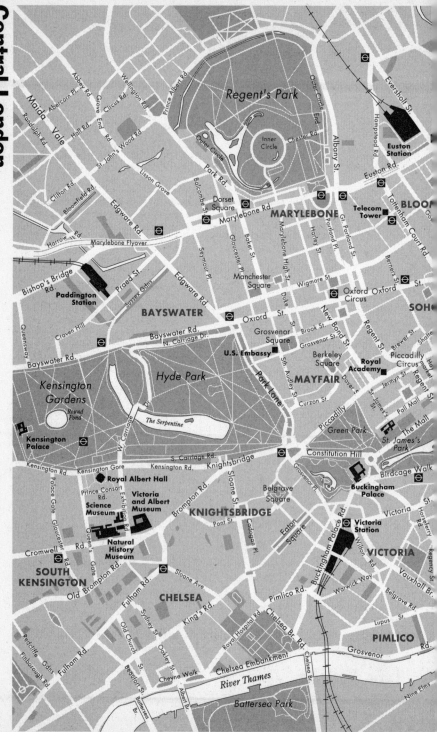

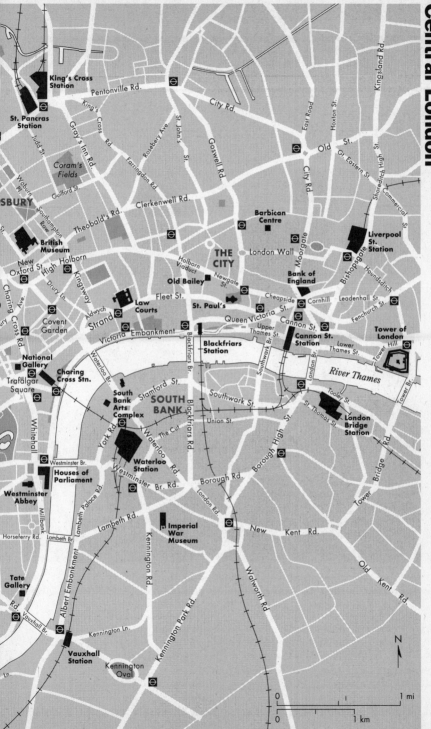

King's Cross
Station

St. Pancras
Station

Pentonville Rd.

King's Cross Rd.

Gray's Inn Rd.

Judd St.

Woburn Pl.

Southampton Row

Guilford St.

Coram's
Fields

SBURY

British
Museum

New
Oxford St.

High Holborn

Drury Ln.

Kingsway

Aldwych

Covent
Garden

Strand

Charing Cross Rd.

National
Gallery

Charing
Cross Stn.

Trafalgar
Square

Whitehall

Houses of
Parliament

Westminster
Abbey

Westminster Br.

Millbank

Horseferry Rd.

Lambeth Br.

Lambeth Palace Rd.

Tate
Gallery

Rd.

Vauxhall Br.

Albert Embankment

Vauxhall
Station

Kennington Ln.

Kennington
Oval

Kennington Park Rd.

Kennington Rd.

Lambeth Rd.

Westminster Br. Rd.

York Rd.

Waterloo
Station

South Bank
Arts
Complex

SOUTH
BANK

The Cut

Stamford St.

Blackfriars Rd.

Union St.

Southwark St.

Borough Rd.

London Rd.

Imperial
War
Museum

Walworth Rd.

New   Kent   Rd.

Borough High St.

St. Thomas St.

London
Bridge
Station

Tooley St.

River Thames

Tower
Bridge Rd.

Old   Kent   Rd.

King's Cross Rd.

Rosebery Ave.

St. John's St.

Farringdon Rd.

Clerkenwell Rd.

Theobald's Rd.

Holborn
Viaduct

Old Bailey

Fleet St.

Law
Courts

Victoria Embankment

Blackfriars Br.

Blackfriars
Station

Waterloo Br.

City Rd.

Goswell Rd.

Newgate
St.

St. Paul's

Queen Victoria St.

Upper
Thames St.

Southwark Br.

Cannon St.
Station

London Br.

Lower
Thames St.

THE CITY

London Wall

Barbican
Centre

Moorgate

Bank of
England

Cheapside

Cornhill

Leadenhall St.

Fenchurch St.

Cannon St.

East Road

Hoxton St.

City Rd.

Old   St.

Gt. Eastern St.

Shoreditch High St.

Kingsland Rd.

Liverpool
St. Station

Bishopsgate

Houndsditch

Commercial St.

Tower of
London

Tower Hill

0   1 mi

0   1 km

N

Introduction

En route to London for the first time, the American novelist Henry James was advised by a fellow train passenger to visit St. Paul's Cathedral. While running an errand in the City on his first morning, he happened to pass St. Paul's. Though the statue of Queen Anne in the forecourt struck him as "very small and dirty," he was still impressed by the scene: "All history appeared to live again, and the continuity of things to vibrate through my mind."

Like James, visitors today will undoubtedly be struck by such images. For the history of London is a rich one, evident in the jumbled layers of its buildings. Low 12th-century fortifications are juxtaposed with soaring 20th-century office blocks, and Victorian churches contrast with Roman city walls. Everywhere you look you'll see a confusion of ages, as well as countless images and symbols of the city that have become ingrained in the global subconscious, whether by Defoe, Fielding, Dickens, and Woolf, or by the Beatles, Stones, Sex Pistols, and Elvis Costello. Even people who have never set foot in London have vivid images of Big Ben, Tower Bridge, red double-decker buses, and pale people brandishing raincoats and umbrellas.

London is not merely a historical pop-up book; it is a living, thriving entity. Take pubs, for example. For every pub serving lovingly hand-pulled traditional ales to gentlemen in tweeds, there's a pub serving overpriced cocktails to city suits with cellular phones, and another pub filled with throbbing techno music and young trendies getting liquored up on bottled "junk booze" before a night at the clubs. But every English stereotype encases a grain of truth; indeed, part of London's appeal lies in discovering the reality behind the preconceptions. Yes, you'll easily find fish and chips, though you're not likely to get them served up in newspaper. And unless you go to "Ye Olde Fish and Chip Shoppe" you'll be more likely to find yourself next to a construction worker on lunch break than an American tourist. If you stray from the well-trodden tourist path, you'll discover another side of London. What do you think you'll remember better—meeting new friends over pints at a cricket match on a Saturday afternoon, or fighting the crowds at Madame Tussaud's Wax Museum? That's not to say that you should miss London's classic sights, for they, too, are the "real" London. A peek at the spoils of empire that are housed within the British Museum reveals more about English imperialism than a stack of history books ever could. By the same token a stroll around Windsor Castle gives a better sense of royal wealth, power, and influence than a thousand stories in the tabloids. Just don't get sucked into the tour-package version of the city that narrowly focuses on traditional and royal London—a Disneyesque montage of busbied sentries, Beefeaters, and pomp and circumstance.

Like any big city, London has its dark side as well, and these problems are compounded by the death throes of an empire beyond "decline." The United Kingdom of Great Britain and Northern Ireland is fraying at the edges—the Scots' demands for devolution and the establishment of an independent Parliament (a demand they might just get if Labour wins the next general election) grow increasingly vociferous; the Welsh National Party is slowly gaining support (and with Prince Charles as their imposed Prince of Wales, it's easy to see why); and Northern Ireland was rocked by the worst violence in over a decade in July 1996 when the Protestant Orangemen were refused (and after a violent protest, granted) permission to march through a Catholic area. With this incipient Balkanization of the U.K., it seems at times that the Ulster Protestants are the only people still clinging to the monarchy and praising "God, Queen, and Country."

As empire faded into commonwealth, large factions of former subjects relocated to the capital, bringing with them their traditions and beliefs. The presence of so many international influences is changing the very essence of what it is to be British. This diversity causes problems, as not all Londoners are embracing the changes wrought by multiculturalism. White supremacist groups, which are exerting their influence in working-class neighborhoods that have been hard hit by unemployment, are criticizing unchecked immigration and crying, "England for the English." The so-called "Little England" movement even targets the Scots and the Welsh as part of the problem. Within a week of arriving in London, you'll no doubt hear at least one wisecrack about "those stupid Irish," Bengali shopkeepers who "just don't belong," or "lazy Jamaicans" who should be sent "home." Violence is on the rise, hate crimes are depressingly regular, and the economy doesn't seem to be getting any better.

The monarchy continues to be buffeted around by the storms of modern life. When Victoria ruled Great Britain, there were already grumblings about disestablishing the monarchy; some even believed that—with the rising importance of Parliament—Victoria would be Britain's last monarch. Queen Elizabeth II soldiers on (she turned 70 in 1996) and shows no sign of relinquishing her crown. One wonders if she feels her eldest son—who once expressed a wish to be his lover's tampon—is unfit to rule this once-great nation, and is holding out until Prince William (Charles's eldest son) reaches 18 in an attempt to skip this sadly flawed generation. As the monarchy grows increasingly symbolic, perhaps the importance of the purity of that symbol increases as well. Elizabeth herself urged Charles and Diana to end their all-too-public mudslinging by finally getting a divorce, hoping to make the nastiness a thing of the past and begin polishing the tarnished reputation of the royal family. Now the divorce has gone through, and life is getting back to normal. It's an intriguing set of images: Charles borrowing money to pay Diana a huge settlement (£17 million it is rumored), Diana still living in Kensington Palace, having lost her H.R.H. title but retaining the trappings of a princess, and Elizabeth and the Queen Mother trying to pretend it all never happened.

Since the 18th century, Britain has often been referred to as "a nation of shopkeepers." Margaret Thatcher, herself the daughter of a greengrocer, went a long way toward fulfilling this bourgeois vision of Britain during her decade-long tenure as prime minister. Under her iron hand and the more timid touch of John Major, Britain's middle class has come into its own, the number of property owners has soared, and business has found a friend in government. Not everyone is pleased by the results, however, and a culture of anti-Tory criticism has sprung up that feels that, under the Conservatives, Britain has abandoned the poor and created a middle class of fat, dumb, and happy consumers. By late March 1997 Britain will have to hold another general election, and things are looking increasingly "rosy" for Tony Blair and the Labour Party. While the Tories continue to attack Labour (with huge billboards all across Britain featuring a pair of red eyes in a black space flanked by red curtains that read "New Labour, New Danger"), some left-wingers have criticized "New Labour's" shift to the center and long-time supporters, including singer-songwriter Billy Bragg, have withdrawn support. Blair and his highly adept (though sadly untelegenic) lieutenant Robin Cook are struggling to regroup, Major seems to be holding on by the skin of his teeth and hoping that some major scandal will cause the tide to turn, and the voters are growing increasingly apathetic, just hoping that regardless of whoever the next prime minister is, the economy will improve.

With all these current hardships and centuries of history, London tends to inspire extreme reactions. James felt that people could be divided into London-lovers and London-haters, and this is even more true today—though your feelings may change from love to hate day by day or even moment by moment. And if you decide one morning that you hate the city, remember that it is ever-changing. As James put it, "Out of London's richness and its inexhaustible good humour it belies the next hour any generalisation you may have been so simple as to make about it."

What to do when your *money* is done traveling before you are.

Don't worry. With **MoneyGram**,^{SM} your parents can send you money in usually 10 minutes or less to more than 18,000 locations in 86 countries. So if the money you need to see history becomes history, call us and we'll direct you to a **MoneyGram**^{SM} agent closest to you.

USA: **1-800-MONEYGRAM**
Germany: **0130-8-16629**

Canada: **1-800-933-3278**
England: **0800-89-7198**
or call collect **303-980-3340**

France: **05-905311**
Spain: **900-96-1218**

MoneyGram
MONEY IN MINUTES WORLDWIDE
_{SM}

BASICS

By Jennifer L. Brewer and Sunny Delaney

1

If you've ever traveled with anyone before, you know the two types of people in the world: the planners and the nonplanners. You also know that travel brings out the very worst in both groups: Left to their own devices, the planners will have you goose-stepping from attraction to attraction on a cultural blitzkrieg, while the nonplanners will invariably miss the flight, the bus, and the point. This Basics chapter offers you a middle ground, providing enough information to help plan your trip without saddling you with an itinerary or invasion plan. Keep in mind that companies go out of business, prices inevitably go up, and sooner or later you're going to miss a train connection. If you wanted predictability, you should have stayed home.

Planning Your Trip

WHEN TO GO

The main tourist season runs from mid-April to mid-October, but the real hordes arrive in June, July, and August—consider yourself warned. In summer, prices predictably go up, and many hostels and cheap hotels stop offering weekly rates. Even so, the daffodils and crocuses are in full bloom, and British high society hits its stride with events like Wimbledon and the Royal Ascot. In winter, London doesn't hibernate simply because all the tourists have gone home. In fact, you're more likely to get an honest—albeit a cold and wet—view of the city during the off-season, without the troops of Americans, Australians, French, Japanese, and everyone else who "does London" in two days as part of "Le Grand Tour."

Even in summer, rain is a threat and layering is de rigueur. Summer also means long, long days—sunrise by 6:30 AM, sunset around 10:30 PM.

CLIMATE London is known for its errant weather. Summer days can be excruciatingly hot (and smoggy) or cool and overcast. Fall is generally mild, and though winter temperatures rarely fall below freezing, the air is damp and the cold seems to go right to your bones. In spring the weather is incredibly schizophrenic: Sun, rain, and hail can follow one another in rapid succession, and temperatures can fluctuate from the mid-40s to high 60s. London's average highs and lows stack up as follows: **January** 37°F/43°F; **April** 42°F/56°F; **July** 56°F/71°F; **October** 45°F/58°F.

PUBLIC HOLIDAYS On the following national holidays, banks and post offices are closed, and public transportation is limited—though some shops, museums, and art galleries may

1

The World At a Discount

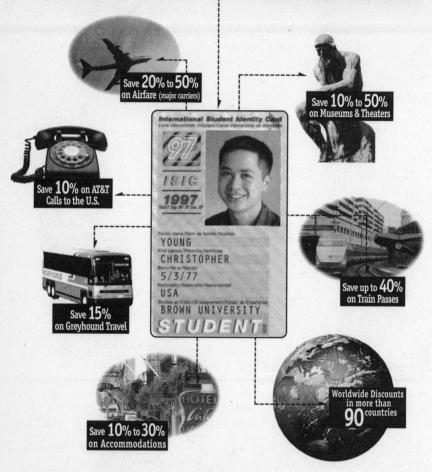

Save 20% to 50% on Airfare (major carriers)

Save 10% to 50% on Museums & Theaters

Save 10% on AT&T Calls to the U.S.

International Student Identity Card
Carte internationale d'étudiant/Carnet internacional de estudiante

97
ISIC
1997

Family name/Nom de famille/Apellido
YOUNG
First names/Prénoms/Nombres
CHRISTOPHER
Born/Né le/Nacido
5/3/77
Nationality/Nationalité/Nacionalidad
USA
Studies at/Etud d'Enseignement/Estab. de Enseñanza
BROWN UNIVERSITY
STUDENT

Save 15% on Greyhound Travel

Save up to 40% on Train Passes

Save 10% to 30% on Accommodations

Worldwide Discounts in more than 90 countries

The International Student Identity Card
Your Passport to Discounts & Benefits

With the ISIC, you'll receive discounts on airfare, hotels, transportation, computer services, foreign currency exchange, phone calls, major attractions, and more. You'll also receive basic accident and sickness insurance coverage when traveling outside the U.S. and access to a 24-hour, toll-free Help Line. Call now to locate the issuing office nearest you (over 555 across the U.S.) at:

Free 40-page handbook with each card!

1-888-COUNCIL (toll-free)

For an application and complete discount list, you can also visit us at **http://www.ciee.org/**

Council

CIEE: Council on International Educational Exchange

remain open: **New Year's Day** (Jan. 1); **Good Friday** (the Friday before Easter); **Easter Monday** (the Monday after Easter); **May Day** (the first Monday in May); **Spring Bank Holiday** (the last Monday in May); **Summer Bank Holiday** (the last Monday in Aug.); **Christmas Day** (Dec. 25); and **Boxing Day** (Dec. 26).

FESTIVALS London has more festivals, street parties, and royal parades than you can shake a gilded scepter at; what's listed below is a mere fraction of what's available. For the scoop while you're in town, check the weekly magazine *Time Out* (£1.70), available at newsstands. Or, dial London Tourist Board's 24-hour **VisitorCall** (tel. 0839/123–456 in U.K. only) service, which offers the latest on events throughout the city for 49p per minute (39p per minute 6 PM–8 AM). Many of the events listed below are free, though biggies like Wimbledon are not.

➤ **JANUARY** • The morning after the huge New Year's Eve bash in Trafalgar Square, the fun continues with the splashy, multinational **London Parade** (Jan. 1), which starts at Westminster Bridge and ends at Berkeley Square. On the last Sunday in January (Jan. 26 in 1997), Londoners dressed in 17th-century garb celebrate the **Charles I Commemoration**—held on the anniversary of the monarch's execution—with a march tracing his last walk from St. James's Palace to the Banqueting House in Whitehall.

➤ **FEBRUARY** • **Accession Day Gun Salute** (Feb. 6) is a spectacular sight: The Royal Horse Artillery gallops through Hyde Park pulling massive gun carriages, then sets up for a noontime 41-gun salute just across from the Dorchester Hotel. **Chinese New Year** is celebrated on the first Sunday of its new year (Feb. 9 in 1997) with lots of firecrackers, lion and dragon dancers, and street performers around Gerrard Street and Newport Place in Soho.

➤ **MARCH** • In early March, the sizzling **Camden Jazz Festival** stirs things up in hip north London; watch for posters around town and check *Time Out* for ticket info. On **St. Patrick's Day** (Mar. 17) raise a celebratory glass of Guinness with resident Irish folk in pubs throughout the city. At the **Head of the River Boat Race** (Mar. 29 in 1997), you can watch 420 eight-man crews from Oxford and Cambridge universities dip their 6,720 oars in the Thames as they race from Mortlake to Putney. The best view is from Surrey Bank above Chiswick Bridge (BritRail: Chiswick); check *Time Out* for the starting time, which depends on the tide. Battersea Park (Tube: Vauxhall) is the place to watch the festive floats and marching bands of the **Easter Parade** (Mar. 30 in 1997) as well as the **London Harness Horse Parade** (Easter Monday), in which trusty steeds are put through their paces to compete for prizes.

➤ **APRIL** • In early April, Londoners don medieval garb and parade from Southwark Cathedral to the Tower of London for the **Chaucer Festival** (tel. 0171/229–0635). The fete continues at the Tower, with food, jugglers, and strolling minstrels galore. The **London Marathon** (Apr. 13 in 1997) is one of the great spectacles of the running world with its enthusiastic crowds and more than 25,000 panting participants. Great places to catch the spectacle include Tower Bridge (Tube: Tower Hill) and at the finish line in The Mall (Tube: Green Park); for more info and entry forms, call 0171/620–4117. In this town the **Queen's Birthday** (Apr. 21) still earns a showy 41-gun salute, at Hyde Park, along the lines of Accession Day (*see* February, *above*).

➤ **MAY** • You may have noticed that Londoners from Prince Charles on down are mad for marigolds and dotty for daisies, but the flora-inspired really bust loose for the ultrahyped, four-day **Chelsea Flower Show** (tel. 0171/834–4333), held May 20–23 in 1997. Tickets must be purchased in advance and usually sell out—check any local newspaper or *Time Out* for details. **Beating the Bounds** (May 9 in 1997) is a quaint Ascension Day tradition dating from medieval days when local parishes marked their spiritual and financial territory by beating young boys at the boundaries. These days only the boundaries get beaten, and it's now a coed affair that culminates with a boy or girl beating the "boundary line" down the middle of the Thames with a cane while upended from the Queen's yacht.

➤ **JUNE** • The **Beating Retreat Ceremony** (June 4–5 in 1997) brings out the best of the Household Division in a floodlit spectacle of marching bands and soldiers on horseback. **Trooping the Colour** (tel. 0171/930–4466), held June 14 in 1997, celebrates the official birthday of the queen and features a contingent of troops accompanied by much pomp and circumstance involving dress uniforms, marching bands, a fly-by by the Royal Air Force, and several gun salutes. The **Royal Meeting at Ascot** (June 17–20 in 1997) brings the horsey set and their enormous hats out in force; *see* Spectator Sports, in Chapter 8, for more information. The vibrant **City of London Festival** (June 22–July 10 in 1997) fills the City with theater, poetry, classical music, and dance performed by a host of internationally known artists. Thespians and their friends flock to London in odd-numbered years for the innovative performances mounted during the **London International Festival of Theatre (LIFT)** (tel. 0171/490–3964), held June 15–July 12 in 1997. Tickets sell out months in advance for **Wimbledon** (tel. 0181/944–1066), the world's most prestigious tennis competition, but you can still get in if you're prepared to wait in line; *see* Spectator Sports, in Chapter 8, for details.

➤ **JULY** • On the first Saturday in July, London's huge **Gay Pride Festival** rallies, parties, and sashays around Clapham Common; check the local gay press or call Pride Trust (tel. 0171/738–7644) for information. From early July until mid-August **The Great Outdoors on the South Bank** (tel. 0171/960–4242) series hosts free weekend entertainment that runs the gamut from ethnic music to French street theater. **The Streets of London Festival** (tel. 01273/821–588) brings free music, theater, art, and comedy to public spaces all over London from July 11 to September 13 in 1997. At the **Royal Tournament** (tel. 0171/373–8141), from July 15 to 26 in 1997, a cast of thousands of wrap jingoism in glittery pageantry at Earl's Court Exhibition Centre. All branches of the armed forces take part in this Las Vegas/Hollywood/Andrew Lloyd Webber–style spectacle. The four-day **Phoenix Festival** (tel. 0181/963–0940) brings some 350 dance, jazz, folk, rock, and comedy acts to Long Marston near Stratford-upon-Avon on the second or third weekend in July. From mid-July through September the Royal Albert Hall is home to one of the world's premier classical music events, the **BBC Henry Wood Promenade Concerts** (tel. 0171/765–4714)—better known as the "Proms"; *see* Classical Music, Opera, and Dance, in Chapter 6, for more info.

➤ **AUGUST** • It's beer heaven at the annual **Great British Beer Festival** (Grand Hall, Olympia, tel. 0172/786–7201), which is organized by the Campaign for Real Ale (CAMRA) and scheduled for August 5–9 in 1997. On the last Sunday and Monday of the month is **Notting Hill Carnival** (tel. 0181/964–0544), the biggest street festival in Europe. The flavor is strongly Afro-Caribbean with more than 100 costumed bands and floats along the carnival route, as well as food, crafts, and spliffs galore.

➤ **SEPTEMBER** • The **Chinatown Mid-Autumn Festival,** held on Gerrard Street in Soho, is a smaller but no less colorful version of the Chinese New Year festival (*see* February, *above*). Less glitzy is **Horseman's Sunday** (tel. 0171/262–1732), the third Sunday of the month, when the good vicar of St. John's Church sits on horseback and blesses more than 100 horses, which then proceed to trot through Hyde Park.

➤ **OCTOBER** • The influential but long-dormant **Soho Jazz Festival** (tel. 0171/437–6437) is trying to make a comeback, and slowly succeeding. It's usually held from the very end of September to the first week of October. The horsey set turns out en masse for the prestigious **Horse of the Year Show** (tel. 0120/369–3088), featuring show jumping and other equestrian hijinks in Wembley Arena on October 1–5 in 1997. The Pearly Kings and Queens, representatives of costermongers (fruit and vegetable vendors), gather at the Church of St. Martin-in-the-Fields for the **Pearly Harvest Festival Service** (Oct. 5 in 1997). England expects that every man will do his duty and attend the **Trafalgar Day Parade** (Oct. 19 in 1997), which takes place around—guess where—Trafalgar Square, to commemorate Admiral Nelson's triumph over the French at, ahem, Trafalgar.

➤ **NOVEMBER** • November 5 marks **Guy Fawkes Night,** a fireworks and bonfire celebration commemorating a foiled attempt to blow up the king and Parliament in 1605. (It all started when James I of Scotland inherited the English throne and began making nasty comments about Catholics. Several plots were hatched against the new king, and just before the 1605 session of Parliament, Guy Fawkes and his accomplices were found in a cellar beneath the House of Lords with enough gunpowder to blow it to bits. The MPs were not amused, and Guy was hanged.) The best place to see fireworks and attend a bonfire is Primrose Hill near Camden Town, but effigies of Guy are burned in various locations around the capital. In mid-November the queen rides in a coach from Buckingham Palace to the House of Lords to read a speech, followed by a procession and pep talk that mark the **Opening of Parliament.** On the second Saturday in November the **Lord Mayor's Show** (tel. 0171/606–3030) makes a big deal of the person who still has some sort of vestigial sovereignty over the one-square-mile chunk of land known as the City. A bunch of floats—including the gold-and-scarlet Lord Mayor's Coach—make a ceremonial trek from Westminster to the Law Courts where the Lord Mayor makes a speech, accepts his duties, and so forth. The evening brings fireworks along the Thames. For something a little more modern, make your way to the National Film Theatre at the South Bank Centre for the smashing **London Film Festival** (tel. 0171/928–3232). Get yourself set for the winter holidays with **London's Grand Christmas Parade** (tel. 0171/240–2468), which winds around London on the last Sunday of November (Nov. 30 in 1997).

➤ **DECEMBER** • The ceremonial heart of London, Trafalgar Square, plays host to an enormous **Christmas Tree** (a gift from the people of Norway) from early December until early January. On December 31, Trafalgar Square is also the site of a huge, freezing, drunken slosh through the fountains to celebrate **New Year's Eve.**

VISITOR RESOURCES

GOVERNMENT TOURIST OFFICES Aside from offering the usual glossy tourist brochures, the **British Tourist Authority (BTA)** can answer general travel questions or refer you to other organizations for more information. Be as specific as possible when writing to request information, or you may just end up with a stack of glossy brochures on cruises or shopping expeditions. If you can get someone to answer questions over the phone, so much the better—the offices are usually staffed by natives. *In the United States: Main Office: 551 5th Ave., New York, NY 10176, tel. 800/462–2748. In Canada: 111 Avenue Rd., Suite 450, Toronto, Ont. M5R 3J8, tel. 416/925–6326. In Australia: 8th Floor, University Centre, 210 Clarence St., Sydney NSW 2000, tel. 02/267–4413. In New Zealand: Suite 305, Dilworth Bldg., cnr Queen and Custom Sts., Auckland 1, tel. 09/303–1446.*

USEFUL WEBSITES Before heading over to this green and pleasant land, a wee bit of websurfing can help you get in the mood and give you up-to-the-second info. An excellent place to start is the **UK Directory** (http://www.ukdirectory.com), which provides pretty comprehensive listings of all websites in the country as well as hundreds of links. Or try **What's New** (http://www.emap.com/whatsnew) for a constantly updated list of the U.K.'s new Internet sites. The online version of the ***Sunday Times*** (http://www.sunday-times.co.uk) won the "Hottest Site on the Net" Award at the 1996 UK Web Awards; you'll be surprised how much British news is missing from U.S. newspapers. The computer version of ***Time Out*** (http://www.timeout.co.uk) doesn't provide you with the week's full listings, but it does have some information and a backfile of stories from previous issues. Like its newspaper equivalent, online ***Loot*** (http://www.lootlink.com) is a free ads service selling everything from cars to Caribbean vacations and fish tanks. It's a good place to begin that search for a flat. For more info on where to find Internet access in London, *see* Media, in Staying in London, *below.*

BUDGET TRAVEL ORGANIZATIONS

Council on International Educational Exchange (CIEE) is a private, nonprofit organization that administers work, volunteer, academic, and professional programs worldwide. Its travel division, **Council Travel,** is a full-service travel agency specializing in student, youth, and budget travel. It offers discounted airfares, rail passes, accommodations, guidebooks, budget tours, and travel gear. It also issues the ISIC, GO25, and ITIC identity cards (*see* Student ID Cards, *below*), as well as Hostelling International cards. Forty-six Council Travel offices serve the budget traveler in the United States, and there are about a dozen overseas, including one in London (28A Poland St., W1, tel. 0171/437–7767). Council also puts out a variety of publications, such as the free *Student Travels* magazine, a gold mine of travel tips (including information on work-abroad, study-abroad, and international volunteer opportunities). *205 E. 42nd St., New York, NY 10017, tel. toll-free 888/COUNCIL, http://www.ciee.org.*

Educational Travel Center (ETC) books low-cost flights to destinations within the continental United States and around the world. Its best deals are on flights leaving from the Midwest, especially Chicago. ETC also issues Hostelling International cards. For more details, request its free brochure, *Taking Off. 438 N. Frances St., Madison, WI 53703, tel. 608/256–5551.*

STA Travel, the world's largest travel organization catering to students and young people, has more than 100 offices worldwide and offers low-price airfares to destinations around the globe as well as rail passes, car rentals, tours, you name it. STA issues the ISIC and the GO25 youth cards (*see* Student ID Cards, *below*), both of which prove eligibility for student airfares and other travel discounts. Call 800/777–0112, or contact http://www.sta-travel.com, for more information.

Student Flights, Inc. specializes in student and faculty airfares and sells rail passes, ISE cards (*see* Student ID Cards, *below*), and travel guidebooks. *5010 E. Shea Blvd., Suite A104, Scottsdale, AZ 85254, tel. 602/951–1177 or 800/255–8000.*

Travel CUTS is a full-service travel agency that sells discounted airline tickets to Canadian students, and issues the ISIC, GO25, ITIC, and HI cards. Its 25 offices are on or near college campuses. Call weekdays 9–5 for information and reservations. *187 College St., Toronto, Ont. M5T 1P7, tel. 416/979–2406.*

Hostelling International (HI), also known as IYHF, is the umbrella group for a number of national hostel associations. HI offers single-sex dorm-style beds ("couples" rooms and family accommodations are available at many hostels) and kitchen facilities at nearly 5,000 locations in more than 70 countries around the world. Membership in any HI national hostel association (*see below*), open to travelers of all ages, allows you to stay in HI-affiliated hostels at member rates (about $10–$25 a night). Members also have priority if the hostel is full and are eligible for discounts around the world, including discounts on rail and bus travel in some countries.

Council Travel Offices in the United States

ARIZONA: Tempe (tel. 602/966–3544). **CALIFORNIA:** Berkeley (tel. 510/848–8604), Davis (tel. 916/752–2285), La Jolla (tel. 619/452–0630), Long Beach (tel. 310/598–3338), Los Angeles (tel. 310/208–3551), Palo Alto (tel. 415/325–3888), San Diego (tel. 619/270–6401), San Francisco (tel. 415/421–3473 or 415/566–6222), Santa Barbara (tel. 805/562–8080). **COLORADO:** Boulder (tel. 303/447–8101), Denver (tel. 303/571–0630). **CONNECTICUT:** New Haven (tel. 203/562–5335). **FLORIDA:** Miami (tel. 305/670–9261). **GEORGIA:** Atlanta (tel. 404/377–9997). **ILLINOIS:** Chicago (tel. 312/951–0585), Evanston (tel. 847/475–5070). **INDIANA:** Bloomington (tel. 812/330–1600). **IOWA:** Ames (tel. 515/296–2326). **KANSAS:** Lawrence (tel. 913/749–3900). **LOUISIANA:** New Orleans (tel. 504/866–1767). **MARYLAND:** College Park (301/779–1172). **MASSACHUSETTS:** Amherst (tel. 413/256–1261), Boston (tel. 617/266–1926), Cambridge (tel. 617/497–1497 or 617/225–2555). **MICHIGAN:** Ann Arbor (tel. 313/998–0200). **MINNESOTA:** Minneapolis (tel. 612/379–2323). **NEW YORK:** New York (tel. 212/822–2700, 212/666–4177, or 212/254–2525). **NORTH CAROLINA:** Chapel Hill (tel. 919/942–2334). **OHIO:** Columbus (tel. 614/294–8696). **OREGON:** Portland (tel. 503/228–1900). **PENNSYLVANIA:** Philadelphia (tel. 215/382–0343), Pittsburgh (tel. 412/683–1881). **RHODE ISLAND:** Providence (tel. 401/331–5810). **TENNESSEE:** Knoxville (tel. 423/523–9900). **TEXAS:** Austin (tel. 512/472–4931), Dallas (tel. 214/363–9941). **UTAH:** Salt Lake City (tel. 801/582–5840). **WASHINGTON:** Seattle (tel. 206/632–2448 or 206/329–4567). **WASHINGTON, D.C.** (tel. 202/337–6464). For U.S. cities not listed, call 800/2–COUNCIL.

A one-year membership is $25 for adults (renewal $20) and $10 for those under 18. A one-night guest membership is $3. Family memberships are available for $35, and a lifetime membership will set you back $250. Handbooks listing all current hostels and special discount opportunities (like budget cycling and hiking tours) are available from some national associations. There are two international hostel directories: One covers Europe and the Mediterranean, while another covers Africa, the Americas, Asia, and the Pacific ($13.95 each). The HI website (http://www.gnn.com/gnn/bus/ayh/index.html) gives addresses and phone numbers for hostels all over the world and notes which ones will let you reserve in advance. *733 15th St. NW, Suite 840, Washington, DC 20005, tel. 202/783–6161.*

National branches of Hostelling International include **Hostelling International–American Youth Hostels (HI–AYH)** (733 15th St., Suite 840, Washington, DC 20005, tel. 202/783–6161); **Hostelling International–Canada (HI–C)** (400-205 Catherine St., Ottawa, Ont. K2P 1C3, tel. 613/237–7884 or 800/663–5777); **Youth Hostel Association of England and Wales (YHA)** (Trevelyan House, 8 St. Stephen's Hill, St. Albans, Herts. AL1 2DY, England, tel. 01727/855–215); **Australian Youth Hostels Association (YHA)** (Level 3, 10 Mallett St., Camperdown, New South Wales 2050, tel. 02/565–1699); and **Youth Hostels Association of New Zealand (YHA)** (Box 436, Christchurch 1, tel. 3/379–9970).

STA Offices

- *UNITED STATES. CALIFORNIA: Berkeley (tel. 510/642–3000), Los Angeles (tel. 213/934–8722), San Francisco (tel. 415/391–8407), Santa Monica (tel. 310/394–5126), Westwood (tel. 310/824–1574). FLORIDA: Miami (305/461–3444), University of Florida (tel. 352/338–0068). ILLINOIS: Chicago (tel. 312/786–9050). MASSACHUSETTS: Boston (tel. 617/266–6014), Cambridge (tel. 617/576–4623). NEW YORK CITY: Columbia University (tel. 212/865–2700), West Village (tel. 212/627–3111). PENNSYLVANIA: Philadelphia (tel. 215/382–2928). WASHINGTON: Seattle (tel. 206/633–5000). WASHINGTON, D.C. (tel. 202/887–0912).*

- *INTERNATIONAL. AUSTRALIA: Adelaide (tel. 08/223–2426), Brisbane (tel. 07/221–9388), Cairns (tel. 070/314–199), Darwin (tel. 089/412–955), Melbourne (tel. 03/349–2411), Perth (tel. 09/227–7569), Sydney (tel. 02/212–1255). AUSTRIA: Graz (tel. 0316/32482), Innsbruck (tel. 0512/588–997), Linz (tel. 0732/775–893), Salzburg (tel. 0662/883–252), Vienna (tel. 0222/401–480). DENMARK: Copenhagen (tel. 031/358–844). FRANCE: Paris (tel. 01/4325–0076). GERMANY: Berlin (tel. 030/281–6741), Frankfurt (tel. 069/430–191), Hamburg (tel. 040/442–363). GREECE: Athens (tel. 01/322–1267). ITALY: Bologna (tel. 051/261–802), Florence (tel. 055/289–721), Genoa (tel. 010/564–366), Milan (tel. 02/5830–4121), Naples (tel. 081/552–7960), Rome (tel. 06/467–9291), Venice (tel. 041/520–5660). NETHERLANDS: Amsterdam (tel. 020/626–2557). NEW ZEALAND: Auckland (tel. 09/309–9995), Christchurch (tel. 03/379–9098), Wellington (tel. 04/385–0561). SPAIN: Barcelona (tel. 03/487–9546), Madrid (tel. 01/541–7372). SWEDEN: Göteborg (tel. 031/774–0025). SWITZERLAND: Lausanne (tel. 0121/617–5811), Zürich (tel. 01/297–1111). TURKEY: İstanbul (tel. 01/252–5921). UNITED KINGDOM: London (tel. 0171/937–9962).*

STUDENT ID CARDS

The **International Student Identity Card (ISIC)** entitles students to discount airfares, special fares on local transportation, and discounts at museums, theaters, and many other attractions. If the popular ISIC card is purchased in the United States, the $19 cost also buys you $3,000 in emergency medical coverage, limited hospital coverage, and access to a 24-hour international, toll-free hotline for assistance in medical, legal, and financial emergencies. In the United States, apply to Council Travel or STA; in Canada, the ISIC is available for C$15 from Travel CUTS (*see* Budget Travel Organizations, *above*). In the United Kingdom, students with valid university IDs can purchase the ISIC at any student union or student-travel company. Applicants must submit a photo as well as proof of current full-time student status, age, and nationality. Upon request, purchase of the ISIC card includes the *International Student Identity Card Handbook,* which details the discounts and benefits available to cardholders.

Go 25: International Youth Travel Card (GO25) is issued to travelers (students and nonstudents) between the ages of 12 and 25 and provides services and benefits similar to those given by the ISIC card. The $19 card is available from the same organizations that sell the ISIC. When applying, bring a passport-size photo and your passport as proof of your age.

International Student Exchange Card (ISE) is available to students and faculty members. You pay $18 and receive a $10 discount on flights within the United States and a $50 discount on certain flights to Europe. Write or call for more information. *5010 E. Shea Blvd., Suite A104, Scottsdale, AZ 85254, tel. 602/951–1177 or 800/255–8000, fax 602/951–1216.*

The $20 **International Teacher Identity Card (ITIC),** sponsored by the International Student Travel Confederation, is available to teachers of all grade levels, from kindergarten to graduate school. The ITIC procures benefits similar to those you get with the student cards. *The International Teacher Identity Card Handbook,* available when you buy the card, has all the details.

PASSPORTS AND VISAS

Visas are not required for U.S., Canadian, Australian, or New Zealand citizens for stays of up to three months in the United Kingdom. If you plan to stay for more than three months, you'll need a visa; talk to the British consulate nearest you before you leave home. If you didn't *plan* to stay but just can't bear to leave your new Euro-boyfriend or girlfriend, contact the country's immigration officials or local police well before your three months are up.

OBTAINING A PASSPORT

➤ **U.S. CITIZENS** • First-time applicants, travelers whose most recent passport was issued more than 12 years ago or before they were 18, travelers whose passports have been lost or stolen, and travelers between the ages of 13 and 17 (a parent must also accompany them) must apply for a passport in person. Other renewals can be taken care of by mail. Apply at one of the 13 U.S. Passport Agency offices a *minimum* of five weeks before your departure. For fastest processing, apply between August and December. If you blow it, you can have a passport issued within five days of departure if you have your plane ticket in hand and pay the additional $30 fee to expedite processing. This method will probably work, but if there's one little glitch in the system, you're out of luck. Local county courthouses, many state and probate courts, and some post offices also accept passport applications. Have the following items ready when you go to get your passport:

- A completed passport application (Form DSP-11), available at courthouses, some post offices, and passport agencies.

- Proof of citizenship (certified copy of birth certificate, naturalization papers, or previous passport issued in the past 12 years).

- Proof of identity with your photograph and signature (for example, a valid driver's license, employee ID card, military ID, student ID).

- Two recent, identical, two-square-inch photographs (black-and-white or color head shots).

See the world

Call

for a

free

Student

Travels

magazine

LOWEST STUDENT/BUDGET AIRFARES ANYWHERE

Boston, MA
(617) 497-1497

Chicago, IL
(312) 951-0585

Dallas, TX
(214) 363-9941

Los Angeles, CA
(310) 208-3551
(213) 463-0655
(818) 905-5777

Miami, FL
(305) 670-9261

New York, NY
(212) 822-2700
(212) 254-2525

San Francisco, CA
(415) 421-3473

Seattle, WA
(206) 632-2448

Washington, DC
(202) 337-6464

London, Britain
(0171) 437.7767

Munich, Germany
(089) 395.022

Paris, France
(1) 44.55.55.65

Council Travel
CIEE: Council on International
Educational Exchange

National Reservation Center
http://www.ciee.org/travel.htm

(800) 226-8624

- A $55 application fee for a 10-year passport, $30 for those under 18 for a five-year passport. First-time applicants are also hit with a $10 surcharge. If you're paying cash, exact change is necessary; checks or money orders should be made out to Passport Services.

Those lucky enough to be able to renew their passports by mail must send a completed Form DSP-82 (available from a Passport Agency); two recent, identical passport photos; their current passport (less than 12 years old); and a check or money order for $55 ($30 if under 18). Send everything to the nearest Passport Agency. Renewals take from three to four weeks.

For more information or an application, contact the **Department of State Office of Passport Services** (tel. 202/647–0518) and dial your way through their message maze. Passport applications can be picked up at U.S. post offices, at federal or state courts, and at U.S. Passport Agencies in Boston, Chicago, Honolulu, Houston, Los Angeles, Miami, New Orleans, New York, Philadelphia, San Francisco, Seattle, Stamford, and Washington, D.C.

➣ **CANADIAN CITIZENS** • Canadians should send a completed passport application (available at any post office, passport office, and many travel agencies) to the **Bureau of Passports** (Suite 215, West Tower, Guy Favreau Complex, 200 Rene Levesque Blvd. W, Montreal, Que. H2Z 1X4). Include C$60; two recent, identical passport photographs; the signature of a guarantor (a Canadian citizen who has known you for at least two years and is a mayor, practicing lawyer, notary public, judge, magistrate, police officer, signing officer at a bank, medical doctor, or dentist); and proof of Canadian citizenship (original birth certificate or other official document as specified). You can also apply in person at regional passport offices in many locations, including Edmonton, Halifax, Montreal, Toronto, Vancouver, and Winnipeg. Passports have a shelf life of five years and are not renewable. Processing takes about two weeks by mail and five working days for in-person applications. For more info, call 514/283–2152.

➣ **AUSTRALIAN CITIZENS** • Australians must visit a post office or passport office to complete the passport application process. A 10-year passport for those over 18 costs AUS$81. The under-18 crowd can get a five-year passport for AUS$41. For more information, call toll-free in Australia 008/131–232 weekdays during regular business hours.

➣ **NEW ZEALAND CITIZENS** • Passport applications can be obtained at any post office or consulate. Completed applications must be accompanied by proof of citizenship and two passport-size photos. The fee is NZ$80 for a 10-year passport. Processing takes about 10 days.

LOST PASSPORTS If your passport is lost or stolen while traveling, you should immediately notify the local police and nearest embassy or consulate (*see* Embassies, in Staying in London, *below*). A consular officer should be able to wade through some red tape and issue you a new one, or at least get you back into your country of origin without one. The process will be slowed up considerably if you don't have some other forms of identification on you, so you're well advised to carry other forms of ID—a driver's license, a copy of your birth certificate, a student ID—separate from your passport, and to tuck a few photocopies of the front page of your passport in your luggage and your traveling companion's pockets.

A United States embassy or consulate will only issue a new passport in emergencies. In non-emergency situations, the staff will affirm your affidavit swearing to U.S. citizenship, and this paper will get you back to the United States. The Canadian embassy or consulate requires a police report, any form of identification, and three passport-size photos. They will replace the passport in four working days. A replacement passport usually takes five working days. New Zealand officials ask for two passport-size photos, while the Australians require three, but both can usually replace a passport in 24 hours.

MONEY

CURRENCY The unit of currency in Great Britain is the pound (£), also known as a quid, broken into 100 pence. Exchange rates change daily, but at press time £1 was equal to $1.55 and $1 was equal to 65p. In Great Britain, pound notes (nobody calls them "bills") come in denominations of £5, £10, £20, and £50. Coins are available in denominations of 1p, 2p, 5p,

10p, 20p, 50p, and £1. Older coins you may come across include the one-shilling coin (worth 5p) and the two-shilling coin (worth 10p). Remember that coins, no matter how valuable, are *not* exchangeable outside the borders of the United Kingdom.

HOW MUCH IT WILL COST For travelers with American dollars, prices in Britain are almost double what they are in the United States. It's more than just a bad exchange rate—the Brits themselves can hardly afford to live in the country. Even if you stay in hostels and eat pub grub, be prepared to drop $50 a day. If you plan to stay in hotels, take cabs, and eat in nice restaurants, that daily bill can easily top $100 per person. To add insult to injury, the British government slaps a whopping 17.5% Value Added Tax (VAT) on almost everything. VAT is usually included in prices, but not always. Lodging will be your greatest expense: Expect to pay around £10–£17 for a dorm bed or £15–£30 per person for a private room.

TRAVELING WITH MONEY Traveler's checks and a major credit card are usually the safest and most convenient way to pay for goods and services on the road, but keep in mind that many of London's cheapie hotels and restaurants accept *only* the coin of the realm—they won't even take traveler's checks in pounds. Obviously, you'll need to carry some cash; protect yourself by carrying it in a money belt, necklace pouch, or front pocket. Don't forget to keep accurate records of traveler's checks' serial numbers and to write down credit-card numbers and emergency phone numbers for reporting the cards lost or stolen.

CHANGING MONEY Banks and bureaux de change (*see* Staying in London, *below*) are everywhere in London, waiting to change your money. Banks usually give better exchange rates. If you do find a bureau de change offering a "fabulous" rate, ask if they charge a commission; most take 2%–3% for themselves (and some bloodsuckers actually skim 5%). You can get around the commission charge if you have American Express or Thomas Cook traveler's checks (*see below*), which you can exchange for free at one of their many respective London offices. Otherwise, you'll have to decide between changing large amounts at a time (which makes the per-transaction commission fee a bit less heinous) or becoming a walking magnet for pickpockets. It's your call. One last tip: It's always cheaper to buy pounds in Britain rather than at home—though you might want to change $50 or so before arriving just in case the exchange booth at the airport is closed or has an unbearably long line.

TRAVELER'S CHECKS Traveler's checks can be used just like cash—except that unlike that lovely stuff, they can be replaced if lost or stolen. Because you *must* produce the purchase agreement and a record of the checks' serial numbers in order to be reimbursed, common sense dictates that you keep the purchase agreement separate from your checks. Caution-happy travelers will even give a copy of the purchase agreement and checks' serial numbers to someone back home. Most issuers of traveler's checks promise to refund or replace lost or stolen checks in 24 hours, but you can practically see them crossing their fingers behind their backs. In a safe place record the toll-free telephone number to call in case of emergencies. The most widely recognized traveler's checks are American Express, Visa, and MasterCard (Thomas Cook is one brand of MasterCard checks). Some banks and credit unions will issue checks free to established customers, but most charge a 1%–2% commission. And in case you were wondering, there's no real advantage to buying checks in pounds rather than dollars—many budget establishments in London don't take traveler's checks of any ilk, so you'll still need to go somewhere to change them into cash.

American Express cardmembers can order traveler's checks in U.S. dollars and pounds by phone, free of charge (with a gold card) or for a 1% commission (with a basic green card). In three to five business days you'll receive your checks; up to $1,000 can be ordered in a seven-day period. Checks can also be purchased through many banks, in which case both gold and green cardholders pay a 1% commission. AmEx also issues **Traveler's Cheques for Two,** checks that can be signed and used by either you or your traveling companion. If you lose your checks or are ripped off, true to Karl Malden's repeated pledges, American Express has the resources to provide you with a speedy refund—often within 24 hours. At their Travel Services offices you can usually buy and cash traveler's checks, write a personal check in exchange for traveler's checks, report lost or stolen checks, exchange foreign currency, and pick up mail. Ask for the *American Express Traveler's Companion,* a handy little directory of their offices, to find out more about particular services at different locations. *Tel. 800/221–7282 in the U.S. and*

*Canada, in U.K., tel. 01222/66–111 for emergency medical and legal referral or 01273/
571–600 to report lost or stolen checks.*

Citicorp traveler's checks are available from Citibank and other banks worldwide in U.S. dollars
and British pounds. For 45 days from date of check purchase, purchasers have access to the 24-
hour International S.O.S. Assistance Hotline, which can provide a doctor, lawyer, assistance with
loss or theft of travel documents, traveler's check refund assistance, and an emergency message
center. *Tel. 800/645–6556 in the U.S. or 813/623–1709 collect outside the U.S.*

MasterCard International traveler's checks, issued in U.S. dollars only, are offered through
banks, credit unions, and foreign-exchange booths. Call for info about acceptance of their
checks in London and for the local number to call in case of loss or theft. *Tel. 800/223–7373
in the U.S.; in Europe, tel. 447/335–02–995 toll-free or 07/335–02–995 collect.*

Thomas Cook brand of MasterCard traveler's check is available in U.S. dollars and British
pounds. If purchased through a Thomas Cook Foreign Exchange office (formerly Deak International), there is no commission. For more info, contact MasterCard (*see above*).

Visa traveler's checks are available in U.S. dollars, British pounds, and various other currencies. *Tel. 800/227–6811 in the U.S. and Canada. Check local listings outside the U.S.*

CREDIT CARDS Many moderately posh restaurants and hotels, most shops and department
stores, and even some hostels in London will accept plastic—look for the card logo on windows. Because a credit card comes in handy for those splurge purchases, financial emergencies, or cash advances when you've plunked down your last pound in a pub, you'd be well
advised to carry one in London. Though you might not want to rely on the plastic too heavily
while traveling (accrued interest on that wild night at the Ritz could put a dent in your student
loans), it never hurts to have a card tucked in your pocket.

GETTING MONEY FROM HOME

Provided there is money at home to be had, there are at least six ingenious ways to get it:

- Have it sent through a large **commercial bank** that has a branch in the town where you're
staying. Unless you have an account with that large bank, though, you'll have to initiate the
transfer at your own bank, and the process will be even slower and more expensive.

- If you're an **American Express** cardholder, cash a personal check at an American Express
office for up to $1,000 ($2,500 for gold cardholders) every 21 days; you'll be paid in U.S.
traveler's checks or, in some instances, in foreign currency.

- **MoneyGram**^{SM} service is a dream come true if you can convince someone back home to go to
a MoneyGram^{SM} agent and fill out the necessary forms. The sender pays up to $1,000 with
a credit card or cash (and anything over that in cash) and, as quickly as 10 minutes later,
it's ready to be picked up. Fees vary according to the amount of money sent, but average
about 3%–10% to send money from the United States to Europe. You have to show ID when
picking up the money. For locations of MoneyGram^{SM} agents, tel. 800/926–9400.

- **MasterCard** and **Visa** cardholders can get cash advances from many banks, even in small
towns. The commission for this handy-dandy service hovers around 7%. If you get a PIN for
your card before you leave home, you can even make the transaction with an ATM machine
(*see* Cash Machines, *below*).

- **Western Union** offers two ways to feed your hungry wallet, both of them requiring a benef-
icent angel with deep pockets on the other side of the wire. Said angel can transfer funds
from a MasterCard, Visa, or Discover card (up to the card's limit or $10,000) by calling
from a home or business (credit card transfers cannot be done at a Western Union office).
Alternatively, your friend can trot some cash or a certified cashier's check over to the nearest office. The money will reach the requested destination in minutes but may not be available for several more hours or days. Fees range from about 5% to 15% depending on the
amount sent.

Stuck for cash? Don't panic. With Western Union, money is transferred to you in minutes. It's easy. All you've got to do is ask someone at home to give Western Union a call on US 1 800 3256000. Minutes later you can collect the cash.

WESTERN UNION | MONEY TRANSFER®

The fastest way to send money worldwide.

- In extreme emergencies (arrest, hospitalization, or worse) there is one more way American citizens can receive money overseas: by setting up a **Department of State Trust Fund.** A friend or family member sends money to the Department of State, which then transfers the money to the U.S. embassy or consulate in the city in which you're stranded. Once this account is established, you can send and receive money through Western Union, bank wire, or mail, all payable to the Department of State. For information, talk to the Department of State's Citizens' Emergency Center (tel. 202/647–5225).

CASH MACHINES Virtually all U.S. banks belong to a network of **ATMs** (Automated Teller Machines), which gobble up bank cards and spit out cash 24 hours a day in cities throughout the world. Some are affiliated with the Cirrus system, some with PLUS and Exchange, and others with STAR. These bank substitutes are better in theory than practice; ATMs may not always function or even exist in smaller towns. If the transaction cannot be completed, chances are the computer lines are busy, and you'll just have to try again later. ATM cards are issued when you open a checking or savings account at a bank and select a PIN (personal identification number). Some foreign ATMs only accept PINs of four or fewer digits; if your PIN is longer, ask your bank about changing it. If you know your PIN as a word, learn the numerical equivalent before you leave since some ATM keypads show no letters, only numbers. On the plus side, you get local currency instantly at a generally excellent rate of exchange. That said, some banks do charge a 1%–3% fee per ATM transaction, so consider withdrawing larger chunks of cash rather than small bundles on a daily basis. To find out if there are any cash machines in a given city, call your bank's department of international banking. Or call **Cirrus** (tel. 800/424–7787) for a list of worldwide locations. **PLUS** also has a toll-free number (tel. 800/843–7587), but for the moment it only lists ATMs in the U.S. and Canada.

A **Visa** or **MasterCard** can often be used to access cash through certain ATMs (provided you have a PIN for it), but the fees for this service are usually higher than bank-card fees. Also, a daily interest charge usually begins to accrue immediately on these credit-card "loans," even if monthly bills are paid up. Check with your bank for information on fees and on the daily limit for cash withdrawals. **Express Cash** allows American Express cardholders to withdraw up to $1,000 in a seven-day period (21 days overseas) from their personal checking accounts via a worldwide network of ATMs. Gold cardholders can receive up to $2,500 in a seven-day period (21 days overseas). Each transaction carries a 2% fee, with a minimum charge of $2.50 and a maximum of $20. You'll want to link your accounts and apply for a PIN two to three weeks before your departure. Call 800/528–4800 for an application.

STAYING HEALTHY

HEALTH AND ACCIDENT INSURANCE Some general health-insurance plans cover health expenses incurred while traveling, so review your existing health policies (or a parent's policy, if you're a dependent) before leaving home. Most university health-insurance plans stop and start with the school year, so don't count on school spirit to pull you through. Canadian travelers should check with their provincial ministry of health to see if their resident health-insurance plan covers them on the road.

Organizations such as STA and Council (*see* Budget Travel Organizations, *above*), as well as some credit-card conglomerates, include health and accident coverage with the purchase of an ID or credit card. If you purchase an ISIC card, you're automatically insured for $100 a day for in-hospital sickness expenses, up to $3,000 for accident-related medical expenses, and $25,000 for emergency medical evacuation. For details, request a summary of coverage from Council (205 East 42nd St., New York, NY 10017, tel. toll-free 888/COUNCIL, http://www.ciee.org). Council Travel and STA also offer short-term insurance coverage designed specifically for the budget traveler. Otherwise, several private companies offer coverage designed to supplement existing health insurance for travelers; for more details, contact your favorite student travel organization or one of the agencies listed below.

Carefree Travel Insurance is, in fact, pretty serious about providing coverage for emergency medical evacuation and accidental death or dismemberment. It also offers 24-hour medical phone advice. Carefree offers basic and deluxe plans available for trips one day and longer.

Basic coverage for an individual ranges from $86 for a 30-day trip to $180 for a 90-day trip. Deluxe coverage ranges from $161 for a 30-day trip to $333 for a 90-day trip. *100 Garden City Plaza, Box 9366, Garden City, NY 11530, tel. 516/294–0220 or 800/323–3149.*

International SOS Assistance offers insurance through Insure America, providing emergency evacuation services, worldwide medical referrals, and medical and trip-cancellation insurance. If all else fails, it also covers the return of "mortal remains." Plan A offers up to $1,000 trip-cancellation insurance for $48. Plan B offers up to $10,000 medical expense insurance and accidental death and dismemberment insurance for varying rates depending on the length of your trip. *Box 11568, Philadelphia, PA 19116, tel. 215/244–1500 or 800/523–8930.*

Travel Guard offers a variety of insurance plans, many of which are endorsed by the American Society of Travel Agents. A basic plan, including medical coverage and emergency assistance, starts at $53 for a five-day trip. Trip-cancellation policies are available for as little as $19. *1145 Clark St., Stevens Point, WI 54481, tel. 715/345–0505 or 800/782–5151.*

Wallach & Company offers two comprehensive medical insurance plans, both covering hospitalization, surgery, office visits, prescriptions, and medical evacuation for as little as $3 per day. Both also buy you access to a network of worldwide assistance centers that are staffed 24 hours a day. *107 W. Federal St., Box 480, Middleburg, VA 20118, tel. 800/237–6615.*

PRESCRIPTIONS Bring as much as you need of any prescription drugs as well as your written prescription (packed separately). Ask your doctor to type the prescription and include the following information: dosage, the generic name, and the manufacturer's name. To avoid problems clearing customs, diabetic travelers carrying syringes should have handy a letter from their physician confirming their need for insulin injections.

FIRST-AID KITS For about 97% of your trip, a first-aid kit may mean nothing to you but extra bulk. However, in an emergency you'll be glad to have even the most basic medical supplies. Prepackaged kits are available, but you can pack your own from the following list: bandages, waterproof surgical tape and gauze pads, antiseptic, cortisone cream, a thermometer in a sturdy case, an antacid, something for diarrhea, and, of course, aspirin. If you're prone to motion sickness, take along some Dramamine. However, self-medicating should only be relied on for short-term illnesses; seek professional help if any medical symptoms persist or worsen.

CONTRACEPTIVES AND SAFE SEX AIDS and other STDs (sexually transmitted diseases) do not respect national boundaries, and protection when you travel takes the same forms as it does at home. If you're contemplating an exchange of bodily fluids, condoms ("rubbers," "johnnys," "macs," and "sheaths" in Britain) and dental dams are the best forms of protection against STDs. In London, condoms are available in pharmacies, supermarkets, and some clubs and bars. The most popular British condoms are Mates and Durex; any reputable brand will display a "Kite" or "CE" mark. Council Travel (*see* Budget Travel Organizations, *above*) distributes a free "AIDS and International Travel" brochure containing information on safe sex, HIV testing, and hotline numbers. **Family Planning Association** (2-12 Pentonville Rd., N1, tel. 0171/837–4004) can also provide more information. Should the unthinkable occur, call **Emergency Contraception Helpline** (tel. 0800/494–847) for 24-hour emergency advice.

RESOURCES FOR WOMEN

This being a notoriously polite culture, women can breathe a bit easier in London than, say, in Rome or Paris. Of course, urban precautions are still necessary, and men do still get "friendly" in pubs and clubs—practice snarling "Piss off!" They should catch your drift at that point.

PUBLICATIONS Along with the lesbian-oriented *Women's Traveller* and *Are You Two... Together?,* major travel publications for women include *Women Travel: Adventures, Advice, and Experience* ($13), published by Prentice Hall. More than 70 countries receive some sort of coverage in the form of journal entries and short articles. As far as practical travel information goes, it offers few details on prices, phone numbers, and addresses. The *Handbook for Women Travelers* ($15), by Maggie and Gemma Moss, has some very good info on women's health and personal safety while traveling.

For England-specific information, pick up **Every Woman** (£2.20), a monthly covering women's groups and centers as well as women-friendly lodging and events. Virago Press publishes the **Woman's Travel Guide: London** (£10), which focuses on women's history and useful hints for women travelers. For many more options and helpful advice on women's events in London, stop by the **Silver Moon Women's Bookshop** (*see* Bookstores, in Chapter 7).

ORGANIZATIONS If you're in need of emergency counseling or support, contact **London Women's Aid** (tel. 0171/251–6537) weekdays 10–1 and 2–4:45 or **London Rape Crisis Centre** (tel. 0171/837–1600) 6–10 weekday nights. **Women Welcome Women (WWW)** is a non-profit organization aimed at bringing together women of all nationalities, all ages, and all walks of life. Membership can put you in touch with women around the globe. Call or fax 01494/465–441, or write to 88 Easton Street, High Wycombe, Bucks, HP11 1LT for more info.

RESOURCES FOR GAYS AND LESBIANS

London has the largest gay community in Britain and a variety of social venues where alternative sexual orientations can be fully expressed. Of course Brits can be bigots with the worst of them, but the general atmosphere is one of tolerance—though gay-bashings seem to be on a slight rise. **Old Compton Street** in Soho, near the Leicester Square tube station, is the heart of London's so-called Gay Village, with lots of gay cafés, nightspots, businesses, and services.

PUBLICATIONS **Are You Two...Together?** ($18), published by Random House, is the best-known, and perhaps most detailed, guide to traveling in Europe. It's fairly anecdotal and skimps on practical details like phone numbers and addresses, but it still makes an excellent read. One of the better gay and lesbian travel newsletters is **Out and About** (tel. 800/929–2268 for subscriptions), with listings of gay-friendly hotels and travel agencies, plus health cautions for travelers with HIV. A 10-issue subscription costs $49; single issues cost about $5. **Spartacus** bills itself as *the* guide for the gay traveler and has practical tips and reviews of hotels and agencies in over 160 countries. It's a bit expensive at $32.95, though you do get snappy color photos and listings in four languages. Write to Box 422458, San Francisco, CA 94142 or call 800/462–6654 for info.

If you're looking for London-specific information, you're in luck: London has a multitude of publications with info on things like meetings, cultural events, gay businesses, and entertainment. Many are free—among them the well-written **Pink Paper**, the fluffier **Boyz**, and the impressive glossy **Freedom**, available at cafés and some newsstands around town. The free **Thud** is a good mag for clubbers to pick up. Other names to watch for are the lifestyle mags **Diva** (lesbian focus; £2) and **Gay Times** (gay focus; £2.50), and, as always, **Time Out** magazine—they're close to unbeatable when it comes to London's gay club scene.

ORGANIZATIONS **International Gay Travel Association (IGTA)** is a nonprofit organization with worldwide listings of travel agencies, hotels, bars, and travel services aimed at gay travelers. *Box 4974, Key West, FL 33041, tel. 800/448–8550, fax 305/286–6633.*

International Lesbian and Gay Association (ILGA) is an excellent source for info about conditions, specific resources, and trouble spots in dozens of countries. *81 rue Marche au Charbon, 1000 Brussels 1, Belgium, tel. 02/502–24–71.*

Gay's the Word (66 Marchmont St., WC1, tel. 0171/278–7654) is a social and intellectual center for London's gay and lesbian community and houses books, magazines, and a bulletin board. Stuff for lesbians to do by and amongst themselves is a bit harder to find, but the **Drill Hall** (16 Chenies St., WC1, tel. 0171/631–1353) is a good start. Aside from hosting women-only Monday nights, for the rest of the week it serves as a cultural center and presents theater and music.

And hotlines? The **Lesbian and Gay Switchboard** (tel. 0171/837–7324) is the main 24-hour info and advice line in the London area. If its lines are busy, you can call **London Friend** (tel. 0171/837–3337), which provides confidential phone counseling for lesbians and gay men daily 7:30 PM–10 PM. It also runs a special **London Friend Women's Line** (tel. 0171/837–2782), open Sunday–Tuesday during the same hours. The **Lesbian Line** (tel. 0171/253–

Your vacation.

Your vacation after losing your hard-earned vacation money.

0924) is there for women Monday and Friday 2 PM–10 PM, Tuesday–Thursday 7 PM–10 PM. There are even more specific hotlines for lesbians and gays who are Jewish, Catholic, in legal trouble, or worried about protecting themselves on the streets; ask any of the folks listed above. The National AIDS Helpline (tel. 0800/567–123) is a toll-free, 24-hour service offering advice and referrals.

TRAVELERS WITH DISABILITIES

Accessibility may soon have an international symbol if an initiative begun by the Society for the Advancement of Travel for the Handicapped (SATH) catches on. A bold, underlined, capital **H** is the symbol that SATH is publicizing for hotels, restaurants, and tourist attractions to indicate that the property has some accessible facilities. While awareness of the needs of travelers with disabilities increases every year, budget opportunities are harder to find. Always ask if discounts are available, either for you or for a companion. London is ahead of the rest of the country in considering the needs of people with disabilities. Many of the big tourist sights and entertainment venues have wheelchair access. Some museums and parks have special attractions, such as touch-tours for the vision-impaired and interpreted events for the hearing-impaired. Whenever possible, our reviews will indicate whether lodgings and tourist sights are wheelchair accessible.

GETTING AROUND **London Regional Transport** publishes a number of helpful pamphlets, one of the best being "Access to the Underground." Wheelchair-accessible **Mobility Bus** services (tel. 0171/918–3312), numbered in the 800 and 900 series, run (albeit infrequently) in many parts of London. **Stationlink** (tel. 0171/918–3312) is a wheelchair-accessible minibus with an hourly circular service that links Waterloo, Victoria, Paddington, Marylebone, Euston, St. Pancras, King's Cross, Liverpool Street, Fenchurch Street, and London Bridge stations; one bus runs clockwise, another counterclockwise. It also connects with the wheelchair-accessible **Airbus A1** at Victoria and **A2** at Euston for Heathrow Airport.

PUBLICATIONS *Access in London* (£8), published by Nicholson, is the premier travel guide in the genre; it's available in most larger bookstores and at many travel bookshops. **Greater London Association for Disabled People (GLAD)** (336 Brixton Rd., SW9 7AA, tel. 0171/274–0107) publishes the wonderfully comprehensive "London Disability Guide." It's free if you pick it up in person; otherwise send them a stamped (80p), self-addressed, large envelope. **RADAR** (*see below*) publishes the useful *Holidays in the British Isles* (£7), which lists wheelchair-accessible lodging and attractions all over Britain.

ORGANIZATIONS **Royal Association for Disability and Rehabilitation (RADAR)** (12 City Forum, 250 City Rd., EC1 V8AF, tel. 0171/250–3222), open weekdays 9–5, is command central for everything people with disabilities could need to know about living and traveling in the United Kingdom. It publishes both travel information and periodicals on political issues. If you're planning an extended stay, check out **Greater London Association for Disabled People (GLAD)** (*see above*), which can put you in touch with folks in your particular neighborhood.

Each London borough also maintains its own information and advice line; two in central London are **Westminster Disability Information Service** (tel. 0171/289–2360) and **Action Disability Kensington and Chelsea** (tel. 0171/937–7073). The **Artsline** (tel. 0171/388–2227), open weekdays 9:30–5:30, can clue you in on accessible goings-on around town. For info about accessible participant sports, call the **British Sports Association for the Disabled** (tel. 0171/490–4919) during normal office hours.

WORKING ABROAD

Getting a job in London or elsewhere in the United Kingdom is no easy matter—prepare for miles of red tape, lengthy booklets of rules and tax regulations, and little respect from British employers who just don't like American and Aussie accents. The most common scenario is perhaps the most bleak: You're in London for a few weeks, decide you love it, and want to stay. Now you need a job. Unless you have a passport from an EU country, however, your only real hope is under-the-table work at pubs and restaurants. These types of thankless positions pay

£3–£5 per hour if you're lucky—and don't count on making much in tips. Some people simply walk in the door, ask if the manager needs assistance, and hope he or she doesn't ask for your papers. If you want to go the legal route, contact one of the following organizations long before you arrive in London.

PUBLICATIONS Council (*see* Budget Travel Organizations, *above*) publishes two excellent resource books with complete details on work/travel opportunities. The most valuable is *Work, Study, Travel Abroad: The Whole World Handbook* ($14), which gives the lowdown on scholarships, grants, fellowships, study-abroad programs, and work exchanges. Also worthwhile is Council's *The High-School Student's Guide to Study, Travel, and Adventure Abroad* ($14). Both books can be shipped to you at book-rate ($1.50) or first-class ($3).

The U.K.-based Vacation Work Press publishes two first-rate guides to working abroad: *Directory of Overseas Summer Jobs* ($15) and Susan Griffith's *Work Your Way Around the World* ($18). The first lists over 45,000 jobs worldwide; the latter has fewer listings but makes a more interesting read. Look for them at bookstores, or you can contact the American distributor directly. *Peterson's, 202 Carnegie Center, Princeton, NJ 05843.*

ORGANIZATIONS **Au Pair Abroad** arranges board and lodging for students between the ages of 18 and 26 who want to work as nannies for three to 18 months. All applicants must go through a somewhat lengthy interview process. *1015 15th St., N.W., Suite 750, Washington, D.C. 20005, tel. 202/408–5380, fax 202/480–5397, 708439@mcimail.com.*

The easiest way to arrange work in Britain is through Council's **Work Abroad Department** (205 E. 42nd St., New York, NY 10017, tel. toll-free 888/COUNCIL, http://www.ciee.org). The program enables you to work in Europe for three to six months. Participants must be U.S. citizens or permanent residents, 18 years or older, and full-time students for the semester preceding their stay overseas. Past participants have worked at all types of jobs, including hotel and restaurant work, office and sales help, and occasionally career-related internships. The cost of the program is $200, which includes legal work-permission documents, orientation and program materials, access to job and housing listings, and on-going support services overseas. Contact Council for their free "Work Abroad" brochure.

Canadians are not eligible for the Council Work Abroad program and should contact **Travel CUTS,** which has similar programs for Canadian students who want to work abroad for up to six months. *187 College St., Toronto, Ont. M5T 1P7, tel. 416/979–2406.*

IAESTE sends full-time students abroad to practice their engineering, mathematics, and computer skills in over 50 countries. You don't get paid much, though the program is designed to cover day-to-day expenses. Applications are due between September and December for travel the following summer, so get going. *10 Corporate Center, Suite 250, 10400 Little Patuxent Pkwy., Columbia, MD 21044, tel. 410/997–2200, fax 410/997–5186.*

STUDYING ABROAD

Studying in London is the perfect way to scope out the local culture. You may choose to study through a U.S.-sponsored program, usually through an American university, or to enroll in a program sponsored by a European organization. Do your homework; programs vary greatly in expense, academic quality, amount of contact with local students, and living conditions. Working through your local university is the easiest way to find out about study-abroad programs in Europe. Most universities have staff members that distribute information on programs at European universities, and they might be able to put you in touch with program participants.

The **American Institute for Foreign Study** and the **American Council of International Studies** arrange semester- and year-long study-abroad programs in universities throughout the world. Applicants must be enrolled as full- or part-time students. Fees vary according to the country and length of stay. *102 Greenwich Ave., Greenwich, CT 06830, tel. 800/727–2437.*

Council's **College and University Programs Division** administers summer, semester, and year-long study-abroad programs at various universities worldwide. To navigate the maze of programs, contact Council (205 E. 42nd St., New York, NY 10017, tel. toll-free 888/COUNCIL, http://www.ciee.org), or purchase its excellent **Work, Study, Travel Abroad: The Whole World Handbook** ($14).

The Information Center at the **Institute of International Education (IIE)** has reference books, foreign-university catalogues, study-abroad brochures, and other materials that may be consulted free of charge if you're in the neighborhood, or you can call for a recorded list of services. IIE also publishes the helpful **Academic Year Abroad** ($43), which lists over 1,900 study-abroad programs for undergraduates and graduates. If you're more interested in summer-abroad and living-abroad programs, check out IIE's **Vacation Study Abroad** ($37). Order either from IIE Books (tel. 212/984–5412). *809 U.N. Plaza, New York, NY 10017, tel. 212/984– 5413. Information Center open Tues.–Thurs. 11–3:45.*

World Learning offers more than 100 different semester-abroad programs, many structured around home stays. *Kipling Rd., Box 676, Brattleboro, VT 05302, tel. 800/451–4465.*

Coming and Going

CUSTOMS AND DUTIES

ARRIVING IN LONDON When going through customs, looking composed and presentable expedites the process. If you're bringing any foreign-made equipment with you from home, such as cameras or video gear, it's wise to carry the original receipt or register it with customs before leaving the United States (ask for U.S. Customs Form 4457). Otherwise, you may end up paying duty on your return.

RETURNING HOME

➤ **U.S. CUSTOMS** • Like most other government organizations, the U.S. Customs Service enforces a number of mysterious rules that presumably make sense to some bureaucrat somewhere. You're unlikely to have run-ins with customs as long as you never carry any illegal drugs in your luggage. When you return to the United States, you will have to declare all items you bought abroad, but you won't have to pay duty unless you come home with more than $400 worth of foreign goods, including items bought in duty-free stores. For purchases between $400 and $1,000 you have to pay a 10% duty. You also have to pay tax if you exceed your duty-free allowances: one liter of alcohol or wine, 100 non-Cuban cigars or 200 cigarettes, and one bottle of perfume. A free leaflet about customs regulations and illegal souvenirs, "Know Before You Go," is available from the **U.S. Customs Service** (Box 7407, Washington, D.C. 20044, tel. 202/ 927–6724).

➤ **CANADIAN CUSTOMS** • Exemptions for returning Canadians range from C$20 to C$500, depending on how long you've been out of the country: for two days out, you're allowed to return with C$200 worth of goods; for one week out, you're allowed C$500 worth. Above these limits, you'll be taxed about 15%. Duty-free limits are up to 50 cigars, 200 cigarettes, 400 grams of tobacco, and 1.14 liters of liquor—all must be declared in writing upon arrival at customs and must be with you or in your checked baggage. To mail back gifts, label the package "Unsolicited Gift—Value under C$60." For more scintillating details, call the automated information line of the **Revenue Canada Customs, Excise and Taxation Department** (2265 St. Laurent Blvd. S., Ottawa, Ont., K1G 4K3, tel. 613/993–0534 or 613/991–3881), where you may request a copy of the Canadian Customs brochure "I Declare/Je Déclare."

➤ **AUSTRALIAN CUSTOMS** • Australian travelers 18 and over may bring back, duty free: one liter of alcohol; 250 grams of tobacco products (equivalent to 250 cigarettes or cigars); and other articles worth up to AUS$400. If you're under 18, your duty-free allowance is AUS$200. To avoid paying duty on goods you mail back to Australia, mark the package "Australian goods returned." For more rules and regulations, request the pamphlet "Customs Information for Travellers" from a local **Collector of Customs** (GPO Box 8, Sydney, NSW 2001, tel. 02/226–5997).

➤ **NEW ZEALAND CUSTOMS** • Although greeted with a "*Haere Mai*" ("Welcome to New Zealand"), homeward-bound travelers face a number of restrictions. Travelers over age 17 are allowed, duty-free: 200 cigarettes or 250 grams of tobacco or 50 cigars or a combo of all three up to 250 grams; 4.5 liters of wine or beer and one 1,125-ml. bottle of spirits; and goods with a combined value up to NZ$700. If you want more details, ask for the pamphlet "Customs Guide for Travellers" from a New Zealand consulate.

GETTING THE BEST DEALS

When your travel plans are still in the fantasy stage, start studying the travel sections of major Sunday newspapers: Courier services, charter companies, and fare brokers often list incredibly cheap flights. Travel agents are another obvious resource, as they have access to computer networks that show the lowest fares before they're even advertised. However, budget travelers are the bane of travel agents, whose commission is based on the ticket prices. That said, agencies on or near college campuses—try STA or Council Travel (see Budget Travel Organizations, above)—actually cater to this pariah class and can help you find cheap deals.

Flexibility is the key to getting a serious bargain on airfare. If you can play around with your departure date, destination, and return date, you will probably save money. When setting travel dates, remember that off-season fares can be as much as 50% lower. Ask which days of the week are the cheapest to fly on—weekends are often the most expensive. An extremely useful resource is Michael McColl's *The Worldwide Guide to Cheap Airfares*, an in-depth account of how to find cheap tickets and generally beat the system. *The Worldwide Guide* also includes a comprehensive listing of consolidators, charter companies, and courier services in travel hub cities all over the world. If you don't find it at your local bookstore, you can mail a check for $14.95, plus $2.50 for shipping and handling, to Insider Publications (2124 Kittredge St., 3rd Floor, Berkeley, CA 94704), or call 800/782–6657 and order with a credit card.

STUDENT DISCOUNTS Student discounts on airline tickets are offered through **Council, Educational Travel Center, STA Travel,** and **Travel CUTS** (see Budget Travel Organizations, above). **Campus Connection** (1100 E. Marlton Pike, Cherry Hill, NJ 08032, tel. 800/428–3235), exclusively for students under 25, also searches airline computer networks for the cheapest student fares. They don't always have the best price, but they do deal with the airlines directly so you won't get stuck with a heavily restricted or fraudulent ticket. Keep in mind that often you will *not* receive frequent-flyer mileage for discounted student, youth, or teacher tickets. For discount tickets based on your status as a student, youth, or teacher, have an ID when you check in that proves it: an International Student Identity Card (ISIC), Youth Travel Card (GO25), or International Teacher Identity Card (ITIC).

CONSOLIDATORS AND BUCKET SHOPS Consolidator companies, also known as bucket shops, buy blocks of tickets at wholesale prices from airlines trying to fill flights. Check out any consolidator's reputation with the Better Business Bureau before starting; most are perfectly reliable, but better safe than sorry. Travel agents can also get you good consolidator fares and will deal with respectable companies.

There are some drawbacks to the consolidator ticket: You can't always be too choosy about which city you fly into. Consolidator tickets are not always refundable, and the flights available will sometimes involve indirect routes, long layovers, and undesirable seating assignments. If your flight is delayed or canceled, you'll also have a tough time switching airlines. However, you can often find consolidator tickets that are changeable, with no minimum or maximum stays required, even at the last minute. Bucket shops generally advertise in newspapers—be sure to check restrictions, refund possibilities, and payment conditions. If possible, pay with a credit card so that if your ticket never arrives, you don't have to pay. One last suggestion: Confirm your reservation with the airline both before and after you buy a consolidated ticket. This not only decreases the chance of fraud but also ensures that you won't be the first to get bumped if the airline overbooks. For more details, contact one of the following consolidators:

Airfare Busters. *5100 Westheimer Ave., Suite 550, Houston, TX 77056, tel. 713/961–5109 or 800/232–8783, fax 713/961–3385.*

Globe Travel. *507 5th Ave., Suite 606, New York, NY 10017, tel. 800/969–4562, fax 212/682–3722.*

UniTravel. *1177 N. Warson Rd., Box 12485, St. Louis, MO 63132, tel. 314/569–2501 or 800/325–2222, fax 314/569–2503.*

Up & Away Travel. *347 Fifth Ave., Suite 202, New York, NY 10016, tel. 212/889–2345, fax 212/889–2350.*

CHARTER FLIGHTS Charter flights have vastly different characteristics depending on the company you're dealing with. Generally speaking, a charter company either buys a block of tickets on a regularly scheduled, commercial flight and sells them at a discount (the prevalent form in the United States) or leases the whole plane and then offers relatively cheap fares to the public (most common in the United Kingdom). Despite a few potential drawbacks—among them infrequent flights, restrictive return-date requirements, lickety-split payment demands, frequent bankruptcies—charter companies often offer the cheapest tickets around, especially during high season. Make sure you find out a company's policy on refunds should a flight be canceled by either yourself or the airline. Summer charter flights fill up fast and should be booked a couple of months in advance.

You're in much better shape when the company is offering tickets on a regular commercial flight. After you've bought the ticket from the charter folks, you generally deal with the airline directly. When a charter company has chartered the whole plane, things get a little sketchier: Bankrupt operators, long delays at check-in, overcrowding, and flight cancellations are fairly common. Other charter troubles: weird departure times, packed planes, and a dearth of one-way tickets. Nevertheless, in peak season, charters are very often the cheapest way to go. You can minimize risks by checking the company's reputation with the Better Business Bureau.

Charter companies to try include **DER Tours** (Box 1606, Des Plains, IL 60017, tel. 800/782–2424), **MartinAir** (tel. 800/627–8462), **Tower Air** (tel. 800/34–TOWER), and **Travel CUTS** (187 College St., Toronto, Ont. M5T 1P7, tel. 416/979–2406). Council Travel and STA (*see* Budget Travel Organizations, *above*) also offer exclusively negotiated discount airfares on scheduled airlines.

COURIER FLIGHTS Courier flights are often the very cheapest way to go. The way it works is simple: You sign a contract with a courier service to babysit their packages (often without ever laying eyes on them, let alone hands), and the courier company pays half or more of your airfare. On the day of departure, you arrive at the airport a few hours early, meet someone who hands you a ticket and customs forms, and off you go. After you land, you simply clear customs with the courier luggage and deliver it to a waiting agent.

Courier flights are cheap, yes, but there are restrictions: (1) flights can be booked only a week or two in advance and often only a few days in advance, (2) you are allowed carry-on luggage only, because the courier uses your checked-luggage allowance to transport the time-sensitive shipment, (3) you must return within one to four weeks, (4) times and destinations are limited, (5) you may be asked to pay a deposit, to be refunded after you have completed your assignment.

Find courier companies in the travel section of the newspaper, the yellow pages of your phone directory, or mail away for a telephone directory that lists companies by the cities to which they fly. One of the better publications is *Air Courier Bulletin* (IAATC, 8 S. J St., Box 1349, Lake Worth, FL 33460, tel. 407/582–8320), sent to IAATC members every two months once they pay the $45 annual fee. Publications you can find in the bookstores include *Air Courier Bargains* ($15), published by the Intrepid Traveler, and *The Courier Air Travel Handbook* ($10), published by Thunderbird Press.

Discount Travel International has courier flights to destinations in Europe, Central America, and Asia from Chicago, Los Angeles, Miami, and New York. The prices are admirably cheap, but some restrictions apply, so call at least two weeks in advance. Couriers must be over 18. *169 W. 81st St., New York, NY 10024, tel. 212/362–3636.*

Now Voyager connects travelers scrounging for cheap airfares with companies looking for warm bodies to escort their packages overseas. Departures are from New York and Newark and occasionally Los Angeles or Detroit; destinations may be in Europe, Asia, or Mexico (City, that is).

Round-trip fares start at $150. A nonrefundable $50 registration fee, good for one year, is required. Call for current offerings. *Tel. 212/431–1616.*

LAST·MINUTE DEALS Flying standby is almost a thing of the past. The idea is to purchase an open ticket and wait for the next available seat on the next available flight to your chosen destination. Airlines themselves no longer offer standby tickets but some travel agencies do. Three-day-advance-purchase youth fares are open only to people under 25 and can only be purchased within three days of departure. Return flights must also be booked no more than three days prior to departure. If you meet the above criteria, expect 10%–50% savings on published APEX fares. Some courier companies keep a last-minute list of travelers who are willing to fly at a moment's notice. Call around to see which do and how you can be listed. There are also a number of brokers that specialize in discount and last-minute sales, offering savings on unsold seats on commercial carriers and charter flights as well as tour packages. If you're desperate to get to London by Wednesday, try **Last Minute Travel Club** (tel. 617/267–9800).

BY AIR

FROM NORTH AMERICA Airlines that serve London with nonstop flights from major U.S. cities include **Aer Lingus** (tel. 800/223–6537), **American** (tel. 800/433–7300), **British Airways** (tel. 800/247–9297), **Continental** (tel. 800/231–0856), **Delta** (tel. 800/241–4141), **TWA** (tel. 800/221–2000), **United** (tel. 800/241–6522), **USAir** (tel. 800/428–4322), **Virgin Atlantic Airways** (tel. 800/862–8621).

FROM AUSTRALIA AND NEW ZEALAND **Quantas** (tel. 800/227–4500 in the U.S. or 02/957–0111 toll-free from Sydney) flies from all major Australian cities to London via Bangkok or Kuala Lampur. From New Zealand (tel. 800/808–767 outside Auckland or 09/379–0306 in Auckland) some flights fly via Australia, but some are nonstop.

TAKING LUGGAGE ABROAD You've heard it a million times. Now you'll hear it once again: Pack light. U.S. airlines allow passengers to check two pieces of luggage, neither of which can exceed 62 inches (length + width + height) or weigh more than 70 pounds. If your airline accepts excess baggage, it will probably charge you for it. Foreign-airline policies vary, so call or check with a travel agent before you show up at the airport with one bag too many. If you're traveling with a pack, tie all loose straps to each other or onto the pack itself, as they tend to get caught in luggage conveyer belts. Put valuables in the middle of packs, wadded inside clothing, because outside pockets are extremely vulnerable to probing fingers.

Anything you'll need during the flight (and valuables to be kept under close surveillance) should be stowed in a carry-on bag. Foreign airlines have different policies but generally allow only one carry-on in tourist class, in addition to a handbag and a bag filled with duty-free goodies. The carry-on bag cannot exceed 45 inches (length + width + height) and must fit under the seat or in the overhead luggage compartment. Call for the airline's current policy. Passengers on U.S. airlines are limited to one carry-on bag, plus coat, camera, and handbag. Carry-on bags must fit under the seat in front of you; maximum dimensions are 9 x 45 x 22 inches. Hanging bags can have a maximum dimension of 4 x 23 x 45 inches; to fit in an overhead bin, bags can have a maximum dimension of 10 x 14 x 36 inches. If your bag is too porky for compartments, be prepared for the humiliation of rejection and last-minute baggage check.

BY TRAIN

London has eight major train stations (as well as a bunch of smaller ones). Each serves a specific part of the country (or the Continent), so be sure to figure out beforehand where your train leaves from. For nation-wide 24-hour train information call 0345/484–950 (accessible from the United Kingdom only). All eight stations have tourist and travel information booths, rip-off bureaux de change, and luggage storage (£2–£5 per day). They are also all served by the London Underground, so it's easy to get around after you arrive in London. **British Travel Centre** (*see* Visitor Information, in Staying in London, *below*) can provide you with train schedules, ticket prices, and other information. *British Rail Passenger Timetable* (£7.50), issued every May and October, contains details of all BritRail services; pick up one at any major train station.

Charing Cross serves southeast England, including Canterbury and Dover/Folkestone, and is on the Northern, Bakerloo, and Jubilee tube lines. *Strand, WC2.*

Euston serves the Midlands, north Wales, northwest England, and western Scotland and is on the Northern and Victoria tube lines. *Euston Rd., NW1.*

King's Cross marks the end of the Great Northern line, serving northeast England, and Scotland. King's Cross is on the Circle, Metropolitan, Piccadilly, Hammersmith & City, Northern, and Victoria tube lines. *York Way, N1.*

Liverpool Street serves East Anglia, including Cambridge and Norwich, and is on the Central, Hammersmith & City, Metropolitan, and Circle tube lines. *Liverpool St., EC2.*

Paddington mainly serves South Wales and the West Country, as well as Reading, Oxford, Worcester, and Bristol. Paddington is on the Circle, Bakerloo, District, and Hammersmith & City tube lines. *Praed St., W2.*

St. Pancras serves Leicester, Nottingham, and Sheffield and is on the Victoria, Northern, Hammersmith & City, Circle, Piccadilly, and Metropolitan tube lines. *Pancras Rd., NW1.*

Victoria serves southern England, including Brighton, Dover/Folkestone, and the south coast. Victoria is on the Circle, District, and Victoria tube lines. *Terminus Pl., SW1.*

Waterloo serves southeastern destinations like Portsmouth and Southampton and is on the Bakerloo and Northern tube lines. *York Rd., SE1.*

RAIL PASSES   If you plan to do a moderate amount of traveling, it may be worth investing in a BritRail Pass as full-price tickets are absurdly expensive. Also note that EurailPass is *not* accepted in Britain (though InterRail is) and that most BritRail passes cannot be purchased in the United Kingdom—you must get them *before* you leave home. An adult **second-class pass** costs $235 for 8 days, $365 for 15 days, $465 for 22 days, and $545 for one month. If you're 16–25 years old, consider a **BritRail Youth Pass.** It allows unlimited second-class travel in the following increments: $190 for 8 days, $290 for 15 days, $370 for 22 days, or $435 for one month. Passes are available from most travel agents or from the BritRail Travel Information Office (1500 Broadway, New York, NY 10036, tel. 800/677–8585). About the only worthwhile pass available in Britain is the **Young Person's Railcard**; it costs £16 from any BritRail office and is good for a third off most train tickets—an investment that will pay you back immediately. However, you must be under age 26 to purchase one.

BY BUS

London's main terminal for all long-distance bus companies is **Victoria Coach Station** (Buckingham Palace Rd., tel. 0990/808–080 or 0171/730–3466), just southwest of Victoria Station. Victoria Coach Station has a bureau de change and luggage storage. Travelers with disabilities, who need or will need disability assistance, should contact **Help Point** (tel. 0171/730–3466, ext. 235).

You can save lots of money by taking a bus instead of a train. **Economy Return** bus tickets, good for travel Sunday through Thursday, can be 30%–50% cheaper than train tickets. Expect to pay about 20% more for **Standard Return** fares, allowing travel on Friday and Saturday. You can also buy cheap **APEX** tickets if you book seven days in advance and adhere to exact times and dates for departure and return. Book tickets on **National Express** (tel. 0990/808–080) buses at Victoria Coach Station or at one of their branch offices at 52 Grosvenor Gardens or 13 Regent Street. It may be cheaper to buy a bus pass ahead of time in the United States. These are valid for 3 days out of 5 ($79, $59 students); and 5 ($139, $105 students), 8 ($200, $149 students), or 15 ($289, $219 students) days out of 30. Contact **British Travel Associates** (tel. 540/298–2232), which sells tickets over the phone and can quote you the latest price in dollars. In Britain, you can buy a pass at any National Express office and at Heathrow and Gatwick airports.

BY FERRY

Provided you are not weak of stomach, ferries with their on-board entertainment, and booze and cigarette-filled duty-free shops, can be the most amusing way to get around. They are the cheapest way to come from France, Belgium, or the Netherlands. They arrive at **Dover** and **Portsmouth** from the French ports of Calais, Boulogne, and Le Havre. The standard round-trip fare is £50, around £25 if you return in fewer than five days. The Netherlands, northern Germany, and Scandinavia are best accessed from the East Anglia town of **Harwich** via ferries bound for Hoek van Holland (Hook of Holland). The Welsh port town of **Holyhead** is the best place to catch ferries to Dublin (£18–£28 single), though there's also service from the Welsh port of **Fishguard** to the Irish port of Rosslare, and from **Stranraer** to **Belfast**. For more info, contact the ferry companies directly: **Hoverspeed and SeaCat** (tel. 01304/240–241), **P&O Ferries** (tel. 01304/203–388), and **Sealink** (tel. 01233/647–047).

BY EUROTUNNEL

Instead of schlepping from airport to airport, you can hop on the **Eurostar** (tel. 01233/617–575) train at its snazzy new terminal in Waterloo Station and, three hours later, wind up in Paris's Gare du Nord. At press time, the lowest, highly restricted Eurostar fares were £69 return from London to either Paris or Brussels. The highest fare was £155 return for a completely flexible, refundable ticket. If you are under 26, you can purchase a return ticket for as little as £79 (£59 for midweek travel) provided you do not change your dates of travel *after the first day* of travel is completed. For reservations or more information, contact **Eurostar Enquiries** (19 Worple Rd., Wimbledon, tel. 0181/784–1333).

HITCHING

Hitching out of London is not difficult, though women traveling solo should carefully consider the risks before attempting it. Make a neat sign indicating your destination, get a good map, and determine which motorway out of London will lead to the area you want; then take a bus or the tube as close to that motorway as possible. Hitchers should stand about 25 yards *beyond* a roundabout, waiting for cars coming off it; never try to get rides from people coming onto a roundabout. You can also work thumb magic around major intersections on the edge of London's metropolis. Hitching is illegal on the actual motorways, but some people do It anyway.

RIDESHARING A rideshare is a (relatively) less risky alternative to hitching and can be fairly cheap: Riders are usually expected to help pay for gas and share any other expenses. *Loot* (£1.30), a want-ads paper, has a section to help those with the means of transport meet those in need of a lift. Also check out the **ride boards** at the University of London's Union (Malet St.) and at University College of London Union (Gordon St.), both of which are near the Euston Square tube station. **Freewheelers** (tel. 0191/222–0090, freewheelers@freewheelers.co.uk) is a Newcastle-based rideshare agency that connects lift-seekers with lift-offerers. There is a £10 annual registration fee, plus £3 match fee for each journey you take; you'll also be required to contribute around 3.5p per kilometer to the driver's costs. A trip from London to Edinburgh costs £14, while London to Oxford is a mere £2.

Getting Around London

TO AND FROM THE AIRPORTS

HEATHROW Heathrow International Airport (tel. 0181/759–4321) handles the vast majority of international flights to and from the United Kingdom. **Terminals 1 and 2** are reserved for European and domestic flights; **Terminal 3** is for most intercontinental and Scandinavian flights; and **Terminal 4** handles all long-distance British Airways flights as well as shuttle flights between major British cities. **Tourist information** counters, accommodations services, and bureaux de change are located in every terminal. Luggage storage, known here as **left lug-**

gage, is also available at every terminal for £2–£3 per item per day; hours are typically 6 AM–10:30 PM daily—but don't count on left luggage counters being open during terrorist bombing campaigns. Passengers in transit or who have gone through passport control can take showers at Terminals 1, 3, and 4 in designated rest-room areas for £2 (including towel and soap).

Don't let Heathrow intimidate you: Thanks to efficient train, tube, and bus service, you can be in central London within 90 minutes of deplaning.

The cheapest and quickest way to get from Heathrow to central London is by Underground, on the **Piccadilly Line:** The 50- to 60-minute trip costs £3.20. There are two Underground stations at Heathrow: one serving Terminals 1–3 and one at Terminal 4. Hop aboard and you can ride directly to many of London's budget accommodation areas, like Earl's Court, South Kensington, and Russell Square. To reach other cheap lodging neighborhoods, such as around Notting Hill Gate or Victoria Station, change to the **District Line** at Earl's Court.

If you have a lot of heavy baggage, taking the tube can be a real hassle: It's crowded, and transfer points usually involve lots of walking and stair-climbing. In this case consider taking London Transport's shiny red, wheelchair-accessible **Airbuses** (tel. 0171/222–1234 or 0181/897–2688), which make 29 stops in central London. Airbuses run daily 6 AM to around 8 PM, at 15- to 30-minute intervals, and for this 60- to 75-minute voyage to the city center, you pay a reasonable £6. From Heathrow, Airbuses make pickups at all four terminals—just follow the AIRBUS or BUSES TO LONDON signs. Heading to the airport, you can catch **Airbus A1** at Victoria Station, **Airbus A2** at King's Cross, or **Airbus Direct,** which stops at the doorstep of many central London hotels. For information, call the Airbus hotline, or grab a brochure at a tourist office or at London Transport's Travel Information Centres (*see* By Underground and By Bus, *below*).

GATWICK Gatwick Airport (tel. 01293/535–353), about 30 miles south of London, accommodates a steady stream of flights from the United States and the Continent. Gatwick has a **tourist information** booth (tel. 01293/560–108), left luggage counter (£2–£3 per item per day; lower rates for long-term storage), accommodation services, and a bureau de change.

The train is your best bet for getting from Gatwick into central London. The **BritRail Gatwick Express train** (tel. 0171/928–5100 or 0171/928–2113) to Victoria Station departs Gatwick every 15 minutes daily 5 AM–8 PM, and once or twice an hour at other times. The 35-minute trip costs £8.90 one-way. The **Network SouthCentral train** (tel. 01273/206–755) goes to Victoria Station for £7.50 one-way; departure and travel times are similar to BritRail's. **Flightline 777** (tel. 0181/668–7261) offers hourly bus service between Gatwick and Victoria Coach Station daily from 6 AM to around 11 PM. The 75-minute trip costs £7.50 single.

STANSTED Stansted Airport (tel. 01279/680–500), 35 miles northeast of central London, opened in 1991 to alleviate the overcrowding at Heathrow. It serves mainly European destinations, plus American Airlines flights to Chicago, AirTransit flights to Toronto and Vancouver, and random charter flights. The airport has a **tourist desk** (tel. 01279/662–520) and a 24-hour bureau de change, but no left luggage service. To reach central London, catch the **Stansted Express** train to Liverpool Street Station; trains run every half hour Monday–Saturday 5 AM–11 PM and Sunday 7 AM–11 PM, and the 40-minute trek costs £10 one-way.

LONDON CITY The little-known London City Airport (tel. 0171/474–5555), about 9 miles southeast of central London in Silvertown, handles mostly European commuter flights. The main terminal has a **tourist info desk,** a left luggage service (£2 per item per day), and a bureau de change. To reach central London, take London Transport's **Bus 473** (80p), which shuttles between the airport and Plaistow tube station on the District Line. Buses depart every 12 minutes Monday–Saturday 5 AM–midnight and every 20 minutes Sunday 6 AM–midnight. Or catch a shuttle bus from the airport to Liverpool Street Station or to the Docklands Light Railway station at Canary Wharf; call **D & J Travel** (tel. 0171/476–6428) for more info.

BY UNDERGROUND, BUS, AND DOCKLANDS LIGHT RAILWAY

London's Underground and bus networks are overseen by **London Transport (LT)** (tel. 0171/222–1200 for recorded info or 0171/222–1234 for 24-hour help with routes, schedules, and fares). London Transport operates **Travel Information Centres** at all Heathrow terminals and in the following tube stations: Euston, King's Cross, Liverpool Street, Oxford Circus, Piccadilly Circus, St. James's Park, and Victoria. You'll want to get your hands on two of LT's free maps (available at all tube stations) when you get into town: the pocket-size **Tube Map** as well as **"Travelling in London,"** which shows Underground stops *and* bus lines for tourist attractions in central London. Travelers with disabilities should get the "**Access to the Underground**" brochure (70p), which includes info on lifts and ramps, as well as Braille maps.

Don't ask Londoners where to catch the "subway." In Britain a subway is an underground passage to allow pedestrians to cross under busy streets— instead, ask for the "tube" or "underground."

Fares for London buses, the Underground, Docklands Light Railway, and BritRail (*see below*) are based on **zones.** The Underground, Docklands Light Railway, and BritRail services are divided into zones 1–6. The bus network is divided into four zones: 1, 2, 3, and Bus Zone 4. (Bus Zone 4 covers approximately the same area as zones 4, 5, and 6 for the Underground and railways.) The more zones you cross through on your trip, the more you pay. With few exceptions, everything you want to see will be within **Zone 1** (which covers Westminster, Piccadilly Circus, Soho, Trafalgar Square, Covent Garden, the City, Victoria, Earl's Court, Kensington, and more) and **Zone 2** (which includes Camden, Hampstead, the East End, Brixton, and Greenwich Park). For more info, pick up LT's free brochures "Buying Your Ticket Made Easier" and "London Transport Fares and Tickets."

The best way to get around London is with a **Travelcard** available at the "Tickets and Assistance" windows at most tube and train stations, from some vending machines in Underground ticket halls, from LT's Travel Information Centres, and from any newsstand or tobacconist displaying the LT PASS AGENT sign. The most popular is the Travelcard for **zones 1 and 2,** which costs £3 daily, £14.80 weekly, and £56.90 monthly. Your Travelcard gets you almost unlimited use of the Underground, London Transport buses (except Airbuses), Docklands Light Railway, and most BritRail services within greater London. (One-Day Travelcards aren't valid on Night Owl buses, but the rest are.) You need a passport-type photo if you're buying a Travelcard good for a week or more, and a local address—a hostel or hotel address should work fine. In 1996, LT introduced a **Weekend Travelcard,** which works like the One-Day Travelcard but entitles you to two consecutive days' discounted travel on weekends or public holidays; for zones 1 and 2 the cost is £4.50.

BY UNDERGROUND The Underground provides comprehensive service throughout central London and more sporadic service to the suburbs. Underground stations are marked by a large red circle overlaid by a blue banner that reads UNDERGROUND. London is served by a dozen Underground lines, each color-coded; it can seem extremely confusing until you get used to it, and you'll find yourself constantly referring to the Underground map.

If you don't plan to use public transport a lot, buy individual tickets for each journey—choose between single and return, the British equivalents of one-way and round-trip. You can also buy a **carnet,** a packet of 10 single tickets. Otherwise, buy a Travelcard (*see above*). Once again, ticket prices are based on **zones.** Zone 1, the cool zone, is a bit pricier than all the other zones: Scooting around inside it costs £1.10 single (£2.20 for a return ticket). Travel inside any one of the other zones is 80p single (£1.60 return), while a trip through all six zones costs £3.20 single. You can buy tickets at electronic vending machines in most stations or at "Tickets and Assistance" windows. Remember to hold on to your ticket since you'll need it to get through the turnstiles at the exit. And beware: Roving inspectors issue an on-the-spot £10 penalty if you're caught without a ticket valid for the zones you're traveling in.

The Underground gets going around 5 AM and closes between 11:30 PM and 12:30 AM depending on which station you're in; you'll find the timetable for each station posted near the turnstiles. Generally the tube is pretty reliable, with trains every 10 minutes—but a multimillion-pound overhaul of the system has recently meant temporary station closures, route changes, and lengthy delays; listen for announcements in each station. You can roughly calculate how long a particular journey *should* take by adding three minutes for each station you'll pass through. Because the tube closes before the rest of London does, it pays to figure out London's Night Owl buses (*see below*) if you plan to party late.

BY BUS Deciphering bus routes can be a bit more complicated than figuring out tube routes. For one, color-coded, comprehensive bus-route maps are only posted at major bus stops; if you really want to master the system, pick up the free "Central London Bus Guide" at an LT Travel Information Centre (*see above*). As with the tube, bus fares are based on zones: Inside Zone 1, the adult one-way fare is 90p, or 60p for a "short hop" of less than ¾ mile; a one-way trip through Zones 1 and 2 is £1.20. But if you're doing a lot of sightseeing, you'll probably want to buy a Travelcard (*see above*).

Out on the street major bus stops are marked by plain white signs with a red LT symbol; buses stop at these points automatically. At some stops, known as **request stops** (marked by red signs with a white LT symbol and the word "request"), you'll need to flag the bus down—waving an arm once will do just fine. There are a few busy intersections in London where all buses seem to go, like Trafalgar Square, Victoria Station, and Piccadilly Circus; for these, you'll need to check a posted bus map to find out *exactly* where you should be standing for the bus to your destination.

On the newer buses, which you board at the front, you pay the driver as you enter (exact change desired but not required). On older buses, in which the driver sits in a separate cab, just hop on, take a seat, and the conductor will swing by to check your Travelcard or sell you a ticket from a coffee-grinder-like apparatus. In 1996 a blue-ribbon city panel discovered something Londoners have known for years: London buses rarely run on time. On most routes they're supposed to swing by every six minutes; in reality it can be a 15- or 30-minute wait. (Please thank the hundreds of pushy BMW owners who drive in the city's bus lanes, rather than cursing the poor bus drivers.) Because of this tarnished service record, Londoners have fled the buses—and tourists like you shouldn't have any trouble getting a seat, even during rush hour (7–9:30 AM and 4–6:30 PM). To get off a bus, pull the cord running the length of the bus above the windows, or press the button by the exit.

➤ **NIGHT OWL BUSES** • From 11 PM to 5 AM, some buses add the prefix "N" to their route numbers and are called **Night Owls.** They don't run as frequently and don't operate on quite as many routes as day buses, but at least they get you somewhere close to your destination without leaving you pence- and poundless. You'll probably have to transfer at one of the night bus nexuses like Victoria, Westminster, and especially either Piccadilly Circus or Trafalgar Square (the main transfer points for late-night buses). Note that weekly and monthly Travelcards are good for Night Owl buses, but One-Day and Weekend Travelcards are not. Night Owl single fares are also a bit more expensive than daytime ones. A final word of advice: Avoid sitting alone on the top deck of a Night Owl bus unless you would like to be mugged. If you're keen on knowing more about Night Owls, ask at an LT Travel Information Centre for the free, handy "Night Bus Guide," which includes several maps.

DOCKLANDS LIGHT RAILWAY The Docklands, the massive area east of central London along the Thames River, is served by **Docklands Light Railway (DLR),** which connects with the Underground at the following stations: Bank, Bow Road, Shadwell, Stratford, and Tower Hill. Dockland's Light Railway trains are overseen by London Transport and use the same system of passes, zones, and fares as the buses and Underground. Its two lines also show up on tube maps. Hours of operation are Monday–Saturday 5:30 AM–midnight and Sunday 7:30 AM–11:30 PM. The **Docklands Travel Hot Line** (tel. 0171/918–4000) offers info 24 hours a day.

BRITRAIL

The BritRail system is a network of above-ground train services that connects outlying districts and suburbs to central London. Recent privatization means its various routes are now handled by a variety of companies; one you're likely to encounter is the **North London** (tel. 01923/245–

001) Line, running from Richmond to North Woolwich with stops at Kew Gardens, Holburn, Hampstead, Hackney, and Docklands. Prices for BritRail trains are comparable to prices for the Underground, and you can easily transfer between the Underground and BritRail at many tube stations (transfer points are marked on tube maps). You can sometimes even use your LT Travelcard (*see* By Underground and Bus, *above*) instead of buying a separate ticket.

BY TAXI

Cabs are the most expensive form of transportation in London, but they can be reasonable if you're splitting the cost with a few other people. Traditional **"black cabs,"** which are not always black, are the most reliable. Drivers of these classy carriages have to pass a rigorous test of London streets, known as "The Knowledge," and are required to take passengers on the most direct route possible. That's not a guarantee that every cabbie is 100% honest, which is why all cabs are equipped with a meter and fare table. Weekday fares start at £1.40 and go up 20p per unit of distance/time (every 257 yards or 56 seconds). There are surcharges for each additional person (40p), each piece of luggage (10p), and booking a cab by telephone (£1.20 minimum). If you're traveling on a weekday after 8 PM or on Saturday or Sunday, rates increase 40p–60p. There's a £2 surcharge for rides during the jolly Christmas and New Year's periods. Ho, ho, ho. It's customary to tip the driver 10% of your fare. If you wish to make a complaint, note the cab number and/or the number of the driver's badge; then contact Metropolitan Police's **Public Carriage Office** (tel. 0171/230–1631 for complaints or 0171/833–0996 for lost property), open weekdays 9–4.

Tired of being chatted up by creepy, leering cab drivers? Ladycabs (tel. 0171/254–3314 or 0171/923–2266) is a northeast-London-based minicab service for women who'd rather be driven by women.

Cabs are easy to hail at all times—except when you really need them, like on weekend nights and when it suddenly begins to pour. To hail a cab on the street, first check that its yellow FOR HIRE sign is switched on, and then flail away. You can also phone ahead for a cab—but keep in mind that companies slap a hefty surcharge on "collections." **Radio Taxis** (tel. 0171/272–0272) is a 24-hour black-cab company that charges a maximum collection fee of £2.40.

MINICABS An alternative to black cabs are minicabs—their fares are normally cheaper, especially if you're traveling long distances or at night. They are run by private companies or individual drivers, and look just like regular cars. Although it's illegal for minicabs to pick up passengers on the street—you're supposed to call or walk into their office—you can usually find them lurking outside of clubs and on West End corners during the weekend wee hours. Because minicabs aren't licensed or regulated like black cabs, bargaining is possible—but to avoid nasty surprises always confirm the price with the driver *before* you get in the car. Some of the reputable, insured minicab companies include **Abbey Cars** (west London, tel. 0171/727–2637), **Greater London Hire** (north London, tel. 0181/340–2450), **London Cabs Limited** (east London, tel. 0181/778–3000), and **Newhame Minicabs** (south London, tel. 0181/472–0400).

Staying in London

AMERICAN EXPRESS American Express has plenty of offices in London that offer the usual array of services, including commission-free currency exchange for cardholders. Only the main office in the Haymarket handles client mail. *6 Haymarket, London SW1Y 4BS, tel. 0171/930–4411. Tube: Charing Cross or Piccadilly Circus. Open weekdays 9–5:30, Sat. 9–4 (until 6 for currency exchange), Sun. 10–6 (currency exchange only). Letter pickup available during weekday business hours and weekends 9–noon.*

Other full-service American Express locations in London include **The City** (111 Cheapside, tel. 010/600–5522; Tube: Bank or St. Paul's); **Knightsbridge** (78 Brompton Rd., tel. 0171/584–6182; Tube: Knightsbridge); **Mayfair** (89 Mount St., tel. 0171/499–4436; Tube: Bond Street); and **Victoria** (102–104 Victoria St., tel. 0171/828–7411; Tube: Victoria). There are also a dozen other AmEx branches that only offer bureaux de change; look in the phone book for the location nearest you.

BUREAUX DE CHANGE While bureaux de change are everywhere in London, actually using them is like flushing money down the toilet—their exchange rates are 10%–15% worse than what the banks offer. The only exceptions are **Thomas Cook,** which has travel offices all over town, and **American Express** (*see above*); both charge bank rates for their respective checks. Otherwise, if you're desperate for cash after-hours, **Chequepoint** has six 24-hour branches with competitive rates: 37–38 Coventry St. (tel. 0171/839–3772); 222 Earl's Court Rd. (tel. 0171/373–9515); 71 Gloucester Rd. (tel. 0171/379–9682); 548 Oxford St. (tel. 0171/723–1005); 2 Queensway (tel. 0171/229–0093); and Victoria Station (tel. 0171/828–0014). Know that exchange rates go up and down daily and even vary from branch to branch of a particular agency, so it pays to shop around.

BUSINESS HOURS Standard business hours are Monday–Saturday 9–5:30. Many major stores stay open later (until 7 or 8) once a week, often Wednesday or Thursday. Most **banks** are open weekdays 9:30–3:30; some have extended hours Thursday evening, and a few are open Saturday morning. **Newsagents** are open daily. Until recently it was (thanks to the Church) a no-no for stores to remain open on Sunday, but plenty of London pharmacies, grocers, department stores, and clothing stores now do.

DISCOUNT TRAVEL AGENCIES If you're looking for discount flights or cheap train, ferry, and bus tickets, check the *Evening Standard* (30p), a daily newspaper, or *Time Out* (£1.70), a weekly magazine, both available at newsstands. Also good is *TNT* (free), a weekly budget-travel magazine with an Aussie bent; it's available at newsstands in Earl's Court and the West End. All have tons of listings, though you'll have to phone around and visit a few shops to track down the best deals. Most of London's bucket shops offer student discounts, InterRail passes (for those living in the United Kingdom longer than six months), as well as flights, ferries, trains to the Continent, and more. One note: Some cheap flights might seem too cheap to be true, and perhaps they are. Watch out for unnecessary "extra" charges, make sure you'll be able to get a full refund in event of a flight cancellation, and don't give out your credit card number until you've agreed on a specific flight (and have details in writing). Also check to see that your agency or tour operator holds a license from the ABTA and/or ATOL.

The following bucket shops are reliable and consistently offer some of the best prices in town: **Travel CUTS** (295A Regent St., W1, tel. 0171/255–1944; Tube: Oxford Circus); **Top Deck Travel** (131–135 Earl's Court Rd., W8, tel. 0171/370–4555; Tube: Earl's Court); and **Trailfinders** (42–50 Earl's Court Rd., W8, tel. 0171/938–3366 or 0171/937–5400; Tube: Earl's Court).

Campus Travel. This independent budget-travel agency has offices in some YHA Adventure Shops and in the student unions of UCL and South Bank University. Call for quotes on airfares, rail passes, you name it. *52 Grosvenor Gardens, SW1, tel. 0171/730–3402. Tube: Victoria. Open weekdays 9–6 (Thurs. until 8), Sat. 10–5, Sun. 10–3. Other locations: UCL Union, 25 Gordon St., WC1, tel. 0171/383–5337; South Bank University Student Union, Keyworth St., SE1, tel. 0171/401–8666; 14 Southampton St., WC2, tel. 0171/836–3343; 174 Kensington High St., W8, tel. 0171/938–2188.*

Council Travel. Off busy Oxford Street, Council caters to budget travelers with its worldwide discount flights, train and coach tickets, car rentals, and ISIC cards. *28A Poland St., W1, tel. 0171/437–7767. Tube: Oxford Circus. Open weekdays 9–6 (Thurs. until 7), Sat. 10–5.*

STA Travel. The four STA offices in London offer deals on just about everything travel-related, including ISIC cards, travel insurance, hostels, and flights. You can also purchase tickets by phone at 0171/361–616 (Europe) or 0171/361–6262 (Africa, Asia, and the Americas). *86 Old Brompton Rd., SW7, tel. 0171/581–4132. Tube: South Kensington. Open weekdays 9:30–6:30 (Fri. until 6), Sat. 10–4. Other locations: 117 Euston Rd., NW1, tel. 0171/465–0484; 11 Goodge St., W1, tel. 0171/436–7779; 38 Store St., WC1, tel. 0171/580–7733.*

EMBASSIES **Australian High Commission.** *Australia House, The Strand, WC2B 4LA, tel. 0171/379–4334. Tube: Temple. Open weekdays 9:30–3:30.*

Canadian High Commission–Consular Section. *38 Grosvenor St., W1X 0AA, tel. 0171/258–6600. Tube: Bond Street. Open weekdays 9–4 (visas issued weekdays 9–11).*

New Zealand High Commission. *New Zealand House, 80 Haymarket, SW1Y 4TQ, tel. 0171/930–8422. Tube: Charing Cross or Piccadilly Circus. Open weekdays 9–5.*

United States Embassy. Passports are handled weekdays 8:30–11 (additional hours Mondays, Wednesdays, and Fridays 2–4) around the corner at the Passport Office, 55 Upper Brook Street. Visas are handled by appointment only. *Main Embassy Offices: 24 Grosvenor Sq., W1A 1AE, tel. 0171/499–9000. Tube: Marble Arch or Bond Street. Open weekdays 8:30–5:30.*

EMERGENCIES AND MEDICAL AID The general emergency number for **ambulance, police,** and **fire** is 999, and you don't need to deposit money to call. The **Samaritans** (tel. 0171/734–2800) 24-hour helpline assists anyone in emotional crisis or feeling suicidal. **National Association of Victims Support Schemes** (Cranmer House, 39 Brixton Rd., SW9, tel. 0171/735–9166) has trained volunteers who can provide advice and emotional support to victims of crime. Hours are weekdays 9–5:30. The **London Rape Crisis Centre** (tel. 0171/837–1600) 24-hour phoneline offers counseling for victims of rape or assault. The nonprofit **Pregnancy Advisory Service** (11–13 Charlotte St., W1, tel. 0171/637–8962) offers a full range of services for women, including pregnancy tests, abortion counseling, morning-after contraception, and PAP smears. The toll-free, 24-hour **National AIDS Helpline** (tel. 0800/567–123) offers confidential counseling and info on AIDS, HIV, and safe-sex practices.

➤ **DOCTORS** • If you're a visitor from one of the EU or Commonwealth countries, rejoice: You can receive free medical treatment while here in London. If you're from some other country and are seeking nonemergency medical treatment, you should check your insurance policy and call first to inquire about rates. Keep in mind that the ISIC comes with hospitalization insurance; read its "Summary of Coverage" card for more info. For serious injuries, the following hospitals have 24-hour emergency wards:

Guy's Hospital. *St. Thomas St., SE1, tel. 0171/955–5000. Tube: London Bridge.*

Royal Free. *Pond St., NW3, Hampstead, tel. 0171/794–0500. Tube: Belsize Park.*

University College London Hospital. *Gower St., WC1, tel. 0171/387–9300. Tube: Euston Square or Warren Street.*

➤ **DENTISTS** • **Eastman Dental Hospital.** Free walk-in emergency dental care. No appointment—it's first come, first served. *256 Gray's Inn Rd., WC1, tel. 0171/837–3646. Tube: Chancery Lane or King's Cross. Open weekdays 8:30–5:30.*

Guy's Hospital Dental School. Provides walk-in emergency dental care, though for nonemergencies you must make an appointment. *St. Thomas St., SE1, tel. 0171/955–5000. Tube: London Bridge. Open weekdays 9–5, weekends 9:30–4 for emergencies only.*

➤ **PHARMACIES** • Chemists (equivalent to an American drugstore) are plentiful in London. Those with late hours include **Bliss Chemists** (5 Marble Arch, W1, tel. 0171/723–6116; Tube: Marble Arch), open daily 9 AM–midnight, and **Boots** (75 Queensway, W2, tel. 0171/229–9266; Tube: Bayswater), open daily until 10 PM. The Boots in Victoria Station (tel. 0171/834–0676; Tube: Victoria) is open weekdays 7:30 AM–8 PM, Saturday 9–7.

LUGGAGE STORAGE Heathrow, Gatwick, and London City airports all offer luggage storage, called "left luggage" (*see* Getting Around London, *above*). In town, the most convenient place to store luggage is in **Victoria Station** (*see* Coming and Going, By Train, *above*). The left luggage counter is between Platforms 7 and 8 and open daily 7 AM–10 PM. Daily rates are £3–£3.50; lockers cost £2.50–£5. Call 0171/928–5151 for more info. The nearby **Victoria Coach Station** (*see* Coming and

Launderettes are all over London, but if you find yourself staying near Russell Square in Bloomsbury, do your laundry in style at Duds 'n Suds (49 Brunswick Shopping Centre, tel. 0171/837–1122). While your clothes circle around, you can play a game of snooker, have a snack at the bar, or watch the large-screen TV.

Going, By Bus, *above*) has a left luggage counter at Gate 6 offering bargain daily rates of £2–£2.50. It's open daily 7 AM–11 PM; call 0171/730–3466 ext. 225, for more info. Both are mere steps from Victoria tube station. **Students-Tourists Storage** (tel. 0800/622–244), with warehouses near Victoria, Earl's Court, and King's Cross, will store your stuff for £5 per item per week.

MAIL The Royal Mail service, though fairly reliable, is very slow. Outbound letters to North America take up to four days longer than incoming ones. Well, at least it's easy to buy stamps: Besides the main offices, you'll find mini–post offices in butcher shops, liquor stores ("off-licenses"), and chemists. Just keep your eyes peeled for POST OFFICE signs bearing a red oval with yellow lettering. For post office addresses, check the London Yellow Pages, or call the **Customer Helpline** (tel. 0345/223–344), which will furnish post office locations, telephone numbers, and hours. Typically, post offices are open weekdays 9–5:30, Saturday 9–12:30.

➤ **SENDING MAIL HOME** • Rates from the United Kingdom are 42p for an international airmail letter (up to 10 grams), 37p for an international aerogramme, and 36p for an international postcard. First-class letters and cards to all EU countries are 25p (up to 20 grams). Be sure to get the free PAR AVION/BY AIR MAIL stickers when you buy your stamps. If you're sending a letter, do it by air mail (a week to 10 days) because surface mail can take from four to nine weeks! Surface mail is really for sending home gifts or heavy items you don't want to carry around. Boxes can be bought at office-supply stores like W. H. Smith and at some post offices. You'll need to fill out a small, green customs sticker that states the weight and contents (so much for surprise gifts).

➤ **RECEIVING MAIL** • If you hold an AmEx card, you can have mail sent to AmEx's Haymarket office (*see above*). Otherwise, you can receive letters from loved ones via poste restante at any London post office (check the list in the London Yellow Pages under "Post Offices"). Have your friends write "Hold for 30 days" in the upper left corner of the package/envelope and address it to: YOUR NAME, Poste Restante, followed by the post office name, address, and postal code. One option is the mammoth, central **Trafalgar Square Post Office.** Don't forget to bring your passport or photo ID when you go to fetch your mail. *Trafalgar Square Post Office, 24–28 William IV St., London, WC2N 4DL, tel. 0171/930–4802. Tube: Charing Cross. Open Mon.–Sat. 8–8 (Fri. from 8:30 AM).*

MEDIA

➤ **INTERNET ACCESS** • Many people are Internet junkies who would shrivel up and die without a regular injection of e-mail and net surfing. Luckily, London has quite a few places where you can check your mail, as well as get your caffeine fix. Visit the amazing **Cyberia** (39 Whitfield St., W1, tel. 0171/209–0982, cyberia@easynet.co.uk; Tube: Goodge Street), which has 10 PCs providing Internet access for £2.50 per half hour (£1.90 for students); a friendly, helpful staff not infected by the "cooler-than-thou" virus; a good range of food; and a varied,

Postal Codes

Postal codes aren't just for mail: London is divided into postal districts, whose corresponding code is a helpful directional. Postal codes are also used to distinguish between two streets with the same name, so be certain of your destination before jumping in a cab or you may find yourself in NW8 instead of W8. Postal codes are almost always listed on street signs, as is the borough the street falls under. A few handy ones to keep in mind while you're exploring: WC1: Bloomsbury; WC2: Covent Garden, The Strand, Leicester Square; W1: Mayfair, Soho; W8: Kensington; SW1: Westminster, Victoria; SW3: Chelsea, Knightsbridge; SW5: Earl's Court; SW7: South Kensington; N1: Islington, King's Cross; NW1: Camden Town.

London Postal Districts

SW6
EARLS
COURT
SW14
Kensington High St.
W6
W12
W11
Holland Park Ave.
KENSINGTON
Nothing
Hill Gate
W10
NW
10
NW6
W9
Westway
A40(M)
PADDINGTON
Maida Vale
NW8
Wellington
Rd.
SW10
SW5
Cromwell Rd.
Old Brompton Rd.
W8
Kensington Rd.
KNIGHTS-
BRIDGE
SW7
Brompton Rd.
Brompton
Rd.
Knightsbridge
Bayswater Rd.
W2
Edgware Rd.
Hyde Park
MARYLEBONE
Marylebone Rd.
Baker St.
Regent's
Park
NW1
Fulham Rd.
SW3
CHELSEA
Chelsea
Embankment
River Thames
Battersea
Park
VICTORIA
MAYFAIR
Piccadilly
ST.
JAMES'S
The Mall
Oxford St.
W1
Gower St.
Tottenham
Court Rd.
SOHO
High Holborn
Euston Rd.
BLOOMS-
BURY
Ferenholl St.
Everholt St.
SW1
PIMLICO
WEST-
MINSTER
Victoria St.
Vauxhall Br.
Westminster Br.
Charing Cross Rd.
Strand
WC2
WC1
Gray's Inn Rd.
FINSBURY
Pentonville Rd.
N1
SW8
Kennington Pk. Rd.
SE11
LAMBETH
Lambeth Rd.
Waterloo Rd.
Fleet St.
HOLBORN
Aldersgate
EC4
EC1
Old St.
City Rd.
SE5
SE17
WALWORTH
BOROUGH
SE1
Cannon St.
London
Br.
THE CITY
London Wall
EC2
EC3
Kingsland
Rd.
Whitechapel Rd.
SE15
SE16
River
Thames
Commercial Rd.
E1
E2

N

32

lively clientele—not all of whom come for the computers. The Cyberians are also the force behind *Cyberia* magazine (£2.20) and Channel Cyberia (http://www.channel.cyberiacafe.net), the world's first Internet service with a 24-hour programming. The stylish **Café Internet** (22 Buckingham Palace Rd., SW1, tel. 0171/233–5786, cafe@cafeinternet.co.uk; Tube: Victoria) has 10 PCs available for £3 per half hour (£2.50 for students). The 10 PCs at **Cyberspy Café** (15 Golden Sq., W1, tel. 0171/287–2242; Tube: Piccadilly Circus) actually seem to clutter up the pristine interior. Internet time costs £5 per hour, £3 per half hour. Basic nibbles and some nice art by local artists can distract you as you wait for a terminal. Lurking in the basement of Dillons bookstore, **Cyber.St@tion** (82 Gower St., WC1, tel. 0171/636–1577, cstation@dillons.co.uk; Tube: Goodge Street) has 8 PCs available for £5 per hour, £3 per half hour. It's seldom busy and the staff is really helpful, but the environment is rather airless. For more info on on-line resources, *see* Useful Websites, in Visitor Resources, *above*.

➤ **MAGAZINES** • *Time-Out* (£1.70), fresh off the press every Tuesday, has more event listings than any other magazine in London as well as fine articles on current events, fashion, and entertainment. *What's On* (£1.20) has fewer listings, but its reviews are often more detailed. Music fans should check out the weekly newspaper-style *Melody Maker* (80p) and *New Music Express* (*NME*, 85p), or the glossy monthlies *Vox* (£2.20), *Select* (£2.20), and *Q* (£2.50), all of which often have free tapes attached. *Wax* (£1.95) focuses on DJ and club culture.

Despite murmurs about its decline, the definitive style mag is still *The Face* (£2). Alongside articles on music and fashion, this monthly also has a new comic strip by Jamie Hewlett, creator of *Tank Girl*. *i-D* (£2.20) is another style bible, which wipes out last month's fashion with every new issue. *Spectator* (£2.20) provides news of the enlightened elite and the latest academic debate, while *Private Eye* (£1) dishes out satire so sharp it's sometimes difficult to feel the blade. *The Economist* (£2.20) provides comprehensive international news, though with a right-wing bent.

➤ **NEWSPAPERS** • Rupert Murdoch is a global name, and the Australian-born American has managed to get his hands on several British newspapers including the *Sun* (30p), which sets the world standard for unscrupulous journalism with daily features like the topless woman known as the "page three girl." Murdoch also has his moneyed fists on the *Times* (30p), a respectable (as far as it goes in journalism these days) newspaper whose Sunday edition (£1) is the perfect accessory for Sunday brunch. The *Daily Telegraph* (40p) is Britain's most conservative paper, the liberal *Guardian* (45p) argues the other side of the story, and the *Independent* (40p) comes down somewhere between the two. The *Evening Standard* (30p) also has all-purpose entertainment info, especially in the free supplement "Hot Tickets," which comes out every Friday. It can't hold a candle to *Time Out*, but some of its features are quite good.

➤ **RADIO** • London has innumerable pirate radio stations on the FM waveband that appear as quickly as they disappear. Some of the stations seem to serve as training grounds for the legal stations; talented DJs are snapped up, while others remain, singing along (off-key) with their favorite tracks. You'll hear some very obscure titles, and the DJs are sometimes amusing. The following FM mainstays aren't nearly as interesting: **BBC Radio 1** (98.8) plays pop and indie music, **BBC Radio 2** (89.1) plays those forty- or fiftysomething faves like Burt Bacharach, **BBC Radio 3** (91.3) is a sleepy classical station, and **BBC Radio 4** (93.5) is talk radio. **Jazz FM** (102.2) plays jazz and blues, **Choice FM** (96.9) features funk and soul, and **Kiss FM** (100) plays dance music and often features celebrity DJs mixing live on the air. **Capital FM** (95.8) and Richard Branson's **Virgin Radio** (105.8) offer a wide range of pop music; Gary Crowley's show on part-time talk-radio station **GLR** (94.9, Monday–Thursday 10 PM–2 AM) is a great place to hear new British pop. For strictly news there's always **London News** (97.3).

PHONES Country Code: 44. After years of near-monopoly, British Telecom (BT) has had to give up some of its market share to competitors Mercury and Inter Phone, and rumors of new companies run rampant. **Mercury** has dropped out of the pay-phone market to concentrate on cellular phones, but you may still see the empty hulks of their oddly shaped phone booths. **Inter Phone** boxes have appeared in scattered locations around London; their phones accept coins only and seem to give you a few more seconds for your 10p. **BT** phones are everywhere, though the old, red phone boxes have largely been replaced with larger, easier-to-clean glass booths. The ones with a red stripe around them accept standard English coins, while those with a green stripe require BT phone cards—a plastic card that's worth a fixed number of 10p units—though some also accept credit cards. **Phone cards** come in denominations of £2, £5, £10, and £20 and are available at newsagents, train and bus stations, tourist-information centers, and numerous other locations; look for green signs saying PHONE CARDS SOLD HERE. BT is introducing a newer model of its phone card with a flashy hologram and easier-to-read "units remaining" strip down the side. To confuse matters more, these new cards and the new-style phones that accept them are only located in scattered areas of town: The new phones are marked with a red stripe (because they also accept coins) and a big green arrow. Over the next few years BT plans to phase out the old phone-card phones. To use either model, lift the receiver, insert your card into the slot, and dial your number. An LED panel indicates how many units you've used. To call the **operator,** dial 100; for **directory inquiries** (information), dial 192.

➤ **LOCAL CALLS** • London has two area codes: 0171 for inner London and 0181 for outer London. If you're phoning from one London area code to another, you must dial the area code. Local calls start at 10p. Modern pay phones display how fast your money is being gobbled up; older phones without displays beep when your money is about to run out. Pay phones will give back any unused coins fed into the slot, but they don't make change, so think twice about using a £1 coin for a local call. If you have credit left and need to make another call, don't hang up. Instead, press the "follow-on call" button—on new phones it's marked, on older phones look for a small, square button away from the keypad—to use the remaining credit. If there's someone waiting, you have credit left, and you're done on the phone, it's good karma to press the follow-on button and hand the receiver to the other person.

➤ **INTERNATIONAL CALLS** • To dial direct from England, first dial 00, then dial the country code (1 for the United States and Canada, 353 for the Republic of Ireland, 61 for Australia, and 64 for New Zealand), then the area code and phone number. Calls to Northern Ireland from England, Scotland, or Wales can be dialed without the international code. To dial direct or collect using American carriers, contact **AT&T Direct Access**^{SM} (tel. 0800/890–011 or 0500/890–303), **MCI** (tel. 0800/890–222), or **Sprint** (tel. 0800/890–877)—the call to the carrier is free. Direct dialing is considerably more expensive from pay phones than from private ones, but many residential phone bills don't itemize calls, so it's difficult to reimburse your hosts. Have a phone card with lots of credit or a ton of change ready, especially £1 coins. To place an incredibly expensive collect call using BT, dial 155 to be connected with an operator.

VISITOR INFORMATION   The main **London Tourist Information Centre** provides details on transportation, lodging, and theater, concert and tour bookings. It doesn't have a public info line—other than a reservations line (tel. 0171/824–8844) for overpriced lodgings at a hefty £5 fee—so go in person and pick up a fistful of brochures. Other information centers are located in **Harrods** (Brompton Rd.; Tube: Knightsbridge), **Selfridges** (Oxford St.; Tube: Bond Street or Marble Arch), **Liverpool Street Station, Waterloo Terminal, Heathrow Airport** (Terminals 1, 2, and 3), and **Gatwick Airport** (International Arrivals Concourse). *Main office: Victoria Station, SW1, no phone. Tube: Victoria. Open daily 8–7.*

British Travel Centre provides details about travel and entertainment for the whole of Britain and makes lodging reservations (£5 fee). It has no phone line for public inquiries, so you must visit in person. The center has different areas for different services, so make sure you're in the right queue. *12 Regent St., SW1, no phone. Tube: Piccadilly Circus. Open May–Sept., weekdays 9–6:30, Sat. 9–5, Sun. 10–4; Oct.-Apr., weekdays 9–6:30, weekends 10–4.*

EXPLORING LONDON 2

By Jennifer L. Brewer and Sunny Delaney

Like most great cities of the world, London is many different things to many different people. Within a few short blocks, concrete monstrosities built after the Blitz give way to swaths of greenery that kings used as their royal hunting grounds hundreds of years ago. The City, the traditional stomping ground for financial movers and shakers, borders the East End, where struggling artists set up shop in run-down warehouses. Viewed from above, London may look like one seething megalopolis, but wander around the twisting streets and you'll discover it's a maze of dense, distinctly flavored neighborhoods.

Londoners tend to be very neighborhood-oriented, spending a lot of time in their particular residential pockets, many of which function as self-contained communities. Indeed, until the Industrial Revolution of the 19th century, what's now called London was a hodgepodge of villages—suburban satellites of the *original* City of London, the financial heart of London that has existed along the banks of the River Thames since the Romans settled it almost 2,000 years ago. Though the City attracts plenty of visitors, it can't compare with Westminster, London's tourist mecca, home to royal palaces past and present and the government buildings surrounding Parliament Square. This has been Royal London with a capital "R" since the 11th century, when King Edward the Confessor moved his court here, away from the cramped quarters of the City.

Apart from a few sights on the outskirts, you're better off checking out London on foot. In the central area, tube stations are abundant and fairly close together, but if you *always* hop on the tube to travel between sights, you won't get a decent idea of the city's layout. Note that the tube map is stylized, so stations that appear distant on the map may actually be within blocks of each other. If you're from a grid-oriented city, it's a safe bet that on foot you'll end up hopelessly lost within minutes, so pick up a copy of the **London A to Z** street atlas (Brits pronounce it "A to Zed"), sold at newsstands and schlock shops throughout the city. The mini-London edition (£3.25) is just the right size to fit in your pocket, but if you'll be in London for a month or more, consider splurging on the wire-bound version (£5)—it's much sturdier and you won't be shedding bits of Kensington as you walk down the street. Don't worry about looking like a tourist: Locals, including cab drivers, swear by it.

GUIDED TOURS

Walking tours are a favorite of London residents and tourists alike. Perennial favorites include the haunts of the Beatles, the trail of Jack the Ripper, and gambols through historic London pubs, but you can find a half-dozen others daily, including tours specializing in arts, architecture, music, gardens, history, you name it. All are listed in *Time Out* (£1.70), in the "Around Town" section. Tours average £4.50 per person (often less for students), last about two hours, and require no

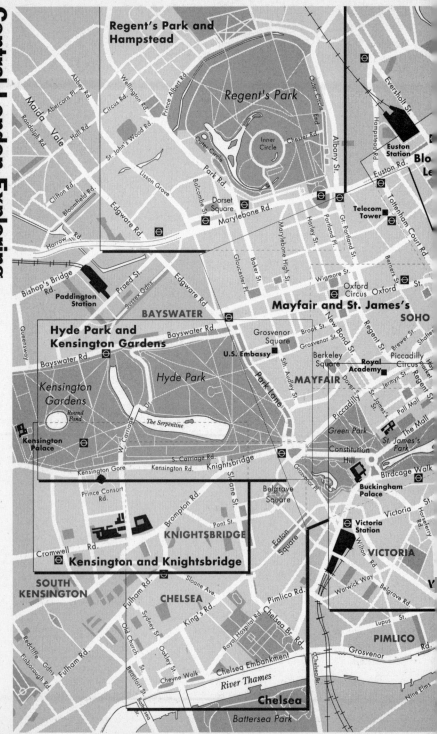

Regent's Park and
Hampstead

Regent's Park

Inner
Circle

Outer Circle

Chester Rd.

Albany St.

Hampstead Rd.

Eversholt St.

Euston
Station

Blo
Le

Euston Rd.

Tottenham Court Rd.

Abbey Rd.

Abercorn Pl.

Wellington Rd.

Circus Rd.

St. John's Wood Rd.

Prince Albert Rd.

Outer Circle

Park Rd.

Maida Vale

Randolph Rd.

Hall Rd.

Clifton Rd.

Bloomfield Rd.

Harrow Rd.

Edgware Rd.

Lisson Grove

Balcombe St.

Dorset
Square

Marylebone Rd.

Marylebone High St.

Harley St.

Portland Pl.

Gt. Portland St.

Telecom
Tower

Berners St.

Bishop's Bridge
Rd.

Paddington
Station

Praed St.

Sussex Gdns.

Edgware Rd.

Gloucester Pl.

Baker St.

Wigmore St.

Oxford
Circus

Oxford

St.

Queensway

BAYSWATER

Bayswater Rd.

Hyde Park and
Kensington Gardens

Bayswater Rd.

Grosvenor
Square

Brook St.

New Bond St.

Regent St.

Mayfair and St. James's

SOHO

Brewer St.

Shaftes

Bayswater Rd.

U.S. Embassy

Grosvenor St.

Berkeley
Square

Royal
Academy

Piccadilly
Circus

Regent St.

Market

Kensington
Gardens

Hyde Park

Sth. Audley St.

Park Lane

Dover St.

MAYFAIR

Jermyn St.

St. James's

Piccadilly

Pall Mall

Round
Pond

The Serpentine

W. Carriage Dr.

Piccadilly

Green Park

The Mall

St. James's
Park

Kensington
Palace

S. Carriage Rd.

Kensington Rd.

Knightsbridge

Constitution
Hill

Birdcage Walk

Kensington Gore

Grosvenor Pl.

Belgrave
Square

Buckingham
Palace

Prince Consort
Rd.

Brompton Rd.

Pont St.

Sloane St.

Victoria
Station

Victoria

Horseferry Rd.

Cromwell Rd.

KNIGHTSBRIDGE

Eaton
Square

Wilton Rd.

VICTORIA

Kensington and Knightsbridge

SOUTH
KENSINGTON

Fulham Rd.

Sloane Ave.

CHELSEA

King's Rd.

Pimlico Rd.

Chelsea Br. Rd.

Warwick Way

Belgrave Rd.

Redcliffe Gdns.

Finborough Rd.

Fulham Rd.

Old Church St.

Sydney St.

Oakley St.

Royal Hospital Rd.

Lupus St.

PIMLICO

Grosvenor Rd.

Nine Elms

Cheyne Walk

Chelsea Embankment

River Thames

Chelsea

Beaufort St.

Chelsea Br.

Battersea Park

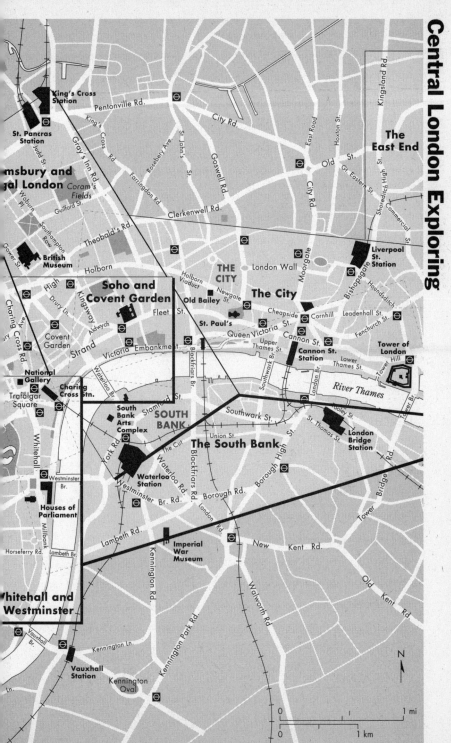

King's Cross
Station

St. Pancras
Station

Pentonville Rd.

King's Cross Rd.

Gray's Inn Rd.

Rosebery Ave.

City Rd.

St. John's St.

Goswell Rd.

East Road

Hoxton St.

Old St.

Gt. Eastern St.

Shoreditch High St.

Kingsland Rd.

Commercial St.

**The
East End**

msbury and
jal London

Woburn Pl.

Southampton Row

Gower St.

Coram's
Fields

Guilford St.

Theobald's Rd.

Farringdon Rd.

Clerkenwell Rd.

London Wall

Moorgate

Liverpool
St.
Station

Bishopsgate

Houndsditch

British
Museum

Holborn

High

Drury Ln.

Kingsway

**Soho and
Covent Garden**

Holborn
Viaduct

Newgate
St.

Old Bailey

**THE
CITY**

Cheapside

Cornhill

Leadenhall St.

Fenchurch St.

The City

Charing Cross Rd.

Covent
Garden

Aldwych

Strand

Fleet St.

St. Paul's

Queen Victoria St.

Cannon St.

Cannon St.
Station

Upper
Thames St.

Lower
Thames St.

Tower of
London

Tower Hill

National
Gallery

Trafalgar
Square

Victoria Embankment

Waterloo Rd.

Blackfriars Br.

Stamford St.

Southwark St.

Southwark St.

Tooley St.

St. Thomas St.

River Thames

London Br.

Tower Br.

Charing
Cross Stn.

South
Bank
Arts
Complex

**SOUTH
BANK**

Union St.

Borough High St.

London
Bridge
Station

The South Bank

Whitehall

Westminster
Br.

Houses of
Parliament

Millbank

York Rd.

The Cut

Waterloo
Station

Westminster Br. Rd.

Blackfriars Rd.

Borough Rd.

London Rd.

New   Kent   Rd.

Old   Kent   Rd.

Tower Bridge Rd.

Horseferry Rd.

Lambeth Br.

Lambeth Rd.

Imperial
War
Museum

Kennington Rd.

Kennington Park Rd.

Walworth Rd.

**hitehall and
Westminster**

Vauxhall
Br.

Kennington Ln.

Vauxhall
Station

Kennington
Oval

N

0   1 mi

0   1 km

advance reservations (just show up at the starting point and pay the guide). The best and biggest conductor of walking tours is **London Walks** (tel. 0171/624–3978), which has humorous, knowledgeable guides and a wide selection of routes, including the London of Oscar Wilde, "Spies' and Spycatchers' London," and a bunch of jolly pub crawls. **Historical Walks of London** (tel. 0181/668–4019) has a menu of pub walks and tours of literary London, legal London, and royal London.

A more flexible (and cost-effective) way to structure your wanderings is to purchase one of the many self-guided walking-tour booklets available at tourist offices. The **Silver Jubilee Walkway** (10 mi) takes you past most of the big-name attractions in central London (the path is marked by a series of silver crowns set into the sidewalks). **Royal Parks Walk** (14.2 mi) takes you past the interesting sights in Hyde Park, Kensington Gardens, Primrose Hill, Regent's Park, Green Park, and St. James's Park. Still under construction is the **London Wall Walk,** which will eventually allow the intrepid to loop around the perimeter of the original city of London.

BY BUS The Original London Sightseeing Tour (tel. 0181/877–1722), **The Big Bus Company** (tel. 0181/944–7810), and **London Pride Sightseeing Company** (tel. 01708/631–122) all offer frequent open-top, double-decker buses to the major sights of central London; charge £10 for a 24-hour ticket; and allow you to hop on and off the company's buses all day long. Additionally, Original London offers £17 combination packages with either Madame Tussaud's Wax Museum or the Tower of London; it saves you a little money and you get to move to the front of the queue at either place. London Pride also offers a route to Greenwich (*see Near London, below*) via Docklands, the developing (and struggling) area along the Thames in east London.

BY BOAT One of the most pleasant (but least hair-friendly) ways to get a feel for the city is to catch a cruise on the mighty Thames. River-tour companies generally offer live commentary, plus snacks, drinks, and even full bars. Most boats can accommodate travelers in wheelchairs. **Westminster Passenger Service Association (WPSA) Upriver** (tel. 0171/930–2062) makes the trip from Westminster Pier to **Kew** (90 min; £5 single, £8 return) and **Hampton Court Palace** (3 hrs; £7 single, £10 return) in Richmond (*see below*) five times daily, Easter–October; call for a current schedule. Catch an early boat so you'll have plenty of time to explore the gardens and/or palace. Just as much fun are its 45-minute **evening cruises** (£5 return), offered daily May–September at 7:30 and 8:30 PM, between Westminster Pier and the Tower of London. As your boat floats along, lounge on the deck with a glass of wine and watch London transform itself by twilight. **Thames Passenger Service Federation** (tel. 0171/930–4097) runs trips

Sightseeing on the Cheap

If you want a motorized overview of London without the droning commentary, save some cash by joining London's commuters on a standard double-decker bus. You can use your Zones 1 and 2 Travelcard on the following routes:

- *Bus 11: King's Road, Sloane Square, Victoria Station, Westminster Abbey, Houses of Parliament and Big Ben, Whitehall, Trafalgar Square, The Strand, Fleet Street, and St. Paul's Cathedral.*

- *Bus 12: Bayswater, Marble Arch, Oxford Street, Piccadilly Circus, Trafalgar Square, Horse Guards, Whitehall, Houses of Parliament and Big Ben, Westminster Bridge.*

- *Bus 19: Sloane Square, Knightsbridge, Hyde Park Corner, Green Park, Piccadilly Circus, Shaftsbury Avenue, Oxford Street, Bloomsbury, Islington.*

- *Bus 88: Oxford Circus, Piccadilly Circus, Trafalgar Square, Whitehall, Houses of Parliament, Westminster Abbey, Tate Gallery.*

downriver from Westminster Pier to **Greenwich** (50 min; £5.30 single, £6.30 return) every 30 minutes from 10:30 to 4, April–October; less frequently in winter. Contact **Port of London Authority** (tel. 0171/265–2656) for information on cruises offered by other companies. For information on boat trips along Regent's Canal, *see box* Camden Cruising, *below.*

Major Attractions

When choosing which of London's major sights to visit, listen closely to your internal tour guide. Your budget will also play a role: Even though the best and most famous museums are free, many other attractions aren't cheap—though an ISIC card may get you a slight discount. Despite London's size, the major sights are relatively close together, so planning a day can be easy. But the best advice of all is to know when you've hit your limit, and head for the pub at the first sign of brain fade. It shows a measure of respect for the great metropolis, which has more to offer than you could possibly take advantage of in a day, a week, or even a year.

BRITISH MUSEUM

The British Museum's collection of artifacts numbers into the millions, and on display within its 2½ miles of galleries is the golden hoard of two and a half centuries of Empire, the booty bought—and flat-out stolen—from Britain's far-flung colonies. Parliament was inspired to found London's first public museum in 1753, after acquiring the extensive ethnographic collection of Sir Hans Sloane, as well as several smaller collections of books and manuscripts. Soon, it seemed everyone had something to donate—George II gave the Royal Library, Sir William Hamilton (husband of Nelson's mistress, Emma) gave antique vases, Charles Townley gave sculptures, the Bank of England gave coins—and the museum's holdings quickly outgrew their original space in Montague House. After the addition of such major pieces as the Rosetta Stone and other Egyptian antiquities (spoils of the Napoleonic War), and the Parthenon sculptures (brought from Greece by Lord Elgin in 1816), Robert Smirke was commissioned to build an appropriately large and monumental building on the same site—though, due to lack of funds, construction was dragged out over 20 years and several architects. The museum has since added the Dead Sea Scrolls, Black Obelisk, Magna Carta, the Lindow Bog Man, and countless other items of worldwide significance.

The collection spans the centuries as well as the globe, featuring artifacts from the prehistoric era, ancient Egypt and Assyria, right on through to Renaissance and contemporary works. The sheer magnitude of the collection (and sometimes the crowd) overwhelms. A good strategy for exploring is to take the 90-minute tour (£6) given Monday–Saturday at 10:45, 11:15, 1:45, and 2:15, Sunday at 3, 3:20, and 3:45, and come back later to whatever intrigued you the most. Another is to buy the £1 souvenir map and follow one of their recommended tours. Visually impaired visitors can call to arrange a special "touch tour" of Roman sculpture. The museum also offers free 45-minute "Eye-Opener" tours focusing on a small section of the collections, gallery talks (11:30), and lectures (1:15); for current listings pick up the "Events" pamphlet at the information desk.

In many ways the **ground floor** is the most impressive in the museum, featuring big-name treasures from Greece and Rome (rooms 1–15). Get up close and personal with the exquisite bas-relief carvings of Bassae Frieze, from the Temple of Apollo in room 6. Rooms 16–24 display sculpture and reliefs from western Asia. And don't miss the huge, human-headed, winged bulls from Assyria (room 16) or the 7th-century BC frieze from Ashurbanipal's palace at Nineveh (room 17), where a royal lion hunt is depicted in amazing detail. The **basement floor** features more antiquities from Greece and Rome, including huge Ionic capitals from the temple of Artemis (room 77), Townley's delightful greyhounds and the poorly restored Discus Thrower (room 84), and one very large foot, taken from a colossal statue of Alexander the Great (room 83). The **upper floors** house collections from all over the world, including exhibits from prehistoric and Roman Britain (rooms 35–40); the Medieval, Renaissance, and Modern Collections (rooms 41–48); and western Asia (rooms 52–59). Rooms 60–65 are among the most popular in the museum, housing the greater part of the Egyptian collection. Easily the two busiest rooms are numbers 60 and 61, where you'll find the mummies—both human and animal, including gazelles, ibises, crocodiles, kittens (looking for all the world like sock puppets), fish, dogs, falcons, and even a small bull. At the very top of the museum sit some of the Asian collections (rooms 91–94), where exhibits change very frequently due to the fragility of the items.

The last year that the **British Library** will share the building with the museum is 1997. By royal decree, the library is entitled to receive one copy of everything published in the United Kingdom—from the Magna Carta and the Lindisfarne Gospels to trashy periodicals and daily newspapers. It's estimated that 2.1 miles of new shelving are needed each year to accommodate the ever-growing collection. Not surprisingly, England's number one library is hurting for space and will move to a larger facility near St. Pancras by the end of 1997. This is your last chance to see the magnificent domed **Reading Room** (tel. 0171/323–7677)— where George Bernard Shaw and Karl Marx (to name but two) warmed seats writing their magnum opuses—before it is transformed into an information center and children's lunch room, as part of the museum's controversial "Great Court" scheme. If you aren't here for serious graduate-level research (with documentation from your university to prove it), pick up a ticket for the free 10-minute tour from the Readers' Admission Office. Tours are usually given weekdays at 2:15 and 4:15 PM, but times are subject to change, so call to confirm. Anyone, however, can visit the library's exhibitions, including the **Manuscript Saloon's** collection of hand-written prose by Milton, Joyce, Woolf, and the Brontës; sheet music by Haydn, Bach, and Schubert; letters written by Henry VIII, Elizabeth I, Edward VI, and a host of other monarchs, and even Lady Jane Grey's prayer book. The **Middle Room** features illuminated manuscripts, including the Lindisfarne Gospels, while the sprawling **King's Library** holds George III's books, early printed works including a Gutenberg bible, and a collection of Asian manuscripts. These exhibits are scheduled to move to the new site in early 1998. *Great Russell St., WC1, tel. 0171/636–1555 or 0171/580–1788 for recorded info. Tube: Tottenham Court Road. Walk north on Tottenham Court Rd., turn right on Great Russell St. Admission free; small charge for special exhibits. Open Mon.–Sat. 10–5, Sun. 2:30–6. Wheelchair access.*

Mad Dash Through the British Museum

You'd need all the time in the world to fully explore the British Museum, but if you only have a few hours to spare, the following should not be missed.

- **Room 7: The Nereid Monument**

- **Room 8: Parthenon sculptures (a.k.a. the Elgin Marbles)**

- **Room 12: The Mausoleum at Halicarnassus**

- **Room 17: Lion hunt reliefs from the palace at Nineveh**

- **Room 25: The Rosetta Stone**

- **Room 30: Handwritten prose of Austen, Joyce, and Wordsworth**

- **Room 37: Lindow Bog Man (a.k.a. Pete Marsh)**

- **Room 41: Sutton Hoo Celtic Art Collection**

- **Room 42: Byzantine relics**

- **Rooms 60–61: Mummies**

BUCKINGHAM PALACE

Since the reign of Queen Victoria, British monarchs have called this big gray fortress their London home. George III bought Buckingham House, as it was called then, in 1762 for a mere £28,000; following his reign, the palace proved to be a sinkhole for expensive remodeling efforts. When George IV took it over, he decided the palace looked far too bourgeois, and in 1824 he set architect John Nash to work on the structure. Nash is responsible for much of what you see now, although the heavy Portland stone facing is the fault of a 1913 remodeling effort—Edwardian architecture at its dullest.

A flag bearing the Royal Standard flies whenever Queen Elizabeth II is in residence, usually on weekdays. The queen opened parts of Buckingham Palace to the public—for a fee, mind you— to pay for the restorations to Windsor Castle (see Near London, below) after a disastrous fire there in 1992. The government initially offered the queen £90 million for restorations, but massive public outcry prompted Her Majesty to foot the bill. With the high cost of castle restorations these days, it's likely the palace will remain open through the summer of 1998, but call for the latest word. They don't let you wander through the whole pad poking into medicine cabinets, but while they're not being occupied by HRH, 17 of the sumptuous **State Rooms,** including the throne room, picture galleries, and dining room, are open for viewing. Needless to say, they're chock-full of treasures—the entire spectacle will either leave you queasy about humankind's acquisitive nature, or drooling with envy. *Queen's Gardens, SW1, tel. 0171/839–1377. Tube: Green Park or St. James's Park. From Green Park, walk ½ mi south on Queen's Walk. From St. James's Park, walk north on Queen Anne's Gate, turn left on Birdcage Walk. Admission: £8.50. Open Apr.–Aug., daily 9:30–4:30. Wheelchair access with advance notice.*

✓ **QUEEN'S GALLERY** A short distance down Buckingham Gate, the Queen's Gallery houses rotating exhibits of pieces from her majesty's private art collection. Gainsborough, Rembrandt, Reynolds, and Rubens are among the regulars featured, but the museum is cluttered and only worth the price if an interesting temporary exhibition is occurring; check *Time Out* for details. *Buckingham Palace Rd., SW1, tel. 0171/930–4832, ext. 3351. Tube: St. James's Park or Victoria. Admission: £3.50. Open daily 10–4. Closed Jan. and Feb. Wheelchair access.*

ROYAL MEWS The Royal Mews houses the royal horses, liveried servants, and gilded carriages. If you visit when both the Queen's Gallery and the Royal Mews are open, you can cop a slightly cheaper combined ticket for £6. Otherwise, it's a lot to pay to look at horses. *Buckingham Palace Rd., SW1, tel. 0171/930–4832, ext. 3351. Tube: St. James's Park or Victoria. Admission: £3.50. Open Apr.–July, Tues.–Thurs. noon–4; Aug.–Sept., Mon.–Thurs. 10:30–4; Oct.–Mar., Wed. noon–3:30. Wheelchair access.*

GUARDS MUSEUM This museum occupies a set of underground rooms in Wellington Barracks, the regimental headquarters of the palace's Guards Division. Exhibits trace the history of the five Foot Guards regiments—Coldstream, Grenadier, Scots, Irish, and Welsh—from the 1660s through the Falklands War. The massive toy soldier shop is definitely worth a look, if you're into that kind of thing. *Wellington Barracks, Birdcage Walk, SW1, tel. 0171/930– 4466, ext. 3430. Tube: St. James's Park. Admission: £2, £1 students. Open daily 10–4.*

✓ **CHANGING OF THE GUARD** One of the biggest tourist shows in town is the Changing of the Guard ceremony, when the soldiers guarding the queen hand over their duties to the next watch. Marching to live music, the old guard proceeds up the Mall from St. James's Palace to Buckingham Palace as the new guard approaches from Wellington Barracks via Birdcage Walk. When the two columns meet, they continue to march around for a half hour before the old guard symbolically hands over the keys to the palace. The ceremony takes place daily at 11:30 AM, April–July, on alternating days August–March, but the guards often cancel due to bad weather; check the signs posted in the forecourt to find out when and if they will march. Unless you arrive by 10:30 AM, you can forget about a decent frontal view of all the pomp and circumstance. Early birds should grab a section of the gate facing the palace, since most of the ceremony takes place inside the fence. If you get there late, try standing along Constitution Hill, the thoroughfare leading to Hyde Park Corner.

HOUSES OF PARLIAMENT

The best view of Parliament is probably the most traditional—from halfway across nearby Westminster Bridge or, as immortalized by Monet in "The Thames Below Westminster," from Albert Embankment on the far side of the Thames. The Empire may be dead, but it's still fascinating to explore the site from which Britain once ruled with imperial impunity. The Houses of Parliament are actually one large building, sprawling along the Thames and home to the chambers of the House of Commons and the House of Lords, who meet on opposite sides of the octagonal Central Hall. The complex is officially known as the **Palace of Westminster,** indicative of the heavy influence the monarchy held over Parliament for centuries. Parliamentarians rebelled against Charles I during the English Civil War (1642–48), but before then, they were very much at the beck and call of the monarch. In fact, many kings summoned Parliament only when they needed money (it was Parliament's responsibility to levy taxes) and then promptly dismissed it.

A major fire in 1834 destroyed almost all of the original Palace of Westminster but the massive **Westminster Hall,** built in 1097–99 by William II and rebuilt by Richard II in 1394–99. The only other remnants of the old parliamentary building are the **Crypt of St. Stephen's Chapel,** where the House of Commons met for 300 years, and the medieval **Jewel Tower** (*see below*), used to store Edward III's collections of furs, jewels, gold, and other royal knickknacks. After the blaze, a competition was held for the design of the new Parliament building, and the winners were Charles Barry, a classical architect, and his assistant Augustus Welby Pugin, a Gothicist. While Barry was responsible for the building's practical plan, the elaborate details are the work of Pugin, a converted Catholic who believed that Gothic was the only "true" Christian architecture.

You can arrange a special "line of route" tour of the Houses of Parliament by writing to the Public Information Office (House of Commons, Westminster, SW1A 2PW) at least a month in advance. The tour takes you through the Queen's Robing Room, Royal Gallery, House of Lords, Central Hall (where MPs meet their constituents), House of Commons, and out into the spectacular Westminster Hall. Watch for the "VR" (*Victoria Regina*) monograms in the carpets and carving belying the "medieval" detailing as 19th-century work. Permits for tours of up to 16 people are available for Friday afternoons while the House is sitting. If you don't arrange for the tour, you can still visit the **Stranger's Galleries** of the House of Commons or the House of Lords. Getting into either gallery is tough, however, so try to get tickets in advance from your embassy or be prepared to wait in line for several hours (lines are shortest after 5:30 PM). The line for the House of Commons is always longer, especially at Question Time (*see below*). *Parliament Square, SW1, tel. 0171/219–4272. Tube: Westminster. For Strangers' Galleries, line up at St. Stephen's Hall Entrance (to the left for the Commons, to the right for the Lords). Admission free. House of Commons open Mon.–Thurs. 2:30–late, Fri. 9:30–3. House of Lords open Mon.–Wed. 2:30–late, Thurs. 3:30–late, Fri. 11 AM–late.*

The Ayes Have It

Parliamentary debates in the House of Commons end with the question being put to a vote, the Speaker asking, "As many as are of that opinion say 'aye,' the contrary 'no.'" (The Lords, on the other hand, declare themselves "content" or "not content.") After "voices" are "collected" the Speaker announces "I think the ayes (or the nos) have it." If the losing side challenges the findings, an order is given to "clear the lobby" of "strangers" (tourists and other nonmembers) and division bells are sounded to indicate an upcoming vote. Members then have eight minutes to enter a division lobby and vote with their bodies: ayes on the west and nos on the east. Apparently eight minutes is sufficient to finish a pint at the adjacent members' pub, which remains open until the House rises for the night. Perhaps this explains the late sittings?

HOUSE OF COMMONS The House of Commons, with roughly 700 elected members from around the country, is where the real power lies. The simple green benches of the Commons are a result of the Blitz: Incendiary bombs destroyed the original chamber in 1941. The sympathetic reconstruction by Sir Giles Gilbert Scott, completed in 1950, modernized the chamber to increase the seating capacity while restoring some of the traditional touches. A pair of red lines running the length of the floor date back to more turbulent times when debate really raged. The lines are placed exactly two sword-lengths apart, and all members must still remain behind them.

Parliament's daily schedule, posted at St. Stephen's Gate, is an amusing look into British life. On a given day, conflicts with the European Union might be allotted, say, an hour of debate, while the hot-button issue of "dog fouling" in London streets gets an entire afternoon's thrashing-out.

Nowadays, you'll mainly see verbal sparring, making a parliamentary session more exciting than many of the "dramas" playing in West End theaters. The ultimate spectacle is quick and cutting repartee during the prime minister's **Question Time,** held in the House of Commons on Tuesday and Thursday between 3:15 and 3:30 PM. This is when the PM defends himself against the slings and arrows of his "right honourable friends." Foreigners are *required* to secure tickets from their respective embassies, and Brits from their MPs. The next best time to visit is either chamber's regular Question Time, held Monday–Thursday between 2:30 and 3:30 PM. It's possible to sit in on other sessions and debates in both houses, but schedules are sketchy since they depend on what crisis the government is currently coping with. You're more likely to get into the Commons during an evening session, starting around 5:30 PM—look for the light shining at the top of Big Ben to see if Parliament is still sitting.

HOUSE OF LORDS The more prestigious but less powerful of Parliament's two houses is composed of both the **lords spiritual** (archbishops and senior bishops of the Church of England) and the **lords temporal** (British peers and peeresses who inherited their titles, were elevated to their ranks by the queen, or are so-called "lords of appeal" who help with judicial duties). As a nonelected body, the Lords wield little parliamentary power: They may amend or delay bills, but what the House of Commons decides becomes law. The Lords do *interpret* the law, however: As the final court of appeal for civil cases in Britain and criminal cases in England, Northern Ireland, and Wales, the Lords hear about 80 cases a year.

The Lords' chamber, masterfully designed by Pugin, is a sumptuous affair, with lots of carved wooden paneling, gilt, and leather. It must have been quite a letdown for the Commons to return to their chamber after meeting here while theirs was rebuilt. The Royal Gallery, adjacent to the Lords' chamber, features frescoes by Daniel Maclise depicting scenes from British history. The line is always shorter to get into the House of Lords, but if you're looking for drama, forget it. The Lords may appear to be snoring the day away, but they are actually leaning their heads close to speakers embedded in the back of the benches—or so they claim. Slumped over like that, it's difficult to picture them being, to use one of their own terms, "not content."

BIG BEN AND VICTORIA TOWER The clock tower on the north end of the Palace of Westminster, perhaps the most enduring symbol of both London and Britain, has come to be known as **Big Ben.** Actually, it's only the 13-ton bell on top that's named Big Ben, though few people make that distinction. Details aside, for the millions of colonials worldwide who've heard the Westminster chimes nightly on the BBC World Service, the 16 tones evoke a wide range of emotions: home, security, a sense of belonging. Especially when Big Ben is lit up at night, its stature dwarfs the other buildings in the Parliament complex, even though it's not the tallest. That distinction belongs to the 336-foot-high **Victoria Tower,** reputedly the largest square tower in the world. It needs to be, as it holds the three-million-document parliamentary archives. A Union Jack flies from the top of Victoria Tower whenever Parliament is in session.

JEWEL TOWER Across the street from Victoria Tower, the stumpy Jewel Tower was built in 1365 to house Edward III's precious gems. It survived the fire of 1834, was severely damaged in the Blitz, was restored in 1956, and is now a very worthwhile museum. On display are relics from the original Palace of Westminster as well as a fascinating display, "Houses of Parliament: Past and Present." Don't miss the 1,200-year-old Westminster Sword, found in the muck of the moat that once surrounded the tower and Palace of Westminster, or the elaborately embroidered Speakers' Robes. *Abingdon St. (also called Old Palace Yard), just south of Parliament Sq., SW1, tel. 0171/222–2219. Tube: Westminster. Admission: £1.50, £1.10 students. Open daily 10–1 and 2–4 (Apr.–Sept., until 6).*

ST. MARGARET'S WESTMINSTER The official church of the House of Commons looks a bit wimpy next to robust Westminster Abbey (*see below*), but its stained-glass windows are worth a quick look. One portrays former parishioner John Milton dictating after the onset of blindness, and above the nave is a stunning depiction of Henry VIII's marriage to Catherine of Aragon (1509), which the church picked up secondhand for a psalm. Above the entrance, you'll find a "gee we're sorry" window depicting the life and death of explorer Sir Walter Raleigh, who was beheaded a few yards away. The whole church received a major renovation in 1992; one of the principal contributors was, inexplicably, New Jersey native Frank Sinatra. *Parliament Sq., SW1, tel. 0171/222–6382. Tube: Westminster. Open daily 9:30–5:15.*

ST. PAUL'S CATHEDRAL

Right in the heart of the City, St. Paul's is instantly recognizable by its huge dome, towering 218 feet above street level. St. Paul's is also the symbolic heart of the City; unlike Westminster Abbey, which is seen as a royal and national church, St. Paul's is really a church for *Londoners*. Postwar construction left the cathedral surrounded by ugly office blocks, but plans have been made to raze nearby buildings and redesign the area. The present structure, the third in a series of cathedrals erected on the site, was built by Christopher Wren between 1675 and 1710, shortly after the Great Fire ravaged London (*see box, below*). Perhaps this fiery finish should have been a warning to Prince Charles and Lady Diana, who married here in the happier summer of 1981.

The cathedral's interior is every bit as exceptional as its silhouette, containing dozens of memorials and other works of art. The **Wellington Monument** looms more than 80 feet high in an arch between the nave and the north aisle. His tomb and remains are in the crypt below. **Samuel John-**

Resurgam!

A lunette on St. Paul's south door pediment features a carving of a phoenix rising from the ashes, symbolic of the cathedral's fiery history. Samuel Pepys reported in his diary that during the Great Fire of 1666 "the stones of St. Paul's flew like grenados, the melting lead running down the streets in a stream." When Wren began rebuilding the new St. Paul's a decade later, he asked a workman to bring him a stone to mark the center of the cathedral. The stone happened to be a piece of an old tombstone with the word RESURGAM (I shall rise again) engraved upon it. Wren took the image of the new cathedral rising from its own ashes to heart, representing it with the aforementioned phoenix.

The next major catastrophe to befall London was the Blitz, during which Londoners used the Golden Gallery in the dome of St. Paul's to spot fires all over the city. The cathedral was in grave danger, but through the efforts of the volunteer St. Paul's Fire Watch, little damage was incurred. Luck also played a role: A bomb landed on St. Paul's on September 12, 1940, but failed to explode. After being extracted, it was driven to Hackney Marsh and detonated, creating a crater more than 115 feet across. The cathedral also escaped damage during a German air raid that destroyed most of the City of London on December 29, 1941. A famous (though fabricated) photograph shows the dome standing serenely amidst plumes of smoke while the surrounding area is consumed by fire.

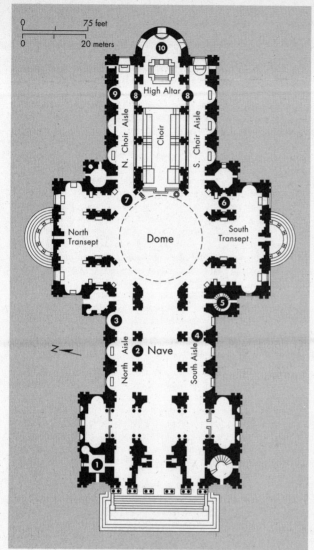

All Souls' Chapel, **1**
American Chapel, **10**
Crypt entrance, **6**
"Light of the World", **4**
"Mother and Child", **9**
Samuel Johnson's Monument, **7**
Staircase to galleries, **5**
Tijou Gates, **8**
Viscounts Melbourne Monument, **3**
Wellington Monument, **2**

son's monument, by the north choir aisle, is as distant from the truth as from his body: Dr. Johnson is actually buried in Westminster Abbey, and his monument idealizes the obese 18th-century lexicographer into a stately Roman dignitary. Two life-size marble angels adorn the monument to the Viscounts Melbourne located in the north aisle. Also notable are Holman Hunt's *Light of the World* in the south aisle, depicting Christ knocking at the bramble-covered door of the human soul; and, in north choir aisle, Henry Moore's *Mother and Child,* a sculpture stunning in its simplicity. The **choir** is the most highly decorated part of the cathedral, with mosaic ceilings, stalls carved by Dutch artist Grinling Gibbons, and iron screens by the French master Jean Tijou. The **High Altar** is stunningly gaudy, all carved wood, gold leaf, and twisty columns. Far below, the **crypt** contains a display on the cathedral's architecture, a small treasury, and dozens of tombs of the famous, including military demigods Nelson, Kitchener, and Wellington, and artists William Blake and Joshua Reynolds. The tomb of the great builder himself, Christopher Wren, is adorned by his son's famous epitaph: LECTOR, SI MONUMENTUM REQUIRIS, CIRCUMSPICE (Reader, if you seek a monument, look around you). Sadly, Wren's **Great Model,** an 18-foot, exquisitely detailed model of the way things might have been had Wren been allowed to build St. Paul's on a Greek-cross (equal-armed) plan, has been removed from the crypt; a new "model room" is being prepared, so check with the staff for details. Wren's classical plan was deemed far too modern and the clergymen demanded a traditional long nave. Ironically, plans for rebuilding the cathedral's neighboring structures have been criticized for being too modern because they *aren't* classical.

If the cathedral's domed ceiling seems lower than you expected, it's because St. Paul's actually has three domes: a shallow, decorated dome seen from inside; a lofty outer dome seen from the street; and a brick cone between them that provides support. The interior of the inner dome's base is encircled by the **Whispering Gallery**; once you've caught your breath from the 259-step climb, whisper into the wall and you'll be heard 100 feet away on the other side of the gallery—if the listener can discern your voice from the dozens of whispering tourists. If your legs can stand it, continue 116 more steps up the dizzying staircase to the **Stone Gallery** outside the dome and the final 141 steps to the **Golden Gallery** at the top of the dome. You'll be rewarded with amazing views of London. If you want every last detail, take a super-informative, slow-paced 90-minute **Supertour** (£3, £2 students) Monday–Saturday at 11, 11:30, 1:30, and 2, or try the 45-minute walkman tour (£2.50, £2 students). Admission to the cathedral and crypt is £3.50, £3 students; admission to the galleries is £3, £2.50 students; or you can buy a combined ticket for £6, £5 students. Sauntering through the free gardens, especially when the roses are in bloom, can be almost as satisfying. Attending services is the only way you'll be able to visit on Sundays; the choir sings at the 11 AM and 3:15 services. *St. Paul's Churchyard, EC4, tel. 0171/236–4128. Tube: Mansion House or St. Paul's. From Mansion House, walk west on Cannon St., turn right on New Change. From St. Paul's, follow signs. Open Mon.–Sat. 8:30–4:30; crypt and treasury open Mon.–Sat. 8:45–4:15; galleries open Mon.–Sat. 10–4:15.*

TATE GALLERY ✔

The Tate is one of England's principal museums—more contemporary and controversial than the National Gallery (*see* Trafalgar Square, *below*), but no less impressive. The Tate is well known for annually rearranging its permanent collection into brilliant and thought-provoking exhibits, often juxtaposing disparate movements, such as pop art and minimalism, to challenge old and new theories of art. The artwork is divided into two collections: the British collection, which features British painting from the 16th century to the present, and the modern collection, featuring con-

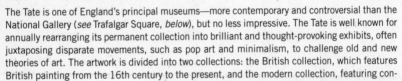

In the eyes of many Brits, a janitor couldn't leave a mop leaning against the wall at the Tate without museum patrons evaluating it with a critical eye.

temporary painting and sculpture from around the world. A major highlight of the British collection is the **Clore Gallery,** dedicated to J. M. W. Turner, hailed as Britain's greatest artist. As with those in the rest of the museum, Clore Gallery exhibits are rotated annually, with selections from the Tate's holdings of more than 300 of Turner's paintings, 300 of his personal sketchbooks, and over 19,000 rough drawings and watercolors. Another feature of the British collection is the work of artist/poet/proto-hippie **William Blake,** who died in poverty during the 19th century—but is now regularly lauded as the greatest of England's geniuses. Tate curators like to liven things up a bit by hanging works by artists Blake inspired next to art by the great man himself.

The Tate is also famous—and infamous—for its modern collection, including works by van Gogh, Matisse, Picasso, Dalí, Rothko, Leger, Duchamp, and Ernst, to name a few. Contemporary artists are championed in the **Art Now** room, which houses exhibits of recent work by new and established artists. Every now and then, the Tate gets itself into hot water by displaying an exhibit that, to the lay art lover, is mind-numbingly dumb. Probably the most famous brouhaha occurred when the gallery paid an ungodly sum for a pile of bricks—nothing more, nothing less. Similar controversies have surrounded displays of such everyday items as milk bottles. Special exhibitions in 1997 include German painter and graphic artist Lovis Corinth (Feb.–May), works by Ellsworth Kelly (June–Sept.), and "Symbolism in Britain" (Oct.–Dec.).

Currently, the gallery offers the following free, guided tours on weekdays: British art from Van Dyck to the Pre-Raphaelites (11 AM); the Turner Collection (noon); modern art from impressionism to surrealism (2 PM); and late-20th-century art (3 PM). On Saturdays at 3 PM, the staff will guide you through the highlights of the entire collection. "Touch tours" of sculptures are also available for visually impaired visitors; call 0171/887–8725 for a schedule. Free lectures, films, and video screenings take place almost daily in the auditorium; pick up a schedule at the info desk. *Millbank, SW1, tel. 0171/887–8000 or 0171/887–8008 for recorded info. Tube: Pimlico. Walk north 1 block, turn right on Vauxhall Bridge Rd. (which becomes Bessboro Gardens), left on Millbank. Admission free; £1–£5 for special exhibits. Open Mon.–Sat. 10–5:50, Sun. 2–5:50. Wheelchair access at Clore Gallery and John Islip St. entrances.*

TOWER OF LONDON

The Tower of London actually refers to the 20 towers that compose London's most famous medieval fortress, covering 18 acres on the bank of the Thames. Besides serving as the residence of every British sovereign from William the Conqueror (he built the original fortress in 1078) to Henry VIII in the 16th century, the Tower also houses a jewel safe, an armory, and a garrison. It is most famous, however, for its role as a prison and place of execution. Some of England's most notable figures met their death here, including Robert Devereux—the Earl of Essex—when he fell out of favor with Elizabeth I, and three queens of England: Lady Jane Grey (crowned in 1553 but deposed and executed after only nine days), Anne Boleyn, and Catherine Howard (Henry VIII's second and fifth wives, respectively). The chapel of **St. Peter ad Vincula,** adjacent to the Tower Green execution site, houses their headless skeletons.

A good way to get a sense of the layout of the Tower grounds is to take a free, hour-long tour led by the witty Yeoman Warders—better known as Beefeaters—dressed to the gills in Tudor costume. Tours leave from just inside the main entrance every half hour until 3:30 (2:30 in winter), but they don't go in bad weather. Every night at 10 PM the Tower is locked during the **Ceremony of the Keys.** Those who planned ahead—and have sent a self-addressed, stamped envelope at least two months in advance to Ceremony of the Keys, Queen's House, HM Tower of London, EC3N 4AB for tickets—are treated to low-key pomp and circumstance and a bugler who sounds the all-clear as the chief Yeoman Warder bolts the front gate. If you think you'd cut a dashing figure in that costume, you've got a long way ahead of you—Warders must have 22 years of honorable service in the Army, Royal Marines, or Royal Air Force before they can even *apply* for the job.

The most impressive and oldest of the towers is **White Tower.** Finished in 1097, it was one of a number of fortified structures erected in London by the justifiably nervous William the Conqueror (angry Saxon kings craved Will's hide after he tanned theirs in 1066). Until renovations are completed, the White Tower will have a small exhibit entitled "Instruments of Torture, Armour for Kings"—a teaser for the larger collection. Once remodeling is complete in Spring 1997, part of the **Royal Armouries** collection will return, with floor upon floor of immaculately polished, beautifully crafted suits of armor, medieval small arms, pikes, and cannonballs. Look out for four suits of Henry VIII's armor marking his transmogrification from a "very fair" and "admirably proportioned" young king to the bloated, middle-aged tyrant he became. The tranquil **Chapel of St. John,** on the tower's first floor, is a haven amidst all the military parapher-

Raven Mad

Perhaps the most important man in the Tower is the Yeoman Ravenmaster, responsible for tending the Tower's ravens. In the 17th century, King Charles II decreed that six ravens should be kept at all times at the Tower, fearing the legend that should the ravens leave the grounds, the Tower would crumble and the monarchy would fall. In recent times, three "reserve" ravens have been added for good measure. Though the ravens are captive (their wings are clipped), they are well cared for and even buried within the tower when they die.

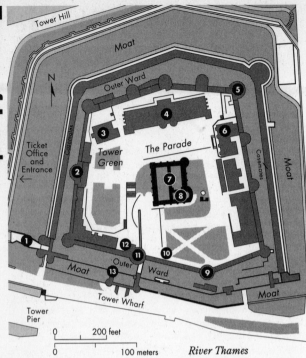

Tower Hill

Moat

Outer Ward

N

Ticket
Office
and
Entrance
←

Tower
Green

The Parade

Moat

Beauchamp
Tower, **2**

Bloody Tower, **12**

Chapel of
St. John, **3**

Chapel of St. Peter
ad Vincula, **8**

Jewel House, **4**

Lanthorn Tower, **9**

Martin Tower, **5**

Medieval Palace, **13**

Ravens'
Lodgings, **10**

Royal Fuseliers'
Museum, **6**

Wakefield Tower, **11**

White Tower, **7**

Yeoman Warder Tour
meeting point, **1**

Outer Ward

Moat

Moat

Tower Wharf

Tower
Pier

0   200 feet

0   100 meters

River Thames

nalia. The curved arches of its Norman architecture are stunning in their simplicity and grace. During construction, you can only visit the chapel accompanied by a Yeoman Warder—pick up a free ticket for the tour from the kiosk near Lanthorn Tower. Always a crowd-pleaser, a small display of **torture instruments** will return to the basement below.

The Crown Jewels, now housed in the **Jewel House,** just north of the White Tower, are the star attraction. The Sovereign Sceptre boasts the largest cut diamond in the world, a 530-carat monster from the Cullinan diamond. The Imperial State Crown, made for the coronation of Queen Victoria in 1838, is studded with 3,000 precious stones, including the second-largest diamond in the world, also cut from the Cullinan stone. This crown is due to be worn at the coronation of England's next monarch, whoever he or she may be. Though the design of the new Jewel House speeds things up a bit, shiny objects tend to attract huge crowds. It's best to visit immediately after the Tower opens or just before it closes. Make the mistake of going at midday, especially on weekends, and the wait could last for hours. And remember, the NO PHOTOGRAPHY ALLOWED signs are very strictly enforced. A new exhibit at nearby **Martin Tower** tells its history as the original Jewel House, including a section on Colonel Blood, the man who nearly successfully stole the Crown Jewels in 1671.

Other points of interest include **Beauchamp Tower,** which has more than 400 eerie notes and doodles carved into the stone (some quite deeply) by prisoners of centuries past, and **Lanthorn Tower,** which contains small but excellent exhibits about life in medieval England. **Bloody Tower** is where the so-called Little Princes, Edward V and his brother, were murdered in the 15th century, probably by henchmen of either Richard III or Henry VII. It is also where Sir Walter Raleigh spent 13 years of imprisonment, during which he wrote the modestly titled *History of the World*. Raleigh's prison life wasn't all that harsh: He had a servant, enjoyed the company of his wife and son, and even fathered a second son whilst imprisoned. Newly opened **Medieval Palace** is the site of Edward's Magna Camera (Great Chamber), from where he ruled the country, and **Wake-**

field **Tower** has an impressive Throne Room with 13th-century replicas showing the opulence of Edward's court. The **Wall Walk,** linking the Wakefield with the Lanthorn towers, offers great views of Tower Bridge. *Tower Hill, EC3, tel. 0171/709–0765. Tube: Tower Hill. Walk south following signs. Admission: £8.30, £6.25 students. Open Mar.–Sept.; Mon.–Sat. 9–6, Sun. 10–6; Oct.–Feb., Mon.–Sat. 9–5, Sun. 10–5 (last admission 1 hr before closing; last entry to exhibits 30 min before closing). Partial wheelchair access.*

TOWER BRIDGE A three-minute walk along the Thames from the Tower of London brings you to Tower Bridge, a Gothic fancy built between 1885 and 1894. Exhibitions in the enor-

London Architecture

Great architectural achievements in London have often been motivated by extreme disaster or misfortune. After the Great Fire of 1666 destroyed four-fifths of a city still reeling from the onslaught of the plague the preceding year, London required almost complete restoration. Three centuries later, much of central and suburban London was flattened by the German air raids of the early 1940s; postwar rebuilding allowed modern architecture to creep into the city. As a result of these intense civic reconstructions, a few individuals had the opportunity to leave significant marks upon the city. Following are architects whose work will literally surround you as you wander through London.

- *Inigo Jones (1573–1652), one of England's first great architects, was almost single-handedly responsible for the resurgence of classical styles of architecture in the early 17th century. Often directly modeling his work after that of Italian architect Andrea Palladio, Jones was highly influential during his time, as the Palladian style quickly spread throughout England. His most famous works include St. Paul's Church at Covent Garden and the magnificent Banqueting House in Whitehall.*

- *Sir Christopher Wren (1632–1723) was given the daunting task of overseeing the rebuilding of London following the Great Fire. His ambitious plans for a complete redesign of the formerly medieval city, drawn up within a week after the fire, were shot down by landowners, businesspeople, and private citizens intent upon a quicker reconstruction. It is questionable whether Wren seriously expected his plans to be accepted; they were very utopian in nature and would have required the strong hand of an absolute monarch to be carried out. Wren was still responsible for 51 new churches (all in the City) and the amazing St. Paul's Cathedral. Only 23 still survive, the finest of which are St. Bride's (Fleet St.), St. Mary Abchurch (Cannon St.), and St. Stephen Walbrook (Walbrook St.). John Betjeman's "City of London Churches" (£2.25), available at many tourist shops, provides a compact and convenient list of all 38 City churches, by Wren and others.*

- *John Nash (1752–1835) completely redesigned a large section of the city stretching from the Mall northward to Regent's Park. He is largely responsible for the look of much of central London; it was his idea to clear Trafalgar Square of its royal stables to make room for the public space as it exists today. He also remodeled Buckingham Palace and designed the fantastic, Indian-inspired Royal Pavilion in Brighton.*

mous twin pillars were renovated for the bridge's centenary and feature excellent animatronic figures speaking on the bridge's history and engineering, as well as on the history of London's bridges from Roman times onward. Hands-on activities include CD-i units where visitors can learn about various sights visible from the two gangways, which afford excellent views. At the bottom of the southern tower, the original steam and hydraulic machinery of the bridge is on polished display. Tower Bridge still opens approximately 500 times a year; if you're lucky you'll catch the spectacle (call 0171/378–7700 for a current schedule). *Tel. 0171/407–0922. Tube: Tower Hill. Admission: £5.50, £3.75 students. Open Apr.–Oct., daily 10–6:30 (last admission 5:15); Nov.–Mar., daily 9:30–6 (last admission 4:45).*

TRAFALGAR SQUARE ✔

To you, Trafalgar Square might seem no more than a huge traffic circle or a place to spend an afternoon poking through some pretty cool museums (*see below*). Many Londoners, however, consider it the heart of their town, and its landmark, **Nelson's Column,** probably makes it the city's most famous square. In 1829, Trafalgar Square was transformed from royal stables to public square in honor of nationally revered naval honcho Lord Horatio Nelson, who died in battle after decimating the French fleet at Cape Trafalgar (on the southwest coast of Spain) in 1805. In 1840, architect E. H. Baily began work on the 185-foot-tall column, Trafalgar Square's most obvious landmark (and a sizable overstatement considering wee "Baron Nelson of the Nile" measured only 5 feet 4 inches in life). Four gigantic **bronze lions** were added by sculptor Sir Edward Landseer in 1868.

For its 150th birthday, the statue atop Nelson's Column received a present: a good scrubbing and a coat of pigeon-proof gel.

The square is also a fine place for people-watching: By day, street performers share the place with occasional protest groups and elderly women feeding flocks of pigeons. Long after sunset, its duty as the main stopping point for late-night buses makes it one of the trippiest, coolest places in London. Packs of clubbers and tourists mill around boozily, making nocturnal hot dog vendors rich and happy. On New Year's Eve, you can multiply the nightlife factor at Trafalgar Square by about 10: It's the most popular place in the city to ring in the new year. This might have something to do with the large clocks around the square, which are perpetually out of sync; loopy crowds end up celebrating the coming of midnight two or three times. All fun and games—until 1995, when two people were crushed to death by crowds.

NATIONAL GALLERY After acquiring the private art collection of a wealthy banker early in the 19th century, Parliament felt compelled to start amassing some culture with a capital "C." To accommodate the growing collection, Parliament bought a plot of land on the edge of Trafalgar Square in 1828 and began to build the National Gallery, a bland classical structure best known for its tall, sandy-brown columns. If you can get past the legions of pigeons guarding the front doors, you'll find one of the world's most impressive collections of Western European art inside, including works by Tintoretto, da Vinci, Caravaggio, della Francesca, Michelangelo, Monet, Titian, Rubens, Van Dyck, Goya, Rembrandt, Constable, Turner, Gainsborough, Seurat, et cetera, et cetera. Ready yourself for a staggering number of Virgins and Sons. Pastorals are also well represented.

The National Gallery's collection is displayed chronologically in the building's four wings. The **Sainsbury Wing** (paid for by the Sainsbury supermarket chain) displays medieval and early Renaissance works (1260–1510). The **West Wing** is devoted to the High Renaissance (1510–1600), the **North Wing** to the Dutch Masters (1600–1700), and the **East Wing** to English portraiture and some of the better known impressionists, spanning the centuries from 1700 to 1920. Free, one-hour guided tours begin in the Sainsbury Wing weekdays at 11:30 AM and 2:30 PM, and on Saturday at 2 PM and 3:30 PM. Those brave souls who do decide to go it alone should pick up a floor plan at the entrance for basic orientation, or stop by the museum's free, technophobe-friendly **Micro Gallery,** where you can use a computer to look at your favorite paintings and print out your own personalized "grand tour." Free lectures on a variety of topics take place weekdays (1 PM) and Saturdays (noon); check at an information desk for more info. *Trafalgar Sq., WC2, tel. 0171/747–2885. Tube: Charing Cross or Leicester Square. Admission free. Open Mon.–Sat.*

10–6, Sun. 2–6 (July–Aug., Wed. until 8 PM). Wheelchair access at Sainsbury Wing and Orange St. entrances.

NATIONAL PORTRAIT GALLERY Painted faces, sculpted faces, drawn faces, photographed faces—the National Portrait Gallery is as much about portraiture as it is about the men and women (mostly men) who made Britannia great. The pieces are arranged chronologically from the top floor to the bottom; take the elevator up and wind your way down through the ages. The final leg of the exhibit brings you right up to the present, and walking out onto the streets of London afterward provides a nice sense of closure. Special events in 1997 include Britain's first major exhibition on that underappreciated art form, the picture frame (Jan.–Feb.); and an exhibition on 18th-century British-African scholar-artist Ignatius Sancho (Jan.–May). The gallery is well known for its impressive free lectures; pick up a calendar at the information desk. *St. Martin's Pl., WC2, tel. 0171/306–0055. Tube: Charing Cross or Leicester Square. Admission free; small fee for some special exhibitions. Open Mon.–Sat. 10–6, Sun. noon–6. Wheelchair access at Orange St. entrance.*

Famous faces in the National Portrait Gallery include Chaucer, Shakespeare, Milton, Lord Byron, the Brontë sisters (minus their brother—look for the smudge), and Virginia Woolf. However, the ones that draw the largest crowds are the royal portraits: Diana in a morose moment, and Charlie looking rather silly in his polo suit.

ST. MARTIN-IN-THE-FIELDS In the northeast corner of Trafalgar Square stands the plain, white-marble church of St. Martin-in-the-Fields. This is where the prestigious Academy of St. Martin-in-the-Fields orchestra was founded in 1726. Handel played on the church's first organ, and Mozart is reputed to have given a concert here on one of his mega-world tours. These days, free music recitals take place Monday–Wednesday and Friday at 1:05 PM—and are probably the best way to take in the church's grim memorials to the British war dead. Evening concerts (£6–£20) usually feature big-name ensembles performing by candlelight. Like most other churches, St. Martin's possesses a **crypt,** but this isn't your typical musty repository of old bones. Instead, the **Cafe-in-the-Crypt** (tel. 0171/839–4342) is one of the coolest, most atmospheric places for latte in all of London. With rough-hewn stone pillars, low vaulted ceilings, and floors tiled with worn grave markers, it's the perfect place to pen moody, intense postcards to the folks back home. Additionally, the crypt houses a modest art gallery and bookstore (both heavy on religious themes), and the **London Brass Rubbing Center** (tel. 0171/930–9306), where for £1.50–£11 (depending on size) you can make rubbings from historic brasses using gold, bronze, or silver wax. *East side of Trafalgar Sq., WC2, tel. 0171/930–0089 or 0171/839–8362 for box office. Open Mon.–Sat. 10–8, Sun. noon–8. Wheelchair access.*

WESTMINSTER ABBEY

Founded in 1065 by Edward the Confessor, who was both king and saint, Westminster Abbey reflects the close relationship of church and state in Britain. The country's monarchs have been crowned and buried here since William the Conqueror assumed the English throne on Christmas Day, AD 1066. Burial in Westminster is one of the highest honors the country can bestow, and accordingly, a walk through this vast, ornate abbey is like perusing a *Who's Who* of British history. Among the deceased sovereigns buried here are Elizabeth I, Mary Queen of Scots, Richard II, and Henry VII. Though you can enter the abbey's nave for free, it costs £4 (£2 students) to see Poets' Corner and the Royal Chapels—the coolest parts of the abbey. Admission to *all* parts of the abbey is free every Wednesday from 6 to 7:45 PM, which is also the only time photography is allowed in the Royal Chapels.

Behind the altar, the **Chapel of St. Edward the Confessor** is home to the Coronation Chair, which is used during the crowning of Britain's kings and queens. In recent years, hooligans have managed to etch graffiti all over the wooden chair; when or if Prince Charles is crowned, his royal derriere will rest on incisive comments like "C loves S forever" and "smoke dope." The chair was built in 1300 to enclose the Stone of Scone (pronounced "Skoon"), which Edward I swiped from Scotland in 1296. The Stone of Destiny, as it is also known, is a symbol of Scottish independence and has been a source of some friction between the two countries. Scottish nationalists stole back the stone in 1950, but Scotland Yard (a misnomer) recovered it six months later. In an attempt to appease the Scottish nationalists, John Major announced

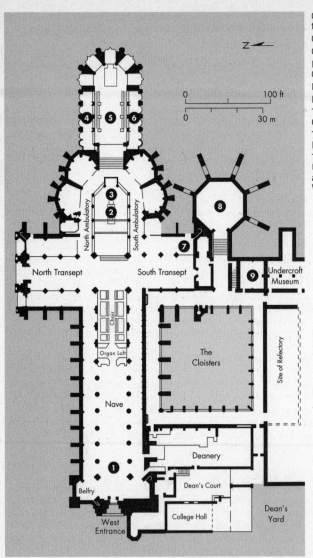

Chapel of Edward
the Confessor, **3**

Chapter House, **8**

Coronation Chair, **2**

Henry VII's
Chapel, **5**

Poets' Corner, **7**

Pyx Chamber, **9**

Tomb of Mary,
Queen of Scots, **6**

Tomb of Queen
Elizabeth I, **4**

Tomb of the
Unknown Warrior
and Memorial to Sir
Winston Churchill, **1**

0   100 ft

0   30 m

North Ambulatory

South Ambulatory

North Transept

South Transept

Undercroft
Museum

Chair

Organ Loft

The
Cloisters

Site of Refectory

Nave

Deanery

Dean's Court

Dean's
Yard

Belfry

West
Entrance

College Hall

in 1996—the 700th-year anniversary of its removal—that the stone should indeed be returned to Scotland. It will, however, be brought back to London for the coronation of future monarchs. Farther back you'll find **Henry VII's Chapel,** one of Britain's most beautiful examples of the rich Gothic style. The tomb of Henry VII and his wife, Elizabeth, was created by Italian artist Torrigiano, best known for popping Michelangelo on the nose during an argument.

Nearly all the deceased greats of English literature are featured in Westminster's **Poets' Corner,** in the south transept. Geoffrey Chaucer was the first to be buried here, in 1400. Memorial plaques pay homage to other luminaries like Shakespeare, T. S. Eliot, Byron, Tennyson, Dylan Thomas, and, more recently, Oscar Wilde. Real monks once wandered through the **Cloisters** on the south side of the nave. Open to the air, they retain a tranquillity that the main portion of the abbey lacks after early morning hours. At the end of a passage leading from the Cloisters is the octagonal, spacious **Chapter House,** the original meeting place of England's Parliament. If you want all the details, 90-minute **Supertours** of the abbey (£7) are given four times a day on weekdays, and twice on Saturday mornings if demand warrants; book ahead by calling 0171/222–7110, or ask at the inquiry desk. *Dean's Yard, SW1, tel. 0171/222–5152. Tube: Westminster. Cross Parliament Sq., follow Broad Sanctuary. Admission free. Open Mon.–Sat. 7:30–6 (Wed. until 7:45), Sun. briefly btw services at 10 AM, 3 PM, and 5:45 PM.*

London Neighborhoods

London is best approached through its highly distinct, diverse neighborhoods, many of which were once towns or villages in their own right. Regardless of who you are or what you're after, London has a neighborhood to fulfill your every whim. If government buildings and famous monuments are what you seek, Whitehall has more than enough for the hardiest tourist. If you prefer a little boho culture, you might want to spend your time in Camden, Notting Hill, or Hampstead. For a vicarious taste of the good (or at least expensive) life, head to ritzy Mayfair, St. James's, or Chelsea. If you're interested in London's legal and financial institutions, make your way to Holborn and the City, respectively. There's great people-watching at Covent Garden, as well as in the various central squares. And for a taste of authentic, workaday London (and an earful of Cockney accents), check out the East End.

West London

CHELSEA

Chelsea, just south of Knightsbridge, is mostly quiet and residential—except for its famous **King's Road** (*see below*), which can be a swell place for a walk if you like to shop. South of King's Road, running along the Thames between Battersea and Albert bridges, is a short strip called **Cheyne Walk** (pronounced "Chainy"), which once boasted such heavyweight residents as

Blue Plaque Attack!

As you wander around London, you'll see lots of small blue plaques on the sides of buildings, describing which famous, semifamous, or obscure but brilliant person once lived there. "The Blue Plaque Guide" (£7), available at larger bookstores, lists plaques throughout the city; a few highlights are listed below. Otherwise, "The Pink Plaque Guide" (£7) points out the homes of prominent gays and lesbians; "The Black Plaque Guide" (£13) gives directions to and gory details about London's famous murder sites.

Elizabeth Barrett Browning (50 Wimpole St., Bloomsbury); Sir Winston Churchill (28 Hyde Park Gate, South Kensington); T. S. Eliot (3 Kensington Ct., Kensington); Mahatma Gandhi (20 Baron's Court Rd., West Kensington); George Frederick Handel (25 Brook St., Mayfair); Karl Marx (28 Dean St., Soho); Piet Cornelis Mondrian (60 Parkhill Rd., Camden); Sir Isaac Newton (87 Jermyn St., St. James); Florence Nightingale (10 South St., Mayfair); George Bernard Shaw (29 Fitzroy Sq., Marylebone); Percy Bysshe Shelley (15 Poland St., Mayfair); Dylan Thomas (54 Delancey St., Camden); Oscar Wilde (34 Tite St., Chelsea); Virginia Woolf (52 Tavistock Sq., Bloomsbury); William Butler Yeats (23 Fitzroy Rd., Camden); Emile Zola (Queen's Hotel, 122 Church Rd., Croydon).

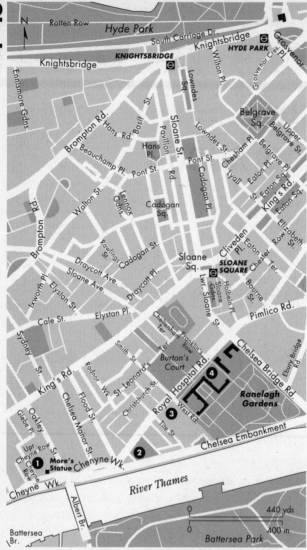

George Eliot (No. 4), Dante Gabriel Rosetti (No. 16), and Mick Jagger (No. 48). Certainly no artists or literary masters roam the streets now; all you'll find are privileged Chelseans walking their pampered Labradors along the manicured streets. You can, however, get a glimpse into the life of one long-gone literary giant. **Thomas Carlyle's House** (24 Cheyne Row, SW3, tel. 0171/352–7087) is just as the Carlyles left it more than 150 years ago—Thomas's hat is still where he put it before he died, and all the furniture, books, and possessions remain intact. It's open April–October, Wednesday–Sunday 11–4:30 (sporadically Nov.–Mar.), and admission is £2.75. The romantic **Ranelagh Gardens,** off the Chelsea Embankment (that's what they call Cheyne Walk east of Albert Bridge), is a fine place to visit, especially on warm summer nights. Mozart gave a concert here in 1764 at the age of eight, and it's easy to imagine the London elite of past centuries putting on airs while meandering along the footpaths. The Chelsea Flower Show is held here in May (*see* Festivals, in Chapter 1).

CHELSEA PHYSIC GARDEN Established in 1673 by the Society of Apothecaries, this garden was used for studying the medicinal properties of herbs and other plants. It's now an important botanical research and education center. The high walls surrounding the garden create a near-tropical oasis, allowing flowers to bloom year-round. Afternoon tea is served between 3:15 and 4:45—it's a real treat to munch crumpets surrounded by riotously blooming rhododendrons. *66 Royal Hospital Rd. (entrance on Swan Walk), SW3, tel. 0171/352–5646. Tube: Sloane Square. Walk south on Lower Sloane St., turn right on Royal Hospital Rd. Admission: £3.50, £1.80 students. Open Apr.–Oct., Wed. 2–5, Sun. 2–6. Wheelchair access.*

KING'S ROAD King's Road has gone yuppie in the last decade or so, but this was where rebel chicks bought the world's first miniskirts (invented by designer Mary Quant, who had a shop on King's Road) in the '60s, and where punk rock was born in the 1970s. Legend goes that the whole punk thing started when the Sex Pistols popped into fashion designer Vivienne Westwood's little King's Road boutique, Sex, for a few pairs of bondage trousers. Voilà! Within a few years the whole boulevard was crammed with counterculture clothing shops, record stores, and disaffected youth. The aggressively weird still assemble on weekends at the northeast end of King's Road, around **Sloane Square.** *Tube: Sloane Square.*

ROYAL HOSPITAL Commissioned by Charles II in 1682 to house veteran soldiers, Wren's Royal Hospital is still home to around 400 "Chelsea Pensioners"—retired servicemen "of good character" who proudly wear their distinctive uniforms: a dark blue overcoat in winter and a scarlet frock coat in summer. The pensioners perform duties—attending church, marching in parades—and in exchange are given food, lodging, clothing, and a daily ration of beer and tobacco. You're welcome to enter the grounds and pay a visit to Verrio's famous painting of Charles II on horseback and Van Dyck's portrait of Charles I and his family. *Royal Hospital Rd., SW3, tel. 0171/730–5282. Tube: Sloane Square. Walk south on Lower Sloane Square St., turn right on Royal Hospital Rd. Admission free. Open weekdays 10–noon and 2–4, Sat. 2–4.*

KENSINGTON AND KNIGHTSBRIDGE

Kensington is museum central: In one large block you'll find three major museums—the Victoria and Albert Museum, the Natural History Museum, and the Science Museum. The neighborhoods of **South Kensington** and **Earl's Court** are riddled with budget lodging and hordes of travelers—Londoners themselves can be a bit thin on the ground around here. As you move northeast toward Knightsbridge, however, the streetscape gets more ritzy and prices go through the roof—only Mayfair and St. James's carry more snob value. Though prices are prohibitive, you can always window-shop on the long east–west thoroughfare of **Knightsbridge** and **Kensington High Street** (different names, same street). Just north of Knightsbridge lie two of London's best parks, Hyde Park and Kensington Gardens (*see below*).

HOLLAND PARK Beautiful Holland Park inhabits a sizable chunk of posh Kensington, just north of the intersection of Kensington High Street and Earl's Court Road. The whole 22 hectares were originally the private grounds of the stately Jacobean **Holland House,** now a youth hostel (*see* Chapter 3), and have only been open to the public since 1952. To the north you'll find stunning gardens and woodlands where wild peacocks, geese, and even a few emus roam. At the park's center is the formal **Dutch Garden** (first planted by Lady Holland in the 1790s) and a glass-walled art gallery, the **Orangery.** At the south side of the park stands the **Commonwealth Institute** (230 Kensington High St., W8, tel. 0171/603–4535), whose small museum dedicated to the 50 member-nations of the former British Empire is scheduled to reopen in March 1997. *Tube: High Street Kensington or Holland Park.*

LEIGHTON HOUSE The former home and studio of Lord Frederick Leighton (1830–1896), a classical painter and avid collector of Islamic art and Asian treasures, is now a beautifully decorated museum. The **Arab Hall,** constructed with intricately detailed tiles and mosaic friezes, is breathtaking. Leighton and pals were not bad painters either, as evidenced by the wonderful Victorian oils in the other rooms. *12 Holland Park Rd., W14, tel. 0171/602–3316. Tube: High Street Kensington. Walk west on Kensington High St., turn right on Addison Rd., right on Holland Park Rd. Admission free. Open Mon.–Sat. 11–5:30.*

Kensington and Knightsbridge

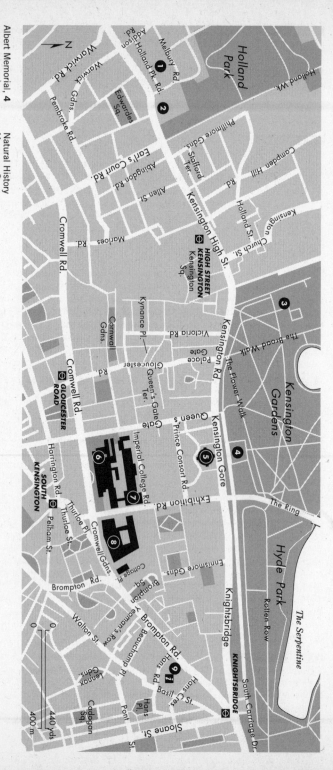

NATURAL HISTORY MUSEUM A thorough collection of plants and animals is housed in the impressive Earth and Life galleries of this fun museum. There are fossils, dinosaur skeletons, stuffed animals (in the literal sense) from every corner of the earth, and amazing interactive exhibits such as a simulated earthquake—the whole shebang. Perhaps more impressive than the contents is the building itself. Designed by Alfred Waterhouse in 1862, the museum resembles a cathedral to science, decorated throughout with images of living and extinct animals and fossils. Stop in during the free hours just to take a peek. *Cromwell Rd., SW7, tel. 0171/938–9123. Tube: South Kensington. Walk north on Exhibition Rd., turn left on Cromwell Rd. Admission: £5.50, £3 students; free weekdays after 4:30, weekends after 5. Open Mon.–Sat. 10–5:50, Sun. 11–5:50. Wheelchair access.*

SCIENCE MUSEUM The Science Museum's six floors are chock-full of groovy, user-friendly exhibits about science, technology, industry, and medicine. In all, they've got 200,000 objects and 2,000 interactive, hands-on exhibits, including video telephones; computers with Internet access; a fully operational radio station; a copy of George Washington's wooden teeth; lots of cool holograms; some of the world's first oral contraceptives; reconstructions of an open-heart surgery and a 1930s dentist's office; the *Vickers Vimy,* the first aircraft to cross the Atlantic; and the command module from the *Apollo 10,* which made the first manned flight around the world. Check at the front desk for info on free daily workshops and guided tours. *Exhibition Rd., SW7, tel. 0171/938–8111. Tube: South Kensington. Walk north on Exhibition Rd. Admission: £5.50, £2.90 students; free daily after 4:30. Open daily 10–6.*

VICTORIA AND ALBERT MUSEUM This stellar museum, affectionately called the V&A, has a vast and eclectic collection of fine and decorative art, crossing all disciplines, all periods, all nationalities, and all tastes. Prince Albert, Victoria's adored consort, was the man with the V&A plan back in the 18th century: It was to be a permanent version of the enormously popular 1851 Great Exhibition, also his creation. Now, nearly a century later, the V&A has stirred up enormous controversy with announcements of a £46 million extension. Called the **Boilerhouse Project,** it will house a state-of-the-art multimedia gallery with computers and virtual reality gizmos, galleries for contemporary exhibits, and it will look like a jumble of glass boxes some seven stories tall. Though ground hasn't yet been broken, traditionalists already loathe the plan on principle.

The best way to take in the V&A's enormous collection is to let yourself get lost for a day in its seven miles of gallery space, then try to find your way out. You'll pass treasures weird and wonderful, like the snuff box believed to have been a gift to Nell Gwyn from Charles II, the great Mughal emperor Shah Jahan's jade cup, or the 12-foot-square, solid-oak, four-poster **Great Bed of Ware,** immortalized by Shakespeare in *Twelfth Night.* The **Art and Design Galleries** exhibit everything from Indian art to Renaissance Italian sculpture and Muslim carpets. The **Materials and Techniques Galleries** illustrate different media of applied art such as jewelry, ornaments, and ceramics. Also worth a stop is the **Fakes and Forgeries Gallery** (room 46), which has a great collection of honest-to-goodness bogus art, and the **Dress Collection** (room 40), with displays of clothing from 1600 to the present day. Stairs from the Dress Collection lead to an exhibit of finely crafted musical instruments. The **Raphael Gallery** displays seven priceless cartoons by the great Renaissance master Raphael, and the **Frank Lloyd Wright Gallery** houses the only re-created Wright interior in Europe. In the brand-new **Silver Galleries,** opened in November 1996, you'll find some 1,500 silver objects dating from 1300 to 1800—including royal flatwear and booty from sunken galleons. Other galleries include the Tsui Gallery of Chinese Art, Nehru Gallery of Indian Art, 20th Century Gallery, Glass Gallery, and Iron Gallery, but that's just a fraction of what this unique museum has to offer.

The V&A offers two varieties of free guided tours daily: Introductory tours leave from the info desk Tuesday–Saturday at 11, noon, 2, and 3; on Monday they leave at 12:15, 2, and 3. Special tours—covering a particular theme, country, or exhibit—leave Tuesday–Sunday at 11:30 and 1:30, Monday at 1:30 and 2:30. During summer months the V&A stays open until 9:30 PM on Wednesday evenings, when it offers fun stuff like live music, a garden wine bar, free gallery talks, and educational lectures. *Cromwell Rd., SW7, tel. 0171/938–8441. Tube: South Kensington. Walk north on Exhibition Rd., turn right on Cromwell Gardens. Admission: £5, £3 students; £7, £5 students on Wed. after 6:30 PM. Open Mon. noon–5:50, Tues.–Sun. 10–5:50 (Wed. until 9:30 PM). Wheelchair entrance on Exhibition Rd.*

HARRODS Originally a small grocer's shop, this most famous London department store is a magnet for every tourist on the planet. Don't come here to shop—it's incredibly expensive—but rather to browse. If you're here around Christmas, definitely check out the decorations and displays—they really do it up. Many of the upper floors are just like any other department store, so you're much better off moseying down to the lavish **food halls** where an amazing array of food is available, including exotic fruits and vegetables, delectable cakes, and over 300 cheeses. Don't be tempted to devour those goodies in the store, however. Apparently Harrods finds eating damaging to its "ambience," and, according to *Time Out*, once ejected someone for eating a chocolate. If you don't mind carnage, visit the meat hall where skilled butchers and fishmongers in crisp aprons bustle under ceiling tiles illustrating *The Hunt*, painted by W. J. Neatby in 1902. *87–135 Brompton Rd., SW1, tel. 0171/730–1234. Tube: Knightsbridge. Walk south on Brompton Rd. Open Mon.–Tues. and Sat. 10–6, Wed.–Fri. 10–7.*

ROYAL ALBERT HALL Looming in the near future for this major-league concert venue (named after Queen Victoria's hubby) is a £40 million-plus refurbishment, paid for in part by British lottery money. Until then, it's home to the acclaimed **Royal Philharmonic Orchestra** and, in summer, busts loose with its enormously popular **Promenade Concerts** (*see* Classical Music, Opera and Dance, in Chapter 6). The interior, a huge amphitheater done up in wine-red and gold, is the height of Victorian imperial architecture and is graced with the largest pipe organ in Great Britain. Unfortunately, such splendors are off-limits to the nonpaying public. To see it you'll need to buy a concert ticket, or take one of the guided tours (£6) offered twice daily. Barring that, pop by for a look at the exterior, if only because it's mentioned in the Beatles song "A Day in the Life." *Kensington Gore, near Exhibition Rd., W8, tel. 0171/589–8212. Tube: Knightsbridge. Walk west on Knightsbridge (which becomes Kensington Rd. and Kensington Gore).*

HYDE PARK AND KENSINGTON GARDENS Hyde Park and Kensington Gardens blend together to form one large 634-acre park, the biggest in London. Though these days it's difficult to tell where one ends and the other begins, each has a unique origin: Hyde Park began as the hunting grounds of Henry VIII (who swiped the land from the monks at Westminster), while Kensington Gardens was first laid out as the grounds for William and Mary's Kensington Palace (*see below*). This is a great place to lounge in one of hundreds of conveniently placed lawn chairs (rentable in summer for only a few pence) or just kick back in the tall grass under a huge shady tree. Small boats cruise on the **Serpentine,** a long, thin lake that arcs through the middle of the two parks. You can rent a rowboat at the boathouse for a few quid (*see* Participant Sports, in Chapter 8).

You're also duty-bound not to miss **Speakers' Corner** on the northeast edge of Hyde Park (Tube: Marble Arch). Since 1873, this has been hallowed ground for amateur orators burning to make a point—originally, speakers ranted and raved atop soapboxes; now they climb aboard aluminum stepladders. It really hits full swing by about 2 or 3 PM on weekends, as spielers spiel, hecklers heckle, and free speech dovetails into street theater. There could be as many as a dozen speakers declaiming to individual crowds of more than 100 people, on subjects as diverse as justice and democracy, the evils of meat-eating, or invaders from Mars. In 1996 Speakers' Corner became a sparring ground for Islamic extremists and Christian evangelists (a handful of speeches ended with knife fights), but an increased police presence has turned the whole thing fairly benign once again. At the southeast corner of the park stands the **Apsley House/Wellington Museum** (149 Piccadilly, tel. 0171/499–5676), onetime home to "Iron Duke" Wellington. Inside you'll find the great man's treasures, uniforms, and weapons, as well as a massive nude-but-for-a-fig-leaf statue of Napoléon Bonaparte, who was Wellington's sworn enemy. The museum is open Tuesday–Sunday 11–5, and admission is £3. Finally, Hyde Park and Kensington Gardens are the place to crash after haggling at the splendid **Portobello Road Market** (*see* Street Markets, in Chapter 7). *Tel. 0171/289–2100 for park info.*

➤ **KENSINGTON PALACE** • Kensington Palace has seen a lot of history since it was converted from plain old mansion to royal homestead by Christopher Wren in 1689. Most recently England's not-so-happy couple Prince Charles and Princess Di lived the dysfunctional family life there, until it was awarded to Diana as part of her divorce settlement. Little bits of the palace are also open for public viewing. Visitors can do the once-over of the **Cupola Room,** where Queen Victoria was baptized; the **King's Gallery,** filled with fine 17th-century paintings;

Hyde Park and Kensington Gardens

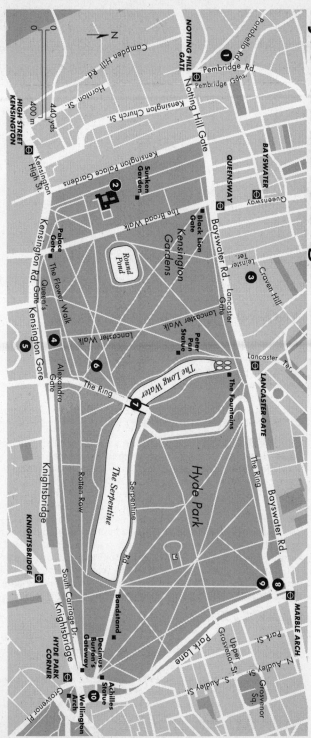

0 ———— 0
0 ———— 400 m
0 ———— 440 yds

NOTTING HILL GATE

Pembridge Rd.
Portobello Rd.
Pembridge Gdns.
Camden Hill Rd.
Hornton St.
Kensington Church St.
Notting Hill Gate

Kensington Palace Gardens
Kensington High St.
HIGH STREET KENSINGTON

BAYSWATER
QUEENSWAY
Queensway

Leinster Ter.
Craven Hill
Bayswater Rd.
Lancaster Gate
LANCASTER GATE
Lancaster Ter.

Sunken Garden
Black Lion Gate
The Broad Walk
Kensington Gardens
Round Pond
Peter Pan Statue

Palace Gate
Queen's Gate
Kensington Rd.
Kensington Gore
The Flower Walk
Alexandra Gate
Lancaster Walk
Lancaster Walk

The Fountains
The Long Water

The Ring
Bayswater Rd.
The Ring

Knightsbridge
KNIGHTSBRIDGE
Knightsbridge
South Carriage Dr.
Rotten Row
The Serpentine
Serpentine Rd.

Hyde Park

Park St.
MARBLE ARCH
N. Audley St.
S. Audley St.
Grosvenor Sq.
Upper Grosvenor St.
Park Lane

Bandstand
Decimus Burton's Gateway
HYDE PARK CORNER
Achilles Statue
Wellington Arch
Grosvenor Pl.

59

and (once renovations are completed in spring of 1997) the **State Apartments,** where the once newly crowned Queen Mary II and William III first shacked up. Also on display is the **Royal Ceremonial Dress Collection,** with clothes worn to regal galas from 1750 to the present day, including Princess Diana's wedding dress. *Kensington Gardens, W8, tel. 0171/937–9561. Tube: High Street Kensington or Queensway. Admission: £5.50, £4.10 students.*

➤ **ALBERT MEMORIAL** • Across from the Royal Albert Hall is the grandiose Albert Memorial, commissioned by Queen Victoria in an expression of her obsessive reverence for her dead husband. Here a 14-foot-tall, gold-plated Albert sits under an ornate canopy, clutching a catalogue of the Great International Exhibition of 1851 (his brainchild). The base is decorated with 169 life-size figures of poets, composers, architects, and sculptors. Currently, the Albert Memorial is undergoing £13 million worth of renovations, though the head-to-toe scaffolding should come off by 1998. *Kensington Gardens, SW7. Tube: High Street Kensington or Knightsbridge.*

✔ ➤ **MARBLE ARCH** • This monument, modeled by Nash after the Arch of Constantine in Rome and carved from 100% Italian marble, originally stood at the entrance to Buckingham Palace. However, fussy Queen Victoria wanted a more robust arch on her front lawn, so in 1851 she ordered Prince Albert to have it moved, stone by stone, to a less conspicuous location. And so it now stands at the northeast corner of Hyde Park. In 1996, the whole shebang was completely renovated (and pigeon-proofed), to the tune of £100,000. To help defray the cost, the Department of National Heritage has been seeking tenants for two tiny rooms built into the sides of the monument. Hey, maybe they're still taking applications. *Tube: Marble Arch (surprise!).*

MAYFAIR

Mayfair, sandwiched between hip and happening Soho and Hyde Park/Kensington Gardens, is an ultraritzy residential neighborhood lined with beautiful 18th-century apartment blocks faced with deep red brick. Many national embassies, and some of London's wealthiest citizens, call Mayfair home. But, unless you have a ton of money, you're likely to get a bit bored here. The sheer number of Rolls-Royces, Bentleys, and Jaguars rolling around Mayfair is staggering; even the delivery vans seem to bear some royal coat of arms, proclaiming them to be purveyors of fine goodies for as long as anyone can remember. The one exception is noisy, rollicking **Oxford Street** (*see below*). To stroll Mayfair, take the tube to Bond Street or Green Park.

BERKELEY SQUARE Shaded by tall trees and populated by cheeky squirrels, Berkeley Square (pronounced "Barkley") is a great place to get the feel of Mayfair. The park is ringed with a high iron fence, and on one side you'll find a Rolls-Royce dealership that stays open late during the annual Berkeley Square Ball—in hopes that wealthy drunks will spring for a new £60,000 roadster. Though the square suffered from a poor redevelopment plan in the 1930s, a line of fine Georgian houses (circa 1737) remains on the west side. No. 44, built in 1740 for one Lady Isabella Finch, has been called London's finest terraced house. Clive of India overdosed on laudanum next door at No. 45 in 1774. Just west of Berkeley Square, **Mount Street Gardens** (also called St. George's Gardens) is a fine place for a picnic. Take a left out of the gardens, walk west along Mount Street, and you'll find **James & Son Purdey** (57 S. Audley St., W1, tel. 0171/499–1801), Britain's famous maker of overpriced guns. You're welcome to browse weekdays 9–5. Next door are the **Counter Spy Shop** and **Lorraine Electronics Spy Shop** for all your espionage needs. *Tube: Green Park. Walk NW 1 block on Piccadilly, turn left on Berkeley St.*

SHEPHERD'S MARKET The May Fair, the market that gave its name to the neighborhood, moved here in 1686 from the Haymarket and was famed for its ribald entertainment; later, the area became a popular haunt of prostitutes. Today, Shepherd's Market is a charming nest of pedestrian-only alleys loaded to the gills with cafés and wine bars. It's a tony, quiet, and exceedingly pleasant place to while away an hour over a cappuccino. At one end, the market opens onto **Curzon Street,** where the British secret service (of 007 fame) had its unmarked headquarters before moving to Gothamesque **Vauxhall Cross** (*see box* London's Modern Architecture, *below*). *Tube: Green Park. Walk west on Piccadilly, turn right on Half Moon St., left on Curzon St.*

GROSVENOR SQUARE The largest square in London, Grosvenor Square has been ruined by the huge, fortresslike **American embassy,** the ugliest government building in town. The rather

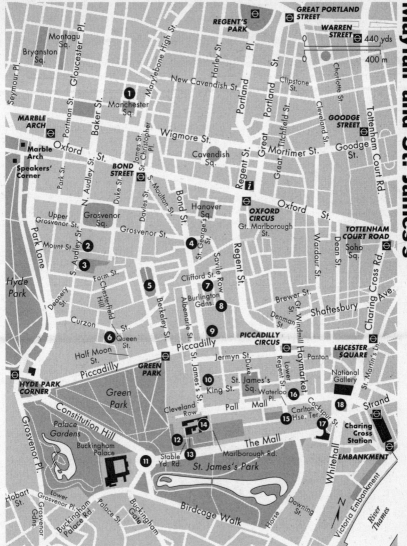

GREAT PORTLAND STREET

REGENT'S PARK

WARREN STREET

0 440 yds
0 400 m

MARBLE ARCH

Montagu Sq.

Bryanston Sq.

Seymour Pl.

Gloucester Pl.

Marylebone High St.

New Cavendish St.

Harley St.

Portland Pl.

Portland St.

Great Portland St.

Clipstone St.

Charlotte St.

GOODGE STREET

Tottenham Court Rd.

Wigmore St.

Manchester Sq. ①

Baker St.

Portman St.

James St.
St. Christopher Pl.

Cavendish Sq.

Regent St.

Great Titchfield St.

Mortimer St.

Great Portland St.

Goodge St.

Marble Arch

Oxford St.

Speakers' Corner

Park St.

N. Audley St.

Duke St.

BOND STREET

S. Moulton St.

Bond St.

Hanover Sq.

OXFORD CIRCUS

Gt. Marlborough St.

Oxford St.

Wardour St.

TOTTENHAM COURT ROAD

Dean St.

Soho Sq.

Charing Cross Rd.

Upper Grosvenor St.

Grosvenor Sq.

Davies St.

St. George's St.

Savile Row

Regent St.

② Purdy's

③

Mount St.

S. Audley St.

Farm St.

Grosvenor St.

④ Sotheby's

Clifford St.

⑦ Cork Street

Brewer St.

Gt. Windmill St.

Shaftesbury Ave.

Charing Cross Rd.

Hyde Park

Deanery St.

Chesterfield Hill

⑤ Berkeley Square

Berkeley St.

Albemarle St.

Burlington Gdns.

⑧ Museum of Mankind

Denman St.

Curzon St.

⑥ Shepherd's Market

Queen St.

⑨ Royal Academy of Arts

Piccadilly

PICCADILLY CIRCUS

LEICESTER SQUARE

Half Moon St.

GREEN PARK

St. James's St.

Jermyn St.

Duke St.

Lower Regent St.

Haymarket

Panton

St. Martin's Ln.

Piccadilly

⑩ Christie's

King St.

St. James's Sq.

National Gallery

Strand

HYDE PARK CORNER

Green Park

Cleveland Row

Pall Mall

⑯ Royal Opera Arcade

Waterloo Pl.

Cockspur St.

⑱ Trafalgar Square

Constitution Hill

Palace Gardens

⑫ ⑭ St. James's Palace

Marlborough Rd.

⑮ Institute of Contemporary Arts

Carlton Hse. Ter.

⑰ Admiralty Arch

Charing Cross Station

Grosvenor Pl.

Buckingham Palace

⑪ Queen Victoria Memorial

Stable Yd. Rd.

⑬ Clarence House

The Mall

Whitehall

EMBANKMENT

Hobart St.

Lower Grosvenor Pl.

Grosvenor Gdns.

Buckingham Palace Rd.

Palace St.

Buckingham Gate

St. James's Park

Birdcage Walk

Horse Gds. Rd.

Downing St.

Victoria Embankment

River Thames

plain statue of Franklin D. Roosevelt, erected in the center of the square in 1948, certainly doesn't help matters. Nearby, look for the plaque commemorating John Adams, first American ambassador to Britain and second president of the United States; he lived at the corner of Brook and Duke streets. *Tube: Bond Street. Walk west on Oxford St., turn left on Duke St.*

OXFORD STREET Oxford Street—which runs from Marble Arch to Tottenham Court Road— is also known as London's Golden Mile. Cramming both sides of the street are some 300 clothing stores, plus lots of steak houses, a few mammoth department stores (*see* Chapter 7), and scads of souvenir shops. No disputing it, Oxford Street is a major tourist attraction in its own right; by some estimates, it also loses around £2 million a week to shoplifters. The shops nearest Hyde Park are the most swank, but everywhere on Oxford Street is loud and crowded with wild-eyed shoppers sucking up £10 Lycra outfits. A worthwhile detour from such Sturm und Drang is **South Molton Street,** a pedestrian arcade at the corner of Oxford and Davies streets. If you ferret around in the little alleys and passageways, you'll find some nice sandwich shops and pubs. *Tube: Bond Street, Marble Arch, Oxford Circus, or Tottenham Court Road.*

BOND STREET Perpendicular to Oxford Street, Bond Street may be the most expensive shopping street in London. It's divided into **New Bond** and **Old Bond** and is just full of the kind of people who coo over £10,000 dresses and £60 silk cravats. As far as shops go, jewelers, antiques dealers, and sellers of original art predominate, and many of them won't give you a second look unless you're trailed by a liveried chauffeur. Maybe you find that shtick sick, but even the impoverished will get a kick out of attending an auction at **Sotheby's** (34–35 New Bond St., W1, tel. 0171/493–8080). Dress nicely, and see who you can fool: They usually have morning lots at least three days a week at 10 and sometimes an afternoon run at 2:30. Or, you can browse through the goods for sale weekdays 9–4:30 and Sunday noon–4. East of Bond Street is **Savile Row,** famous for its many accomplished tailors and the site of the Beatles' last public appearance: an impromptu performance on the roof of the Apple Records building in 1969. *Tube: Bond Street, Green Park, or Piccadilly Circus.*

CORK STREET Parallel to Bond Street is Cork Street, the center of the established commercial art scene in London, with more than a dozen private galleries between **Burlington Gardens** and **Clifford Street.** They're close together, so it's easy to hit them all within a few hours—and though they sometimes look intimidating, all are open to the public free of charge. You'll find that Cork Street galleries tend to fixate on contemporary Western art, although a handful emphasize material ranging from 20th-century canonical "avant garde" to Australian aboriginal art and contemporary Russian realism. *Tube: Green Park or Piccadilly Circus. From Green Park, walk east on Piccadilly, turn left on Old Bond St., right on Burlington Gardens. From Piccadilly Circus, walk NW 1 long block on Regent St., turn left on Vigo St. (which becomes Burlington Gardens).*

SOHO

Back in the days when all of Soho was just Whitehall Palace's parklands, royal huntsmen filled the air with their cries of "So-ho! So-ho!" Though nobody knows for sure, the direct translation into modern English is probably "Hey, guys, let's quit hunting foxes and go grab some beers."

Soho began its life as one of the leading bohemian neighborhoods of London during the 1950s, as a beatnik stomping ground and the heart of the London jazz scene. In the 1960s, rock took over and the area became home to a new counterculture, with clubs featuring headliners like the Rolling Stones, the Who, and the Kinks in their respective heydays. With the coming of punk and seminal bands like the Sex Pistols, Generation X, the Clash, and X-Ray Specs, King's Road (*see* Chelsea, *above*) replaced Soho as the home of London's pop culture, leading to a resurgence in the Soho jazz scene that continues to this day. Sadly, much of Soho has suffered from the yuppification and commercialization that are, ironically, so common in former bastions of urban hipness. Its streets are lined with an odd amalgam of fashionable clothing stores, gourmet restaurants, high-power hair salons, trendy cafés, theaters, and nightclubs, plus a smattering of XXX-rated sex shops (remnants of the 'hood's long-ago incarnation as the red-light district of London). Additionally, a huge number of Hollywood studios have their postproduction facilities here, so you'll also see names like Tri-Star, Warner Bros., and Lucasfilm etched over dozens of Soho doors.

Soho and Covent Garden

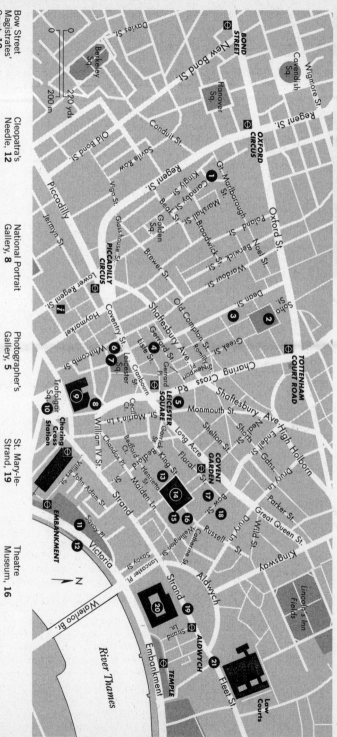

Soho has an international flavor that many of central London's neighborhoods lack; generally, you have to go to the city outskirts to find such a polyglot community. French Huguenots arriving in the 1680s were the first foreigners to settle the area en masse, followed by Germans, Russians, Poles, and Greeks—though Soho today displays more Chinese and Italian influences. The Chinese community is crowded around **Gerrard Street** (*see* Chinatown, *below*). If you're looking for traditional Italian restaurants and cafés, head for **Old Compton Street,** which is also a major center for gay life in the city. **Berwick Street** is home to a market popular with tourists and locals alike (*see* Street Markets, in Chapter 7). If you catch the tube to Leicester Square, Oxford Circus, Piccadilly Circus, or Tottenham Court Road, you'll find yourself right on the edge of Soho.

LEICESTER SQUARE Leicester Square is often compared to New York's Times Square, but it isn't as big, as bright, or as sleazy. Still, just like any other major entertainment district, Leicester (pronounced "Lester") has some shady characters and an off-and-on drug scene. Huge movie houses, many converted from grand old theaters, surround the square, showing the latest releases. Tacky tourist attractions line some of the side streets, and weird street theater is often staged on the pedestrian mall at the western edge of the square (although you may get tired of that punker playing the same six notes over and over on his sax). On the west side is the **Society of West End Theatres** ticket kiosk (*see* Theater, in Chapter 6), where you can buy half-price, same-day tickets for many London shows. Just off Leicester Square on Leicester Place stands the oasis-like **Notre Dame de France,** a modern French Catholic church worth visiting if only to see an impressive Jean Cocteau mural in a chapel dedicated to the Virgin.

PICCADILLY CIRCUS Only the most gullible of tourists (surely not you) still believe Ringling Brothers tigers and acrobats perform at Piccadilly Circus. Rather, the weird name comes out of the dark days of the 17th century, when men wore *picadils* (ruffled collars) and one smart young tailor grew rich enough on the proceeds to build a fine house. Snobs sneeringly labeled it Piccadilly Hall, and when the mansion was later ripped down to build a circular junction for five major roads, the name morphed into Piccadilly Circus. Despite the lack of rainbow-haired clowns, the circle offers plenty of fine people-watching, especially on the steps of the famous **Eros** statue (disappointingly, this is supposed to represent the angel of Christian charity, *not* the Greek god of erotic love) or on the wall of the fountain beneath the bronze **Horse of Helios** sculpture. Note to rockers, kitsch-seekers, and lovers of the Pop Life: Piccadilly Circus is also home to treasures like an animatronic Janis Joplin, a 100% wax Artist-Formerly-Known-As-Prince, a wondrous "Wall of Hands," lots of laser lights, and plenty of taped guitar solos, all at **Madame Tussaud's Rock Circus** (The London Pavilion, 1 Piccadilly Circus, tel. 0171/734–8025). You wouldn't want to miss the self-proclaimed "No. 1 Rock Attraction in Britain," would you? Admission: £7.50, £7 students. *Tube: Piccadilly Circus.*

CHINATOWN Known as **Tong Yan Kai** (Chinese Streets) by residents, Chinatown has some purely tourist trappings—telephone booths topped by pagodas, for example. But before you work yourself into a tizzy thinking you've rediscovered Shanghai in Greenwich Mean Time, understand that London's Chinatown is very small. In fact, it's really only two short streets, **Gerrard** and **Lisle,** which run between Leicester Square and Shaftesbury Avenue. Even so, it's home to many of London's 50,000 Chinese residents—most came to Britain from Hong Kong in the '50s and '60s, and quite a few more have arrived as Britain prepares to hand Hong Kong over to China in July 1997. It's fascinating to poke around in the tiny stores that sell Chinese herbs and oddly shaped vegetables, or feast on a meal of dim sum in one of the many restaurants (*see* Chapter 4). February's New Year's Celebration and September's Mid-Autumn Festival (*see* Festivals, in Chapter 1) fill the air with the cacophony of firecrackers—if you're in town at either time, don't miss the fun. *Tube: Leicester Square. Walk north on Charing Cross Rd., turn left on Lisle St.*

SHAFTESBURY AVENUE Cutting through the center of Soho, Shaftesbury Avenue is one of London's three principal theater streets (along with the Haymarket and Coventry Street). Built side by side in the early 1900s, many of the theaters survived the war and retain the grand look espoused by Edwardian theater. Sir Noël Coward, Sir John Gielgud, and Sir Laurence Olivier all made it big in Shaftesbury Avenue theaters like the Apollo, the Lyric, the Globe, and the Queen's. Today, you're likely to find these same theaters hosting the works of such playwrights as Tom Stoppard and Peter Shaffer. For more info, see West End Theaters, in Chapter 6. Tube: Leicester Square or Piccadilly Circus.

London's 1851 census lists a "Charles Mark, Doctor (Philosophical Author)" living at 28 Dean Street, southwest of Soho Square. Today, a blue plaque commemorates the site of Karl Marx's residence from 1851 to 1856.

CARNABY STREET During the '60s, this pedestrian mall was a groovy place to hang out, buy flowery fashions, and pick up the latest tunes. All that's gone now, and Carnaby Street survives solely on the basis of its past fame. Come in the late afternoon to miss the worst of the crowds, but don't spend much time on Carnaby Street itself—it's nothing more than trendy stores and tourist schlock. Put down that plastic "bobby" helmet and explore the small alleys and streets to the east, which have some hip clothing stores (particularly if you're in the market for leather) and tiny crafts shops; try **Marshall** and **Broadwick** streets. Tube: Oxford Circus. Walk south on Regent St., turn left on Great Marlborough St., right on Carnaby St.

SOHO SQUARE Built in the 1670s to honor Charles II, Soho Square is one of the oldest public squares in London. Nowadays this pleasant village green is a welcome open space in the middle of hectic Soho. It's shared in perfect harmony by businesspeople on their lunch breaks, pram-pushing nannies, tourists, elderly folks, and homeless people—all under the watchful gaze of a dilapidated 19th-century statue of King Charles himself. Tube: Tottenham Court Road. Walk west on Oxford St., turn left into Soho Sq.

Central London

ST. JAMES'S ✔

When Henry VIII's lovely **Whitehall Palace** burned down in 1698, all of London turned its attention to St. James's Palace (see below), the new royal residence. In the 18th and 19th centuries, the area around the palace became the fashionable place to live, and many of the estates surrounding the palace disappeared in a building frenzy, as mansions were built, streets laid out, and expensive shops established. Today, St. James's—along with Mayfair and Sloane Square in Chelsea—remains London's most elegant and fashionable address. For a detail of the area, see the map Mayfair and St. James's, above.

PALL MALL Pall Mall, pronounced "Pal Mal," is a haven of quiet and refined elegance that has managed to survive from more regal days. The street gets its name from *paille maille,* a French version of croquet that was popular during the reigns of Charles I and II. A number of gentlemen's clubs, those quintessentially snobby English institutions, line Pall Mall, including the Athenaeum, United Oxford and Cambridge University Club, Travellers' Club, and the Reform Club. Many clubs went under after World War II, though several made comebacks in the conservative, free-market '80s. Surrealistic **Christie's** (8 King St., SW1, tel. 0171/839–9060), the premier art auctioneers of the Western world, resides north of Pall Mall. The auctions are open to the public and are free, but loitering is discouraged—unless, of course, you look like you're pocketing a platinum card. Pall Mall runs almost parallel to the Mall from Trafalgar Sq. and dead-ends at St. James's Palace. Tube: Charing Cross, Green Park, or Piccadilly Circus.

ST. JAMES'S PALACE This elegant brick palace lies at the end of Pall Mall on the former site of a women's leper hospital. The ever-sensitive Henry VIII bought the hospital in 1532 and erected a hunting lodge in its stead. Only the **Chapel Royal** and four-story **Gatehouse** remain of Henry's original manor—most of the palace was rebuilt after a fire in 1809. For much of its existence, the palace has played second fiddle to the now-gone Whitehall Palace and to Buckingham Palace, though all foreign ambassadors to Britain are still officially accredited to "The Court of St. James's." Alas, the palace is not open to the public. Pall Mall, at St. James's St., SW1. Tube: Green Park. Walk east on Piccadilly and turn right on St. James's St.

THE MALL The red-Tarmac Mall cuts a wide swath all the way from Trafalgar Square to Buckingham Palace. It was laid out in 1904, largely because it was felt that the British monarchy should have a processional route in keeping with its imperial status. After all, the French had the fine Champs-Elysées, and they didn't even have a sovereign anymore. The 115-foot-wide Mall is no Champs-Elysées, however; without a royal procession clomping down it, the Mall seems soulless. **Admiralty Arch,** a triumphal arch bordering Trafalgar Square, marks the start of the Mall. Built in 1911, the central gate is opened only for royal processions. From here, the Mall sweeps past St. James's Park and **Carlton House Terrace,** a stately 1,000-foot-long facade of white stucco arches that is home of the ICA (*see* Museums and Galleries, *below*), a first-rate contemporary gallery. Farther down on the right is **Clarence House,** raised by genius John Nash between 1812 and 1830, and now home of the Queen Mother. She alone seems to bob along high above the tiresome sex scandals, divorces, and assorted rubbish that have plagued the royal family for far too long. The Mall ends in front of Buckingham Palace at the **Queen Victoria Memorial,** an irritatingly didactic monument to the glory of Victorian ideals. The broad avenue of the Mall replaced a much smaller, gravel boulevard that now lies a little to the north. Together with St. James's Park, the Mall was the place to see and be seen in 17th- and 18th-century London. Nowadays, the best time to explore the Mall is Sunday, when it's closed to traffic.

ST. JAMES'S PARK Sitting amid London's grandest monuments, this 93-acre park is remarkably peaceful—it enjoys an almost librarylike quiet. It is a stroller's park, a place to wander among the flowers, feed the ducks, and sit and read. The focal point is an ornamental canal, added by Charles II and redesigned by George IV, filled with geese and lined with weeping willows. For the better part of the 17th and 18th centuries, the park was the playground for England's elite, who would gather here to stare down their noses at one another before heading off to be idle elsewhere. At night—when the fountains, Westminster Abbey, and the Houses of Parliament are illuminated—the scene is honestly breathtaking. *Tube: Charing Cross, St. James's Park, or Westminster.*

GREEN PARK Across the Mall from St. James's Park, Green Park is a grassy expanse crisscrossed by walking paths. You can never totally escape the traffic noise from Piccadilly here, but it's still a popular spot to doze in the sun or read the paper. Green Park tube station lets you off at the northeastern corner of the park, at the top of Queen's Walk. This asphalt path leads south toward St. James's Park and The Mall, passing several large mansions behind protective fences. One of these mansions, **Lancaster House,** is used for government functions and negotiations. The talks that led to black-majority rule in Zimbabwe, formerly Rhodesia, were held here. *Tube: Green Park.*

WHITEHALL AND WESTMINSTER

Whitehall is both a street and a vast, faceless bureaucracy. Whitehall the street runs from Trafalgar Square to Parliament Square through the heart of official London—which means it's a major tourist stomping ground. Whitehall the bureaucracy can't be so easily defined. Essentially, the term applies to the central British government, whose ministries fill many of the buildings off Whitehall and around Carlton Terrace. Adjacent Westminster is a small section of London most noted for its abbey, bridge, and palace, each named Westminster—though the palace is more commonly known as the **Houses of Parliament** (*see* Major Attractions, *above*). Southern Westminster is a sleepy residential area with charming old homes—worth wandering through if you're on your way to the splendid **Tate Gallery** (*see* Major Attractions, *above*).

HORSE GUARDS AND PARADE GROUND As you walk down Whitehall toward Parliament Square, you pass the Horse Guards on the right. This low building, constructed between 1745 and 1755, is the backdrop for a smaller version of the **Changing of the Guard** performed at Buckingham Palace. Each day at 11 AM (10 AM Sundays), a mounted contingent of the Household Cavalry clops its way down the Mall from Hyde Park Barracks to Whitehall. It takes about a half hour before they arrive in front of Horse Guards and relieve the soldiers standing in sentry boxes facing the Banqueting House. If you don't feel like battling the crowds at Buckingham Palace, this is the next-best ceremonial relic. If it's raining significantly or there is a State event, the whole thing's canceled. For no apparent reason, two more sentries guard **Horse**

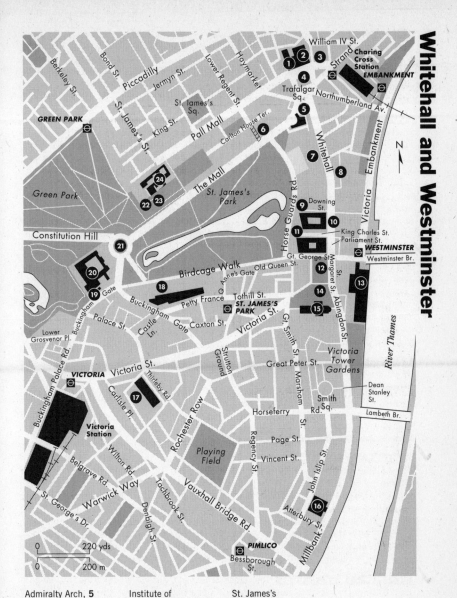

Admiralty Arch, **5**

Banqueting House, **8**

Buckingham Palace, **20**

Cabinet War Rooms, **11**

Cenotaph, **10**

Clarence House, **23**

Downing Street, **9**

Horse Guards and Parade Ground, **7**

Houses of Parliament, **13**

Institute of Contemporary Arts, **6**

Lancaster House, **22**

National Gallery, **1**

National Portrait Gallery, **2**

Nelson's Column, **4**

Parliament Square, **12**

Queen Victoria Memorial, **21**

Queen's Gallery and Royal Mews, **19**

St. James's Palace, **24**

St. Margaret's Westminster, **14**

St. Martin-in-the-Fields, **3**

Tate Gallery, **16**

Wellington Barracks (Guards Museum), **18**

Westminster Abbey, **15**

Westminster Cathedral, **17**

Guards Arch, which leads to the **Parade Ground.** Once the site of Henry's VIII's jousting arena, this massive square looks a little bleak when nothing's going on. In June, however, the parade ground comes alive with some of London's biggest ceremonies—**Trooping the Colour** and **Beating Retreat** (*see* Festivals, in Chapter 1). To the west of the parade ground lies St. James's Park, and to the north looms **Admiralty Arch** (look for all the incongruous high-tech antenna equipment on top), an interesting combination of pomp and practicality.

BANQUETING HOUSE Designed by Inigo Jones and built between 1619 and 1622, Banqueting House is one of the earliest examples of Renaissance architecture in England. It's also the only surviving building from the original Whitehall Palace, the onetime home of Henry VIII, which burned in 1698. The House's main room was originally used as a venue for the court entertainments of Charles I and in 1649 was the backdrop for his beheading. These days, it's a popular spot for state banquets. The chief attractions are Rubens's ceiling paintings, commissioned by Charles I, which portray him and his father, James I, in a favorable, even divine, light. *Whitehall, across from Horse Guards Arch, SW1, tel. 0171/930–4179. Tube: Charing Cross or Westminster. Admission: £3, £2.25 students. Open Mon.–Sat. 10–5 (last admission 4:30). Closed occasionally for government functions.*

DOWNING STREET If it weren't for the massive security measures and the ogling tourists, you would never suspect the importance of the rather ordinary homes on this street. The mammoth iron gate is the first hint, but the guys checking under every car for bombs are a dead giveaway. The prime minister lives at **10 Downing Street,** guarded by a black door and more than one policeman. The most recent occupant has been John Major, whose bland suburban demeanor looks right at home in this mundane setting—it's easy to picture him running next door to borrow a cup of sugar from the Chancellor of the Exchequer (Britain's finance honcho), who lives at No. 11.

CENOTAPH Built in 1919, the Cenotaph is a simple white-stone memorial to those slain in World War I. This Whitehall monument is the focus of the annual Remembrance Day ceremonies (equivalent to the American Veterans' Day), which take place at 11 AM on the Sunday closest to the 11th day of the 11th month, when the queen and other dignitaries lay wreaths of poppies on the Cenotaph. The blood-red poppy, which proliferated on the battlefields of Flanders, has become a symbol for the nation's war dead. *Whitehall, btw Downing and King Charles Sts. Tube: Westminster.*

CABINET WAR ROOMS Winston Churchill, the Cabinet, and the Chiefs of Staff coordinated Britain's war effort from this fortified basement in a civil-service building—definitely worth a few hours' exploration. A free audiotape tour guides you through rooms that have been reconstructed to look as they did at the close of World War II. Especially interesting is a map covered with pushpins representing advancing Allied armies in the final weeks of the war. Old American vets and young German tourists roaming the war rooms together make for a curious spectacle beyond the exhibits. *Clive Steps, at end of King Charles St., SW1, tel. 0171/930–6961. Tube: Westminster. Walk west on Bridge St., turn right on Parliament St., left on King Charles St. Admission: £4.20, £3.10 students. Open daily 9:30–6 (last admission 5:15).*

WESTMINSTER CATHEDRAL The center for Roman Catholicism in England was designed by J. F. Bentley to satisfy three requirements: The building had to have a wide nave to accommodate large congregations (it's the widest nave in Britain); an architectural style that wouldn't out-Gothic the ultra-Gothic Westminster Abbey; and a design that could be built quickly (and decorated later). The resulting "London Byzantine" style prompted Norman Shaw, another Victorian architect, to describe the cathedral as "the finest church which has been built for centuries." Although consecrated in 1910, the cathedral remains unfinished inside. The walls are decorated with marble from around the world, but the domes and arches lack the glittering mosaics that would catapult this building into the same class as, say, St. Mark's in Venice. Of special note is **St. Andrew's Chapel** (third on the right), decorated in 1910–15 by a team of artists led by the Arts and Crafts architect Robert Weir Schultz. Eric Gill's carvings of the stations of the cross are some of the finest sculptures to be seen in London. Take the elevator to the top of the 273-foot **campanile** (£2, £1 students; open daily 9–5) for a spectacular view of London and beyond. *Victoria St., SW1, tel. 0171/798–9055 or 0171/798–9097 for recorded info.*

Tube: Victoria. Walk west on Victoria St., look for the cathedral piazza on your right. Admission free. Open daily 7–7.

COVENT GARDEN

Just east of Soho lies Covent Garden, London's first public square. These days the name also applies to the nest of narrow streets, arcades, and pedestrian malls surrounding the square. For penniless travelers, this is one of the best places in London to come for free entertainment: Musicians, buskers, jugglers, and comics all perform in the streets and squares; look for a daily schedule of events posted on the railings of St. Paul's Church (*see below*). Historically speaking, the original Covent Garden was just that—a plot of land used to grow fruit and vegetables for the 13th-century Abbey of St. Peter at Westminster. With the 16th-century dissolution of the monasteries, the land passed into the hands of the Earls of Bedford. Covent Garden then evolved into London's principal produce market, a bustling maze of stalls and shops. In 1830 the **Central Market Building** was built, but increasing traffic congestion forced produce-sellers to relocate south of the Thames in 1974. The original market building has been completely renovated and is now filled with boutiques, health-food shops, and trendy restaurants. For a detail of the area, *see* the map Soho and Covent Garden, *above.*

Facing away from the market, **St. Paul's Church** (Bedford St., WC2, tel. 0171/836–5221) is often called the "actor's church" because of the walls lined with memorials to well-known thespians such as Ellen Terry, Charlie Chaplin, and Noël Coward. The rest of the church, built by Inigo Jones in 1631 and rebuilt in 1795 after a fire, is rather stark. The rear portico, site of the opening scene with Eliza Doolittle and Professor Higgins in *My Fair Lady,* serves as a great stage for the daily program of free entertainment—everything from mimes to fire-eaters. On the southeast corner of the square are the **London Transport Museum,** housed in the former flower market building, and the **Theatre Museum** (*see* Museums and Galleries, *below*). **Neal Street** pedestrian mall, just north of the market across Long Acre, has a young, laid-back, bohemian crowd; plenty of happy shoppers; and tiny **Neal's Yard,** a courtyard full of funky world- and natural-food cafés. Have a pint in front of one of the many pubs and take a gander at the folks who walk by.

East of the market is Bow Street, famous for the **Royal Opera House,** home to the Royal Ballet and the Royal Opera Company (*see* Classical Music, Opera, and Dance, in Chapter 6). In July 1997 it will close for £78 million-plus worth of renovations and won't reopen again until around 2000. Opposite the opera house stands the **Bow Street Magistrates' Court** (28 Bow St., WC2, tel. 0171/379–4713), established in 1749 by Henry Fielding, who was a magistrate, journalist, and author. Fielding employed a group of detectives known as the Bow Street Runners and paid them with fines levied by the court. Eighty years later, Home Secretary Sir Robert ("Bobby") Peel used the Bow Street Runners as the basis for his newly formed battalion of London police, called "bobbies" or "peelers" after his name. Attend a session in London's oldest magistrate court weekdays 10:30–1 and 2–4:30, Saturdays 10:30–noon.

North London

MARYLEBONE AND REGENT'S PARK

It may not come as a shock that Marylebone (pronounced MARE-ra-le-bun), one of the main tourist zones outside the West End, is boring and crowded. Away from the main drags, however, you'll find pleasant cafés along **Marylebone High Street,** cheap take-out stands north of Marylebone Road, and some nice terrace houses around **Regent's Park.** For reasons unknown, people have been flocking to **Madame Tussaud's Wax Museum** (Marylebone Rd., tel. 0171/935–6861) for eons. Madame Tussaud's is full of dummies: both the waxy sort and the sort who are willing to pay £8.75 to get in. Don't say we didn't warn you. The **London Planetarium** in the same building as Tussaud's is less hokey, and the virtual-reality effects of space and motion are good, but did you really come to London to look at a simulation of the night sky? In case you did, shows start every 40 minutes, and tickets are £5.45 (£11 for combined ticket with wax museum). Don't be taken in by the official-looking blue plaque mounted at

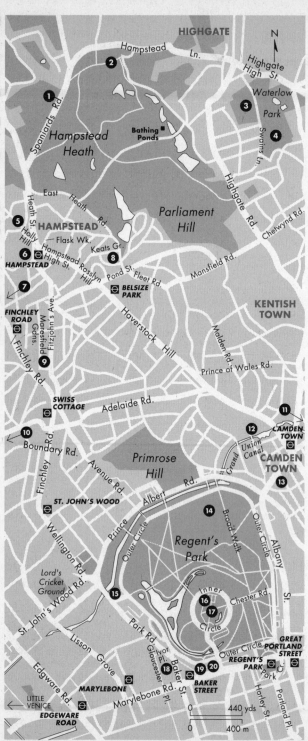

Regent's Park and Hampstead

Camden Arts Centre, **7**

Camden Lock, **12**

Church Row, **6**

Fenton House, **5**

Freud Museum, **9**

Highgate Cemetery East, **4**

Highgate Cemetery West, **3**

Jewish Museum, Camden Town, **13**

Keats House, **8**

Kenwood House, **2**

London Canal Museum, **11**

London Central Mosque, **15**

London Planetarium, **19**

London Zoo, **14**

Madame Tussaud's Wax Museum, **20**

Open-Air Theatre, **16**

Queen Mary Gardens, **17**

Saatchi Collection, **10**

Sherlock Holmes Museum, **18**

Spaniards Inn, **1**

70

221B Baker Street (tel. 0171/935–8866), purportedly the home of the (fictional) detective **Sherlock Holmes.** The "museum" here strives to make Holmes real by scattering a few "artifacts" throughout the four-story Victorian. While it's not interesting enough to warrant the £5 admission, you may well ponder why the address receives letters almost every day for Holmes—up to 50 per week.

REGENT'S PARK Once yet another one of Henry VIII's hunting grounds, Regent's Park was developed in the early 19th century by architect John Nash for his pal the Prince Regent as an elite residential development for "the wealthy and the good." Today it is one of central London's biggest parks, with a small lake and an even tinier pond, both of which can be traversed by rented rowboats, pedal boats, and canoes (*see* Participant Sports, in Chapter 8). The **Inner Circle,** a perfectly round lane, encloses the beautiful **Queen Mary Gardens.** The presence of the **London Central Mosque,** on the western edge of the park, ensures that on weekends large numbers of Muslims from the ex-dominions are out promenading in their finest. For a relaxing (some would say boring) day out, catch a match at nearby Lord's Cricket Grounds (*see* Spectator Sports, in Chapter 8). *Tube: Baker Street, Great Portland Street, or Regent's Park.*

LONDON ZOO The northern end of Regent's Park is the site of the London Zoo, opened in 1828 as the world's first institution dedicated to the display *and* study of animals. The zoo fell on hard times at the start of the decade, but a successful "Save Our Zoo" campaign raised sufficient funds to keep the zoo open and modernize its facilities. The zoo has since turned its focus to wildlife conservation and breeding programs. Every day at 2:30 is feeding time at the **Penguin Pool.** The abstract building by Bernard Lubetkin makes an interesting backdrop for the playful birds—though the white concrete structure is sadly unsuitable for the cold-loving creatures. The reptile house is extensive, as is the aquarium. Make a special trip to the **Aviary** to see Josephine—a quiet hornbill who is at least 47 years old. Pick up a schedule of daily events at the entrance; one of the best is "Duck!" (4 PM), where birds of prey swoop over the audience. The most direct way to get here is Bus 274, heading west from the Camden Town tube station (get off the bus at Ormonde Terrace); or take a canal boat from Little Venice or Camden Lock (*see box* Camden Cruising, *below*). It's also a nice walk from Camden Town along the canal—just walk up the dirt path after you've passed the looming aviary and cross the bridge. *Regent's Park, NW1, tel. 0171/722–3333. Tube: Baker Street or Camden Town. Admission: £7.50, £6.50 students. Open daily 10–5:30.*

CAMDEN TOWN

One of the most bohemian and diverse neighborhoods in London, Camden Town developed around Regent's Canal during the industrial revolution. In this former working-class neighborhood, successive waves of immigrants helped shape Camden's cosmopolitan atmosphere—though it's becoming increasingly gentrified. It becomes a serious mob scene on weekends, when tens of thousands of people flock to shop the Camden markets, particularly **Camden Lock** (*see* Street Markets, in Chapter 7). The crowds don't thin much at night, either, since Camden has some great bars and clubs.

Our favorite day out in Camden would include an early morning poke around the markets, followed by a walk down the canal to Little Venice when things get too crowded, a canal-boat trip back to Camden Lock in the afternoon, and dinner at the Lansdowne (see Camden, in Chapter 4).

The Camden Town tube station is on **Camden High Street,** which runs north–south through the heart of the district. Take a right from the station to reach Camden Lock. If crowds give you claustrophobia, visit during the week when you can snooze on the banks of Regent's Canal or enjoy the village's many cool cafés, restaurants, and pubs in relative peace. The spectacle of the crowd is absent, as are many of the vendors, but it's still a great place to spend a sunny day in London. Another quick getaway is a cruise down the canal past Regent's Park and on to Little Venice, near Paddington Station (*see box* Camden Cruising, *below*).

PRIMROSE HILL Like Regent's Park, Primrose Hill was once part of Henry VIII's hunting grounds. A tall hill commands a fine view of central London—check out the plaque identifying the buildings on the skyline. A young, cool crowd, many from nearby Camden Town, hangs out here, as do plenty of dogs. Every November 5, the park is the focus of huge Guy Fawkes Night celebrations (*see* Festivals, in Chapter 1) complete with fireworks and a huge bonfire. *Tube: Chalk Farm. Walk south on Regent's Rd.*

ISLINGTON

The Borough of Islington is an increasingly stylish area occupying about 6 square miles east of Camden and north of the City. Before the great amalgamation of London, the village of Islington was a popular stopover for travelers on their way to the budding metropolis, and lots of inns and watering holes cropped up to serve the transient visitors. During Tudor times, the lush, low hills in the wilderness around the village were prime royal romping and hunting grounds, supposedly the favorite of Henry VIII. As London grew and modernity arrived with a bang, Islington was not what you'd call a preferred address. Ugly industrialization consumed a great deal of the countryside, especially along Regent's Canal, which runs through the borough. The excellent **London Canal Museum** (*see* Museums and Galleries, *below*), not far from the center of Islington, has displays showing the way "canal people" have lived their lives on and along Regent's Canal.

In the 18th century, Islington was home to a fashionable spa, but once the railroads came in the 1860s, the wealthy left the area and their houses filled up with the poor, often living in terrible conditions. Many immigrant groups—Italian, Lebanese, Bengali, Turkish—have settled in Islington over the past 100 years, giving it a cultural richness in which Islingtonians still take pride. The area has also been a haunt for artists, students, writers, and various other intelligentsia over the years, including some of the bad boys of social commentary—George Orwell, Salman Rushdie, Lenin, and Trotsky. In the 1960s, Islington was still very working class; however, in the 1970s, it became regentrified as artsy liberals flocked here for the boho atmosphere and palatable housing prices. By the 1980s, property values had skyrocketed as people who spent their days nearby in the City getting rich off junk bonds moved in. Much of the recent press on Islington revolves around its image as the homeland of sun-dried-tomato-eating "champagne socialists." Tony Blair, leader of the Labour Party, makes his home in the borough, along with sizable poor and working-class communities.

Ascending from the depths of the Angel tube station—on what is allegedly the longest escalator in Europe—you stumble upon on the main drag, **Islington High Street,** in the heart of the old village. Just north, **Upper Street** (*see below*) is a busy thoroughfare lined with art galleries, antiques stores, and swanky shops and eateries, as well as some great pubs and fringe theaters—easily

Camden Cruising

Spend a sunny afternoon drifting along in one of the narrow boats traditionally used on Regent's Canal. The following companies offer trips between Little Venice and Camden Lock.

- *Jason's Trip (tel. 0171/286–3428) has three to four boats departing daily. Live commentary directs your attention to sights along the way and informs you about the history of the canal. A full bar keeps the 45-minute (each way) journey all too brief. Tickets are £4.50 single, £5.50 return.*

- *Cruise with the London Waterbus Company (tel. 0171/482–2660 for recorded info) from Little Venice to the London Zoo (35 min). The £9.80 price includes zoo admission. Alternatively, stay on board to Camden Lock (50 min, £3.50). The peace is unbroken by commentary, though the gung-ho can peruse the free information leaflets available on board. Boats leave Little Venice daily from 10 to 5 on the hour.*

Islington at its trendiest. Islington is trying to promote itself as a cultural attraction, especially on the basis of its artistic bent. The extremely friendly and helpful staff at the **Discover Islington Visitor Information Centre** (44 Duncan St., off Upper St., tel. 0171/278–8787), open Monday 2–5 and Tuesday–Saturday 10–5, can provide info on all sorts of things going on around the borough. **Angel Walks** (tel. 0171/226–8333) also offers interesting tours (£4, £3 students) of Islington such as "Orwell's Islington" and "The Angel and Joe Orton." The latter walk is especially entertaining and informative—guide Peter Powell knew the playwright personally.

CANDID ARTS TRUST Set in an alley behind the Angel tube station, Candid Arts Trust wants to revitalize the area through the arts. It is home to three galleries with changing exhibits, a theater, and **Candid Café** (tel. 0171/278–9368), where tasty food is served in a warm, funky atmosphere. Book ahead for one of its increasingly popular four-course meals (£13.50)—even Björk has been sighted dining here. On weekends, an art market is held in the alley. *3 Torrens St., EC1, tel. 0171/837–4237. Tube: Angel. Walk left on Islington High St., turn left on City Rd., left on Torrens St. Gallery hours vary; café open Tues.–Sun. noon–11.*

CRAFTS COUNCIL This is the primary national organization for promoting contemporary crafts in Britain. Though they celebrate "the mark of the hand," the council is willing to go against the popular grain in their rotating displays of different craft mediums: In 1996 while the rest of England swooned, quivered, and displayed their Strawberry Thief wallpaper in celebration of the William Morris centenary, they held an exhibition entitled "William Morris Revisited: Questioning the Legacy." They also have an art reference library, small café, and the scoop on the best artisans' shops in the city. *44A Pentonville Rd., N1, tel. 0171/278–7700. Tube: Angel. Walk left out of station, turn right on Pentonville Rd. Admission free. Open Tues.–Sat. 11–6, Sun. 2–6.*

UPPER STREET If you head north from the Angel tube station along bustling, semibohemian Upper Street, you'll soon pass the flashy **Business Design Centre** (52 Upper St., tel. 0171/359–3535) on the left. While it's no great thrill in and of itself, the large hall was built on the site of the formerly important **Royal Agricultural Hall** (nicknamed "the Aggie") and still retains a large part of the older structure. The Aggie was built in 1862 to house cattle, after Victorian urban planners deemed it uncouth to keep parading live animals all the way from the hinterlands to the Smithfield Meat Market in the city. A thousand tons of cast iron were used to support the magnificent glass roof of the central hall, which also served as a venue for gala balls and receptions, and odd sporting events like the six-day race, where men would try to complete 500 miles' worth of laps around the Aggie's hall. Now the refurbished hall (open weekdays 9–5:30) hosts changing exhibitions, many of which are free.

Continuing north brings you to **Islington Green,** a serene, well-kept grassy spot and the hub of village life for Islingtonians of yesteryear. The small **Islington Museum Gallery** (268 Upper St., tel. 0171/354–9442), a few blocks north, hosts temporary exhibits on themes reflecting the cultural and artistic diversity of Islington. In 1997 these include "Eels, Pie, and Mash" (Jan. 10–Mar. 3), an exhibit of photographs taken by Chris Clunn in eel and pie shops around Islington; and a collection of Osama Khatlan's textured photo-drawings (Mar. 13–23). The museum is open Wednesday to Saturday 11–5, Sunday 2–4, and admission is free.

Islington Markets

Islington High Street (Tube: Angel) is the beginning of the serious antiques-selling area that eventually funnels into the pedestrian-only Camden Passage, one of the hottest markets around for antiques and plain old junk. If a £45 teaspoon is out of your price range, follow Liverpool Road to Chapel Market, home of a daily street market featuring everything from stationery and clothes to flowers, produce, and sweets; come in the morning to see it at its boisterous best.

Houses of Detention (Clerkenwell Close, EC1, tel. 0171/253–9494) was once the busiest 18th- and 19th-century underground prison in town. The incredible research center has a library with over 19,000 prison records and accounts. Unfortunately, at press time it was closed for remodeling with hopes to reopen in early 1997; call for an update.

MARX MEMORIAL LIBRARY In the southern reaches of the borough, **Clerkenwell** was an early suburb of the City and is now the heart of Islington's Italian community. Off **Clerkenwell Green**—the centuries-old hangout of London's political radicals, including John Stuart Mill and Vladimir Lenin—is Marx Memorial Library, commonly known as Marx House, housed in a beautiful Georgian building with a long history of radicalism. Marx and his fellow council members met here to plan the 1864 International, and in 1886 and early 1887 Marx's daughter Eleanor was involved in the London Patriotic Club, which was headquartered here. The upstairs reading room is decorated with a 1935 fresco called "The Worker of the Future Clearing Away the Chaos of the Present"; a banner made by William Morris for the Socialist League hangs downstairs. You can also see the office from which Lenin published the Russian Social Democratic newspaper *Iskra* and fermented ideas leading to the 1917 Bolshevik Revolution. The library itself has one of the world's premier collections of radical books and written artifacts of Marxist history. *37A Clerkenwell Green, EC1, tel. 0171/253–1485. Tube: Farringdon. Walk north on Farringdon Rd., turn right on Clerkenwell Rd. Admission free. Open Mon. 1–6, Tues.–Thurs. 1–8, Sat. 10–1. Closed in Aug.*

BLOOMSBURY AND LEGAL LONDON

The **British Museum** (*see* Major Attractions, *above*) and the **University of London** (*see below*) impart something of an intellectual atmosphere to the residential neighborhood of Bloomsbury. Yet apart from some blue plaques on **Gordon Square,** you're far more likely to find a schmaltzy B&B than any reminders of Virginia Woolf, Vanessa Bell, Lytton Strachey, J. M. Keynes, E. M. Forster, and G. E. Moore—the so-called Bloomsbury Group, which would assemble in the 1920s and 1930s on most Thursday nights to drink and discuss why the Victorian era could not handle sexual, religious, and artistic enlightenment. Few traces remain of the personalities that brought Bloomsbury renown as the cradle of British philosophical and aesthetic modernism, yet it still has an active café and pub scene fortified by the students who liven up the area after classes. Plan your day sitting in one of the many charming coffeehouses or wine bars on **Lamb's Conduit Street** or, if weather permits, enjoy the outdoor cafés on **Russell Square. Sir John Soane's Museum** makes a nice, eclectic visit, and hard-core fans will enjoy poking about **Dickens's House** (*see* Museums and Galleries, *below*). If you're wandering around Euston Street near King's Cross Station, definitely check out the newly restored exterior of the hotel atop St. Pancras train station—Sir George Gilbert Scott's most stunning feat of architecture. Russell Square tube station puts you right in the belly of the beast; otherwise, it's just a short walk north from Tottenham Court Road or Holborn tube stations to Russell Square.

When you hear the word "lawyer," the immediate tendency is to yawn, grimace, or check your wallet. It's surprising, then, just how pleasant it can be to wander around the **Inns of Court** in Holborn, the heart of legal London. In the 15th and 16th centuries, the Inns of Court were exactly what they sound like—crash pads for lawyers who had business at the city's courts. Eventually, the lawyers took over the hotels and added offices and dining halls. Over time, the various inns were consolidated into just four—Lincoln's, Gray's, Middle Temple, and Inner Temple—and became the focal point of legal work in the city. Today, London barristers (trial lawyers) are still required to maintain an association with one of the inns, such as having an office there or dining in the hall a certain number of times each year. Law students must take their examinations at an inn and dine in one of the halls 24 times before they are admitted to the bar. Similar in style to the courtyards of Cambridge and Oxford, the inns still retain a dignified academic air. Hang out on **Chancery Lane** and watch all the wigged and gowned lawyers heading for court. The legal attire is just one indicator of how differently British and Americans approach the question of law: It's tough to imagine these guys coming on TV and saying, "Have you or a loved one been injured lately?"

LINCOLN'S INN Beautiful gardens and immaculate lawns surround Lincoln's Inn, the only inn unaffected by World War II bombings. The impressive architectural features of Lincoln's

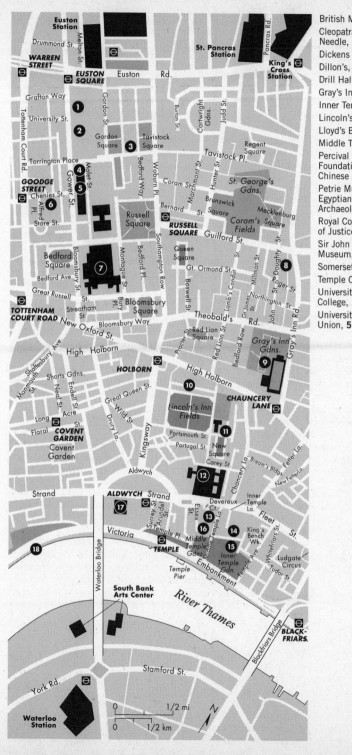

British Museum, **7**
Cleopatra's
Needle, **18**
Dickens House, **8**
Dillon's, **4**
Drill Hall, **6**
Gray's Inn, **9**
Inner Temple, **15**
Lincoln's Inn, **11**
Lloyd's Bank, **13**
Middle Temple, **16**
Percival David
Foundation of
Chinese Art, **3**
Petrie Museum of
Egyptian
Archaeology, **2**
Royal Courts
of Justice, **12**
Sir John Soane's
Museum, **10**
Somerset House, **17**
Temple Church, **14**
University
College, **1**
University of London
Union, **5**

Bloomsbury and Legal London

Inn range from the 15th-century Old Hall to New Square, the only surviving 17th-century square in London. Don't miss the chapel, redesigned by Inigo Jones between 1619 and 1623. *Chancery Ln., WC2, tel. 0171/405–1393. Tube: Chancery Lane or Holborn. Admission free. Chapel open weekdays noon–2:30, grounds open weekdays 9–6.*

GRAY'S INN Gray's Inn, on the other side of High Holborn from Lincoln's Inn, was blown to bits during the Blitz, and everything—except the stained glass and carved oak screen in the main hall—was completely rebuilt in the 1950s. Before he was caught taking bribes and imprisoned in the Tower of London, Francis Bacon (1561–1626) kept chambers here and is thought to have designed the impressive gardens. Charles Dickens looked "upon Gray's Inn generally as one of the most depressing institutions of brick and mortar, known to the children of men." *Gray's Inn Rd., WC1, tel. 0171/405–8164. Tube: Chancery Lane or Holborn. Grounds open weekdays 10–4.*

THE TEMPLE South of Fleet Street and technically in the City, the Middle and Inner Temples (collectively known as the Temple) got their name from the Knights Templar, an 11th-century chivalric order that owned the land here. Sadly, about the only part of the complex that is open to the public is the gardens of the Middle Temple. If you can sneak a peek inside the Middle Temple Hall, look for the 29-foot-long Bench Table, donated by Elizabeth I. A smaller table, the "Cupboard," is reputedly made from wood taken from Sir Francis Drake's ship, the *Golden Hind.* Though little of the original church survives, nearby **Temple Church** (open Wed.–Sat. 10–4), built by the Knights Templar in the 12th century, is one of only three round churches in England and one of Britain's finest examples of early English Gothic. *The Temple, EC4, tel. 0171/797–8250. Tube: Temple. Grounds open Mon.–Sat. 10–4, Sun. 1–4.*

ROYAL COURTS OF JUSTICE G. E. Street's impressive Law Courts lie on the Strand, a block away from the Temple. To watch the proceedings, walk (quietly) into a public gallery at the rear of any of the 58 courts. Don't come expecting tales of horror and gore, however: The murder trials you read about in the tabloids are held at the Old Bailey (*see* The City, *below*), while the Law Courts deal with more mundane cases involving fraud and swindle. It's still fun to wander around the cavernous, neo-Gothic building with all the judges and lawyers in their wigs and gowns, carrying their papers bound with the traditional red ribbon. Directly across the street is the Law Courts branch of **Lloyds Bank** (222 Strand), whose glorious Victorian interior is well worth a visit. Designed as a restaurant for the legal profession, it's decorated with Doulton tile panels with scenes of Ben Johnson's plays and many varieties of chrysanthemum. Outside of normal banking hours, you can still see the glazed-terra-cotta entryway—it houses the ATM. *The Strand, WC2, tel. 0171/936–6000. Admission free. Open weekdays 10–4:30. Closed Aug.–Sept.*

UNIVERSITY OF LONDON University College, the oldest of several colleges and schools that make up the University of London, was once accused of being that "godless college in Gower Street." Today, the college and the university as a whole continue to be places where you can act in ways that the vicar would never condone. Its students have access to probably the best nightlife in the nation—pubs, cafés, and cheap restaurants dot the residential streets around the university, and the lively clubs and action of Soho are nearby. University College was founded in 1827 by educators who objected to the fact that Oxford and Cambridge would accept only students indoctrinated by the Church of England. With a curriculum modeled after those of German universities, University College was the first English school to accept Jews, Catholics, and Quakers. In 1878, the university became the first in England to accept women.

One of several collections administered by the university, the **Percival David Foundation of Chinese Art** (53 Gordon Sq., WC1, tel. 0171/387–3909), open weekdays 10:30–5, has a magnificent collection of 10th- to 18th-century Chinese ceramics. The top floor features some jewel-like colored pottery—sort of like 17th- and 18th-century Fiestaware. Inside the D. M. S. Watson Library, the small **Petrie Museum of Egyptian Archaeology** (tel. 0171/387–7050) houses a justly famous collection of Roman-era mummy portraits and an amazing array of objects relating to Egyptian everyday life. The museum is open weekdays 10–noon and 1:15–5 but closes frequently in August and September, so call ahead. The college's main courtyard and portico are on Gower Street, opposite the redbrick University College Hospital. Head inside to check out what remains of Jeremy Bentham (*see box, below*). *Gower St., WC1E, tel. 0171/ 387–7050. Tube: Euston Square. Walk south on Gower St.*

HAMPSTEAD AND HIGHGATE

Four miles north of central London, Hampstead is a posh, stylish area popular with writers, musicians, and artists. Cool cafés, chic restaurants, trendy boutiques, and a growing number of chain stores line the two main drags, **Hampstead High Street** and **Heath Street,** both right by Hampstead tube station. Hampstead is well known for its grand houses, winding streets, country lanes, and the beautiful **Hampstead Heath** (*see below*). On **Church Row** just off the bottom end of Heath Street, you'll find some of the finest 18th-century houses in London. Besides the houses of Freud and Keats (*see below*), the more famous Hampstead abodes include **Fenton House** (Hampstead Grove, tel. 0171/435–3471), a National Trust building that houses the Benton Fletcher collection of early keyboard instruments. Hampstead also has some cool little pubs, including the **Holly Bush** (22 Holly Mount, tel. 0171/435–2892), north of Hampstead High Street off Holly Hill, and **Spaniard's Inn** (Spaniard's Rd., tel. 0171/455– 3276), where Keats, Shelley, and Byron tipped pints, as did highwayman Dick Turpin. North-east of Hampstead across the Heath, **Highgate** is another tony residential area. **Highgate High Street** is lined with boutiques and a few cafés that give it a bohemian flair. If you want to avoid paying the extra 80p it costs to get off at Highgate station (it's in Zone 3), get off at Archway and hike up Highgate Hill past Waterlow Park. On your way you'll pass **Dick Whittington's Stone,** supposedly placed at the point where young Dick Whittington heard the bells pealing, telling him to "turn round" and return to London.

FREUD MUSEUM The pad of the father of psychoanalysis still feels eerily lived in. Freud spent the last year of his life here, having fled Vienna in 1938 to escape Nazi persecution. After he died, his daughter Anna—a pioneer in the field of child psychology—maintained the house as a shrine to him, and after her death it was turned into a museum. Take a peek into Freud's life and try to analyze *his* psyche by inspecting the strange toys, art, and curious knick-knacks. You can also check out his library and study—complete with the (in)famous couch— where he spent his final year doing some of his most important theorizing. On the landing there is a remarkable drawing of Freud by Dalí, who sketched Freud secretly and later completed this portrait. Ask about the schedule of special exhibits, lectures, and showings of archival films. *20 Maresfield Gardens, NW3, tel. 0171/435–2002. Tube: Finchley Road. Walk south on Finchley Rd., turn left on Trinity Walk, left on Maresfield Gardens. Admission: £3, £1.50 students. Open Wed.–Sun. noon–5.*

KEATS HOUSE The great Romantic poet John Keats wrote many of his poetic masterpieces during his two-year stay at this Hampstead home. It was also here that he met and fell in love with the girl next door, Fanny Brawne, for whom he pined for years. Though they became

The Head of University College

Social reformer Jeremy Bentham (1748–1832) was the foremost proponent of utilitarianism, the doctrine that defines an action's usefulness by the measure of happiness it brings. After his death, the founder of University College decreed that his body should be donated to science and kept in the college. Now Jeremy's skeleton (with a wax replica for a head) sits quietly in his favorite chair, wearing his clothes and holding his cane. Jeremy is kept in a case at the southern end of a hallway in the main building. In recent years, Jeremy's decaying head, once placed on the floor between his feet, was removed from the case—presumably to ensure greater happiness to viewers. The head is now kept in the college safe; one can only wonder how they've stored it (Tupperware?).

engaged in 1819, Keats's declining health prevented the marriage from ever taking place. He sailed to Italy in 1820 hoping to recuperate, but instead his condition worsened and he died in Rome at the ripe young age of 25. Their two houses have since been combined to form an all-encompassing Keats museum, furnished just as it was during the poet's lifetime. Be sure to check out the full-scale plaster "lifemask" of Keats's head, created by a painter friend, and other goodies like the engagement ring Keats gave to Fanny, his letters, and first editions of *Poems* (1817) and *Endymion* (1819). The adjacent **Keats Memorial Library** (open by appointment only; tel. 0171/794–6829) contains all the poet's compositions, as well as scholarly studies dedicated to him. *Keats Grove, NW3, tel. 0171/435–2062. Tube: Hampstead. Walk SE on Hampstead High St., turn left on Downshire Hill, veer right on Keats Grove. Or take BritRail to Hampstead Heath, walk north on South End Rd., turn left on Keats Grove. Admission free. Open Apr.–Oct., weekdays 10–1 and 2–6, Sat. 10–1 and 2–5, Sun. 2–5; Nov.–Mar., weekdays 1–5, Sat. 10–1 and 2–5, Sun. 2–5.*

HAMPSTEAD HEATH If you dig traipsing through hill and dale, following narrow paths to nowhere, and crashing through bushes, the 800-acre Hampstead Heath is the place for you. For a big-city park, Hampstead Heath is surprisingly rural—even despite the omnipresent litter. There are some fine views of central London from Parliament Hill, but beware the deadly stunt kites flown by well-meaning novices. Swimming, tennis, cricket, and even the occasional softball game are some of the sports you can watch or participate in; for more info *see* Chapter 8. Otherwise, the principal sight is **Kenwood House** (Hampstead Ln., tel. 0181/348–1286), a 17th-century mansion by Robert Adam with landscaped gardens and the **Iveagh Bequest,** a fine collection of paintings, including works by Gainsborough, Van Dyck, Rembrandt, Turner, and Vermeer. The house is open daily 10–6 (Oct.–Mar. until 4), and admission is free. *Tube: Hampstead. Walk ½ mile north on Heath Street. Or take Brit Rail to Hampstead Heath or Gospel Oak.*

HIGHGATE CEMETERY A light drizzle (not unlikely in London) creates a wonderful gloom in Highgate Cemetery, where a maze of narrow footpaths cuts through a forest of vine-covered Victorian tombstones. The cemetery is divided into two parts: The **Eastern Cemetery** is still in use and contains the somber tombs of George Eliot (a.k.a. Mary Ann Evans) and Karl Marx, the German philosopher with whom political theorists all over the world would like to have a chat. Coincidence makes strange bedfellows: Just a few feet away, across the gravel path, lies Marx's dialectical opposite (and one of George Eliot's lovers), social Darwinist Herbert Spencer, who once wrote that "socialism is slavery." The **Western Cemetery,** open only for tours (£3), has a spectacular Egyptian Avenue, incredible landscaping, and eerie catacombs. Buried here are Radclyffe Hall, author of *The Well of Loneliness,* the poet Christina Rossetti, and bare-knuckle prizefighter Tom Sayers, whose tomb is guarded by a sculpture of Lion, his devoted dog. **Waterlow Park,** at the northern border of the cemetery, is one of the only parks in London where you'll encounter some formidable hills, which run down to rush-bordered ponds full of waterfowl. *Swains Ln., N6, tel. 0181/340–1834. Tube: Archway. Walk north on Highgate Rd., turn left on Bisham Gardens, left on Swains Ln. Admission to East Cemetery: £1. Open weekdays 10–5, weekends 11–5. Tours of West Cemetery offered weekends, hourly 11–4 (also Mar.–Nov., weekdays at noon, 2, and 4).*

In a moment of grief, Dante Gabriel Rossetti buried some unpublished love poems in his wife Elizabeth Siddal's coffin. A few years later, Rossetti had a change of heart and had poor Lizzie's corpse exhumed to recover the manuscript so the poems could be published—as part of "The House of Life."

East London

STRAND AND EMBANKMENT

Strand, which turns into Fleet Street about ½ mile from Charing Cross, is smelly, noisy, and dirty. And not in an interesting way either—just a lot of cars in a boring concrete canyon that's crowded by sidewalks and mediocre restaurants. Tea-totalers may be interested in the oldest tea shop in London, **Twinings** (216 Strand, tel. 0171/353–3511), but unless you're a very methodical sightseer or really into carbon monoxide, you could forgo this particular area with no adverse effect. The Embankment, on the other hand, is a bit more intriguing. Constructed between 1868 and 1874 by Sir Joseph Bazalgette (the same man who designed London's sewers), the Embankment, which runs all the way from Westminster to the City, was designed to protect the city from flooding (a job now handled by the Thames Barrier). For a detail of the area, *see* the map Soho and Covent Garden, *above.*

CHARING CROSS "Charing" is an old English word derived from the French for "dear queen" (*chère reine*). The story goes that Edward I erected 13 crosses in 1290 to mark the funeral route of his beloved queen, Eleanor of Castile, entombed in Westminster Abbey. Londoners cast copies of the crosses in the 19th century and sunk one in front of Charing Cross station, hence the name. These days, few people notice the somber memorial in what's essentially a tube station parking lot. *Tube: Charing Cross.*

CLEOPATRA'S NEEDLE Although it's not the most dramatic monument in London, Cleopatra's Needle brings home the reality of how vast and far flung the British Empire was in its heyday. Here, on the gray Embankment, stands a pink granite Egyptian obelisk carved with hieroglyphics and flanked by benches supported by sculptures of camels. Carved in Heliopolis in 1450 BC to record the victories of Ramses the Great, it was given to the British in 1819 by the viceroy of Egypt. Even so, it took another 59 years for the obelisk to make its way to Britain: Weighing 180 tons, the needle couldn't be put on a ship, so it was towed behind in a torpedolike case, which was lost during a storm at sea. To everyone's surprise, it was recovered soon afterward and towed to London for immediate display. Its twin is in New York's Central Park. *Victoria Embankment, opposite Victoria Embankment Gardens, WC2. Tube: Embankment.*

Quirky Victorians buried a time capsule beneath the Embankment's obelisk, including such oddities as a railway guide, a portrait of Queen Victoria, and a baby's bonnet.

SOMERSET HOUSE Constructed between 1776 and 1786 by William Chambers, Somerset House replaced a Renaissance palace used by members of the royal family. Until 1973, Somerset House was the home of the Registrar General of Births, Deaths, and Marriages, as well as a number of other government offices. Today, the building houses Inland Revenue (the British equivalent of the IRS) and the **Courtauld Institute Galleries,** affiliated with the University of London. The gallery has a collection of oils from the 15th to 20th centuries of which the impressionist and postimpressionist movements (displayed in rooms 8 and 10) are the best represented. The Cézanne collection is considered the finest in London, as is the collection of Manet's works, including *A Bar at the Folies-Bergère* (you know, the one with the bored-looking waitress). Modigliani's wonderful *Female Nude* coyly looks away from poor van Gogh's *Self-Portrait with Bandaged Ear,* while Degas's dancers stand en pointe. Classical works by such artists as Lely, Giovanni Bellini, and Rubens are also exhibited. In 1997, special exhibitions from the Courtauld's collection of prints and drawings will include "The Art of Etching" (Feb.–May) and "Women and Men" (June–Aug.), which will challenge viewers to reconsider their assumptions about gender and its relationship to art. *Strand, WC2, tel. 0171/873–2526. Tube: Temple. Walk west on Temple Pl., turn right on Surrey St., left on Strand. Admission: £4, £2 students; free after 5 PM. Open Mon.–Sat. 10–6, Sun. 2–6.*

ST. MARY-LE-STRAND Constructed between 1714 and 1717, St. Mary-le-Strand was the first of 50 churches that devout Queen Anne ordered built to lure London's growing population away from wantonness and back to religion following the twin whammies of the plague (1665) and the Great Fire (1666)—though only 12 churches ever materialized. The architect was Scotsman James Gibbs, who melded elements of Italian baroque with Christopher Wren's distinctive style. Gibbs probably never intended to surround his church with an unceasing flow of traffic, but those are the breaks. *Strand, across from Somerset House, WC2, tel. 0171/836–3126. Tube: Aldwych. Open daily 11–3.*

ST. CLEMENT DANES An inscription in Latin on the barrel-vaulted ceiling translates to read "Built by Christopher Wren 1682. Destroyed by thunderbolts of air warfare 1941. Restored by the Royal Air Force 1958." That pretty much sums up the history of this church, also an island in a sea of traffic. Photographs on the stairway up to the gallery show the damage done to the church, revealing its remarkable restoration. The church's distinctive bells were the inspiration for the nursery rhyme "Oranges and lemons, say the bells of St. Clement's." They ring most days at 9 AM, noon, 3 and 6 PM. *Strand, by Royal Courts of Justice, WC2, tel. 0171/242–8282. Tube: Aldwych. Open daily 8:30–4:30.*

THE CITY

The City is to London what Wall Street is to New York. It smells of money and deals. And like all other good capitalist animals, the City answers to the markets and nothing else, not even the rest of London—it's an administrative and legal entity in itself. Taking up just over a square mile in east London, the City is home to the stock exchange, the Bank of England, Lloyd's, and a host of large banking and trading firms. The traditional view of the City has always been that of upper- and upper-middle-class gentlemen in bowler hats carrying brollies and briefcases. That all changed in the headlong rush for money during the Thatcher '80s, when once-staid companies began hiring employees who could produce the goods, even though they may not have attended the right schools. Of course, the Old-Boy network hasn't dried up and blown away—the snobbery has just grown a little more subtle. In fact, the City's newly made millionaires are still referred to by their upper-class brethren as "barrow boys." The '90s have brought recession to the area, and competition from lower-rent areas like Docklands has resulted in a lot of vacant buildings. Still, on weekdays the City vibrates with tension, cellular phones, and power ties, and it makes for some interesting people-watching and eavesdropping.

Although the City lies to the east of central London, it actually rests on the original Celtic settlement that the Romans conquered and built up into Londinium. Vestiges of this ancient heritage pop up all over the City, even though the Great Fire of London, which started in a baker's shop on Pudding Lane in September 1666, destroyed almost every building in the area. In the years that followed, architect Christopher Wren redesigned the entire district, building 51 new churches, including **St. Paul's Cathedral** (*see* Major Attractions, *above*), which stood as the focal point of a new city of spires. German bombers wrecked most of Wren's work, however (fewer than half remain), and postwar London architects managed to brutalize much of the rest. Unfortunately, the once-dramatic views of St. Paul's have slowly disappeared behind concrete behemoths. For a calendar of events and recommended walks in the area, contact the **City Information Center** (tel. 0171/332–1456) at the south side of St. Paul's Cathedral.

✔ **FLEET STREET** Until a decade ago, Fleet Street was synonymous with newspapers and journalists. Almost all of Britain's major papers had their offices here, and Fleet Street pubs were the lairs of hoary old journalists and their sources. The newspapers are all gone now, scattered to cheaper neighborhoods with lower overheads, more computers, and fewer unionized employees. Even so, many people still refer to the British press as Fleet Street. It's not surprising really, since the printed word has a long history here. Wynkyn de Worde printed about 800 books in the area around St. Paul's between 1500 and 1535. Most of the books were for the clergy, the only literate bunch back then, but in later centuries, printers, binders, and stationers all set up shop in the area. London's first daily newspaper, the *Daily Courant,* began publishing here in 1702, and *Punch,* the leading Victorian satirical magazine, was published at 85 Fleet Street.

At various times, Fleet Street has acted as everything from a cheerleader for the Empire to a scurrilous Peeping Tom looking to catch Princess Di without a bra. Nowadays, however, there's nothing to do here but marvel at the architecture. Just across the street from St. Bride's (*see below*) is the sleek black office block with curved corners that once housed the *Daily Express,* a conservative tabloid that has since moved its offices to the south side of Blackfriars Bridge. The *Daily Telegraph,* Britain's most conservative paper, had its offices in a modernistic building next to Peterborough Court just up the street. Fleet Street hasn't completely lost its publishing connection: Reuters is headquartered at number 85—on the site of the former home of *Punch.* Designed by Lutyens, the L-shaped building bends around St. Bride's.

✔ ➤ **ST. BRIDE'S FLEET STREET** • Known as the printers' church, St. Bride's is surrounded by now predominantly empty newspaper offices. Our old friend Wynkyn de Worde's first printing press was situated next to the old St. Bride's, which was destroyed in the Great

The City

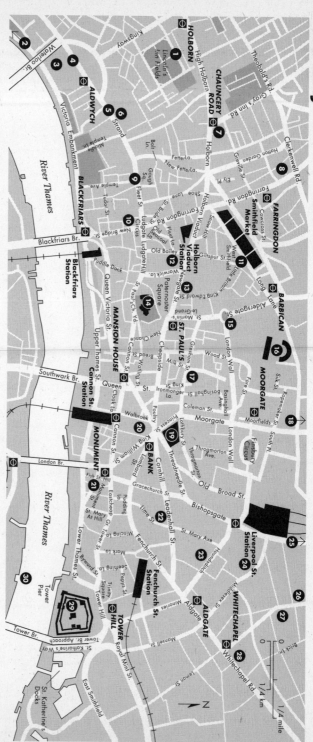

Fire. Rebuilt by Wren, St. Bride's spire is the highest he ever built; its distinctive shape is said to have been the inspiration for the first tiered wedding cake. Though gutted in the Blitz, with only the steeple and outer walls surviving, the church has been nicely restored and provides a welcome haven from the anxiety of City life. The **crypt** contains an excellent exhibition about the history of the church, revealing its Roman and medieval foundations, and a history of Fleet Street itself. Free lunchtime recitals are held Tuesday, Wednesday, and Friday at 1:15 PM, and evensong is held at 6:30. *Bride Ln., EC4, tel. 0171/583–0239. Tube: Blackfriars. Walk north on New Bridge St., turn left on Fleet St., left on Bride Ln. Open weekdays 8:30–5.*

GUILDHALL The City's strong tradition of trade is evidenced by the Guildhall and the 40-plus livery company halls (the modern-day equivalent of the medieval trade guilds) scattered within its square-mile limit. The Guildhall was constructed between 1411 and 1440 as a central meeting place for craftsmen of various trades, and although the original building was damaged by the Great Fire of 1666 and again by the Blitz in 1940, it has been carefully reconstructed to its original splendor. The stained-glass windows display the name of every Lord Mayor since 1189, and the hall is adorned with the elaborate banners of the 12 major livery companies and the arms of all 101 of the livery companies of the city of London. New livery companies are still being added—number 101 was the Worshipful Company of Information Technologists. The livery companies gained a considerable amount of wealth, property, and political power over the centuries, playing a pivotal role in the election of the Lord Mayor. The Guildhall is still the site of the Court of Common Council meetings, and the ceremonial induction of the Lord Mayor and other city officials. Adjacent to the Guildhall is the **Museum of the Worshipful Company of Clockmakers** (open weekdays 9:30–4:45), which contains over 700 exhibits about the history of timekeeping including a silver, skull-shaped watch, which probably belonged to Mary Queen of Scots. *Guildhall Yard, EC2, tel. 0171/606–3030. Tube: Bank. Walk north on Prince's St., turn left on Lothbury, right on Guildhall Yard. Admission free. Open daily 10–5; closed Sun. Oct.–Apr. Wheelchair access.*

✔ **MONUMENT** The Monument, designed by Christopher Wren, is now rather dwarfed by the City's office buildings, though it used to loom majestically as one of the world's tallest columns. Built in 1677 to commemorate the Great Fire, the column is 202 feet high—the exact distance westward from the fire's Pudding Lane origin. For amazing views of the city, climb the spiraling 311 steps to the platform at the top. The platform was enclosed in 1847, following several shocking suicides. *Monument St., EC2, tel. 0171/626–2717. Tube: Monument. Admission: £1. Open Apr.–Sept., weekdays 9–6, weekends 2–6; Oct.–Mar., Mon.–Sat. 9–4.*

Famous defendants tried at the Old Bailey include Oscar Wilde, convicted of homosexuality in 1895; William "Lord Haw Haw" Joyce, who did pro-Nazi radio shows from Berlin during World War II; and Peter "Yorkshire Ripper" Sutcliffe, a serial killer convicted in 1981.

OLD BAILEY If you can't afford theater tickets or you're a fan of "Rumpole of the Bailey," go and watch a trial at the Old Bailey, officially known as the Central Criminal Court. You can't beat the drama (it's all for real) or the price (it's free). Just line up outside and scan the offering of trials—they're posted on a sort of legal menu du jour at the Newgate Street entrance; start with something light, perhaps a mugging, and then move on to a main course of murder and mayhem. The juiciest trials usually go down in Courts 1–3, the old courts. In the modern Courts 4–19, it's difficult to see unless you're in the front row or actually on trial yourself. No bags or cameras are allowed in the building, and there's nowhere to safely store them nearby, so come empty handed. While you're waiting for the show to begin, check out Pomeroy's famous bronze statue of Justice atop the building, overlooking the spot where prisoners of notorious Newgate Prison were once executed. Rough justice indeed. *Old Bailey, at Newgate St., EC4, tel. 0171/248–3277. Tube: St. Paul's. Walk NW on Newgate St. Public Gallery open weekdays 10–1 and 2–4.*

BARBICAN CENTRE This large complex of residential towers and cultural venues was built between 1959 and 1981 in an attempt to resurrect central London as a living city instead of merely a place of work. Though the complex's modern concrete blocks are inordinately ugly and look more like something you would find in Eastern Europe than London, the recent creation of a grand entrance portal softens the blow a little. The seemingly ill-fated Barbican Centre has managed to evolve into one of the city's principal cultural institutions. Varied musical performances are held in **Barbican Hall** (*see* Classical Music, Opera, and Dance, in Chapter 6), **Barbican Theatre** is the London home of the Royal Shakespeare Company, which also stages smaller performances in the **Pit** (*see* Theater, in Chapter 6), and the **Barbican Cinema** shows mostly mainstream films. There are also some impressive visual arts displays at the **Barbican Art Gallery.** Free music and art exhibitions are usually held in one of the many foyers, and the huge, glass-encased **conservatory,** filled with exotic plants and trees, is open to the public (80p) on weekends noon–5:30. *Silk St., EC2, tel. 0171/638–4141 or 0171/638–8891 for box office. Tube: Barbican. Admission to Barbican Art Gallery: £5, £3 students. Gallery open Mon.–Sat. 10–6:45 (Tues. until 5:45), Sun. noon–6:45.*

LLOYD'S BUILDING Like it or not, the Lloyd's building is the most aggressively "modern" building in the City and certainly one of the most architecturally important structures built in the '80s. The duo that put it up, celebrity-architect Richard Rogers and structural engineer Peter Rice (engineer of the Sydney Opera House), also worked together on the equally revolutionary Centre Georges Pompidou in Paris. The Lloyd's building makes no effort to hide its "builtness," a key element in Rice's project of "humanizing" architecture by reintroducing evidence of human participation in construction. Indeed, you might mistake Lloyd's for a building still under construction. The bright blue structures protruding from the roof look like cranes, and the many tubes and ducts exposed on the exterior look as though they're waiting for their facade. Ironically, this futuristic building is home to the very traditional Lloyd's of London, an insurance market founded in the 1680s. Lloyd's hit hard times in the early '90s, resulting in a number of its investors, the so-called Names, going bankrupt. There used to be an observation deck that was open to the public, but for security reasons, it's now completely closed. *1 Lime St., EC3, tel. 0171/623–7100. Tube: Monument. Walk north on Gracechurch St., turn right on Fenchurch St., right on Lime St.*

ST. BARTHOLOMEW-THE-GREAT Behind a 13th-century stone gateway topped with a 16th-century Tudor gatehouse hides beautiful St. Bartholomew-the-Great. Built in 1123 by Henry I's court jester Rahere (whose tomb is to the left of the altar), St. Bart's is the oldest

London's Modern Architecture

Though contemporary architects are not allotted the enormous spaces of their predecessors, their work is often just as noticeable—for better or worse. One good example is Vauxhall Cross at the Albert Embankment, the new home of MI6, otherwise known as the British Secret Service. Despite its theme-park appearance, this center of espionage is absolutely inaccessible. Terry Ferrel designed the moated, cream-and-green building in a style vaguely reminiscent of the background settings of 1960s comic books. Of the rash of skyscrapers that went up in the mid-1980s boom, Minster Court on Mark Lane stands out garishly. Best described as "notionally Gothic," the home of the London Underwriting Centre is really just a boring office block with "Gothic" pretensions. Not surprisingly, no individual will take responsibility for this architectural anomaly—a plaque reads GMW Partnership. A better compromise of old and new is Waterhouse Square, on Holborn near the Chancery Lane tube station. Formerly known as the Prudential Assurance building, Alfred Waterhouse's bright-red terra-cotta structure was built between 1879 and 1906 and has recently been remodeled. The amazing Gothic exterior hides a sunny courtyard, so don't be afraid to go inside. The Docklands area (see below) is another good place to scout out interesting new buildings.

standing parish church in London, from where the oldest bells in the city ring. The quaint lady's chapel was once a printing shop where Benjamin Franklin was employed as a youngster. If the church looks familiar, it's because it was featured in *Four Weddings and a Funeral* as the site of the fourth wedding. *West Smithfield, EC1, tel. 0171/606–6171. Tube: Farringdon. Walk south on Farringdon, turn left on West Smithfield. Open weekdays 8:30–5, Sat. 10:30–3:30, Sun. 8–8.*

ST. STEPHEN WALBROOK Considered by many to be Wren's most perfect church, St. Stephen Walbrook has a high-domed ceiling supported by 16 Corinthian columns. The dark wood of the organ and pulpit contrasts wildly with the church's most controversial feature: a gray, marshmallowy, marble altar sculpted by Henry Moore from Roman travertine marble and dedicated in 1987. The Samaritans organization was founded here in 1953; the original helpline telephone sits on a pedestal in the southwest corner of the church. *Walbrook, EC4, tel. 0171/283–4444. Tube: Bank. Open weekdays 9–4.*

THE EAST END

Though often shunned by tourists and derided by Britons, the East End of London is well worth a visit. It's certainly not the "Queen's London," but it is the *people's* London—an ethnically diverse, hardened, and vibrantly alive district. Historically it has been one of London's poorest areas, home to successive waves of immigrants, many of whom came to avoid religious persecution. A building on the corner of Brick Lane and Fournier Street in Spitalfields is the perfect illustration of the area's changing character: Built in 1743 as a Protestant church for French Huguenots, the building became a Methodist chapel in 1809, then a synagogue serving the Orthodox Machzikei Hadath sect in 1897, and more recently a mosque serving the large Muslim community. As a new mosque is being built a few blocks north, one wonders what incarnation the building will take on next—perhaps housing for artists, the most recent wave of immigrants to the East End, who have come to take advantage of the large studio/living spaces in the many dilapidated warehouses.

Brick Lane is one of the best dining thoroughfares in the city, lined with places selling authentically prepared and reasonably priced Bangladeshi, Indian, and other savory cuisines.

Like the rest of London, the East End is a jumble of grown-together villages. Much of the area is well served by public transit. **Spitalfields,** the district that encompasses Brick Lane and a couple of amazing markets, fans out eastward from the front door of Liverpool Street Station. To the south and southeast of Spitalfields, **Whitechapel** is home to Whitechapel Gallery (*see* Museums and Galleries, *below*) and best served by the Aldgate and Aldgate East tube stations. **Bethnal Green,** northeast of Spitalfields, has its own tube station on the Central Line. The massive **Docklands** area, far to the east along the Thames, is served by the **Docklands Light Railway,** which makes connections at Bank, Tower Hill, Shadwell, Stratford, and Bow Road tube stations. Stop by the **Tower Hamlets Environment Trust** (150 Brick Ln., tel. 0171/377–0481) weekdays 10–5 to pick up info on the sights, sounds, tastes, and history of the East End.

SPITALFIELDS Spitalfields takes its name from St. Mary Spital, a hospital founded in 1197. The area has a long history of involvement with the clothing trade; Huguenots fleeing Catholic France after the revocation of the Edict of Nantes settled in the area in the 1680s, bringing with them their silk-weaving skills. Many of these silk-weaving workshops survive, though the workers shifted from French Protestants to Jewish refugees to Bangladeshis, and the textiles from silk to cotton, Lycra, and leather. At Bishopsgate, the thoroughfare in front of Liverpool Street station, flamboyant office buildings and construction projects that reflect City-style gentrification meet the western border of the East End. To the east is one of Spitalfields's main commercial avenues, the ugly and appropriately named **Commercial Street,** with the sprawling **Spitalfields Market** building to the left (*see* Street Markets, in Chapter 7). At the intersection of Commercial and Fournier streets is Hawksmoor's definitively steepled **Christ Church,** built in 1720 when the area was populated mostly with French immigrants—check out the old French gravestones in the churchyard. Christ Church is also the venue for an amazing lineup of concerts that are part of the annual **Spitalfields Festival** (tel. 0171/377–1362), held June 4–25 in 1997.

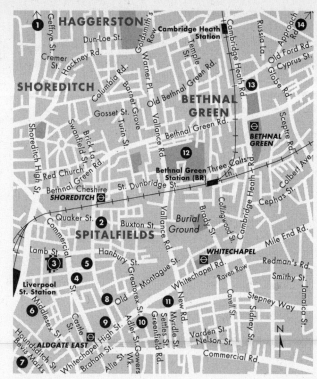

Bethnal Green
Museum of
Childhood, **13**

Bevis Marks
Synagogue, **7**

Brick Lane, **8**

Christ Church, **4**

East London
Mosque, **11**

Geffrye Museum, **1**

Petticoat Lane
Market, **6**

Spitalfields Heritage
Centre, **5**

Spitalfields
Market, **3**

Tower Hamlets
Environmental
Trust, **2**

Victoria Park, **14**

Weavers Fields, **12**

Whitechapel Art
Gallery, **9**

Whitechapel Bell
Foundry, **10**

Head east on Fournier Street to reach **Brick Lane**; a visit to one or more of the ethnic restaurants lining the street is almost obligatory for food lovers. As evidenced by its name, the area was once a brickmaking center; now it seems Brick Lane is built on restaurants and leather shops. A left on Brick Lane and then another quick left will put you in front of the **Spitalfields Heritage Centre** (19 Princelet St., tel. 0171/247–0971), which researches the history of the area's immigrants. Continue north on Brick Lane, past the Shoreditch tube station—be warned that it only operates peak hours on weekdays and Sunday mornings—to reach the large, flavorful **Brick Lane Market** (*see* Street Markets, in Chapter 7), which roars to life on Sunday mornings.

WHITECHAPEL   In the Victorian era, Whitechapel was the site of some of the most terrible slums in London. The area was already notorious when, in August 1888, the mutilated body of Polly Nicholls was found. The Whitechapel Murders, perpetrated by the mysterious Jack the Ripper, had begun. Nowadays, there's little evidence of these grisly crimes, apart from the clusters of tourists being led on "Jack the Ripper" tours every evening. Along **Whitechapel High Street** and its continuance, **Whitechapel Road** (which runs in front of the Aldgate and Aldgate East tube stations), you will, however, find evidence of the area's changing demographic makeup. Whitechapel was the heart of London's Jewish community until the 1950s; prior to World War II the district had about 90,000 Jews compared with today's 6,000. Those interested in East End Jewish culture shouldn't miss the **Bevis Marks Synagogue** (Bevis Marks, off Creechurch Ln., EC3, tel. 0171/626–1274), London's oldest. In 1699 the growing community of refugees fleeing persecution in Spain and Portugal commissioned Joseph Avis, a Quaker, to build this beautiful structure, completed in 1701.

Orthodox Hassidim still walk the streets in their somber black attire, but the area's blocky flats are slowly being filled by immigrants from Asia. Hundreds of Bangladeshi residents congregate at the tremendous **East London Mosque** (84–86 Whitechapel Rd., tel. 0171/247–1357), the first building in London built specifically for use as an Islamic place of worship. Just west of the mosque is **Whitechapel Bell Foundry** (34 Whitechapel Rd., tel. 0171/247–2599), established in 1570. One of the most famous bells to be cast here is Philadelphia's Liberty Bell—though don't let that make you think they do bad work. Big Ben, the 13-ton bell in the famous clocktower at Westminster, was cast here in 1858 and is still perfectly sound. On Sunday mornings, the colorful and value-packed **Petticoat Lane Market** (see Street Markets, in Chapter 7) on Middlesex Street is a favorite destination for thousands of Londoners.

BETHNAL GREEN Northeast of Whitechapel lies Bethnal Green, a downtrodden area dotted with pretty green parks. Sprawling **Victoria Park** was the first park in London created specifically for public use (1842); social reformers felt that the poor needed space, fresh air, and light—none of which they had in their tiny, grim tenements. To get here head north on Cambridge Heath Road, turn right on Old Ford Road and follow it east about ½ mile. On the way you'll pass **Bethnal Green Museum of Childhood** (Cambridge Heath Rd., E2, tel. 0181/983–5200), an offshoot of the Victoria and Albert Museum. A huge collection of toys, games, puppets, dolls, and an amazing assortment of dollhouses, some dating as far back as 1760, is housed in this free museum. Look for the box containing the musical wooden sheep, just up the right stairs to the lower galleries; playing "Mary Had a Little Lamb" may be the best 20p you spend all day. Another monstrous, grassy expanse (Frisbee heaven) is **Weavers Fields,** accessible by heading south on Cambridge Heath Road and continuing right on Three Colts Lane, past the garages where London taxicabs come to die.

DOCKLANDS Sprawling eastward along the Thames from Tower Bridge, Docklands is a marvelous and sad ode to "progress." Despite being hard hit in the Blitz, the London docks remained very busy up until the 1960s, carrying 61.6 million tons of cargo as late as 1964. Abrupt dock closures in the '70s sank the area into economic decline, but by the '80s the wide-open spaces (read "cheap land") of the Docklands seemed like a possible solution to inner-city decline. The London Docklands Development Company took over, and money was lavished on several developments, most notably **Canary Wharf.** One Canada Square, the complex's 800-foot tower (the tallest building in Britain), remains half empty, despite being the home of several newspapers that used to line Fleet Street. The Docklands is a great place to see modern and postmodern architecture. Some interesting buildings to look out for are the red-fronted, oddly shaped **China Wharf** (29 Mill St., Bermondsey), John Outram's Lego-meets-ancient-Egypt **Storm Water Pumping Station** (Stewart St., Isle of Dogs), and the parabolic roof of the Canary Wharf Docklands Light Railway station. **Docklands Light Railway** (tel. 0171/363–9700) glides through much of the area, offering stunning views as well as efficient service.

The wise traveler will take the DLR immediately to the Crossharbour/London Arena stop and visit **London Docklands Visitor's Centre** (3 Limeharbour, E14, tel. 0171/512–1111) on the **Isle of Dogs.** The center, open weekdays 9–6 and weekends 10–5, has loads of information, an interesting exhibition of the area's history, and free pamphlets on walks in the area that take you past some of the more hidden architectural gems and points of interest. **Butler's Wharf** (Shad Thames, Rotherhithe)—a more aesthetically (and financially) successful project than Canary Wharf—used to be warehouses but is now a stunning ultramodern building housing trendy bistros, the **Design Museum** (see Museums and Galleries, below), and private industries. Another converted warehouse area is **St. Katherine's Dock,** just east of the Tower of London, now a peaceful stomping ground for tourists, yachting enthusiasts, and City professionals.

South of the Thames

THE SOUTH BANK

Many visitors never venture across the Thames unless they're heading to or from Waterloo Station, but the South Bank is well worth a visit. The South Bank was bombed flat during World War II and is fairly industrial, but the area is also on the rise. The stunning new **Eurostar Terminal** at Waterloo Station is located here, as are the **South Bank Centre** (see below), one of London's major cultural venues, and several museums and galleries. New development projects seem to be proposed every week as lottery-financed Millenium Fund money is thrown at the

The South Bank

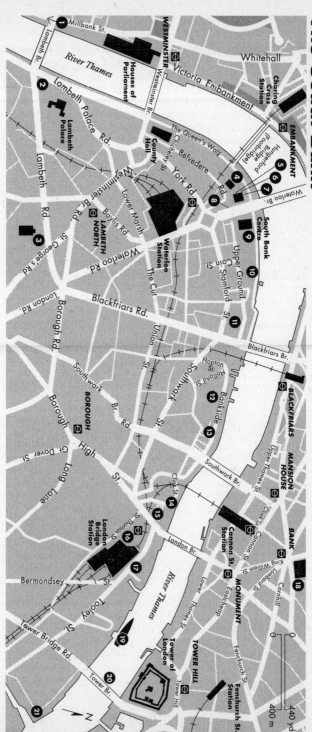

Bank of England
Museum, 18
Bankside Power
Station, 12
Clink Exhibition, 14
Design Museum, 21

Gabriel's Wharf, 10
Hayward Gallery, 5
H.M.S. Belfast, 19
Imperial War
Museum, 3

International
Shakespeare
Globe Centre, 13
London
Dungeon, 17
Museum of
Garden History, 2

Museum of the
Moving Image, 8
National Film
Theatre, 7
Old Operating
Theatre
Museum, 16

Oxo Tower
Wharf, 11
Queen Elizabeth
Hall, 6
Royal Festival
Hall, 4

Royal National
Theatre, 9
Southwark
Cathedral, 15
Tate Gallery, 1
Tower Bridge, 20

area. Some projects are definitely worthwhile (the Tate Gallery's Bankside project), though others seem a bit odd (the proposal for a giant Ferris wheel next to Tower Bridge).

SOUTH BANK CENTRE This sprawling, multitier monument to modernist poured concrete is home to the **Royal National Theatre, National Film Theatre,** and **Royal Festival Hall** (*see* Chapter 6), as well as the **Hayward Gallery** and **Museum of the Moving Image** (*see* Museums and Galleries, *below*). This progressive institution hosts a number of free foyer events; pick up a thick monthly brochure listing these and other attractions at the various buildings of the complex. The complex is awkward and fragmented, though Richard Rogers's controversial Crystal Palace plan aims to unify the site by throwing a wavy blue-tinted glass roof over the area, turning it into something between a cultural shopping mall and Disneyland by the end of 1999. *South Bank, Belvedere Rd., SE1, tel. 0171/960–4242. Tube: Embankment or Waterloo. Wheelchair access.*

SOUTHWARK It is difficult to tell that Southwark (pronounced "Suth-uk"), directly opposite the Tower of London, is London's oldest suburb, dating back to Roman times. Most of the buildings today are post–World War II, with a few notable exceptions. The site of London's entertainment district in Tudor times, Southwark is again set to become a popular area through projects like the rebuilt **Globe Theatre,** part of the **International Shakespeare Globe Centre** (*see below*), and the Tate Gallery's new Modern Art Museum, which is slated to open in the **Bankside Power Station** (past Blackfriars Bridge) by 1999. Clink Street, east of Southwark Bridge, was the site of the notorious prison that gave its name—the Clink—to jails everywhere. Inmates were those who ran afoul of the Bishops of Winchester, who controlled this part of Southwark and licensed prostitutes ("Winchester Geese") and brothels among other entertainments—taxing the profits heavily. **The Clink Exhibition** (1 Clink St., SE1, tel. 0171/403–6515) seeks to tell the story of the prison and its inmates but looks a bit run-down for your £2.50 (£1.50 students) admission. If you like your gore a little more graphic, you might want to visit **The London Dungeon** (Tooley St., tel. 0171/403–7221). It's tacky, expensive (£7.75, £6.50 students), and packed with tourists—like a lower-brow Madame Tussaud's with more blood—but kids love this place.

➤ **INTERNATIONAL SHAKESPEARE GLOBE CENTRE** • Shakespeare staged many of his plays in Southwark at the old Globe Playhouse, which burned down in 1613 when a spark from a cannon used in *Henry VIII* ignited the thatched roof. Though the theater was rebuilt immediately after the fire, the brimstone of the Puritans proved too much and the Globe was closed in 1642. The theater was part of a vibrant entertainment district that featured everything from bearbaiting to dive bars. In those days, people didn't pay £20 a ticket for a theater seat, and they didn't look for neo-Marxist-feminist symbolism in Shakespeare's works. Going to the theater, it seems, was more like going to a baseball game, with people in the cheap seats acting oafish. Yet instead of peanuts, the playgoers cracked hazelnuts (whose hulls will again be scattered on the floor of the new Globe).

The reconstruction of the **Globe Theatre** is the work of the late American filmmaker Sam Wanamaker, who slaved for two decades to raise funds for the project, which even uses the same construction materials and techniques as 16th-century craftsmen. The "wooden O" is scheduled for a grand opening on June 14, 1997, Wanamaker's birthday. A second indoor theater, the **Inigo Jones Theatre,** is also being built, based on the venerable architect's 17th-century designs. Once complete, both theaters will be used for performances of old and new plays in 16th- or 17th-century style. The *New York Times* reports that Mark Rylance, the artistic director of the Globe, would be "delighted" if the audience shouted during performances or even threw fruit at the actors, as they did in Shakespeare's time. The new **Shakespeare's Globe Exhibition** offers a fascinating look at the archaeological research on this reconstruction and the building techniques being used—plaster made from sand, lime, and goat's hair, oak carved into mortise and tenon joints. *Bear Gardens, SE1, tel. 0171/928–6342. Tube: London Bridge. Walk south on Borough High St., quick right on Southwark St., right on Southwark Bridge Rd. Admission: £5, £4 students. Open Mon.–Sat. 10–5, Sun. 2–5.*

➤ **SOUTHWARK CATHEDRAL** • Southwark Cathedral is the largest Gothic church in London after Westminster Abbey. Construction of this whopper—the fourth church on this site since the 7th century—started in 1220, but it was substantially rebuilt in the 19th century. Just west of the south transcept there's a large memorial to William Shakespeare (though his bones are far, far away in Stratford-upon-Avon). His unfortunate brother, Edmund, who was actually buried here in 1607, suffers the ignominy of an "unknown" grave. *Montague Close, off Borough High St., tel. 0171/407–3708. Admission free. Open daily 8–6.*

➢ **OLD OPERATING THEATRE MUSEUM** • Don't come to this museum if you or a family member is facing surgery anytime soon. The display of a 19th-century operating room, complete with sawdust to soak up the blood, is enough to turn any visitor into a Christian Scientist. The operating room, glimpsed in *The Madness of King George,* is all that remains of the original St. Thomas's Hospital, which occupied the site from the 13th to the mid-19th century before moving to Lambeth. Though the other buildings were destroyed, the operating theater, which is in a remote loft, was blocked off and forgotten for more than a century. It's been restored to its original, gruesome, and doubtlessly unsterile state. *9A St. Thomas St., SE1, tel. 0171/955–4791. Tube: London Bridge. Follow signs from station. Admission: £2, £1.50 students. Open Tues.–Sun. 10–4.*

➢ **HMS BELFAST** • Part of the Imperial War Museum, HMS *Belfast* was the pride of the Royal Navy during the mid-century. It remains the largest cruiser ever built for the British and is the only warship of the British fleet still afloat. It helped shell the Normandy beaches on D-day and later served in the Far East. Roam around the decks, which feature dioramas reconstructing life on the ship; climb in the "A" turret near the fo'c'sle (the ship's front to you, landlubber) and aim the big empty gun; or sit in the Captain's Chair and bark orders at wax dummies or other tourists. A nice way to arrive (or leave) is to ferry across from Tower Pier (60p each way). Ferries leave daily, April–October, every 15 minutes from 11 to 5. *Morgan's Ln., off Tooley St., SE1, tel. 0171/407–6434. Admission: £4.40, £3.30 students; free Fri. Open daily 10–6 (Nov.–Feb. until 5); last admission 45 min before closing. Partial wheelchair access.*

BRIXTON

Brixton, southeast of central London, is a funky working-class, Afro-Caribbean community rarely visited by the casual tourist. Young Londoners love the neighborhood for its all-night raves and innumerable clubs. By day, the big draw is the excellent open-air **Brixton Market** (*see* Street Markets, in Chapter 7), where some of the more exotic offerings include cassara bread, akara balls, bootleg reggae tapes, and Afro wigs made from yak hair (£10). The market fills most of the blocks around the Brixton tube station and along rockin' Electric Avenue (yes, the one in the Eddy Grant song). One of the best places to get in touch with Brixton's African and West Indian community is at the **Black Cultural Archives** (378 Coldharbour Ln., SW9, tel. 0171/738–4591), open Monday–Saturday 10–6. It houses a small collection of photographs, letters, storyboards, artwork, and other cool stuff chronicling the plight and achievements of black immigrants from Roman times until today. You'll also find changing displays of works by locally and widely known black artists.

In the recent past Brixton's dealt with more than its share of urban blight: In 1981 and 1985, it was rocked by a series of riots that—even though they were dubbed "race riots"—were probably sparked by worsening socioeconomic conditions. Westminster did take notice, however, and has tried to perk up Brixton's economy by investing some £180 million in the neighborhood during the last five years. These days the streets are bustling, and residents, for the most part, are hopeful.

RICHMOND

The borough of Richmond-upon-Thames, southwest of central London, is filled with culture and money. The startlingly lavish Victorian mansions you'll see around Richmond have belonged to the families of various countesses and earls for generations; the rest house a sprinkling of rock stars and TV celebrities. One of the highlights of any visit here is a climb up **Rich-**

mond Hill for sweeping views over the river. From Richmond Hill it's an easy walk to **Richmond Park,** one of the largest parks in Europe, with about 2,500 acres of heathland still roamed by herds of wild deer. Richmond's **Tourist Information Centre** (Town Hall, Whitaker Ave., tel. 0181/940–9125) is open weekdays 10–6, Saturdays 10–5. In July the **Richmond Festival** kicks in for a few weeks of music and street theater on and around the Richmond Green and Richmond Bridge. *Tube or BritRail: Richmond.*

KEW GARDENS Founded in 1759 by Princess Augusta (wife of Frederick, Prince of Wales), the amazing 300-acre Kew Gardens (also known as the Royal Botanic Gardens) is the mother of all botanical gardens. Wild thickets, manicured flower beds, lakes, ponds, and paths abound. Half a dozen glass greenhouses—many huge and architecturally magnificent—house some of Kew's 60,000 species of plants, from arctic to tropical vegetation, and from huge trees to humble ground cover. Although it's hard to choose favorites, the **Princess of Wales's Conservatory** is especially charming. Here in a modernist structure, a tropical jungle has been re-created in lush detail: Mist blows out of pipes every 45 seconds, birdcalls resound from hidden speakers, and the atmosphere is hot and sultry. Another wonder is **Kew Palace,** a 1631 Jacobean mansion that was home to George II and Queen Caroline in the 1720s and vacation residence of George III in the late 18th century. It's open April–September, daily 9:30–5:30, and worth the £1 admission (50p if you pay at the entrance to the gardens) to poke around the small museum of items from the Georgian era and relax in its peaceful café. *Kew and Wakehurst Pl., tel. 0181/332–5000 or 0181/940–1171 for recorded info. Tube: Kew Gardens. Follow the signs to Victoria Gate. Admission: £4.50, £3 students. Open weekdays 9:30–6, weekends 9:30–7 (shorter hrs in winter); greenhouses close 30 min before the gardens.*

MARBLE HILL HOUSE Marble Hill House was the former home of Henrietta Howard, the mistress of King George II. Later occupants of this riverside abode included another royal concubine—Mrs. Fitzherbert, who was later secretly wedded to King George IV. The house has been recently restored, and the details—from the furnishings to the moldings—are exquisite. There's a small park in back where concerts are held July–August. *Richmond Rd., tel. 0181/892–5115. Tube: Richmond. Walk SW on Kew Rd. (which becomes George St.), cross Richmond Bridge to Richmond Rd., follow path on Beaufort Rd. Admission: £2.50, £1.90 students. Open Apr.–Sept., daily 10–1 and 2–6; Oct.–Mar., Tues.–Sun. 10–1 and 2–4.*

✓ **HAMPTON COURT PALACE** Up the Thames west from Richmond is Hampton Court Palace, party house of English royalty since the early 16th century. The palace was built in 1514 for Cardinal Wolsey, Henry VIII's primary adviser. The jealous king compelled Wolsey to give him the palace, and added the great hall in 1532. Henry is said to have rushed construction of the hall by having laborers toil 24 hours a day in shifts, working by candlelight at night. Centuries later, William III and Mary II toyed with tearing the whole thing down and building an imitation British Versailles but contented themselves instead with adding the graceful South Wing, designed by Wren. The amazing extravagance of the palace is evident in its size, but the ornate interior and exterior decoration puts its value far beyond comprehension. Within the grounds are the world's first indoor tennis court, massive state bedrooms, kitchens capable of feeding a thousand a day, plus gardens, canals, a maze of hedges better than the one in *The Shining,* and the oldest known grapevine in the world (it's more than 220 years old). *Hampton Court Bridge, tel. 0181/781–9500. Take London Transport Bus R68 from central Richmond, BritRail to Hampton Court, or the ferry from Westminster Pier. Admission: £8, £5.75 students. Open Mon. 10:15–6, Tues.–Sun. 9:30–6 (Oct.–Mar. until 4:30).*

Near London

GREENWICH ✓

If you're nearing saturation point with the traffic and crowds of London, go to the village of Greenwich (pronounced "GREN-itch"). Despite being only a few miles from the City, it feels worlds apart. You have two options for getting there: The slow and scenic way, by river (*see* Guided Tours, By Boat, *above*), or a quick 25-minute ride on Docklands Light Railway from Tower Hill or Bank station to the Island Gardens station, on the Isle of Dogs. Check out the view from the park before crossing the Thames, and then head for the squat, circular brick building with a glass roof—this marks the entrance to the Greenwich Foot Tunnel, a claustrophobia-inducing passage, which is the final leg of your journey. You'll emerge at Greenwich Pier, very near where the *Cutty Sark* sits in dry dock. Now more familiar as the symbol of a brand of rum, this 19th-century, tea-trading clipper was once the fastest ship in the world: In 1871, it completed the journey from China to London in only 107 days. For £3.25 (£2.25 students), you can climb aboard the decks, peruse the world's largest collection of figureheads, or grab hold of the wheel and play captain. A short distance away stands the much smaller *Gipsy Moth IV*, the 54-foot vessel used by Sir Francis Chichester on the first solo circumnavigation of the world in 1966–67. Climb aboard for 50p (30p students), or just marvel at the diminutive size for free. For more info on either ship call 0181/858–3445. For landlubbers, there's **Greenwich Royal Park** (tel. 0181/858–2608), the oldest of London's Royal parks, containing incredible flower gardens, a Victorian tea pavilion, a boating lake, the Royal observatory (*see below*), and a stunning view of London from Greenwich Hill.

Greenwich's markets have become a very popular alternative to Camden's. The small, covered **Bosun's Yard Market** (59 Greenwich Church St., tel. 0181/293–4804) is packed with stalls selling arts and crafts, books, and other small items; it's open daily in summer (weekends only in winter). **Greenwich Market** (College Approach, Stockwell Street, High Road, and surrounding alleys) is held weekends 9–6 and features a wide range of antiques, old books and records, and odd bits of bric-a-brac. Fewer tourists means better deals; still, you should bargain hard. For information on guided walks and the like, stop by the **Greenwich Tourist Office** (46 Greenwich Church St., tel. 0181/858–6376); it's open daily 10:15–4:45 (shorter hours in winter).

✓ **NATIONAL MARITIME MUSEUM** When King Charles II ordered Christopher Wren to build "a small observatory within our part of Greenwich" in 1675, few realized the impact this unassuming building would have on the future of world navigation.

Although the **Royal Greenwich Observatory** is no longer used for astronomical observations (London's bright lights obscure the view), this is the place the BBC is talking about when it announces "**Greenwich Mean Time (GMT)**"; it's also the point from which sailors around the globe determine their bearings, using Greenwich as the prime meridian (0° longitude). The building holds a remarkable collection of beautiful antique timepieces and several antique telescopes. The observatory is now part of the nearby **National Maritime Museum,** which boasts the world's largest collection of maritime artifacts, including paintings, medallions, and other reclaimed wreckage from England's mighty days of thalassocracy. The £5.50 admission (£4.50 students) gets you into the observatory, the museum, and the Queen's House (*see below*). *Romney Rd., SE10, tel. 0181/ 858–4422. Open daily 10–5 (last admission at 4:30).*

The line in the Royal Greenwich Observatory's courtyard divides the world into two halves, the Eastern and Western hemispheres. Straddle it and you're standing in both hemispheres simultaneously.

QUEEN'S HOUSE Designed by Inigo Jones in 1616, the Queen's House was Britain's first classical building. The royal apartments have been restored to their 1660 state and feature a surprisingly vibrant color scheme. The highlight of the building is the **Great Hall,** a perfect cube, 40 feet in all three directions, decorated with paintings of the Muses, the Virtues, and the Liberal Arts. For admission prices, *see* National Maritime Museum, *above. Romney Rd., SE10, tel. 0181/858–4422. Open May–Sept., Mon.–Sat. 10–6, Sun. noon–6; Oct.–Apr., Mon.–Sat. 10:30–3:30, Sun. 2:15–4.*

ROYAL NAVAL COLLEGE Founded by William III as the naval equivalent to Chelsea Royal Hospital (*see* Chelsea, *above*), these Wren buildings were converted into a college for aspiring sailors in 1873. The symmetrical blocks were designed to preserve the view from the Queen's House to the river, and wandering around the grounds and the two buildings open to visitors makes a nice diversion. Students dine in the **Painted Hall,** decorated with baroque murals (1707–17) of William and Mary by Sir James Thornhill, who also painted the interior of the dome at St. Paul's. The **College Chapel** was rebuilt after a fire in 1779 in a neo-Grecian style. Nelson's body lay in state here after his death at the battle of Trafalgar in 1805. *King William Walk, tel. 0181/858–2154. Admission free. Open daily 2:30–4:45.*

WINDSOR

Windsor, west of central London along the Thames, is the sort of place where rowboats roll gently upriver, where geese along the riverbank noisily lap up crumbs, and where families stroll with ice cream. Of all the day trips you could make from London, this is one of the nicest; Windsor Castle and the royal pomp are simply bonuses. That said, the royal presence draws throngs of foreign and English visitors, packing the narrow, cobbled streets of what would otherwise be a charming village. BritRail makes the trip from London's Waterloo to **Windsor and Eton Riverside Station** (Datchet Rd., tel. 01753/861–244) and from London's Paddington to **Windsor and Eton Central Station** (Thames St., tel. 01753/859–644). Both trips leave about every half hour, last 50 minutes, and cost £5.30 return. **Green Line** (tel. 01923/673–121) Buses 700, 701, 702, and 703 also travel from Eccleston Bridge, near Victoria Station, to Windsor (1 hr, £4.55 return). Windsor is an easy day trip from London, but if you want to spend the night, there's a **YHA hostel** (Mill Ln., tel. 01753/861–710) a mile west of the castle. It's open mid-January through mid-December, and beds cost £9.10. The **Tourist Information Centre** (24 High St., tel. 01753/852–010) is just around the corner from the castle.

Across from the tourist office is Christopher Wren's **Guildhall,** begun in 1687. Look carefully at the pillars in the center of the forecourt—Wren added them later when townsfolk expressed their concern that the slender outer pillars weren't strong enough to support the upper story. Note that they don't rise all the way to the ceiling, proving Wren's design to be sound. In pleasant contrast, nearby **Market Cross House** slants sharply to one side and now houses the Earl's Sandwich Shop (51 High St., tel. 01753/857–534), where you can buy tasty and reasonably priced sandwiches (£1.10–£2.60). Running the length of the Market Cross House is **Queen Charlotte Street,** recognized as the shortest street in Britain at 51 feet, 10 inches long.

WINDSOR CASTLE What William the Conqueror originally built out of dirt and wood (and what Henry II rebuilt in stone) has survived countless alterations over the centuries to become today's Windsor Castle. The process of restoration continues: A 1992 fire heavily damaged several rooms in the State Apartments, most of which were for the private use of the queen, who spends most of her weekends here (the castle remains open even when she's in residence). Whenever the queen is at Windsor, the Union Jack that usually flies from the Round Tower is replaced with the royal coat of arms.

Overheard at Windsor Castle (think heavy midwestern accent): "Why on earth would the queen build her house so close to an airport?"

The castle is divided into the Lower, Middle, and Upper Wards. Many of England's kings and queens are buried in the 15th-century **St. George's Chapel,** the principal structure of the Lower Ward. The tomb of Henry VIII is located in the choir—a simple slab in the floor that he shares with Charles I, and a remarkably meager monument to such a megalomaniac. The Gothic chapel is the shrine of the Order of the Garter, a chivalric order founded in 1438 by Edward III. The **State Apartments** are in the Upper Ward and feature an amazing collection of royal portraiture and other paintings, including works by Dürer, Rubens, and Van Dyck. Check out the Gobelin tapestries, too, and the Louis XVI bed. The **Gallery** hosts changing exhibitions taken from the Royal Collection, one of the finest art collections in the world. For an additional £1 fee you can visit **Queen Mary's Dolls' House,** a masterpiece by the architect Edwin Lutyens. The Dolls' House, measuring 8 by 5 feet, is a fully functional marvel of miniature engineering with electric lights, running faucets, and elevators. Prominent authors and artists of the day contributed miniature paintings and handwritten books to the house's library, and seamstresses invested some 1,500 hours stitching monograms on the tiny little linens. Be aware that the State Apartments are closed when the queen is in residence; call ahead before making the trek to avoid disappointment. The Gallery closes in January and reopens in May; St. George's Chapel and the Albert Memorial Chapel are closed every Sunday. The **Changing of the Guard** takes place Monday–Saturday at 11 AM. *Castle Hill, tel. 01753/831–118. Admission: £8.50; £5.50 when State Apartments are closed. Open Mar.–Oct., daily 10–5:30 (last admission 4), Nov.–Feb., daily 10–4 (last admission 3). Wheelchair access with advance notice.*

ETON Just across the Thames from Windsor, Eton is home to one of England's most exclusive public (read: private) schools. Don't be too impressed: Academic standards are no higher here than at other public schools, though the Old-Boy network is, indeed, intimidating. Since the school was founded by Henry VI in 1440 for the expenses-paid education of "poor scholars," many Eton graduates have gone on to Oxford, Cambridge, and fame in public life. Eighteen prime ministers, the King of Siam, Henry Fielding, Percy Bysshe Shelley, Aldous Huxley, George Orwell, and Ian Fleming have all studied at Eton, but who's counting? Eton's 15th-century **chapel** is a highlight, with its famous gold-inlaid pipe organ, though the modern stained glass near the altar is a bit disturbing. The **Museum of Eton Life** provides a brief glimpse into a day in the life of an Eton brat, while the **Brewhouse Gallery** displays changing exhibitions. *Brewhouse Yard, tel. 01753/863–593. Admission to grounds and museums: £2.50. Open daily 2–4:30, from 10:30 during school holidays.*

Museums and Galleries

In addition to the museums reviewed below, the following museums are discussed above: **Barbican Art Gallery** (*see* The City); **Bethnal Green Museum of Childhood** (*see* The East End); **Black Cultural Archives and Museum** (*see* Brixton); **British Museum** (*see* Major Attractions); **Cabinet War Rooms** (*see* Whitehall and Westminster); **Candid Arts Trust** (*see* Islington); **Commonwealth Institute** (*see* Kensington and Knightsbridge); **Courtauld Institute Galleries** (*see* Somerset House, in Strand and Embankment); **Crafts Council** (*see* Islington); **Fenton House** (*see* Hampstead and Highgate); **Freud's House** (*see* Hampstead and Highgate); **Guards Museum** (*see* Buckingham Palace, in Major Attractions); **HMS *Belfast*** (*see* The South Bank); **International Shakespeare Globe Centre** (*see* The South Bank); **Jewel Tower** (*see* Houses of Parliament, in Major Attractions); **Keats House** (*see* Hampstead and Highgate); **Kensington Palace** (*see* Hyde Park and Kensington Gardens, in Kensington and Knightsbridge); **Kenwood House** (*see* Hampstead and Highgate); **Leighton House** (*see* Kensington and Knightsbridge); **London Dungeon** (*see* The South Bank); **Madame Tussaud's Wax Museum** (*see* Marylebone and Regent's Park); **National Gallery** (*see* Trafalgar Square, in Major Attractions); **Natural History Museum** (*see* Kensington and Knightsbridge); **National Maritime Museum** (*see* Greenwich); **National Portrait Gallery** (*see* Trafalgar Square, in Major Attractions); **Old Operating Theatre Museum** (*see* The South Bank); **Percival David Foundation of Chinese Art** (*see* University of London, in Bloomsbury); **Queen's Gallery** (*see* Buckingham Palace, in Major Attractions); **Science Museum** (*see* Kensington and Knightsbridge); **Tate Gallery** (*see* Major Attractions); **Thomas Carlyle's House** (*see* Chelsea and King's Road); **Victoria and Albert Museum** (*see* Kensington and Knightsbridge).

Bank of England Museum. Housed in the Bank of England Building, this multimedia museum has some cool historical artifacts, early photographs, collections of old coins and bank notes, original artwork from Britain's currency, and interactive videos about the history of bank notes. The collection lays out the bank's history and functions, chronicling the institution's importance in helping to build England's financial and trading empire of yore. Special exhibits, which change every few months, feature topics like "All Change"—a history of the decimalization process. *Bartholomew Ln., EC2, tel. 0171/601–5545 . Tube: Bank. Walk east on Threadneedle St., turn left on Bartholomew Ln. Admission free. Open weekdays 10–5.*

Camden Arts Centre. This is one of the best places in London to see contemporary European art. Exhibits rotate frequently through the center's three galleries, and on-site projects provide the opportunity to meet and discuss works in progress with rotating resident artists. The center will undergo a major renovation in 1997, with some of the galleries closed for part of the year. Call ahead to see what's on. *Arkwright Rd., NW3, tel. 0171/435–2643. Tube: Finchley Road. Walk north (uphill) on Finchley Rd., turn right on Arkwright Rd. Admission free. Open Tues.–Thurs. noon–8, Fri.–Sun. noon–6.*

Dickens House. During the three years (1837–39) he lived at 48 Doughty Street, Charles Dickens churned out *Oliver Twist* and *Nicholas Nickleby* and finished up *Pickwick Papers*. The house is now an interesting museum and library, containing a large collection of Dickens's household goods, his desk, and the ubiquitous lock of hair. *48 Doughty St., WC1, tel. 0171/405–2127. Tube: Russell Square. Walk east on Bernard St., turn right at Coram's Fields, left on Guilford St., right on Doughty St. Admission: £3.50, £2.50 students. Open Mon.–Sat. 10–5.*

Design Museum. This elegantly laid-out museum houses two floors of 20th-century international design, with an emphasis on mass-produced consumer goods. The hypermodern **Review Gallery** displays a constantly changing survey of contemporary design, while the **Collection Gallery** has a more historical emphasis; there's even a computer database connecting objects with the historical circumstances in which they were produced. Exhibitions in 1997 include the work of modernist architect Charlotte Perriand (Oct. 1996–Apr.), who worked with Le Corbusier, and an exhibition on the role of the erotic in all forms of design (spring 1997). *Butler's Wharf, Shad Thames, SE1, tel. 0171/403–6933 or 0171/378–6055 for recorded info. Tube: Tower Hill. Cross Tower Bridge and head east along the Thames. Admission: £4.75, £3.50 students. Open weekdays 11:30–6, weekends noon–6. Wheelchair access.*

Dulwich Picture Gallery. Britain's oldest public art gallery (opened in 1817) is from a grand design by the neoclassical architect Sir John Soane. Housed within is a breathtaking display of old masters, such as Rembrandt, Rubens, Canaletto, and Van Dyck, still hung as tightly together as they would have been in the 19th century. The gallery alters its exhibition from time to time with visiting collections. *College Rd., SE21, tel. 0181/693–5254. BritRail: West Dulwich. Or take Bus 3 from Oxford Circus, Trafalgar Square, or Westminster. Admission: £2, £1 students; free on Fri. Open Tues.–Fri. 10–5, Sat. 11–5, Sun. 2–5.*

Geffrye Museum. This wonderful museum features excellent displays of 11 complete period rooms, dating from the 16th century to the 1950s. Sir Robert Geffrye, a merchant and once Mayor of London, left part of his fortune to the Ironmongers' Company to build almshouses to house the elderly poor. When the buildings were sold in 1911 (to build healthier homes in outer London), they became a museum to educate local craftsmen in interior fashions. There's also a beautiful herb garden (open April–October). *Kingsland Rd., E2, tel. 0171/739–9893. Tube: Liverpool Street. From station, walk east to Bishopsgate and take Bus 22A, 22B, or 149. Admission free. Open Tues.–Sat. 10–5, Sun. 2–5. Wheelchair access.*

Hayward Gallery. The forte of this flagship art gallery of the South Bank Centre is assembling retrospectives of modern artists such as Magritte, Jasper Johns, Dalí, and Toulouse-Lautrec. Paintings by British post-war painter Howard Hodgkin and the Prinzhorn Collection, featuring works by the mentally ill, will be displayed December 1996–February 1997, followed by an exhibition on the Harlem Renaissance (June–Aug.), and "The Twentieth Century: The Age of Modern Art" (Sept.–Jan.) *South Bank, Belvedere Rd., SE1, tel. 0171/960–4242. Tube: Embankment or Waterloo. Admission: £5, £3.50 students. Open daily 10–6 (Tues. and Wed. until 8).*

Imperial War Museum. Housed in the former home of the Royal Bethlehem for the Care of the Insane, or "Bedlam," this museum outlines the history of Britain's 20th-century wars using weaponry, mementos, and reconstructions. Don't think the lunatics have taken over the asylum—despite a bristling array of planes, field guns, and other war toys in the entrance hall, the museum's exhibits focus on the *horror,* rather than the "glory" of war. Two galleries upstairs house large collections of art from the two world wars. Downstairs you can visit "The Trench Experience," re-created from the Great War, and "The Blitz Experience," an excellent eight-minute trip through London's Blitz. The "Secret War" exhibit details the world of espionage, especially the work of MI5 and MI6, Britain's intelligence forces. For an extra £1.50, you can fly with "Operation Jericho" and witness a 1944 raid over France. *Lambeth Rd., SE1, tel. 0171/416–5000. Tube: Elephant & Castle. Walk NW on St. George's Rd., turn left on Lambeth Rd. Admission: £4.50, £3.50 students; free after 4:30. Open daily 10–6. Wheelchair access.*

Institute of Contemporary Arts (ICA). Lectures, avant-garde films, and rotating exhibits of photography, painting, sculpture, and architectural drawings by international and homegrown talent make ICA the headquarters for lusty cultural bolshevism. Its café and bar are hangouts for black-clad, hip intellectuals, who love to smoke, drink, and discuss German expressionist films or vernacular architecture. There's also a video library where you can watch films, and a bookshop (offering choice bargains). *Nash House, The Mall, SW1, tel. 0171/930–6393 for recorded info or 0171/930–3647 for box office. Tube: Charing Cross or Piccadilly Circus. From Charing Cross, walk SW on The Mall. From Piccadilly Circus, walk south on Regent St., turn right on The Mall. Admission for exhibits: weekdays £1.50, £1 students; weekends £2.50, £1.50 students. Gallery open daily noon–7:30 (Fri. until 9); café open Mon.–Sat. 2–3 and 5:30–9; bar open Mon. noon–11, Tues.–Sat. noon–1 AM, Sun. noon–10:30.*

Jewish Museum, Camden Town. This collection of art and artifacts illustrates Jewish rituals and culture and the history of Jews in Britain. The items are beautifully displayed and carefully labeled. The upstairs gallery contains many precious antiques, including manuscripts, embroidery, silver, ceremonial dress, and the oldest English-made "Hanucah" lamp. *129–131 Albert St., NW1, tel. 0171/284–1997. Tube: Camden Town. Head SW on Parkway, turn left on Albert St. Admission: £3, £1.50 students. Open Sun.–Thurs. 10–4. Closed national and Jewish holidays. Wheelchair access.*

Jewish Museum, Finchley. London's East End was the gateway for most Jewish immigrants arriving in Britain over the centuries, but a larger Jewish community now exists here in Golders Green. This wing of the Jewish Museum features their social history collections, which use photographs, storyboards, and historical artifacts to trace the immigration, settlement, and lifestyles of local Jews. The museum will undergo a major refit in 1997, adding reconstructions of an early immigrant home and a garment workshop. The upstairs gallery is devoted to Holocaust education. *80 East End Rd., N3, tel. 0181/349–1143. Tube: Finchley Central. Turn right on Station Rd., left on Regent's Park Rd., left on East End Rd. Admission: £2, £1 students. Open Mon.–Thurs. 10:30–5, Sun. 10:30–4:30.*

London Canal Museum. Located in a former ice storage house, this museum illustrates the growth and decline of London's canal network. These waterways were once important venues for trade and transportation, and a distinct way of life evolved for the "canal people" who lived and worked on them. Make sure to look at the trippy narrow boats of modern canal-dwellers on nearby Regent's Canal. *12–13 New Wharf Rd., N1, tel. 0171/713–0836. Tube: King's Cross. Walk north on York Way, turn right on Wharfdale Rd., left on New Wharf Rd. Admission: £2.50, £1.25 students. Open Tues.–Sun. 10–4:30 (last entry 3:45).*

London Transport Museum. After an expensive overhaul in 1993, the London Transport Museum is more fascinating than ever. Dozens of buses, trams, and trains from the early 1800s to the present day are on display (including an improbable-looking double-decker tram once pulled by a single, overworked horse). The accompanying info tells the story of mass transportation's impact on both the growth of London and the class stratification within it. If that sounds dry, you can gambol with costumed actors, watch multilingual videos, or "test-drive" your own bus or tube train. *39 Wellington St. (entrance on The Piazza), WC2, tel. 0171/836–8557. Tube: Covent Garden. Admission: £4.50, £2.50 students. Open daily 10–6 (Fri. from 11). Wheelchair access.*

London Toy and Model Museum. This museum's collection of dolls, teddy bears, and other antique toys (including an ancient Roman gladiator doll) is pretty fascinating even if you've abandoned your own Barbies and model airplanes. If you've got tykes in tow, they'll go nuts over the carousel, mini-steam train, and penny slot machines—but sorry, kids only on the choo-choo. *21 Craven Hill, W2, tel. 0171/706–8000. Tube: Bayswater, Lancaster Gate, or Paddington. Admission: £5, £4 students. Open daily 10–5:30 (Sun. from 11).*

Museum of Garden History. This peaceful little spot of green is hidden away from the smoggy, concrete world. Housed in the former St. Mary-at-Lambeth Church—an interesting sight in itself—the churchyard contains a replica of a 17th-century garden, built to honor Charles I's royal gardeners, the Tradescants, who are buried here, as is William Bligh, captain of the *Bounty.* If you're wondering why gardeners would be buried in such splendor, chew on this: John Tradescant the Elder collected rare objects from around the world on his plant-hunting travels and displayed them in a museum in his home, The Ark, which opened to the public in 1629. His collection became the basis of the collection of the Ashmolean Museum at Oxford. *St. Mary-at-Lambeth, Lambeth Palace Rd., SE1, tel. 0171/261–1891. Tube: Lambeth North. Walk SW on Hercules Rd., turn right on Lambeth Rd. Admission free. Open Mar.–Dec., weekdays 10:30–4, Sun. 10:30–5. Wheelchair access.*

Museum of London. Come here for an extremely thorough look at the history of the city, from the Stone Age to the present. A lot of the older material on display was found in the Thames or at modern building sites. Be sure to see the sculptures from the Temple of Mithras, god of heavenly light. Worshipers of Mithras buried the sculptures so they wouldn't be destroyed by their rival cult, the Christians. Other "don't miss" items include the amazing Cheapside Hoard of jewelry, a beautiful art deco elevator from Selfridge's, and the glitzy Lord Mayor's Coach. The ticket is good for three months, so you can visit over and over. *London Wall, EC2, tel. 0171/600–3699. Tube: Barbican or St. Paul's. From Barbican, walk south on Aldersgate St. From St. Paul's, walk north on St. Martin's-Le-Grand. Admission: £3.50, £1.75 students; free after 4:30. Open Tues.–Sat. 10–5:50, Sun. noon–5:50.*

Museum of Mankind. Otherwise known as "The Ethnography Department of the British Museum," the Museum of Mankind features exhibits exploring non-Western cultures—particularly the indigenous people of Africa, Australia, the Pacific Islands, North and South America, Asia, and certain areas of Europe. Displays are rotated frequently from its massive collection in storage. *6 Burlington Gardens, W1, tel. 0171/437–2224. Tube: Piccadilly Circus. Walk NW on Regent St., turn left on Vigo St. (which becomes Burlington Gardens). Admission free. Open Mon.–Sat. 10–5, Sun. 2:30–6.*

Museum of the Moving Image (MOMI). This impressive television and film museum traces the history of man's manipulation of light and shadow. Tons of interactive exhibits—plus snippets from groundbreaking flicks—make this a definitively cool museum. The museum also has a wide collection of movie memorabilia, like the goldfish models from *The Meaning of Life* and Charlie Chaplin's costume from *Modern Times.* Mildly embarrassing actors employed by the museum float around, trying to add period flavor—*some* of them succeed. *South Bank, Belvedere Rd., SE1, tel. 0171/401–2636. Tube: Embankment or Waterloo. Admission: £6, £4.85 students. Open daily 10–6 (last admission 5 PM). Wheelchair access.*

National Army Museum. Admirably, the National Army Museum is nondidactic in its presentation on the life of British soldiers from the Tudor period to the present day. One of the highlights is a huge model—with more than 70,000 toy soldiers—of the Battle of Waterloo. The museum is not afraid to take on current events, either, with exhibitions examining the Gulf War, Bosnia, and women in the military; the last will continue to be on display through 1997. *Royal Hospital Rd., SW3, tel. 0171/730–0717. Tube: Sloane Square. Admission free. Open daily 10–5:30. Wheelchair access.*

National Museum of Cartoon Art. Changing exhibits display everything from the notorious political cartoonists of England's past to contemporary comic book artists from around the world. Don't feel guilty about spending an entire afternoon looking at cartoons—you can learn a great deal about social history from the exhibits here. The museum hopes to move from its current bleak building to a much grander location in Covent Garden in 1998. *Baird House, 15–17 St. Cross St., EC1, tel. 0171/405–4717. Tube: Farringdon. Walk north on Farringdon St., turn left on St. Cross St. Admission free. Open weekdays noon–6.*

National Postal Museum. Even if you've never collected stamps, stop by this philatelic extravaganza—it's one of the most important collections of postage stamps in the world. The interesting exhibit "Post Haste" details the history of the British postal service and its ever-increasing speed. Upstairs there are changing exhibitions and racks and racks of stamps. Look for the Penny Black, the world's first adhesive stamp, and Freddie Mercury's childhood stamp collection. *King Edward St., London Chief Post Office, EC1, tel. 0171/239–5420. Tube: St. Paul's. Walk west on Newgate St., turn right on King Edward St. Admission free. Open weekdays 9:30–4:30.*

Photographer's Gallery. This is the leading locale in London for contemporary British and international photography. Exhibitions change several times a year, and symposia on various topics are occasionally held. Just as fascinating is the gallery store, with an excellent selection of prints for sale. *5 Great Newport St., WC2, tel. 0171/831–1772. Tube: Leicester Square. Walk north on Charing Cross Rd., turn right on Great Newport St. Open Mon.–Sat. 11–6. Wheelchair access.*

Royal Academy of Arts. The venerable Royal Academy, an art school founded in 1769, is the oldest institution in London devoted to the fine arts. It houses a permanent collection of works by Royal Academicians and stages impressive special exhibitions throughout the year: In 1997, these include late works by cubist Georges Braques (Jan.–Apr.), the Berlin of George Grosz (Mar.–June), and works by Hiroshige (July–Sept.). The Academy's annual Summer Exhibition of contemporary art is as famous as it is discriminating—anyone can submit work, though only 1,300 are chosen from an average of 14,000 applicants. The Academy's postgraduate students show off their final exam projects to the public in January. *Burlington House, W1, tel. 0171/439–7438. Tube: Green Park or Piccadilly Circus. From Green Park, walk NE on Piccadilly. From Piccadilly Circus, walk west on Piccadilly. Admission varies; average £5, £4 students. Open daily 10–6. Wheelchair access.*

Royal Air Force Museum. Located within two hangars on the Hendon Airfield, this museum tells the story of the Royal Air Force, from its beginnings in 1917 to the present. Aviation and war buffs will appreciate the ensemble of planes, photographs, and quotes detailing the Royal Air Force battles in World War II. Others will probably be more interested in the "Battle of Britain Experience," with dioramas of Blitz damage and a talking head of Winston Churchill. It's a long way out here—the Imperial War Museum (*see above*) is a better bet for the casual observer. *Grahame Park Way, NW9, tel. 0181/205–2266. Tube: Colindale. Walk NE on Grahame Park Way. Admission: £5.20, £2.60 students. Open daily 10–6. Partial wheelchair access.*

Saatchi Collection. The megabucks of adman Charles Saatchi fuel this huge gallery, one of the most coveted venues in the land. As one of the most influential private collectors, Saatchi has made the careers of a number of artists and has spent the '90s focusing on British artists like Damien Hirst (the dead-animals-in-formaldehyde guy) and Rachel Whiteread (the plaster-casts-of-rooms-and-buildings woman). Exhibits change frequently; the annual Young British Artists show is always thought provoking. *98A Boundary Rd., NW8, tel. 0171/624–8299. Tube: Swiss Cottage. Walk ⅓ mi south on Finchley Rd., turn right on Boundary Rd. Admission: £3.50; free Thurs. Open Thurs.–Sun. noon–6.*

Serpentine Gallery. Search for this tea pavilion turned art gallery just north of the Albert Memorial in Kensington Gardens. Consult *Time Out* to see what's new here (usually some sort of cool modern multimedia work), because the gallery closes sporadically throughout the year. Free "gallery talks" are offered Sundays at 3 PM during exhibitions. *Kensington Gardens, W2, tel. 0171/723–9072. Tube: Lancaster Gate or South Kensington. Admission free. Open daily 10–6; closed occasionally for 2- to 3-week periods.*

Sir John Soane's Museum. This fascinating ex-abode of one of Britain's greatest architects is full of antiquities, gargoyle heads, pediments, and a plethora of other chunks of buildings. Soane had so much stuff that special walls—which open on hinges to reveal other walls—were constructed so that he could hang three times as many paintings in his small Picture Room. Fortunately, Soane liked Hogarth's *Rake's Progress* enough to put it on the outside. The Sepulchral Chamber holds the alabaster sarcophagus of Seti I; Soane was so pleased with his purchase that he held a three-day party to celebrate its installation in 1825. As you walk around the museum, make sure you peep out the windows and over the railings—Soane left bits and pieces everywhere. *13 Lincoln's Inn Fields, WC2, tel. 0171/405–2107. Tube: Holborn. Walk south on Kingsway, turn left on Remnant St. Admission free. Open Tues.–Sat. 10–5.*

Theatre Museum. With fascinating goodies galore, the Theatre Museum illustrates life on the British stage from Shakespeare's time through the present. On exhibit are theatrical memorabilia of every kind, including prints and paintings of the earliest London theaters, early scripts, costumes, and props. It's not all high-brow drama stuff either—the galleries include art and artifacts of the circus, modern musicals, puppetry, and even rock music (Mick Jagger's jumpsuit always draws a small crowd). For the price of admission you can also attend stage-makeup demos and costume workshops. The box office sells tickets for West End theatrical events. *1E Tavistock St. (entrance on Russell St.), WC2, tel. 0171/836–7891. Tube: Covent Garden. Admission: £3.50, £2 students. Open Tues.–Sun. 11–7.*

Wallace Collection. Hertford House makes a suitably impressive gallery for this incredible art collection, including 18th- and 19th-century French paintings and furniture; Dutch, Italian, English, and Spanish paintings; medieval, Renaissance, and Baroque works of art; and even arms and armour. Titian, Rembrandt, and Poussin are among the bigger names here; but the collection is very strong on Greuze's doe-eyed, soft-focused maidens, and Franz Hals's *Laughing Dutchman* hangs in an upstairs gallery. Try to be in Room 5 at the top of an hour; the Eleonora di Toledo clock chimes one of 14 tunes. The Wallace Collection is a perfect place to contemplate the art, since the place is relatively quiet and not crammed with tourists. *Hertford House, Manchester Square, W1, tel. 0171/935–0687. Tube: Bond Street. Walk west on Oxford St., turn right on James St., left on Manchester Square. Admission free. Open Mon.–Sat. 10–5, Sun. 2–5.*

Whitechapel Gallery. This large, well-designed venue with lots of natural light was built in the 1890s to bring culture to the East End; these days cheap studio spaces have attracted more than 7,000 artists to the area. Besides their regular exhibits, they have a great lineup of art talks and other special events—even "touch tours" for visually impaired visitors. From January through March, the gallery will feature work by leading British sculptor Tony Cragg. *80 Whitechapel High St., E1, tel. 0171/522–7888 or 0171/522–7878 for recorded info. Tube: Aldgate East. Follow signs to museum. Admission free; small charge for some exhibits. Open Tues.–Sun. 11–5 (Wed. until 8).*

Cheap Thrills

Yes, London is an expensive city, but you can find tons of ways to get the most out of the metropolis for a few quid or less. In addition to poking around the host of free museums, you can spend a very pleasant day in one of London's many parks and squares. Picnicking, reading, zoning out, basking in the sun, and, of course, people-watching are only some of the activities you can pursue at Hyde Park, Kensington Gardens, St. James's Park, Green Park, Holland Park, Hampstead Heath, and Regent's Park—to name just a few. Another boon for the poor in London is the large number of street performers. Prime locales to see buskers (as they're called in Britain) include Leicester Square, Covent Garden, Carnaby Street in Soho, the Church of St. Martin-in-the-Fields Market, and, of course, the tube, particularly at West End stops. The West End is also a good spot for late-night people-watching. Hang out in Trafalgar Square, Leicester Square, or Piccadilly Circus and watch tourists, clubbers, prophets of the coming apocalypse, and red-nosed juiceheads stumble past one another under the bright lights and glowing neon.

If you're looking for a good rambling walk, a path runs from the southeastern corner of St. James's Park (Tube: Westminster) through Green Park, Hyde Park (pass through the pedestrian subway at Hyde Park Corner), to the northwestern corner of Kensington Gardens; this 3-mile trail traverses the very heart of the city. Another long, pleasant walk is the 8-mile path along Regent's Canal. A particularly nice stretch runs from just south of Warwick Avenue tube along the northern edge of Regent's Park to Camden Lock. The walk along the South Bank of the Thames from Southwark Bridge (opposite St. Paul's) to Lambeth Bridge (south of Whitehall) affords brilliant views of the skyline from St. Paul's to the Houses of Parliament. At dusk, stick around for the great sunsets; you can mull over life's little joys and tragedies as you watch the sky slowly turn a pale magenta.

Not just for the morbid, London's cemeteries make for interesting visits. Strolling though the cemeteries was quite a popular activity in Victorian times. Many were established in the mid-19th century by which time London's churchyards were literally filled with bodies. Though **Highgate Cemetery** (*see above*) is the most famous, **Kensal Green** (Harrow Rd., W10), just west of the Kensal Green tube station, was the first private cemetery, opening its gates in 1832, and the burial place of novelists Henry Makepeace Thackeray, Wilkie Collins, and Anthony Trollope. The colonnaded catacombs of often empty **Brompton Cemetery** (Old Brompton Rd., SW7) can be quite creepy on a cloudy day. Residents of note include suffragette Emmeline Pankhurst and artist Frederick Leyland, whose exquisite tomb was designed by his Pre-Raphaelite buddy Edward Burne-Jones. To reach the cemetery walk west on Old Brompton Road from the West Brompton tube station. Both cemeteries are free to visit, open daylight hours, and feature tidy paths and over a century's worth of elaborate sepulchral art—it's just as rewarding to find a nicely carved tomb as it is to locate the small memorial of an eminent Victorian.

WHERE TO SLEEP   3

By Jennifer L. Brewer and Sunny Delaney

Budget lodging in London is likely to fall significantly short of your expectations. Instead of cozy bed-and-breakfasts (B&Bs) with plump matrons stuffing you with scones and cream, you're more likely to find damp, dim, and dingy rooms and breakfasts of rolls and tea. Furthermore, finding a tolerable double room for less than £35 a night will be a coup; your best bet is to look around **Bloomsbury,** the streets around the **Victoria** and **King's Cross** stations, and the less attractive **Earl's Court,** and **Notting Hill Gate.** Even many hostels charge up to £18 for a dorm bed in a room crammed with nine other people. Winner of the "too good to be true—there must be a catch" category, **Tonbridge Club** (120 Cromer St., WC1, tel. 0171/837–4406), near King's Cross Station, provides safe, spartan, dormitory accommodation, along with showers, luggage storage, and use of a kitchen for a mere £5 per night. The catches: You must show a foreign passport, check in between 10 PM and midnight, abide by the midnight curfew, and check out by 9:30 AM. The club's 50 beds are understandably in high demand, so call ahead. The only other bargains are the city's three campgrounds (*see* Camping, *below*), where hard-core penny-pinchers can camp for £5–£5.50 a night in London's outskirts.

If you find yourself without a place to stay in London, sleeping in the open is highly discouraged. Shelter Nightline (tel. 0800/446–441) can provide advice for stranded visitors.

If you're visiting during the off-season, don't hesitate to haggle, since most places also lower their rates anywhere from £2–£5 per night to 10% per week. Your cheapest option is a dorm bed in a hostel or B&B for as little as £50–£90 per week. During summer, most places stop offering a weekly rate and charge a straight £10–£20 per night for a dorm bed. Reserve as far in advance as possible for hotels and hostels from June to August—March is not too early. Reservations usually require a credit card number or a deposit for the first night. If you do arrive without reservations, the **Tourist Information Centre Accommodations Service** (26 Grosvenor Gardens, tel. 0171/824–8844), at the north end of hectic Victoria Station (look up and follow the signs), sells the handy guide *Where to Stay in London* (£3), which lists hundreds of B&Bs and hotels throughout the city. Though the staff caters to wealthy tourists, they can book a bed in the £15–£25 range for a £5 fee. They have other locations at Heathrow

Don't be afraid to haggle for reduced rates on multinight stays; you shouldn't be forced to pay the daily rate if you're staying somewhere for a week or more.

Airport in the tube station that serves Terminals 1, 2, and 3 and at the Liverpool Street station. There are also lodging hustlers in Victoria Station hoping to whisk you from the station to a local hotel via their free van service. Of course, you should never pay for *anything* without

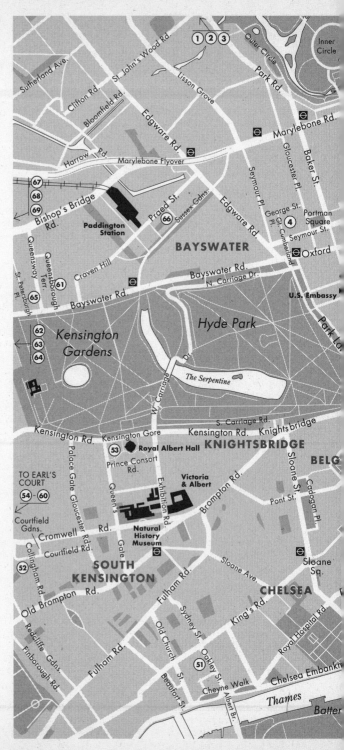

London Lodging

John Adams Hall, **8**

Kandara Guest House, **24**

Limegrove Hotel, **44**

Lords Hotel, **69**

Luna and Simone Hotel, **42**

Lynton House Hotel, **49**

Magnolia Hotel, **51**

Melita House Hotel, **40**

Museum Inn Hostel, **35**

The Oxford Arms, **23**

Oxford Street (YHA), **37**

Palace Hotel, **64**

Parkland Walk Guest House, **7**

Philbeach Hotel, **59**

Primrose Hill B&Bs, **6**

Quest Hostel, **61**

Rasool Court Hotel, **60**

Repton Hotel, **32**

Ridgemount, **30**

Rotherhithe (YHA), **39**

St. Athan's Hotel, **17**

St. David's/Norfolk Court Hotels, **66**

St. Margaret's, **33**

Tonbridge Club, **20**

Vicarage, **63**

Victoria Hotel, **41**

Windermere Hotel, **46**

University of London Accommodations Office, **31**

seeing your room first, and do not accept a ride with anyone who gives you the creeps. For women traveling solo, it's generally best to avoid these vultures altogether. University residence halls (*see* Student Housing, *below*) offer a clean, cheap alternative to dodgy hotels and noisy hostels. And those of you whose weeklong visit turns into a yearlong commitment should take a gander at Longer Stays, *below*.

Hotels and B&Bs

The ever-growing demands of the tourist market have caused a revolution in London lodging. In the past most rooms had very basic facilities, but nowadays, most have sinks and TVs, quite a few provide tea- and coffee-making facilities, and many hoteliers are installing showers or en-suite bathrooms. For the purposes of this guide "with bath" means with en-suite toilet and shower or tub, while "with shower" means there is a shower in the room (often in the middle, like a misplaced phone booth) and a toilet down the hall. Breakfasts vary widely, from dry toast and tea, with butter and jam if you're lucky ("continental breakfast"), to toast with butter and jam, egg, cereal, tea or coffee, and maybe bacon, sausage, fried tomatoes, beans, or the dreaded blood pudding ("English breakfast"). We've listed the type of breakfast provided (if any) at the end of each review. The categories below refer to the total price for a double room, including VAT.

AROUND VICTORIA STATION

The area around Victoria Station—including the neighborhoods of **Belgravia, Pimlico,** and **Westminster**—has a billion cheapish hotels, all of which make their living off this mammoth, sprawling BritRail terminal–bus depot–tube station. Most hotels are less than a 10-minute walk from the station along residential streets, and the farther from the station you go, the cheaper rooms become. The good news is that B&B owners here compete fiercely for customers. If you are willing to bargain, you can get excellent rates, especially during the off-season and/or if you agree to stay more than a few nights. A good strategy is to walk down one of the main budget hotel drags, like **Belgrave Road, Ebury Road,** or **Warwick Way,** offer everybody £10 less than the asking price, and see who makes the best counteroffer. The tiny **Windsor Guest House** (36 Alderney St., SW1, tel. 0171/828–7922) has shared-bath doubles for £32.

➢ **UNDER £40 • Georgian House Hotel.** For backpackers with sound limbs and strong lungs, the tidy Georgian House offers a half-dozen bargain "student rooms": singles £18, doubles £31, triples £42, and quads £50. You don't have to be a student, but you do have to be able to hike up to the fourth floor. Less demanding are their regular singles (£28), doubles (£43–£53), and triples (£48–£65), all with private bath. All rooms have TVs and coffee-makers; some have phones. *35 St. George's Dr., at Warwick Way, SW1, tel. 0171/834–1438, fax 0171/976–6085. Tube: Victoria. Walk south on Buckingham Palace Rd., turn left on Elizabeth St. (which becomes St. George's Dr.). 35 rooms, 29 with bath. English breakfast. MC, V.*

Limegrove Hotel. While this minuscule guest house can't offer much in the way of beauty or luxury, it handsomely compensates with friendly, caring management. Some rooms are newly renovated, while others are a bit run down; all come with a TV. Singles are £24, doubles £34, triples £45. *101 Warwick Way, SW1, tel. 0171/828–0458. Tube: Victoria. Walk SE on Wilton Rd., turn right on Warwick Way. 9 rooms, 1 with bath. English breakfast.*

Luna & Simone Hotel. This family-run hotel looks just like the others on Belgrave Road, but it's probably one of the best (plus, it's only 300 yards from Victoria Station). The immaculate, comfortable rooms all have TVs, phones, and hair dryers. Singles are £22–£28 (£35–£42 with bath), doubles £34–£40 (£46–£54 with bath), and triples with bath £56–£65. *47–49 Belgrave Rd., SW1, tel. 0171/834–5897, fax 0171/828–2474. Tube: Victoria. Walk SE on Wilton Rd., turn right on Bridge Pl., left on Belgrave Rd. 36 rooms, 25 with bath. English breakfast. MC, V.*

➢ **UNDER £50 • Elizabeth House (YWCA).** One of the nicest places to bed down near Victoria Station is run by the Young Women's Christian Association (YWCA), but don't let that scare you away: It's coed and nondenominational. The whole place is clean and cheery, with excellent 24-hour security and a heavenly garden patio. Handsome singles cost £21, doubles £42 (£45 with bath). Dorms (£15 per person) sleep three or four to a room. *118 Warwick Way, SW1, tel. 0171/630–0741, fax 0171/630–0740. Tube: Victoria. Walk south on Buckingham Palace Rd., turn left on St. George's Dr., right on Warwick Way. 31 rooms, 9 with bath. Laundry, safe, TV lounges. English breakfast. MC, V.*

Melita House Hotel. This comfortable, family-run hotel is on a quiet, residential street. The small rooms—all with TV, phone, and hair dryer—are clean, though the furniture is strictly garage sale. Singles cost £30 (£33–£38 with bath), doubles £45 (£48–£52 with bath). Triples (£65), quads (£75), and quints (£85) all have private baths. *33–35 Charlwood St., SW1, tel. 0171/828–0471, fax 0171/932–0988. Tube: Victoria. Walk SE on Wilton Rd., turn right on Bridge Pl., left on Belgrave Rd., right on Charlwood St. 20 rooms, 16 with bath. English breakfast. AE, MC, V.*

➤ **UNDER £60 • Collin House.** The Thomases, the friendly owners of this spotless Victorian B&B, maintain a quiet, nicely conservative atmosphere (no late-night revelers here, please). Come for the top-notch rooms, each with a sink, a handsome wood-frame bed, and framed photos of Wales taken by the proprietor. Singles cost £38, doubles £52 (£62 with bath), and triples £75 (£80 with bath). *104 Ebury St., SW1, tel. and fax 0171/730–8031. Tube: Victoria. Walk south on Buckingham Palace Rd., turn right on Eccleston St., left on Ebury St. 13 rooms, 8 with bath. English breakfast.*

Ebury House. At this small, pleasant place you can relax and make yourself at home—rooms certainly aren't palatial, but they're clean and tastefully decorated in pastel florals. The wood-paneled breakfast room is a great place for a chat with friendly owner David Davies. Singles (£40), doubles (£55), and triples (£75) all have TVs and sinks. *102 Ebury St., SW1, tel. 0171/730–1350, fax 0171/259–0400. Tube: Victoria. Walk south on Buckingham Palace Rd., turn right on Eccleston St., left on Ebury St. 13 rooms, none with bath. English breakfast. AE, MC, V.*

Lynton House Hotel. For over 30 years, the friendly Batey family has welcomed travelers to its cozy B&B, where even the radiators have floral slipcovers. Comfy singles (£35) and doubles (£50–£55) come equipped with TVs and washbasins. There's a small common terrace and excellent security. *113 Ebury St., SW1, tel. 0171/730–4032, fax 0171/730–9848. Tube: Victoria. Walk south on Buckingham Palace Rd., turn right on Eccleston St., left on Ebury St. 14 rooms, none with bath. English breakfast.*

➤ **UNDER £80 • Elizabeth Hotel.** This elegant hotel once served as the private home of aristocrats (including relatives of Edward VII). These days it offers luxuriously appointed rooms overlooking an attractive square. Singles (£55), doubles (£66–£70), triples (£93), and quads (£105) come with bath, a TV, and a knockout English breakfast. A less luxurious, shared-bath single (£40) and double (£65) are also available. *37 Eccleston Sq., at Warwick Way, SW1, tel. 0171/828–6812, fax 0171/828–6814. Tube: Victoria. Walk SE on Wilton Rd., turn right on Bridge Pl., left on Belgrave Rd., right on Eccleston Sq. 40 rooms, 38 with bath.*

Windermere Hotel. The Windermere's brochure gushes about "home comforts in an elegant setting" and trust us, they aren't kidding. The impeccably furnished rooms have TVs, phones, high ceilings, and ethereal white curtains. They're housed in a pair of Victoria-era buildings at the far end of the Warwick Way budget-hotel strip. Rooms with private bath are £60–£80, but basic, shared-bath singles are £46, doubles £54. *142–144 Warwick Way, SW1, tel. 0171/834–5163 or 0171/834–5480, fax 0171/630–8831. Tube: Victoria. Walk SE on Wilton Rd., turn right on Warwick Way. 24 rooms, 19 with bath. English breakfast. AE, MC, V.*

BAYSWATER AND NOTTING HILL GATE

Bars and cheap eateries on **Bayswater Road** cater to the budget and middlebrow travelers who pack the neighborhoods' innumerable hotels. **Queensway,** perpendicular to Notting Hill Gate and Bayswater, is a party-hearty tourist strip lined with pubs that blare "You Shook Me All

Night Long" and other sing-along favorites. Luckily, the more sedate environments of Kensington Gardens and Hyde Park are just across Bayswater Road.

➤ **UNDER £40** • **Hyde Park House.** The Hyde is one of the nicer hotels in the area, close to the Bayswater and Queensway tube stations and a short walk from leafy Hyde Park. It's on a side street, so noise is not a problem. Simple singles are £26, doubles £38. *48 St. Petersburgh Pl., W2, tel. 0171/229–9652 or 0171/229–1687. Tube: Queensway. Walk west on Bayswater Rd., turn right on St. Petersburgh Pl. 14 rooms, none with bath. Continental breakfast.*

Lords Hotel. Rooms here are basic and a bit shabby, although some have wide windows and balconies (definitely ask for one). Singles are £26 (£40 with bath), doubles £35 (£55 with bath), triples £45 (£66 with bath). *20–22 Leinster Sq., W2, tel. 0171/229–8877, fax 0171/229–8377. Tube: Bayswater. Walk north on Queensway, turn left on Moscow Rd., right on Chester Gardens. 67 rooms, 40 with bath. Continental breakfast. AE, MC, V.*

➤ **UNDER £50** • **The Gate Hotel.** This tiny B&B at the top of Portobello Road is friendly and clean with reasonably sized rooms furnished with conveniences like refrigerators, TVs, and phones. Singles go from £36, doubles from £48. *6 Portobello Rd., W11, tel. 0171/221–2403, fax 0171/221–9128. Tube: Notting Hill Gate. Walk north on Pembridge Rd., turn left on Portobello Rd. 6 rooms, 5 with bath. Small charge for AE, MC, V.*

St. David's/Norfolk Court Hotels. The Regency-style Norfolk Court joined the neighboring art deco–style St. David's hotel a few years ago, resulting in a simple, comfortable guest house. Some second-floor rooms have French windows and balconies that overlook Norfolk square. Singles are £28 (£40 with bath), doubles £44 (£55 with bath). *20 Norfolk Sq., W2, tel. 0171/723–4963, fax 0171/402–9061. Tube: Paddington. Walk north on Praed St., turn right on London St., left on Norfolk Sq. 70 rooms, 25 with bath. English breakfast. AE, MC, V.*

➤ **UNDER £60** • **Glynne Court Hotel.** The Glynne Court is actually in the Marble Arch area adjacent to Bayswater, right off Oxford Street (London's main shopping drag). For late-night runs to Virgin Records, this is the place to stay. Although it's not the Ritz, the rooms are clean, and discounts are offered for longer stays. Singles are £55, doubles £65, triples £75. *41 Great Cumberland Pl., W1, tel. 0171/262–4344, fax 0171/724–2071. Tube: Marble Arch. Walk west on Bayswater Rd., quick right on Great Cumberland Pl. 15 rooms, 12 with bath. Small charge for AE, MC, V. Continental breakfast.*

Vicarage. Run by the same family for nearly 30 years, the Vicarage feels like a real home. It's beautifully decorated, quiet, and overlooks a garden square near Kensington's main shopping streets. Expect to pay about £36 for a single and £58 for a double. *10 Vicarage Gate, W8, tel. 0171/229–4030, fax 0171/792–5989. Tube: High Street Kensington. Walk right on Kensington High St., turn left on Kensington Church St., veer right at fork onto Vicarage Gate. 18 rooms, none with bath. English breakfast.*

BLOOMSBURY AND KING'S CROSS

The former stomping ground of the Bloomsbury Group—the famed literary clique that included Virginia Woolf, E. M. Forster, Lytton Strachey, and John Maynard Keynes—is today the stomping ground of thousands of students from the nearby University of London and an equal number of tourists marching toward the British Museum. It is also prime lodging territory: Several student dorms, one great (and one not-so-great) hostel, and dozens of B&Bs line the streets all the way up to King's Cross station. Try **Cartwright Gardens, Tavistock Place,** or **Gower Street** if you're having trouble finding a bed for the night. Whereas Bloomsbury has a quiet, academic atmosphere, King's Cross is busier, noisier, and a touch seedy. **Argyle Street,** across from King's Cross Station, is a good street to try for clean budget accommodations. If you're desperate for a private room, try **Goodwood Hotel** (38–40 Tavistock Pl., WC1, tel. 0171/837–0855), which offers dark, dingy, minuscule doubles for £26. **The Generator** (*see* Hostels, *below*), just down the street, is a much cleaner, larger, and funkier bet.

➤ **UNDER £40** • **The Alhambra.** This is the best B&B bargain in Bloomsbury. The singles (£25), doubles (£34, £45 with bath), and triples (£45, £60 with bath) are all clean and spacious, and Mrs. Valoti is a friendly and gracious host. *17–19 Argyle St., WC1, tel. 0171/837–9575, fax 0171/916–2476. Tube: King's Cross. Head west on Euston Rd., turn left on Argyle St. 55 rooms, 13 with bath. English breakfast.*

Hotel Cavendish. This is a nice, simple, family-run B&B just down the road from Dillon's bookstore. Singles cost £25–£28 and doubles are £34–£42, depending on the size of the room and whether it faces the street or their lovely garden. The friendly owners will make a full vegetarian breakfast on request. *75 Gower St., WC1E, tel. 0171/636–9079, fax 0171/580–3609. Tube: Goodge Street. Turn right on Tottenham Court Rd., quick left on Chenies St., left on Gower St. 22 rooms, none with bath. English breakfast. AE, MC, V.*

Jesmond Dene Hotel. The Jesmond Dene has possibly the smartest decor in London—many rooms feature stylish combinations of pale blues or black and white, and even the hallway carpeting is chic chic chic. It's a real gem, and well priced to boot: Singles cost £25, doubles £35 (£10 more with bath), and every room has a sink and TV. *27 Argyle St., WC1, tel. 0171/837–4654, fax 0171/833–1633. Tube: King's Cross. Head west on Euston Rd., turn left on Argyle St. 24 rooms, 6 with bath. English breakfast.*

➢ **UNDER £50** • **Arosfa Hotel.** Mr. and Mrs. Dorta, the friendly owners, are what make this B&B a cut above the others on Gower Street. The rooms are simple yet spotless; ask for one facing away from the street. Bibliophiles will be happy to know that Dillon's is directly across the road. Singles cost £27, doubles £40, triples £53 (£10 more with shower). *83 Gower St., WC1E, tel. and fax 0171/636–2115. Tube: Goodge Street. Turn left on Tottenham Court Rd., right on Torrington Pl., right on Gower St. 15 rooms, 2 with bath.*

County Hotel. The County is huge by budget standards with 175 rooms. Smallish singles (£31) and more spacious doubles (£43) are clean but bleakly decorated in '60s-institutional style. The lobby is quite nice (revolving wooden door!), but the clientele at the downstairs pub is mainly foreign businessmen—you may want to tipple elsewhere. *Upper Woburn Pl., WC1H, tel. 0171/387–5544 or 0171/278–7871, fax 0171/837–4653. Tube: Euston. Walk south on Ersholt St., cross Euston Rd. to Upper Woburn Pl. 175 rooms, none with bath. English breakfast. AE, MC, V.*

Garth Hotel. The simple rooms are softened by a very friendly staff. Potter William de Morgan was born in this building—pity none of his glorious tile work graces the showers here. Singles go for £34 (£40 with bath), doubles £47 (£55 with shower). As the hotel caters to many Asian guests, it also offers a Japanese breakfast on request. *69 Gower St., tel. 0171/636–5761, fax 0171/637–4854. Tube: Goodge Street. Turn right on Tottenham Court Rd., quick left on Chenies St., left on Gower St. 18 rooms, 7 with bath. English breakfast. MC, V.*

Ridgemount. The kindly owners, Mr. and Mrs. Rees, make you feel at home, and the public areas—especially the family-style breakfast room—have a friendly, cluttered Victorian feel. Ask for a room that overlooks the leafy garden. Singles are £28, doubles £40 (£11 more with bath). *65–67 Gower St., WC1E, tel. 0171/636–1141. Tube: Goodge Street. Turn right on Tottenham Court Rd., quick left on Chenies St., left on Gower St. 34 rooms, 4 with bath. English breakfast.*

St. Athan's Hotel. This simple but appealing Edwardian guest house is close to Russell Square. The sloping walls and sagging staircases have a certain charm, and your hosts, Hans and Lucia Geyer, are delightful. If you stay for more than a day, you may find yourself playing "straight man" to the wickedly funny Hans. Singles are £36, doubles £46, triples £60; add £10–£12 for a private bath. *20 Tavistock Pl., WC1, tel. 0171/837–9140, fax 0171/833–8352. Tube: Russell Square. Exit station to the left, turn right on Herbrand St., right on Tavistock Pl. 50 rooms, 8 with bath. English breakfast. AE, MC, V.*

➢ **UNDER £60** • **Euro Hotel.** The big, bright rooms of the Euro complement the airy bistro atmosphere of the breakfast room. The staff is young and eager to please. Singles cost £40, doubles £55. *53 Cartwright Gardens, WC1H, tel. 0171/387–4321, fax 0171/282–5044, eurohotel@dial.com. Tube: King's Cross. Walk west on Euston Rd., turn left on Mabledon Pl., veer right on Cartwright Gardens. 35 rooms, none with bath. English breakfast. AE, MC, V.*

Gresham Hotel. The Gresham is large and slightly impersonal, but the rooms are clean and pale-blue sinks mediate the '70s earthtone decor. The singles (£32, £50 with bath) are narrow, but the doubles (£50, £65 with bath) are large enough to easily turn around in. Rooms at the back are quieter, though there isn't a view to speak of. *36 Bloomsbury St., WC1B, tel. 0171/580–4232, fax 0171/436–6341. Tube: Tottenham Court Road. Walk north on Tottenham Court Rd., turn right on Great Russell St., left on Bloomsbury St. 45 rooms, 13 with bath. English breakfast. AE, MC, V.*

Jenkins Hotel. If you're afraid of or allergic to dogs, move on to the next review. The Jenkins is home to two big, friendly Labradors, Charlie and Georgie, and two friendly humans, Felicity and Sam. Rooms are nicely furnished and all have a TV, phone, fridge, and tea- and coffee-making facilities. Singles cost £39 (£52 with bath), doubles £52 (£62 with bath), and triples with bath are £76. If the entrance looks familiar, it's because it was featured in the Agatha Christie television series *Poirot*. *45 Cartwright Gardens, WC1H, tel. 0171/387–2067, fax 0171/383–3139. Tube: King's Cross. Walk north on Tottenham Court Rd., turn right on Great Russell St., left on Bloomsbury St. 15 rooms, 7 with bath. English breakfast. MC, V.*

Repton Hotel. The Repton, on a breezy road between Bloomsbury and Russell squares, has small but well-equipped rooms—note the TVs, phones, and tea- and coffee-making facilities. If you want the Georgian terrace experience in central London, this is your best and cheapest bet. It's in high demand, so call ahead. Singles cost £45–£48, doubles £55, and dorm beds £15 per person. *31 Bedford Pl., WC1B, tel. 0171/436–4922, fax 0171/636–7045. Tube: Russell Square. Exit station to the left, turn left on Herbrand St., quick right on Guilford St., left on Southampton Row, right on Russell Sq., left on Bedford Pl. 29 rooms, all with bath. Continental breakfast. MC, V.*

St. Margaret's. This hotel has been run by a friendly Italian family for years. The spacious rooms, towering ceilings, and prime location by Russell Square are the main draws. The back rooms have pleasant garden views. Singles cost £41, doubles £52 (£66 with bath), slightly less for multinight stays. *24 Bedford Pl., WC1B, tel. 0171/636–4277, fax 0171/323–3066. Tube: Russell Square. Exit station to left, turn left on Herbrand St., quick right on Guilford St., left on Southampton Row, right on Russell Sq., left on Bedford Pl. 64 rooms, 6 with bath. English breakfast.*

EARL'S COURT

The area around Earl's Court and Gloucester Road tube stations has the highest concentration of inexpensive lodging in London. Unfortunately, the rooms are also some of the skankiest, though we've tried to pick some winners for you. If you want to troll the neighborhood for bargains, try **Hogarth Road, Earl's Court Gardens, Penywern Road,** and **Eardley Crescent**; all are chockablock with budget sleeping options. Once you're settled you can explore the area's fast-food restaurants and pubs and laugh with glee at how close you are to the museums in neighboring South Kensington. The tiny **Sara Hotel** (15 Eardley Crescent, SW5, tel. 0171/244–9500, fax 0171/381–0180) has 12 rooms (all with bath), which go for around £40 per double.

➤ **UNDER £40** • **The Albert Hotel.** Just down the street from Kensington Gardens, this old house serves as an inviting, inexpensive haven for London travelers. Rooms come in many shapes and sizes: singles (£26), doubles (£35), four- to six-person rooms (£12.50–£13.50 per person), and 9- to 11-bed dorm rooms (£10 per person). Beds are given on a first-come, first-served basis. *191 Queen's Gate, SW7, tel. 0171/584–3019. Tube: Gloucester Rd. Walk east 3 blocks on Cromwell Rd., turn left on Queen's Gate. 30 rooms, 22 with bath; 32 dorm beds. Continental breakfast.*

Fieldcourt House. The Fieldcourt is a grand old Victorian place with clean, pleasant rooms and befuddled French management. Add a number of permanent residents (who have their tab picked up by the dole), and you'll agree that all it's missing is Barton Fink. Singles cost £15 (£90 weekly), doubles £28 (£170 weekly), triples £39, and quads £48. *32 Courtfield Gardens, SW5, tel. 0171/373–0153. Tube: Earl's Court. Walk south 2 blocks on Earl's Court Rd., turn left on Barkston Gardens (which becomes Courtfield Gardens). 40 rooms, none with bath. Continental breakfast.*

Green Court Hotel. The "green" in Green Court is the management's fondness for plastic potted flowers. Rooms here are extremely worn but clean, and each is furnished with TV, phone, and clashing floral fabrics. For the price, it's the best of the crew of bargain-basement digs on Hogarth Road. Singles run £16–£22, doubles £32, and triples £42. *52 Hogarth Rd., SW5, tel. 0171/370–0853, fax 0171/370–3998. Tube: Earl's Court. Cross Earl's Court Rd., turn right on Hogarth Rd. 26 rooms, 24 with bath. Continental breakfast. AE, MC, V.*

Hunter's Lodge Hotel. There's absolutely nothing fancy or luxurious about this low-key hotel, but the bathrooms are clean and the staff is friendly. Singles cost £20 (£30 with bath), doubles £28 (£45 with bath), and triples £36 (£55 with bath). They also offer dorm beds for £10 per night (£60 weekly). *38 Trebovir Rd., SW5, tel. 0171/373–7331. Tube: Earl's Court. Walk north 1 block on Earl's Court Rd., turn left on Trebovir Rd. 26 rooms, 6 with bath. English breakfast. AE, MC, V.*

Rasool Court Hotel. Though this place looks frightfully upscale from the outside, its clean but bland rooms are reasonably priced. Singles are £26 (£29–£32 with bath), doubles £37 (£40–£43 with bath), and all rooms come with a TV and phone. Graffiti carved into the doors of the shared bathrooms testifies to its popularity with legions of horny backpackers from around the world. *19–21 Penywern Rd., SW5, tel. 0171/373–8900 or 0171/373–4893, fax 0171/244–6835. Tube: Earl's Court. Exit Underground at Warwick Rd., walk south ½ block, turn left on Penywern Rd. 57 rooms, 20 with bath. Continental breakfast. AE, MC, V.*

➤ **UNDER £60** • **Magnolia Hotel.** This family-run guest house, just south of Earl's Court in Chelsea, is immaculate, quiet, secure, and pleasantly furnished. Rooms, many with new TVs, are small but full of homey touches. Best of all, it's spitting distance from the trendy shopping paradise of King's Road. The only drawback is that it's a long trek from the nearest tube station. Singles are £33–£43, doubles £43–£56. *104–105 Oakley St., SW3, tel. 0171/352–0187. Tube: Sloane Square. Walk SW about ¾ mi on King's Rd., turn left on Oakley St.; or take Bus 11, 19, 22, 211, 249, or 319. 20 rooms, 10 with bath. English breakfast. AE, MC, V.*

Philbeach Hotel. This 19th-century building houses London's best established gay hotel, as well as a bar and a restaurant called **Wilde About Oscar.** And, it occasionally hosts diversions like cabaret shows and garden parties. Singles are £45 (£50 with bath), doubles £55 (£60 with bath). *30–31 Philbeach Gardens, SW5, tel. 0171/373–1244 or 0171/373–4544, fax 0171/244–0149. Tube: Earl's Court. Follow directions to Beaver Hotel (see below). 35 rooms, 18 with bath. Continental breakfast. AE, MC, V.*

➤ **UNDER £70** • **Beaver Hotel.** If you're looking to splash out in Earl's Court, book at the Beaver. It's on a charming, tree-lined street of late-Victorian town houses. Rooms, all with TV and phone, are spiffy and modern, and you get access to lounges with cable TV, a self-serve bar, and pool table. No wonder they sell T-shirts (£8). Private-bath singles are £49, doubles £65; a few shared-bath singles are £28, doubles £40. *57–59 Philbeach Gardens, SW5, tel. 0171/373–4553, fax 0171/373–4555. Tube: Earl's Court. Exit Underground on Warwick Rd., walk north 1 block, turn left on Philbeach Gardens. 38 rooms, 30 with bath. English breakfast. AE, MC, V.*

NORTH LONDON

For a taste of bohemian suburbia (i.e., nice neighborhoods with cool cafés) and a homier and less-touristy atmosphere than Earl's Court or Bayswater, try the neighborhoods north of central London, which roughly encompass the massive expanse of trees, ponds, and rolling hills known as the Heath. You may have to sit on the tube an extra few stops or even catch a bus to central London, but that's the price you pay for a quieter, more residential, less stressful experience. Hotel rates are about the same in north London as in most other areas, but you're more likely to get what you pay for here.

If you want a taste of English country–style living while still being near central London, definitely contact the **Primrose Hill Agency.** This small B&B association believes that "travel shouldn't be a rip-off"; to prove it, they book guests into beautiful family homes at reasonable rates—£20–£30 per person in single or double rooms. All houses are in or around leafy Primrose Hill and Hampstead, where you'll find London's best parks. Expect cozy rooms, your own latchkey, and scrumptious breakfasts. There's a three-night minimum, and you should book ahead to be safe. *Contact Gail O'Farrell, 14 Edis St., London, NW1 8LG, tel. 0171/722–6869, fax 0171/916–2240. 25 rooms in various locations.*

➤ **UNDER £40** • **Five Kings Guest House.** Although the surrounding neighborhood is quintessentially residential, you're only 15 minutes by foot from both Camden and the Heath. The friendly proprietors run a tight ship—nothing fancy, but very inviting. Singles are £20 (£27 with bath), doubles £32 (£38 with bath). *59 Anson Rd., Kentish Town, N7, tel. 0171/607–3996 or 0171/607–6466. Tube: Tufnell Park. Turn left on Brecknock Rd., left on Anson Rd. 16 rooms, 10 with bath. English breakfast. MC, V.*

Kandara Guest House. The main reason to stay here is location—just a short bus ride from the heart of lively Islington. The guest house is small and tidy, with recently remodeled singles (£26), doubles (£36), and triples (£46). This is a much better bet than the nearby Elena Hotel. *68 Ockendon Rd., Islington, N1, tel. 0171/226–5721 or 0171/226–3379. Tube: Angel. From station, take Bus 38, 56, 73, or 171A NE on Essex Rd. to Ockendon Rd. 10 rooms, none with bath. English breakfast. MC, V.*

➤ **UNDER £50** • **The Oxford Arms.** This traditional pub and inn is the place to stay if you want a neighborhood atmosphere and easy access to local brew. The double rooms (£40) are equipped with showers and toilets, and the lone single (£26) has a shower and a toilet down the hall. All rooms feature TVs and tea- and coffee-making equipment. Depending on your cholesterol level, the lack of a cooked breakfast may be a blessing or a curse—but they do offer self-service cold cereal. *21 Halliford St., Islington, N1, tel. 0171/226–6629. Tube: Angel. From station, take Bus 38, 56, 73, or 171A NE up Essex Rd. to Halliford St. 5 rooms.*

Parkland Walk Guest House. The luxurious Parkland Walk is near Crouch End, which is an ideal escape for people who prefer country living to life in the hectic city. Modern renovations haven't sanitized the style and character of the Parkland, nor have they obstructed the great views of London. The fresh, delicious food is yet another reason to come. Singles are £26 (£32 with bath), doubles £46 (£55 with bath), a bit less if you stay more than two nights. *12 Hornsey Rise Gardens, N19, tel. 0171/263–3228, fax 0171/831–9489. Tube: Archway or Finsbury Park. From Archway, take Bus 41 to Crouch End. From Finsbury Park, take Bus 210 to Crouch End. 6 rooms, 4 with bath. English breakfast, no smoking. Reservations advised.*

Hostels

England's **Youth Hostel Association (YHA)** (tel. 0171/248–6547 or fax 0171/236–7681 for reservations) operates seven hostels in central London (some are more central than others) and a number out in the boonies (only one of which is really accessible by tube). These Formica-and-linoleum wonders tend to be clean to the point of sterility. Even if the outside looks cool, it's a safe bet that the rooms are basic and bland and packed to the rafters with space-age bunk beds. None of the seven YHA hostels listed below have a lockout, only Highgate Village has a curfew, and the reception desks are usually open daily 7 AM–11 PM, though some provide 24-hour access. Purchase a YHA membership card at any hostel for £9.30 (£3.20 under 18), or pay an extra £1.55 per night for a guest stamp; after accruing six stamps you're granted full membership. **Astor,** a private hostel firm, runs three places in London that cater to international cheapo travelers; show your ISIC card to shave 10% off the tab. Astor also provides free continental breakfasts of juice, cereal, and toast. Wherever you stay, reservations are *imperative* June through August, particularly if you want a single or double room in one of the few hostels that offer such things (don't let this scare you, but many are booked solid for summer by the end of May). Unless otherwise noted, the non-YHA hostels listed below do not have curfews or lockouts and are open 24 hours for check-in.

You do not need a YHA hostel card if you already have a Hostelling International (HI) card. In England the two cards are essentially interchangeable.

Some London B&Bs also offer dorm-style accommodations in addition to their more expensive singles and doubles. B&Bs can be a welcome respite from snoring bunk mates, noisy school groups, and 8 AM wake-up calls. The following B&Bs charge £10–£15 for dorm beds and are reviewed above: **The Albert Hotel** (*see* Earl's Court, *above*), **Elizabeth House (YWCA)** (*see* Around Victoria Station, *above*), **Hunter's Lodge** (*see* Earl's Court, *above*), and **Repton Hotel** (*see* Bloomsbury and King's Cross, *above*).

Chelsea Hotel. This huge Earl's Court hostel is incredibly popular with backpackers, and for good reason: Rooms (though worn) are clean and cheap, from the dorm rooms (beds £10) to singles (£16), doubles (£25–£27), triples (£36), and quads (£44). But wait, there's more, including a common room with a video games, a pool table, CD jukebox, and special party nights. They'll even haul your ass from Victoria Station by minibus (free). *33–41 Earl's Court Sq., SW5, tel. 0171/244–6892 or 0171/244–7395, fax 0171/244–6891. Tube: Earl's Court. Walk south 3 blocks on Earl's Court Rd., turn right on Earl's Court Sq. 180 beds. Continental breakfast, laundry, luggage storage (£1), safe deposit boxes (50p).*

City of London Hostel (YHA). Formerly the home of the St. Paul's boys choir, this hostel has a great location in the middle of town. Unfortunately, it has zip for character and attracts more of a middle-aged set than comparable budget accommodations. Dorm beds cost £16–£23 per person (£12.50–£19.15 under 18), depending on the number of beds in the room; doubles are £40.50, triples £56. *36–38 Carter Ln., EC4, tel. 0171/236–4965, fax 0171/236–7681. Tube: Blackfriars or St. Paul's. From Blackfriars, walk east on Queen Victoria St., turn left on St. Andrew's Hill, right on Carter Ln. From St. Paul's, follow signs to cathedral, cross in front of cathedral entrance to Dean's Ct., turn right on Carter Ln. 191 beds. English breakfast, laundry, luggage storage. MC, V.*

Earl's Court (YHA). From the outside, this Victorian town house turned hostel looks deceptively small and cozy. Inside you'll find up to a dozen beds stuffed into each of the institutional-looking dorm rooms. You won't get sparkly clean bathrooms, but you will get convenience to the tube, a giant common room, and an in-house tourist info center where you can make travel arrangements or buy theater tickets. Beds cost £17.70 (£15.55 under 18). *38 Bolton Gardens, SW5, tel. 0171/373–7083, fax 0171/835–2034. Tube: Earl's Court. Walk south approx. 6 blocks on Earl's Court Rd., turn left on Bolton Gardens. 155 beds. Bureau de change, continental breakfast, kitchen, laundry, lockers (bring lock), safe deposit boxes. MC, V.*

The Generator. This new hostel is easily the grooviest in town, with a friendly, funky vibe, lots of young people, and vibrant decor—blue neon and brushed-steel decor downstairs and upstairs dorm rooms painted in bright blue and orange. The Generator Bar has cheap drinks, and the Fuel Stop cafeteria provides inexpensive meals. Rooms are simple but clean; singles are £37, doubles £44, dorm beds £17.50–£18.50. *MacNaghten House, Compton Pl., WC1H, tel. 0171/388–7666, fax 0171/388–7644, generator@lhdr.demon.co.uk. Tube: Russell Square. Turn right on Bernard St., left on Marchmont St., right on Tavistock Pl., left on Compton Pl. 800 beds. Bar, cafeteria, continental breakfast, luggage storage, TV lounge. MC, V.*

Hampstead Heath (YHA). This great hostel is well out of the hustle and bustle of central London yet convenient to the tube. The grounds are beautiful (only Holland Park's are comparable), and on sunny days you can play in nearby Hampstead Heath. Doubles are £35.40, dorm beds £14.40 (£12.30 under 18) or £17.20 (£15.10 under 18). *4 Wellgarth Rd., NW11, tel. 0181/458–9054, fax 0181/209–0546. Tube: Golders Green. Walk SE on North End Rd., turn left on Wellgarth Rd. 200 beds. Bureau de change, English breakfast, kitchen, laundry, TV lounge. MC, V.*

Highgate Village (YHA). If you're not bothered by a midnight curfew, this hostel will reward you with lodgings in an attractive Georgian house in a quiet neighborhood. It's also just a hop, skip, and jump away from Highgate Cemetery, the Heath, and the Flask (a cool pub just up the road). Dorm beds cost a mere £12.25 (£8.50 under 18), so reservations are a good idea. It's a long uphill trek from the Archway tube station, or you can take Bus 143, 210, or 271 to the top of Highgate Hill. *84 Highgate West Hill, N6, tel. 0181/340–1831, fax 0181/341–0376. Tube: Archway. Walk north on Highgate Hill, turn left on South Grove. 70 beds. Midnight curfew. Reception open 7 AM–midnight. Kitchen, TV lounge. MC, V.*

Holland House/King George VI Memorial Youth Hostel (YHA). Here's a hostel with a funky twist: It incorporates part of a Jacobean mansion, and it's set right in the middle of woodsy Holland Park. Unfortunately, it's also a hike from the nearest tube station. For £17.70 per person (£15.55 under 18) you can take a spot in the 12- or 20-bed dorm rooms, or scrap for the single and double rooms (there's one of each). *Holland Walk, Kensington, W8, tel. 0171/937–0748, fax 0171/376–0667. Tube: High Street Kensington or Holland Park. From High Street Kensington, walk west on Kensington High St., turn right on Holland Walk; or take Bus 9, 9A, 10, 27, 28, or 49 west to Commonwealth Institute, then walk north on Holland Walk. From Holland Park, walk east on Holland Park Ave., turn right on Holland Walk. 201 beds. English breakfast, kitchen, laundry, lockers (bring lock), luggage storage (£1.50). MC, V.*

Museum Inn Hostel (Astor). The best thing about this hostel is its location, right across the street from the British Museum and convenient for exploring Bloomsbury and the West End. Dorm beds in rooms that have seen much better days are £13–£15 per person; doubles are £32–£34. *27 Montague St., WC1, tel. 0171/580–5360, fax 0171/589–1590. Tube: Tottenham Court Road. Walk north on Tottenham Court Rd., turn right on Great Russell St., left on Montague St. 64 beds. Continental breakfast, key deposit (£5), kitchen, safe deposit boxes. MC, V.*

Oxford Street (YHA). The big draw at this hostel is its location: smack in the center of hip Soho. It's so convenient (imagine staggering home from the pubs instead of dealing with the tube) you'll overlook the cramped rooms. You'll also battle hordes of other backpackers who want to stay here, so make reservations. Beds go for £17.30 (£14.10 under 18); most rooms are doubles, triples and quads. *14 Noel St., W1, tel. 0171/734–1618, fax 0171/734–1657. Tube: Oxford Circus. Walk east on Oxford St., turn right on Poland St., left on Noel St. Bureau de change, kitchen, lockers, luggage storage, TV lounge. 82 beds. MC, V.*

Palace Hotel. This tidy, cheerful Bayswater hostel just completed a major renovation of its kitchen and bathrooms, now with sparkling new loos. It's situated just north of Kensington Gardens on a pleasant street lined with redbrick buildings. Beds in the six- to eight-bed dorms are £10. November–May they offer an amazing weekly rate of £50. Reservations are strongly recommended June–August. *31 Palace Ct., W2, tel. 0171/221–5628, fax 0171/243–8159. Tube: Notting Hill Gate. Walk east on Notting Hill Gate (which becomes Bayswater Rd.), turn left on Palace Ct. 74 beds. Continental breakfast, key deposit (£2), safe deposit boxes.*

Quest Hostel (Astor). This private hostel near the Queensway tourist strip is a fun place to stay: It has a roomy lounge with TV/VCR and pool table, plus an exceptionally friendly staff. The lone double costs £30, while four- to eight-bed dorm rooms cost £14 per person. Year-round they offer a limited number of beds for £63 per week; reserve far in advance. *45 Queensborough Terr., W2, tel. 0171/229–7782, fax 0171/727–8106. Tube: Bayswater or Queensway. From Bayswater, turn right on Queensway, left on Bayswater Rd., left on Queensborough Terr. From Queensway, walk east on Bayswater Rd., turn left on Queensborough Terr. 98 beds. Continental breakfast, kitchen, safe deposit boxes. MC, V.*

Rotherhithe (YHA). Although this hostel is really cool architecturally, it's tucked away near the Docklands, quite a trek from central London. Fortunately, the neighborhood is interesting in its own right and the rooms, while pretty shrimpy, all have private baths. Doubles are £45.50 and dorm beds are £14.45–£20.15 (£11.40–£17.10 under 18), depending upon the number of beds in the room. Until the East London Underground Line reopens in August 1997, you'll have to take an orange bus marked "ELT" that drives along the route. The ELT stops in front of the hostel (the "ELX" does not). *Island Yard, Salter Rd., SE16, tel. 0171/232–2114, fax 0171/237–2919. Tube: Rotherhithe. Walk NE on Brunel Rd. (which becomes Salter Rd.). Bureau de change, laundry, restaurant. Wheelchair access. MC, V.*

Victoria Hotel (Astor). The Victoria, less than 500 yards from Victoria Station, is terrific if you just want to collapse at the end of a long journey. Rooms are small and dark, and the carpets are threadbare, but at least it's cheap: Dorm beds cost £12.50–£14 daily, £65 weekly. The common room is crowded, smoky, loud, and congenial, like a cool pub without the beer. *71 Belgrave Rd., SW1, tel. 0171/834–3077, fax 0171/932–0693. Tube: Victoria. Walk south on Buckingham Palace Rd., turn left on Eccleston Bridge (which becomes Belgrave Rd.). 70 beds. Kitchen, safe deposit boxes, TV lounge. MC, V.*

Student Housing

Many university residence halls earn some extra pounds by throwing their doors open to backpackers and the great unwashed during school vacations. Life in college dorms will give you the pleasure of rubbing shoulders with like-minded young expatriates, but the most significant advantage is location: Student housing is often in northwest Bloomsbury, an easy 10-minute walk from London's West End. Though the dorms are often spartan, they are usually much cleaner than cheap hotels, and you get access to such amenities as saunas, tennis courts, laundry rooms, kitchens, gyms, and cheap eats at university pubs and cafeterias. These places fill up fast in summer, and reservations are a must. Student identification, however, is not: Nonstudents typically pay a small supplement (a pound or two a night) to stay in dorms. If you're having trouble finding space in one of the following student dorms, contact the **Vacation Bureau** at King's College (127 Stamford St., SE1, tel. 0171/836–5454). It offers bed and breakfast in six halls around central London, April 13–May 4 and June 14–September 16 in 1997. The student rate for a single room is £14; nonstudents pay £17–£23. There's no minimum stay, and a 10% discount by the week. Unless otherwise specified, the following dorms rent available space year-round.

Campbell House. This is definitely one of London's nicer residence halls. The rooms are large (especially the doubles), many have fireplaces, and those in the back overlook a pleasant courtyard. Excellent kitchen facilities make this a great place to settle in for a while. Singles cost £16 nightly, £100 weekly; doubles are £28 nightly, £185 weekly. *5–10 Taviton St., WC1, tel. 0171/391–1479, fax 0171/388–0060. Tube: Euston Square. Walk east on Euston Rd., turn right on Gordon St., left on Endsleigh Gardens, right on Taviton St. 100 rooms, none with bath. Kitchen, laundry.*

Canterbury Hall. The attractive wood-paneled lobby goes a long way toward disguising the building's true nature as an apartment block. An advantage is that most bathrooms are shared by only two or three rooms. Singles cost £21.15 with breakfast, £25 with breakfast and dinner. Students with ID pay only £17.50 for bed, breakfast, and dinner. *12–18 Cartwright Gardens (address not marked on building), WC1, tel. 0171/387–5526, fax 0171/383–7729. Tube: King's Cross. Walk west on Euston Rd., turn left on Mabledon Pl. 228 rooms, none with bath. English breakfast, kitchen, laundry, tennis courts. Open mid-Mar.–mid-Apr. and June 10–Aug. 15.*

Central University of Iowa Hostel. Nestled amongst the B&Bs on Bedford Place, this spot has an excellent location and simple, clean rooms. Dorm beds are £16 in a three- or four-person room, £18 in a two-person room. *7 Bedford Pl., WC1, tel. 0171/580–1121, fax 0171/580–5638. Tube: Russell Square. Exit station to the left, turn left on Herbrand St., quick right on Guilford St., left on Southampton Row, right on Russell Sq., left on Bedford Pl. 31 beds. Reception open 8–8 (sometimes closed 1–3). Check-in 11 AM. Continental breakfast, kitchen, laundry, TV lounge. Open mid-May–mid-Aug. MC, V.*

Centre Français. This Bayswater outpost of the Centre Français language-school chain offers cheap, clean lodging for weary francophiles. Practice saying "*J'aime les croissants*" and "*Vive* *la France!"* with those who've come here to master "scones with marmalade, please" and "God save the queen." Singles are £26.50 (£159 weekly), doubles £42 (£252 weekly), triples and quads £18 per person (£108 per person weekly). Dorm beds are £15 each (£87 weekly). *61– 69 Chepstow Pl., W2, tel. 0171/221–8134. Tube: Notting Hill Gate. Walk north on Pembridge Rd., turn right on Pembridge Sq., left on Chepstow Pl. 169 beds. Laundry.*

College Hall. This hall in the center of London's student ghetto gives you easy access to university pubs and facilities—it's across the street from the student union and just down the block from Dillon's bookstore. Students can stay in singles for £15 with breakfast, £18 with breakfast and dinner. Nonstudents pay £20 with breakfast, £25 with breakfast and dinner. *Malet St., WC1, tel. 0171/580–9131, fax 0171/636–6591. Tube: Goodge Street or Russell Square. From Goodge St., turn left on Tottenham Court Rd., right on Torrington Pl., right on Malet St. From Russell Square, walk SW across square to Montague Pl., turn right on Malet St. 200 rooms, none with bath. English breakfast, laundry, library, no smoking, TV room. Open mid-June–mid-Aug.*

Commonwealth Hall. Fringe benefits in this modern (read: ugly) high-rise dorm include the use of the library, Ping-Pong table, tennis courts, and bar. Singles are £18.50, £22.50 with dinner. *1–11 Cartwright Gardens (address not marked on building), WC1, tel. 0171/387– 0311, fax 0171/383–4375. Tube: King's Cross. Walk west on Euston Rd., turn left on Mabledon Pl. 420 rooms, none with bath. English breakfast, kitchen, laundry. Open June– late Aug.*

Connaught Hall. This newly refurbished residence hall overlooks pleasant Tavistock Square. Singles cost £17, £20 with dinner; nonstudents add £3. *36–45 Tavistock Sq., WC1, tel. 0171/387–4120 (front desk) or 0171/387–6181 (reservations), fax 0171/383-4109. Tube: Euston or Russell Square. From Euston, walk SW on Eversholt St. From Russell Sq., walk NW on Woburn Pl. 200 rooms, none with bath. English breakfast, kitchen, laundry, TV. Open July 1–mid-Sept.*

Hughes Parry Hall. This high-rise dorm has basic, clean singles for £20.50 with breakfast, £24 with breakfast and dinner. *19–26 Cartwright Gardens, WC1, tel. 0171/387–1477, fax 0171/383–4328. Tube: King's Cross. Walk west on Euston Rd., turn left on Mabledon Pl. 300 rooms, none with bath. Bar, English breakfast, laundry, library, pool table, tennis courts. Open mid-Mar.–mid-Apr. and June 27–late Aug.*

International Hall. The building is uninspired, but you're near Russell Square and the Renoir, a good arty film house. Singles go for £17.50 with breakfast and dinner; nonstudents add £2. *Brunswick Sq., WC1, tel. 0171/837–0746, fax 0171/278–9720. Tube: Russell Square. Turn right on Bernard St., left on Brunswick Sq. 535 rooms, none with bath. Bar, laundry, TV lounge.*

International Student House. This fun, monstrously huge establishment sits at the southeast corner of Regent's Park, right across from Great Portland Street tube station. Popular with international students, this place fills up fast despite its size, and reservations are almost obligatory. A dorm bed in a clean four-bunk room costs £14; a bed in an "economy" dorm with six or more beds is £10. Singles are £24, doubles £39. The best deal, however, is for stays of three months or longer: If you pay in advance for an entire month, a dorm bed costs a mere £42 a week without breakfast. *229 Great Portland St., W1, tel. 0171/631–8300, fax 0171/636–8315. Tube: Great Portland Street. 120 short-term beds. Bar, continental breakfast, fitness center, key deposit (£10), laundry, restaurant. MC, V.*

John Adams Hall. This group of Georgian houses has been converted into student lodging, and rooms are available at bargain rates during school vacations. Though there's nothing luxurious about the complex or the small and dim (but clean) rooms, the residence is only a short walk from the British Museum and Euston Station. Singles are £21.40, doubles £37, less if you stay a week or more. *15–23 Endsleigh St., WC1, tel. 0171/387–4086 or 0171/387–4796 (ask for Ms. Stubbs), fax 0171/383–0164. Tube: Euston Square. Walk west on Euston Rd., turn right on Gordon St., left on Endsleigh Gardens, right on Endsleigh St. 151 rooms, none with bath. English breakfast, laundry. Open July–mid-Sept. MC, V.*

Camping

Camping in London is a weird enough idea to be interesting, and if you don't mind a longish commute, it's practical, too. God knows, it's cheap enough. Both Tent City locations are actually inside Zones 1 and 2, which is great for Travelcard holders (*see* Getting Around, By Underground and Bus, in Chapter 1). Halfway there, the Underground trip turns into a pleasant train ride through the country. The campgrounds do fill up in the summer months, so call ahead.

Lee Valley Cycle Circuit and Campsite. This 48-acre nature reserve doubles as a cycling racetrack. It's a 20-minute tube ride from central London and a 15-minute walk from the station, so stock up on groceries before coming; the only thing nearby is an expensive snack bar in the sports center across the street. The rates are £5 per person, and you have to bring your own tent. Reservations are a good idea in July and August. *Temple Mill Ln., E15, tel. 0181/534–6085. Tube: Lepton. From station, turn left and follow Lepton High Rd. to first set of traffic lights, turn right on Temple Mill Ln. and follow it around the turn to the right. 100 sites. Reception open 8–7. Laundry, luggage storage, showers, toilets. Open mid-Mar.–mid-Oct.*

Tent City Acton. Have you ever want to live the *M*A*S*H* experience? This west London institution has 450 cots in 14 large tents spread across Wormwood Scrubs. You can choose between men's, women's, and mixed tents, or else pitch your own tent for the same daily price of £5.50. A fun and friendly crowd comes here, and all profits go to Tree of Life, a charity that works to revitalize the community. *Old Oak Common Ln., W3, tel. 0181/743–5708. Tube: East Acton. Walk NE on Erconwald St., turn left on Wulfstan St. (which merges with Old Oak Common Ln.). 450 beds. Kitchen, laundry, luggage storage, showers, snack bar, toilets. Open June–early Sept.*

Tent City Hackney. This huge park on the outskirts of London is ideal for cheap sleeping in a small enclosed grove. Formerly called Hackney Camping, it recently joined forces with the Tent City folks and now donates all its profits to charity. BYOT (bring your own tent) and camp for a mere £5 per person, or call ahead and try to get one of the 30 dorm beds. *Millfields Rd., E5, tel. 0181/985–7656. Tube: Liverpool Street. From station, take Bus 22A to Millfields and Mandeville Sts., cross bridge, and follow signs. 200 sites, 30 dorm beds. Luggage storage, showers, snack bar, toilets. Open June–Aug.*

Longer Stays

London may be one of the world's most overtouristed cities, but it's also a damn fine place to live, attracting students, writers, artists, and other international folks in droves. While this is great for the town's cosmopolitan flair, it leads to one pressing question: Is it even remotely possible to find a cheap flat? Yes and no. If you arrive on a Saturday and expect to rent something cheap by Monday, you're utterly mad. But if you have a bit of time and money, you will inevitably find something suitable. The trick is, you'll probably have to camp out in a hostel (or on a friend's couch, if you're lucky) for a week or two to conduct a proper housing search.

One warning: The competition for living space is fiercest in September, when London universities start their terms and students are desperate for a place to call home.

If you're just looking for a place to crash for a few weeks to a month or two, consider a university hall (*see* Student Housing, *above*); rates are typically around £100 per week. Additionally, many hotels and hostels offer cheap weekly rates, even if they don't advertise them—should you find a place that seems cool, it doesn't hurt to ask. One option for females aged 18–25 is the **Earl's Court YWCA** (227 Earl's Court Rd., SW5 9BL, tel. 0171/373–2851, fax 0171/370–5275), which offers semi-private rooms (with kitchen, bath, and shared common room) for £67.40 per week. However, you must stay a minimum of six months and undergo a lengthy application process. Send them an SASE for more info and an application.

Otherwise, your options for renting include a **bedsit** (very modest studios, where you have your own teensy "kitchenette" but share toilet and shower with three or four other people), **studio** (self-contained living spaces with combo living room/bedroom/kitchen, plus bath), or **flat** (apartment with separate bedroom, kitchen, and bath). Generally, these are all advertised by their weekly rate. Most places will ask for one or two weeks' rent as deposit and require a minimum stay of three months (bedsits) to six months (studios and flats). You can get a room for as little as £50 a week if you don't mind having your bathtub in the kitchen and living behind train tracks in Zone 3 or 4. Though this has a certain romantic ring to it, you'd be better off paying £60–£90 a week for accommodations in central London—you'll still have to shower in the sink, but at least you'll live within a short walk of the tube in Zone 1 or 2. Keep in mind that the farther you live from the city center, the more expensive your monthly tube pass will be: Anything beyond Zone 3 will cost you so much money and time that you might as well live in Paris.

PUBLICATIONS The best newspaper for finding a home is *Loot* (£1.30), which appears at local newsstands six times a week (it's a different color each day). Since it's free to place an ad in *Loot,* it often has the best—and the cheapest—selection of flats and bedsits in London; it also has special sections on student housing and short-term stays. Otherwise, *TNT* (free; published every Monday) offers a good selection, while the classifieds of the weekday newspaper the *Evening Standard* (30p) are a bit less helpful.

ACCOMMODATION SERVICES Accommodation services are terrific if you're an impatient, type A person, or if you don't know the city well enough to conduct a search on your own; they advertise in the publications described above. Know that many services charge a fee of one or two weeks' rent that is usually nonrefundable and payable *before* you see your first prospect. Sounds like a raw deal, doesn't it? And so it is. However, **Jenny Jones Accommodation Agency** (40 S. Molton St., W1, tel. 0171/493–4801), in Mayfair, is a *no-fee* agency—it charges the landlord instead of bleeding poor folks like you dry. Another option is **Kensington Studios** (39 Thurloe St., SW7, tel. 0171/581–8292), which specializes in central and west London. It charges a £49 registration fee and then makes appointments for you with prospective landlords; if you fail to find a place after three months it'll refund your money. **Flatsearch** (31 King's Rd., SW3, tel. 0171/730–7888) doesn't do bedsits, but it'll set you up with a studio or flat for a fee of one-and-a-half week's rent.

FOOD

4

By Jennifer L. Brewer and Sunny Delaney

There are more than 8,000 restaurants in London, many serving so-called British cuisine. Though the phrase "traditional English food" stereotypically means a stale shepherd's pie, greasy sausages, and soggy peas, it can also mean a delicate seafood dinner that even a gourmet would approve of. Of course, that seafood dinner may cost upwards of £15, so if you're on a strict budget, you're more likely to explore the greasy depths of pub grub, chips (what Americans call french fries), and deep-fried burgers.

Then again, in London you can also choose from a nearly endless variety of ethnic cuisine—one of the benefits of the city's having been an imperial capital with far-flung dominions. Italian, Continental, and Middle Eastern restaurants are ubiquitous; other regional cuisines cluster in particular parts of London. You'll find Bengali on Spitalfields's **Brick Lane** (Tube: Aldgate East), Indian on Bloomsbury's **Drummond Street** (Tube: Euston Square), and Vietnamese on **Lisle Street** (Tube: Piccadilly Circus). Wander along **Gerrard Street,** in Soho, and enter a Hong Kong street scene with crates of fresh produce, skinned ducks hanging in shop windows, and the omnipresent stench of yesterday's fish.

British food has been described as cold, fattening, unhealthy, expensive, life-threatening, tear-provoking, and gut-wrenching—literally. Some restaurants seem to be in cahoots with the pharmaceutical companies.

Trouble is, London is expensive. The cheapest sit-down meals cost at least £4, more likely £6–£9. If you want any sort of ambience you'll pay £8–£14, not including the cover charge (50p–£1) that some restaurants add to the bill. Usually that vexatious 17.5% VAT (Value Added Tax) is already included in the prices, but you may want to read the menu just to be sure. Some restaurants also include a mandatory service charge; inspect the check to avoid paying twice. Otherwise, the standard tip is 10%.

Any lengthy stay in London requires a strategy for eating on the cheap—like making lunch the biggest meal of the day to take advantage of discounted lunch specials. London's pubs (*see* Chapter 5) typically serve soups and sandwiches for less than £5, and fish and chips or steak and peas for £4–£7. If you can't afford to eat out all the time, acquaint yourself with ubiquitous London department store **Marks & Spencer** (*see* Department Stores, in Chapter 7), which sells surprisingly yummy and diverse prepared meals at decent prices. A good and relatively inexpensive grocery chain is **Sainsbury's,** with convenient locations at 158 Cromwell Road, Canal Way at Ladbroke Grove, and 4 Kings Gate Parade. You'll also find chains like **Safeway** and **Tesco** all over town. Alternatively, most of London's neighborhoods have regular fruit and vegetable markets (*see* Markets and Specialty Stores, *below*).

One final note: If you're looking for a specific restaurant but don't know which neighborhood it's in, check the handy index at the back of this book. If you're looking for a type of cuisine, check the reference listings at the end of this chapter.

Restaurants

BAYSWATER AND NOTTING HILL GATE

Bayswater is crowded with kebab joints, chippies, and mediocre delis that cater to an undemanding American tourist crowd. Good restaurants are a bit thin on the ground here, and those in the know join British trendsetters in Notting Hill Gate, which is a cut above Bayswater when it comes to food. If you're poking around Portobello Road, avoid the scary beef-burger vans and stop in at **The Grain Shop** (269B Portobello Rd., W11, tel. 0171/229–5571) for an ever-changing menu of stews and pasta dishes (£2–£4), quiche (£1.35), and yummy spinach pie (£1.20). *Make* room for a cheese croissant (£1).

➤ **UNDER £5 • Manzara.** This place doubles as a pâtisserie in the early hours, but come noon, the kitchen kicks into high gear and starts serving good-size portions of tasty Turkish food like grilled lamb with pine nuts on hummus (£3.35) and grilled chicken skewers with rice (£3.85). After 7 PM, splurge on their buffet (£6), where you pick what you want from an array of ingredients and the chef cooks it in front of you. *24 Pembridge Rd., W11, tel. 0171/727–3062. Tube: Notting Hill Gate. Walk north on Pembridge Rd. Open daily 8 AM–11:30 PM (Fri.–Sat. until midnight). AE, MC, V.*

Norman's. This neighborhood spot serves up simple café food in a friendly environment—the kind of place where diners at different tables strike up conversations with each other. Full English breakfasts run £2.70, and staples like omelets with chips (£2.40–£3), sandwiches (£1.15–£2), and spaghetti bolognese (£3.50) round out the menu. *7 Porchester Gardens, W2, tel. 0171/727–0278. Tube: Bayswater. Walk north on Queensway, turn left on Porchester Gardens. Open Mon.–Sat. 8:30 AM–11:30 PM, Sun. 8:30 AM–9:30 PM.*

Portobello Café. The staff can be a bit snippy, but this café has outside tables and a great location in the flea market area at the top of Portobello Road. Veggie chili with rice (£4.25) is good and spicy, or try one of their baguette sandwiches (£3.50–£4). The famished should order the Portobello Fry-up (£4.75), with two eggs, beans, mushrooms, tomatoes, and your choice of veggie or pork sausage. *305 Portobello Rd., W10, tel. 0171/969–1996. Tube: Ladbroke Grove. Walk left on Ladbroke Grove, turn right on Cambridge Gardens, left on Portobello Rd. Open daily 9:30–5:30 (Fri.–Sat. from 8).*

➤ **UNDER £10 • Churchill Thai Kitchen.** This excellent Thai restaurant is hidden in an enclosed patio at the rear of a traditional British pub. Chow on spicy *khao rad na ga prao* (rice with a choice of chicken, prawn, or meat sauce) or *kwaitiew pad thai* (Thai noodles with prawns), both for around £5. *Churchill Arms, 119 Kensington Church St., W8, tel. 0171/727–1246. Tube: Notting Hill Gate. Walk east on Notting Hill Gate, turn right on Kensington Church St. Open Mon.–Sat. 12:30–2:30 and 6–9:30, Sun. noon–2:30.*

No chippie worth its salt is open on Monday; with most fishermen sitting at home on Sunday, Monday's fish would be more than a day old.

Geales. If you fancy fish and chips, wildly popular Geales has been serving some of the best in London for more than 50 years. The homemade fish soup makes an excellent appetizer (£2); follow it with a small fillet of haddock, plaice, or cod for £4.50 and an order of chips (£1.20) or peas (£1). Huge fillets run £7.50–£8.50, depending on the market price of the fish. It's not hypergreasy either, despite the fact that Geales fries its fish in beef drippings. *2 Farmers St., W8, tel. 0171/727–7969. Tube: Notting Hill Gate. Walk west on Notting Hill Gate, turn left on Farmers St. Open Tues.–Sat. noon–3 and 6–11. AE, MC, V.*

Khan's. Cane chairs, high ceilings, and cool murals make this neighborhood institution a great place to linger over some of London's cheapest Indian food. Chicken *shahi* (in a mild curry sauce) costs a mere £3, lamb tikka £3.60, and the veggie curry is a steal at £2.50. Though you could easily fill up for less than £5, Khan's now has a minimum charge of £5.75 per person—eat up! *13–15 Westbourne Grove, W2, tel. 0171/727–5420. Tube: Bayswater or Queensway. From either station, walk north on Queensway, turn left on Westbourne Grove. Open daily noon–3 and 6 –midnight. AE, MC, V.*

Osteria Basilico. It's peopled with the painfully stylish, and you may hear more talk about cosmetic surgery than you might like, but the food at Basilico is worth listening to the tribulations of Fiona's nose job. Try the hearty and filling minestrone soup (£3.50), a variety of tasty pastas with tasty sauces (£5.20–£6.50), or pizza (£5.50–£6), which is also available for takeaway. *29 Kensington Park Rd., W11, tel. 0171/727–9372. Open weekdays 12:30–3 and 6:30–11, Sat. 12:30–4:30 and 6:30–11, Sun. 12:30–3:15 and 6:30–10:30.*

BLOOMSBURY

Once London's literary slum, Bloomsbury is now better known for its thriving Asian and Indian communities. Bloomsbury's cramped lanes and alleyways harbor the highest concentration of Indian restaurants in the United Kingdom. Near Euston station, **Drummond Street** is lined with East Indian curry houses and southern Indian vegetarian restaurants. A variety of cuisine is available on **Lamb's Conduit Street** and **Goodge Street.** Bloomsbury is also home to the original **Wagamama** (*see* Soho, *below*), if you need your ramen fix.

➢ **UNDER £5 • Anwars.** Superlow prices make this simple canteen especially popular with students from nearby colleges. Though the interior has seen better days (the 1970s, by the looks of things), the prices are right: You can get a bowl of chicken or meat curry (£2.80) and a large plate of rice (£1.20), or a yummy mutton biryani (£3). *64 Grafton Way, W1, tel. 0171/387–6664. Tube: Warren Street. Walk south on Tottenham Court Rd., turn right on Grafton Way. Open daily 11–11.*

Diwana Bhel Poori House. They serve up fresh southern Indian (read: vegetarian) cuisine on big plates at Diwana. Try the *thali,* a set meal with rice, dal, vegetables, chapatis, and pooris (£4.10), or come between noon and 2:30 daily for their all-you-can-eat buffet (£4). The mango milkshakes (£1.60) will kindly distract you from the Indian pop music whining in the background. *121–123 Drummond St., NW1, tel. 0171/387–5556. Tube: Euston. Walk right on Melton St., turn left on Drummond St. Open daily noon–midnight. BYOB. AE, MC, V.*

Greenhouse. This subterranean veggie heaven is located beneath the Drill Hall, a gay and lesbian theater and cultural center, and gets quite crowded just before performances. Main courses like lentil stew with rice or a pasta bake with veggies go for £4 and change daily; salads range from £1.10 to £3.70. Greenhouse is "womyn only" on Monday nights and always nonsmoking. *16 Chenies St., WC1, tel. 0171/637–8038. Tube: Goodge Street. Walk south on Tottenham Court Rd., quick left on Chenies St. Open Mon.–Sat. noon–8:30.*

➢ **UNDER £10 • La Bardigiana.** It's simple, it's small, and the staff is sometimes curt, but the price is right—especially if you can't face another biryani. A wide selection of yummy pizzas and pastas runs £4.60–£5.20. *77 Marchmont St., tel. 0171/837–5983. Tube: Russell Square. Turn right on Bernard St., left on Marchmont St. Open Mon.–Sat. 11:30–10. AE, MC, V.*

Chutney's. It's on everybody's short list for London's best vegetarian Indian restaurant. The £5 buffet (Mon.–Sat. noon–2:45, Sun. noon–10:30) is one of the city's few culinary steals. If you come for dinner, start with the vegetable kebab (£2.20) and continue with spicy mixed vegetables (£2.60) or *muttar panir* (tofu and peas in a hot sauce; £2.80) over a plate of rice (£1.80). Cool off with a glass of passion fruit, mango, or pineapple juice (95p). If you're catching a train at Euston Station, Chutney's is definitely worth the 10-minute walk. *124 Drummond St., NW1, tel. 0171/388–0604. Tube: Euston. Walk right on Melton St., turn left on Drummond St. Open Mon.–Sat. noon–2:45 and 6 –11:30, Sun. noon–10:30. MC, V.*

BRIXTON

Brixton is brimming with Afro-Caribbean joints. Most are within several blocks of the Brixton tube station and cater to the crowds who swarm Brixton Market (*see* Street Markets, in Chapter 7). If you're in the mood for a quick nosh, try **Miss Nid's Good Food** (397 Coldharbour Ln., tel. 0171/274–5605), which serves cheap West Indian–style snacks. Tucked away between market stalls, tiny **Bushman Kitchen** (36 Brixton Station Rd., tel. 0171/737–0015) serves West African snack foods and "natural medicinal herbs and root drinks."

➢ **UNDER £5** • **The Jacaranda Garden.** No, it doesn't actually have a garden—but there are fresh flowers on the tables. Otherwise, the Jacaranda is a spare and mellow café, where Brixtonians come for their world-food fix: Jamaican-style rice and peas with salad (£3.50), focaccia sandwiches (£3), quiche (£1.35), and vegetarian gumbo (£5). And if you want to linger a few hours over coffee, penning poetry or reading a few chapters from *Heart Sutra,* hey, that's OK. *11–13 Brixton Station Rd., SW9, tel. 0171/274–8383. Tube: Brixton. Walk north on Brixton Rd., turn right on Brixton Station Rd. Open weekdays 10–7, Sat. 10–6.*

Phoenix Restaurant. You'll find aging, cheap, and cheerful diners like this all over London, but for the price you can't find a better roast lamb with two veggies (£3.60) or cheese omelet with chips (£3.60). The classic greasy English breakfast is under £3; toast and tea are served all day. *441 Coldharbour Ln., SW9, tel. 0171/733–4430. Tube: Brixton. Walk south on Brixton Rd., turn left on Coldharbour Ln. Open Mon.–Sat. 6–5.*

Pizzeria Franco. "London's most famous pizzeria" is high on atmosphere and good on garlic-intensive pizza—from the *margherita* (tomato and mozzarella; £3.70) to the *quattro stagioni* (ham, mushrooms, artichokes, olives, and anchovies; £5.20). Owner Franco, from southern Italy, also makes a mean calzone (£5). You'll find this tiny trattoria tucked away in one of Brixton Market's covered arcades, between a vendor of ladies' polyester panties and a guy hawking electronic gizmos. In neighboring Clapham, chi-chi sister restaurant **Eco** (162 Clapham High St., SW4, tel. 0171/978–1108) caters to resident yuppies. *4 Market Row, SW9, tel. 0171/738–3021. Tube: Brixton. Walk south on Brixton Rd., turn left on Electric Ave., right on Electric Ln., and look for Market Row arcade entrance on left. Open Mon.–Tues., and Thurs.–Sat. 9–4:45.*

➢ **UNDER £10** • **Asmara.** The swankiest restaurant in London for Eritrean and Ethiopian cuisine is all gussied up in a dozen shades of crimson. Take a seat and prepare to feast on traditional dishes like *shiro* (finely ground chickpeas; £3), *derho* (richly spiced chicken stew; £5), and *zigeni* (spiced hot lamb or beef; £6), all served with spongy *injera* bread. Beware the *dullet* (mixed roasted offal; £3). *386 Coldharbour Ln., near Atlantic Rd., SW9, tel. 0171/737–4144. Tube: Brixton. Walk south on Brixton Rd., turn left on Coldharbour Ln. Open Mon.–Sat. 10 AM–2 AM, Sun. 5:30 PM–2 AM. MC, V.*

CAMDEN TOWN

There's no shortage of food in Camden, with dozens of stalls in the markets selling all kinds of cheap grub. **Camden High Street**—surprise—is the main drag, interspersed with stands selling kebabs, pizza, and sausage, and the odd café. **Inverness Street, Parkway,** and **Bayham Street** have eateries that are slightly less clogged with Camden shoppers.

➢ **UNDER £5** • **The Bagel Bar.** This is the perfect place to grab a filling, cheap breakfast before hitting the markets. Full English breakfasts are a mere £2–£3. Freshly made sandwiches are a bargain at 85p–£2, but the beef or veggie burger for 99p looks iffy. Hot salt-beef (that's "corned beef" to you) bagels (£1.90) make a mighty good snack. *12 Inverness St., NW1, tel. 0171/284–0974. Tube: Camden Town. Walk north on Camden High St., turn left on Inverness St. Open daily 7–5:30.*

➢ **UNDER £10** • **Daphne's.** Daphne's is a carnivore's delight, with excellent food and fast, friendly service. Appetizers like deep-fried calamari and *loukanika* (grilled spicy sausages) run £2.25–£3.25, and main dishes of moussaka, *tavvas* (cubes of lamb baked with herbs), and *ortikia* (quail with lemon and oregano) cost £6.25–£7. If the weather is even remotely pleasant, sit in the rooftop garden. *83 Bayham St., NW1, tel. 0171/267–7322. Tube: Camden Town. Walk SE on Camden High St., turn left on Greenland St., right on Bayham St. Open Mon.–Sat. noon–3 and 6–midnight. MC, V.*

The Engineer. Honored by *Time Out* as Best Bar in '95, the Engineer makes a wonderful place to hang out after a walk along the canal. The menu changes every other week, but you can expect fresh and filling portions of dishes like cheddar potato cakes with greens (£7), and mainstay starters such as caesar salad (£4.50) and antipasto (£5–£6). The atmosphere is lively and noisy at this popular spot. Reserve ahead if you're coming for dinner; try for an outside table if the weather's warm. *65 Gloucester Ave., NW1, tel. 0171/722–0950. Tube: Camden Town or Chalk Farm (recommended after dark). From Camden Town, walk north on Camden High St., at bridge turn left on the Canal and watch for signs. From Chalk Farm, walk south across Adelaide Rd., veer left on Gloucester Ave. Open noon–3 and 6–midnight. MC, V.*

The Lansdowne. A sign over the entrance reading "no mobile phones" sets the tone for this mellow, upmarket pub on the fringe of Camden Town. Sit next to north London's young affluents at huge wooden tables and sample food from a menu that changes daily. The linguine with pine nuts, chili, garlic, and parmesan (£6) and the grilled lamb with ratatouille and rice (£8) are both excellent with glasses of house wine (£2–£3). *90 Gloucester Ave., NW1, tel. 0171/483–0409. Tube: Chalk Farm. Walk SE on Chalk Farm Rd., turn right on Regent's Park Rd., cross bridge, veer left on Gloucester Ave. Bar open Mon.–Sat. noon–11, Sun. noon–3 and 7–10:30; restaurant open daily 12:30–2:30 and 7–10.*

Le Bistroteque. A friendly but frenzied staff serves "cuisine méditerranée" amongst bright green walls and an airy skylight. Ample portions of main dishes like grilled lamb with soya noodles, vegetarian pasta, and grilled chicken and vegetables are a mere £5. Large breakfasts (£4) are served until 5 PM. *4 Inverness St., NW1, tel. 0171/428–0546. Tube: Camden Town. Walk north on Camden High St., turn left on Inverness St. Open daily 9:30 AM–midnight. MC, V.*

Luna. Luna is a welcome respite from the bustle of Camden Stables market. Sandwiches (£4) like grilled chicken and arugula or sausage on focaccia bread come with a small salad; or try the large portions of pasta (£6), "big salads" like avocado, pancetta, and spinach (£5.50), or spiced scallops with stir-fried vegetables (£9). Weekends they serve brunches like eggs Benedict or scrambled eggs with smoked salmon for £6, including orange juice and coffee. *48 Chalk Farm Rd., NW1, tel. 0171/482–4667. Tube: Chalk Farm. Walk SE on Chalk Farm Rd. Open weekdays noon–11:30, Sat. 11 AM–11:30 PM, Sun. 11–10:30.*

Thanh Binh. Just north of Camden Lock, Thanh Binh is deservedly a longtime *Berkeley Guide* favorite. Sit down and enjoy the delicate Vietnamese prawns (£5.50) or finger-licking-good Mongolian lamb (£5) if you're wistful for Vietnamese decor; otherwise order a chicken with lemongrass lunch box (£3) to take away and eat by the loch. On weekends, they sell lunch boxes (£2.50) with curried chicken or beef and rice or noodles from the front of their restaurant all day. *14 Chalk Farm Rd., NW1, tel. 0171/267–9820. Tube: Chalk Farm. Walk SE on Chalk Farm Rd. Open Tues.–Sat. noon–2:30 and 6–11:30, Sun. noon–10. AE, MC, V.*

CHELSEA

Trendy Chelsea is loaded with good places to graze, but many of the restaurants price entrées like they're major investments. If you're looking to dine on a budget, stick to the restaurants at the top of **King's Road,** between the Sloane Square tube station and Beaufort Street. Or, try **Fulham Road,** where the pace is less frenetic and the prices more reasonable.

➤ **UNDER £5 • Chelsea Bun Diner.** The oddly named Bun Diner is always jam-packed with locals, and here's why: damn good breakfasts. They serve breakfast the whole day long (on Sundays some folks bring champagne and make a day of it), but if you show up before 10 AM you can get the "Early Bird Breakfast" for £2.30. PS: Lunch and dinner are terrific here, too. *9A Limerston St., SW10, tel. 0171/352–3635. Tube: Earl's Court or Sloane Square. From either tube station, take Bus 11, 19, 22, or 31. Open daily 7 AM–11 PM (Sun. from 8 AM). BYOB.*

Sydney Street Cafe. On warm days, it's worth wandering into the über-touristy Chelsea Farmer's Market—a bunch of schlocky shops with nary a farmer in sight—for a decent breakfast (£3.50) or lunch (£3–£5) at one of this café's peaceful, outdoor tables. During summer evenings it's home to a very popular all-you-can-eat BBQ feast-o-rama (£13). *215 Sydney St., SW3, tel. 0171/352–5600. Tube: South Kensington. Walk south on Onslow Sq., turn right on Fulham Rd., left on Sydney St. Open Apr.–Oct., daily 9 AM–midnight; Nov.–May, Tues.–Sun. 11–5.*

➤ **UNDER £10 • Ambrosiana Creperie.** This hip, attractive Chelsea restaurant dishes out a variety of both sweet and savory crepes. Start with a savory one like salami, ratatouille, and cheese (£5.50), or chicken, spinach, tomato, and cheese (£5.80). Or hey, why not skip straight to a dessert crepe, like pears and cinnamon (£3.50). Serious crepeophiles dine on Thursdays, when all crepes are half-price. *194 Fulham Rd., SW10, tel. 0171/351–0070. Tube: South Kensington. Walk SW on Old Brompton Rd., turn left on Sumner Pl., right on Fulham Rd. Open weekdays noon–3 and 6–11:30, weekends noon–11. MC, V.*

Brahms. In Pimlico, the neighborhood just east of Chelsea, is this funky cross between an elegant bistro and a sleek, very hip, very David Lynch diner. It offers special touches like acres of green velvet curtains, drippy candles in old wine bottles, and sweeping views of the Battersea Power Station. The menu is just as eccentric, featuring lots of vaguely French and British dishes, all under £9. Dine before 7:30 PM and you can get three courses for £5. *147 Lupus St., SW1, tel. 0171/834–9075. Tube: Pimlico. Walk west on Lupus St. for 10 min, or take Bus 24 or C10. Food served Mon.–Sat. noon–3 and 6–midnight, Sun. noon–midnight.*

Buona Sera at the Jam. The Jam is a classy little '70s-era restaurant with a surprise: There appear to be only six tables at first, but then the host will direct you to climb above those already seated into a little cubby that makes a romantic, cozy setting for diving into the special pastas (£5–£6) and new-British dishes (£7–£8). The effect is like dining in a double-decker bus, and, best of all, you can do it until 1 AM. *289A King's Rd., SW3, tel. 0171/352–8827. Tube: Sloane Square. Walk SW on King's Rd. Open Mon.–Sat. noon–1 AM. MC.*

Chapter 11. Huge neo-expressionist paintings provide the backdrop for this dinner-only restaurant. Appealing—albeit pricey—entrées include grilled lemon and pepper chicken (£7.50) and seafood risotto (£8). *47 Hollywood Rd., SW10, tel. 0171/351–1683. Tube: Earl's Court. Walk SE on Earl's Court Rd. (which becomes Redcliffe Gardens), turn left on Tregunter Rd., right on Hollywood Rd. Open Mon.–Sat. 7 PM–11:30 PM. AE, MC, V.*

Pucci Pizza. This kitschy, Italian-run pizzeria is decked out with blue-checkered tablecloths and tacky Old World artifacts. Even so, Pucci's creative pizzas—such as the Four Seasons (mushroom, pepperoni, anchovy, and tomato; £6) and the Siciliana (with eggplant and olives; £5.50)—will have you singing "That's *amore!*" *205 King's Rd., SW3, tel. 0171/352–2134. Tube: Sloane Square. Walk SW ½ mi on King's Rd. Open Mon.–Sat. 9:30 AM–1 AM.*

THE CITY AND ISLINGTON

Restaurants in the City mainly cater to suited office folk; after all, this is the financial heart of London. Predictably, the area is busiest on weekdays from dawn until early evening, and it slows to a crawl on weekends. There's no lack of sandwich shops, delis, pubs, and restaurants, but if you're not desperately hungry as you explore the City, consider a short tube ride to nearby Islington. Once the center for '70s dropouts, Islington is now a community on the rise, with a surfeit of happening places to dine, especially along **Islington High Street.**

➤ **UNDER £5 • Alfredo's.** Virtually unchanged since the 1920s, Alfredo's is more than your average neighborhood café. Join the crowd of regulars for hearty English breakfasts (£2.20–£2.80), sandwiches (90p–£2), and homemade pies with two veggies (£2.40), served in a homey, chrome and mirrored interior. *4–6 Essex Rd., N1, tel. 0171/226–3496. Tube: Angel. Walk north on Islington High St., veer right on Essex Rd. Open weekdays 7–2:30, Sat. 7–4.*

Ravi Shankar. Filling, cheap food is served in this airy space with pale yellow walls. A potato dosa filled with veggies and rice goes for £3.60. If you're especially hungry order Mysore thali (£4.70), with dal, *bhaji* (deep-fried veggies), rice, and chapati. Partake in the all-you-can-eat lunch buffet (£4.50), served noon–2:30 (Sunday until 5), or take-away lunch packs with veggie curry, rice, and salad (£2). In the evenings, students get a 20% discount. *422 St. John St., EC1, tel. 0171/833–5849. Tube: Angel. Walk south on St. John St. Open Mon.–Sat. noon–2:30 and 6–11 (Fri.–Sat. until 11:30), Sun. noon–5 and 6–11. AE, MC, V.*

➤ **UNDER £10** • **The Eagle.** Originator of the "good food in a pub" genre (and copied by The Engineer and The Landsdowne, to name but two), The Eagle has the requisite open kitchen, young City folk, and changing menu of Mediterranean edibles. Spanish ham, bruschetta, and tomato salad (£8) and home-salted cod with mash (£7.50) are both good bets. They also serve a tasty homemade soup du jour (£3.50), almost a meal in itself. At lunchtime this place is packed with journalists from the nearby *Guardian* offices. *159 Farringdon Rd., EC1, tel. 0171/837–1353. Tube: Farringdon. Walk right on Cowcross St., turn right on Farringdon Rd. Kitchen open weekdays noon–2:30 and 6:30–10:30, Sat. 12:30–4 and 6:30–10:30.*

The Place Below. It takes some gumption to bill yourself as "London's best vegetarian restaurant," but The Place Below—set in the crypt beneath St. Mary-le-Bow church—may be justified. The changing menu features large portions of salads (£4–£7), and hot dishes like ratatouille (£6) and quiche with salad (£4.50). For a light meal consider a bowl of soup with bread (£2.80). Prices are less for takeout, which is a fine idea on a nice day. *St. Mary-le-Bow, Cheapside, EC2, tel. 0171/329–0789. Tube: Mansion House. Walk north on Bow Ln., left on Cheapside. Open weekdays 7:30–2:30. MC, V.*

The Quality Chop House. Once a quiet little chop house, The Quality Chop House went upmarket a few years ago and never looked back. While it still serves large portions of hearty British grub like eggs, bacon, and chips (£6), some of what it offers is almost a parody of the traditional: bangers and mash becomes Toulouse sausages with mash and onion gravy (£8). Try to ignore the sounds of the Cityfolk and imagine what it would have looked like when it was, indeed, a "progressive working-class caterer"—same wood and cast-iron booths and black-and-white tile floor, but the suits would have been shabbier. *94 Farringdon Rd., EC1, tel. 0171/837–5093. Tube: Farringdon. Walk right on Cowcross St., turn right on Farringdon Rd. Open Sun.–Fri. noon–3 and 6:30–11:30, Sat. 6:30–11:30.*

COVENT GARDEN

There's no "garden" at Covent Garden, and the lively open-air market that once captivated visitors (and fed Londoners) is long, long gone. Alas, this is now the land of pricey crafts shops and a boggling array of almost identical yuppie bistros. Your strategy? Get your food from produce and snack sellers on **Endell Street** or **Neal Street,** then picnic on the Covent Garden piazza—filled with street performers vying for your pocket change on weekday evenings and Sunday afternoons. Otherwise, **Neal's Yard** (a tiny courtyard sandwiched between Monmouth and Endell streets, just north of Shorts Gardens) is a cool, peace-love-and-granola kinda place, packed with juice bars, natural-foods shops, and idyllic outdoor tables.

➤ **UNDER £5** • **Food for Thought.** Covent Garden hipsters frequent Food for Thought for the large portions of fresh, inventive vegetarian and vegan food like roast pepper and almond soup (£2), tomato herb bread (35p), and pasta with mushrooms and sage (£2.80). Everything on the menu is under £3—which explains why this snug basement café is never empty. *31 Neal St., WC2, tel. 0171/836–9072. Tube: Covent Garden. Walk right on Long Acre, turn left on Neal St. Open Mon.–Sat. 9:30–9, Sun. noon–4.*

The Rock & Sole Plaice. This family-run diner—a cross between your basic fish and chips bar and a pre-theater bistro—has no aspirations to be anything other than traditionally British, with options like cod and chips (£4.50) and chicken mushroom pie (£3.60). Expect small crowds after the pubs close. *47 Endell St., WC2, tel. 0171/836–3785. Tube: Covent Garden. Walk right on Long Acre, turn left on Endell St. Open Mon.–Sat. 11:30–11:30, Sun. noon–9:30.*

➤ **UNDER £10** • **Calabash.** Re-creating Kenya in a London basement isn't easy, but this excellent African restaurant does the job with bright woven tablecloths, colorful paintings, and lots of leafy plants. Go for *yassa* (onion stew with pepper and lemon juice; £6.50), lamb couscous (£7.50), or hearty groundnut stew with peanut sauce (£6.25). Chase it all down with a Nigerian beer (£2) or a bottle of Algerian or Zimbabwean wine (£7.50 and up). *38 King St., Africa Centre, WC2, tel. 0171/836–1976. Tube: Covent Garden. Walk south on James St., turn right on King St. Open weekdays 12:30–2:30 and 6–10:30, Sat. 6–10:30. AE, MC, V.*

Cranks. The Covent Garden outpost of this no-meat-allowed chain trumpets itself as "the largest vegetarian restaurant in Europe." Indeed, you can chow down at one of a bazillion tables spread over two bright, airy floors, or take a seat outside on the piazza. The menu changes weekly and usually includes a vegan soup (£2.30) and enterprising but occasionally disappointing entrées (£4). Never less than heavenly are the desserts (£1–£3). Note: If you're looking to conserve cash (and time—speedy waitpersons are an endangered species here), get your grub from the self-service counter upstairs. *1 The Market, WC2, tel. 0171/379–6508. Open Apr.–Oct., Mon.–Sat. 9 AM–11 PM, Sun. 10–10; Nov.–Mar., daily 9–8 (Sun. from 10). AE, MC, V. Other locations: 23 Barrett St., W1, tel. 0171/495–1340; 5 Cowcross St., EC1, tel. 0171/490–4870; 9 Tottenham St., W1, tel. 0171/631–3912.*

Mars. Mars is definitely on a planet of its own: It's got funky blue and orange walls, broken-china mosaics, and strangely named, vaguely French food. Menu highlights include Soupe Egberte le Sensitive (a fine-tasting lentil soup; £3.50) and Mr. Jones Goes Back to Basics (avocado, spinach, and ricotta parcels; £6.50). The post-work crew comes here in droves. *59 Endell St., WC2, tel. 0171/240–8077. Tube: Covent Garden. Walk right on Long Acre, turn left on Endell St. Open Mon. 6 PM–midnight, Tues.–Sat. noon–midnight, Sun. noon–10.*

Neal's Yard Dining Room. Let the drifting sounds of mellow reggae music lead you upstairs from Neal's Yard to this "world food" café. On the changing menu you'll find a roundup of Turkish *meze* (appetizers), Egyptian falafel, Indian thali, Mexican enchiladas, and West African groundnut stew, typically priced £3.85 (small portion) or £5.85 (large). *14 Neal's Yard, WC2, tel. 0171/379–0298. Tube: Covent Garden. Walk right on Long Acre, turn left on Neal St., left on Shorts Gardens, right on Neal's Yard, and look for stairway on right. BYOB, no smoking. Open Mon.–Tues. noon–5, Wed.–Sat. noon–8.*

EARL'S COURT AND SOUTH KENSINGTON

Earl's Court has the dubious honor of being home to London's only Taco Bell. Add loads of cut-rate kebab shops, greasy chippies, and generic sandwich shops to the mix and you'll see why many refer to this neighborhood as a "culinary black hole." If you're really hankering for fish and chips, grease and all, get thee to ancient **Maxwell's** (263 Old Brompton Rd., SW5, tel. 0171/373–5130). If you're at all concerned about healthy eating, your choices are better in neighboring South Kensington, particularly in the blocks surrounding the museums and South Kensington tube station, and along **Pelham Street** and **Brompton Road.**

➣ **UNDER £5 • Al Rawshi.** Quick and greasy satisfaction is guaranteed from the chicken or lamb schwarma (£2) and falafel (£1.50) at this tiny Lebanese snack bar. Wash it all down with a variety of fresh fruit juices (£1). *3 Kenway Rd., SW5, no phone. Tube: Earl's Court. Walk north on Earl's Court Rd., turn right on Kenway Rd. Open daily 11:30–11.*

Don't leave Kramps without a two-for-one coupon. On your next visit (sorry, you've got to wait at least 24 hours), this handy coupon gets you two plates of crepes for the price of one.

Benjys. The deal at divey Benjys is breakfast: It's big, it's cheap, and it's served all day. If you're ravenous, you'll covet the Builder's Breakfast (£3.50), a freight-load of baked beans, two sausages, two pieces of toast, bacon, one egg, and as much tea and coffee as you can put down. Would you like extra sausage (£1.40) with that? *157 Earl's Court Rd., SW5, tel. 0171/373–0245. Tube: Earl's Court. Open daily 7 AM–9:30 PM.*

Kramps Creperie. This unfortunately named restaurant serves up dozens of delicious crepes, both sweet and savory. If you've never had a crepe before, steady yourself: The selection stretches from chicken Creole (£5) to sugar and lemon (£1.50). And know that crepes aren't really designed for big eaters like yourself—if you're *really* hungry, order up a mess of 'em, or maybe get a side salad (£1.75). *6 Kenway Rd., SW5, tel. 0171/244–8759. Tube: Earl's Court. Walk north on Earl's Court Rd., turn right on Kenway Rd. Open daily noon–11. MC, V.*

➢ **UNDER £10** • **Spago.** This enthusiastically Italian restaurant has a delightful array of pasta dishes (most £5), including penne with Gorgonzola and spinach, and baked rigatoni. *6 Glendower Pl., SW7, tel. 0171/225–2407. Tube: South Kensington. Walk west on Old Brompton Rd., turn right on Glendower Pl. Open Sun.–Tues. noon–midnight, Wed.–Sat. noon–1 AM.*

Texas Lone Star Saloon. This over-the-top shrine to Texas will cure the homesick Lone Star Staters before they can say "Sam Houston." Respectable barbecue ribs (£6) and messy chili burgers (£5.50) are the best deals. The good selection of Mexican beers (£1.80 a bottle) may force you to postpone your research into English ale. *154 Gloucester Rd., SW7, tel. 0171/370–5625. Tube: Gloucester Road. Walk south on Gloucester Rd. Open Sun.–Wed. noon–11:30, Thurs.–Sat. noon–12:30 AM.*

Thai Taste. In a wasteland of fluorescent-lit chip shops, Thai Taste is an elegant oasis of white tablecloths, proper silverware, and subdued lighting. On the menu you'll find expertly prepared traditional dishes like pad thai (£4.80), red curry chicken (£5.25), and beef with black beans, ginger, and mushrooms (£5.50). Note: The entrance is easy to miss, so keep a sharp eye out. *130 Cromwell Rd., SW7, tel. 0171/373–1647. Tube: Gloucester Road. Walk north on Gloucester Rd., turn left on Cromwell Rd. Open daily noon–2:30 and 6–11. AE, MC, V.*

THE EAST END

Spitalfields, in the heart of the East End, was once the center of London's Jewish community, but as the Jews left, so did **Bloom's,** a much beloved kosher restaurant that recently moved north to Golders Green (130 Golders Green Rd., NW11, tel. 0181/450–1338). The area is now better known for Asian shops, restaurants, and markets; **Brick Lane** and surrounding streets are where you'll find the best choices. There are a number of reasonable sandwich shops and cafés in the Docklands; but it's very much a lunch venue, as the place empties after 6 PM.

➢ **UNDER £5** • **Brick Lane Beigal Bake.** This East End institution churns out freshly baked bagels around the clock. Add smoked salmon and cream cheese to your bagel for 90p, or go for succulent slices of salted beef and mustard (£1.50). This place gets packed with clubbers coming down after a night of e-induced raving, and on Sunday during the Brick Lane market. On New Year's Day the queue stretches down the block. *159 Brick Ln., E1, tel. 0171/729–0616. Tube: Aldgate East. Walk east on Whitechapel High St., turn left on Osborn St. (which becomes Brick Ln.). Open daily 24 hrs.*

Clifton. It's one of the more stylish Pakistani eateries on Brick Lane, but still cheaper than most; chicken vindaloo or lamb *phal* (hotter than hell) will set you back £3.10. The late open hours attract a zany clientele; Bez (the man who did little but dance in the Happy Mondays, and now in Black Grape) has been spotted here. *126 Brick Ln., E1, tel. 0171/377–9402. Tube: Aldgate East. Walk east on Whitechapel High St., turn left on Osborn St. (which becomes Brick Ln.). Open Sun.–Wed. noon–1 AM, Thurs.–Sat. noon–3 AM. AE, MC, V.*

A sign outside the Clifton reads "All the spices our chef uses are aphrodisiac." Perhaps that explains the lascivious murals.

Dino's Grill. Who knew Formica came in so many faux wood grains? City suits and folks from nearby garment factories come for surprisingly tasty lasagna (£3.40), cod or plaice and chips (£4.20), and specials like the roast of the day with two veggies (£4). Go ahead and have a Budvar (£2) with your lunch—you're on vacation, right? The same food is served downstairs (open weekdays 11:30–3) in a more stylish setting, but you'll miss Dino's singing and banter. *76 Commercial St., E1, tel. 0171/247–6097. Tube: Aldgate East. Walk north on Commercial St. Open weekdays 6–4:30, Sun. 6–2. AE, MC, V.*

Lahore Kebab House. Lahore serves excellent tandoori dishes in purely functional surroundings. There's a bare sink to wash your hands in before eating, and the staff makes no bones about hurrying customers in and out. Well-spiced lamb *karahi* (seared on a sizzling plate) costs £4, vegetable curry £3, and meat kebabs are a steal at 50p. Solo women will be stared at by the predominantly male clientele and may feel more comfortable heading elsewhere. *2 Umberston St., E1, tel. 0171/488-2551. Tube: Aldgate East. Walk NE on Whitechapel High St., turn right on Commercial Rd., right on Umberston St. Open daily noon-midnight.*

HAMPSTEAD AND HIGHGATE

The wealthy, genteel surroundings—Hampstead Heath is but a step away—ensure that Hampstead is littered with overpriced bistros and trendy cafés. Don't restrict yourself to **Hampstead High Street**; explore the side streets for tearooms and a smattering of mellow cafés. On busy **Heath Street,** fill up on delicious Hungarian poppy-seed cake at **Louis Patisserie** (32 Heath St., NW3, tel. 0171/435-9908). Highgate is much of the same, with little beyond the usual faux French or Italian chain cafés on Highgate High Street. If **Café Vert** (*see below*) is closed, you'd be better off catching a bus to Hampstead.

➤ **UNDER £5** • **Café Vert.** Tucked away in a community center inside a converted church, Café Vert serves up delicious vegetarian food. Try a huge portion of spinach and mushroom lasagna served with a tasty salad (£3.75), quiche and salad (£3), or a big veggie breakfast (£2.50). There's even live jazz on Sundays. *Jacksons Lane Centre, 269A Archway Rd., N6. Tube: Highgate. Open Tues.-Fri. 10-9, Mon. and Sat. 10-3:30, Sun. noon-3:30.*

➤ **UNDER £10** • **Byron.** This beautiful restaurant has brightly painted walls, heavy silk draperies, and a rich blue exterior. It's quite spendy in the evening, but they serve a great two-course set lunch Monday–Saturday noon–3 for £5. The menu changes daily, but it is always delicious and elegantly presented. *3A Downshire Hill, NW3, tel. 0171/435-3544. Tube: Hampstead. Walk SE on Hampstead High St., turn left on Downshire Hill. Open Mon.-Sat. noon-3 and 6-11, Sun. noon-10:30. AE, MC, V.*

Viva Zapata. The £5 all-you-can-eat Tex-Mex buffet is highly recommended for anyone with a taste for chili and beans. It's a long trek from Hampstead tube, but there's a good selection of cocktails and food—mussels, shrimp, fish, and vegetables in addition to the usual tacos, rice, sour cream, and guacamole. The staff can be offhand, but they fit in with the laid-back atmosphere. *7 Pond St., NW3, tel. 0171/431-9134. Tube: Hampstead. Walk SE on Hampstead High St., turn left on Pond St. Open daily noon-midnight.*

Zamoyski's. Start off your meal by sampling some of the 30 different vodkas (£1.60 a shot)—those with a sweet tooth should try the honey vodka. Then get to work on the Polish *mezze,* nine dishes for a bargain £5.50, or the amazing *pieczeń po husarsku* (marinated lamb roasted with wild mushroom sauce; £8). Portions lean toward the small side, but the food is rich and perfectly seasoned. Candles, dark wood, and that tempting array of vodkas make this spot very popular; phone ahead on weekend nights or expect a long wait. *85 Fleet Rd., NW3, tel. 0171/794-4792. Tube: Hampstead. Walk south on Hampstead High St., turn left on Pond St., veer right on Fleet Rd. Open weekdays 5:30 PM-11 PM, Sat. 6 PM-11 PM, Sun. noon-11. AE, MC, V.*

KENSINGTON AND KNIGHTSBRIDGE

Kensington and Knightsbridge are posh neighborhoods, full of lavish designer boutiques and "my god, you're joking"-priced restaurants. Best bets for cheap noshes in Knightsbridge are the pubs and sandwich shops on **Beauchamp Place** (off Brompton Road), and in Kensington, the fast-food joints scattered along **Kensington High Street.** Just for thrills, you might also want to stalk the food halls at Harrods and Harvey Nichols, the area's two tony department stores (*see* Markets and Specialty Stores, *below*).

➤ **UNDER £5** • **La Barraca.** The menu at this mellow, attractive place features tons of tapas (Spanish appetizers) like calamari with white beans (£3.90), garlic chicken (£3.65), and steamed mussels (£3.90); order several and then share among friends. Weekends, La Barraca is popular with young Londoners as a late-night watering hole. *215 Kensington Church St., W8, tel. 0171/229-9359. Tube: Notting Hill Gate. Walk east on Notting Hill Gate, turn right on Kensington Church St. Open Mon.-Sat. 11 AM-1 AM, Sun. 2 PM-12:30 AM. AE, MC, V.*

➤ **UNDER £10** • **Caravela.** This Portuguese basement bistro, done up like an old fishing village, is a great place if you can stomach the outrageous £1.25 cover charge and mandatory 12.5% service charge. Your choices include traditional dishes like *sardinhas assadas* (charcoal-grilled sardines; £7), *lulas á marinheira* (squid simmered in tomatoes and onions; £8), and the ultradelicious *cataplana* (thick seafood stew served in a giant copper bowl; £9). Most nights you'll be serenaded by Portuguese folk guitarists. *39 Beauchamp Pl., SW3, tel. 0171/ 584–2163. Tube: Knightsbridge. Walk SW on Brompton Rd., turn left on Beauchamp Pl. Open Mon.–Sat. noon–3 and 7 PM–1 AM. AE, MC, V.*

Beyond Mickey D's

If the thought of dining in a chain restaurant makes you break out in a rash, relax— we're not suggesting McDonald's. The places listed below all have great food, decent prices, attractive decor, and, hey, they just happen to have more than one location. Maybe it's one near you.

• *Aroma. This bright, vibrant string of cafés was recently voted best in a "Time Out" reader poll. Its specialty coffee is a hit, perhaps because it's served with a little piece of chocolate. Pastries and snacks are £1–£3. 273 Regent St., W1, tel. 0171/495–4911; 120 Charing Cross Rd., WC2, tel. 0171/240–4030; 1B Dean St., W1, tel. 0171/ 287–1633; 381 Oxford St., W1, tel. 0171/495–6945; 168 Piccadilly, W1, tel. 0171/ 495–6995; 36A St. Martin's Ln., WC2, tel. 0171/836–5110; 115–123 Bayham St., NW1, tel. 0171/482–6666.*

• *Dôme. One of the best deals in town is the £5 three-course meal available all day long at this string of hip French bistros. The selection changes daily, with possibilities like ginger-carrot soup, onion tart, liver pâté, roast chicken, and many delicious desserts. 32 Long Acre, Covent Garden, WC2, tel. 0171/379–8650; 35A Kensington High St., W8, tel. 0171/937–6655; 289–291 Regent St., W1, tel. 0171/636–7006; 354 King's Rd., SW3, tel. 0171/352–2828; 57–59 Charterhouse St., EC1, tel. 0171/ 336–6484.*

• *Pizza Express. For a pizza chain, this place ain't bad: Pies arrive at your table hot and tasty, and the prices (£3.40 and up) are pretty cheap. Some of the branches even host live jazz. There are approximately 25 locations throughout London.*

• *Prêt à Manger. For quick sandwiches (£1.20–£2), salads (£1.50–£2.80), and even sushi (£5–£5.85), Prêt à Manger cannot be beat. Everything is prepared hourly on the premises, with the emphasis on fresh, natural ingredients (no grease, no preservatives). There are approximately 40 locations.*

• *The Stockpot. Count on these old-time café-diners for inexpensive English and Continental fare like soups (80p), omelets (£2.50), and casseroles (£2.75). 6 Basil St., SW3, tel. 0171/589–8627; 273 King's Rd., SW3, tel. 0171/823–3175; 40 Panton St., SW1, tel. 0171/839–5142; 18 Old Compton St., W1, tel. 0171/287–1066; 50 James St., W1, tel. 0171/486–1086.*

Curry Inn. In a city packed with Indian restaurants vying for the title of "best," it's easy to overlook this tiny, tastefully decorated contender. The dishes here, like biryani (£4.85–£7) and curries (£3–£6), are generous and expertly prepared and the staff will cheerfully make suggestions or explain ingredients. *41 Earl's Court Rd., W8, tel. 0171/937–2985. Tube: High Street Kensington. Walk west on Kensington High St., turn left on Earl's Court Rd. Open Mon.–Sat. noon–2:30 and 6–11:30, Sun. 6–11:30. AE, MC, V.*

Scandies. You may want to kneel and kiss the ground before entering this tidy eatery, because if you're hungry and you're in Knightsbridge, it's gonna save your ass. The Continental menu changes fortnightly, but regular delicacies include salmon salad (£4.50) and spicy lamb casserole (£6). When weather permits, they set out sidewalk tables. *4 Kynance Pl., SW7, tel. 0171/589–3659. Tube: Gloucester Road. Walk north on Gloucester Rd., turn left on Kynance Pl. Open weekdays noon–2:30 and 5:30–10:30, weekends 5:30–10:30. AE, MC, V.*

SOHO AND MAYFAIR

Soho, the heart of tourist London, is a happy hunting ground when it comes to restaurants, cafés, trattorias, and food stands—in fact, it's tops for just about every type of eatery imaginable. In London's small Chinatown, on **Lisle Street** (pronounced "Lyle") and **Gerrard Street** between Leicester Square and Shaftesbury Avenue, you'll find the city's best Asian restaurants, as well as plenty of stores selling bulk herbs, produce, fresh fish, meats, Asian teas, and miracle cures. **Wardour Street** has an amazing array of international cuisine: Asian, American, French, Italian, you name it. **Old Compton Street** is *the* place to go for a traditional (though often expensive) Italian meal. Mayfair, on the other hand, is mainly a ritzy residential neighborhood, with a sprinkling of sandwich shops along **Piccadilly** and around the **Marble Arch** tube station, and fast-food stands of all types along **Oxford Street**; while you're there, drop by Selfridges (*see* Markets and Specialty Stores, *below*) to gape at its splendid food halls.

➤ **UNDER £5 • Café Sofra.** If you're looking to escape the fast-food frenzy of Piccadilly, duck down windy, historic Shepherd Street and start hunting for this cozy café. On the menu are Middle Eastern–type snacks and light meals, like mixed mezze (£3.10) or lentil casserole (£3.50), plus standard sandwiches and desserts. *10 Shepherd St., W1, tel. 0171/495–3434. Tube: Green Park. Walk SW on Piccadilly, turn right on White Horse St., left on Shepherd St. Open daily 7:30 AM–midnight.*

Govinda's. There's no proselytizing at this friendly Hare Krishna restaurant, just tasty vegetarian grub at rock-bottom prices. On the regular menu are basics like baked potato with cheese (£1.85), lasagna (£3.50), and vegetable curry (£3). Every night from 7:30, it's all-you-can-eat for £4, and if that isn't good enough, on Sunday at 5 PM the Krishnas serve a free—yes, free—feast. No alcohol is allowed. *9–10 Soho St., W1, tel. 0171/437–4928. Tube: Tottenham Court Road. Walk west on Oxford St., turn left on Soho St. Open Mon.–Sat. noon–8.*

Malaysia Hall Dining Hall. It's no big secret among hungry Londoners that Malaysia Hall's student cafeteria serves excellent food at dirt-cheap prices. Fortunately, the public is welcome, and you can't do better for so little money. The set meal (£1.80) is rice, vegetables, and a main dish, like sweet-and-sour fish or spicy noodles. Breakfast includes tasty traditional *roti canai* (deep-fried bread with curry dipping sauce). As you can imagine, lines are long. *46 Bryanston Sq., W1, tel. 0171/723–9484. Tube: Marble Arch. Walk west on Oxford St., turn right on Great Cumberland Pl. Open daily 8–10 (breakfast), noon–3 (lunch), 5–9 (dinner).*

Mildred's. This eatery offers above-average, 100% organic veggie food, a genial staff, and a boho hipster clientele. The menu changes daily, but entrées like stir-fried vegetables, frittatas, or a chili bean burrito are all £4–£6.50. For dessert, spoon into a bowl of yogurt, honey, and nuts for £2.40. *58 Greek St., W1, tel. 0171/494–1634. Tube: Leicester Square. Walk north on Charing Cross Rd., turn left on Shaftesbury Ave., right on Greek St. Open Mon.–Sat. noon–11, Sun. 12:30–6:30.*

The New Piccadilly. The decor in this hole-in-the-wall is so weird it's interesting: red and yellow Formica furniture, an old unfinished floor, and a curious collection of "art." Simple, no-frills, British-Italian food like omelets, pizzas, casseroles, steaks, and pastas is all under £6.

8 Denman St., W1, tel. 0171/437–8530. Tube: Piccadilly Circus. Walk NE on Shaftesbury Ave., turn left on Denman St. Open daily 11–9:30.

New World. It's a world unto itself at this Chinese dim-sum-o-rama, which seats 700 comfortably. Love it for the paper tablecloths, schlocky Chinese lanterns, and tacky Muzak. And then there's the dim sum, a variety of dumplings, noodles, steamed buns, even chickens' feet, all for around £1.50. It's a great bargain, and if you're not stuffed to the gills for £5, you'd better have that tapeworm checked out. 1 Gerrard Pl., W1, tel. 0171/734–0677. Tube: Leicester Square. Walk north on Charing Cross Rd., turn left on Little Newport St., and continue 1 block to alley. Open daily 11 AM–11:45 PM. AE, MC, V.

Pollo. At this Soho institution, you can pick from an extensive menu of incredibly cheap pastas: basic spaghetti runs £3, with chicken £4. The atmosphere is jovial and noisy, and you may have to share a table with the herds of hungry university students. 20 Old Compton St., W1, tel. 0171/734–5917. Tube: Leicester Square. Walk north on Charing Cross Rd., turn left on Moor St. (which becomes Old Compton St.). Open daily noon–midnight.

Poons. Once a hole-in-the-wall, now a smart restaurant, Poons offers more than just stir-fry. Try the special "wind-dried" duck with rice (£4.80–£6.60), hotpot (soup with stuffed bean curd; £3.50), or deep-fried oysters (£5.50). The staff are friendly, and they'd like you to be so, too—when the place gets busy, waiters don't ask before seating people at your table. 27 Lisle St., WC2, tel. 0171/437–4549. Tube: Leicester Square. Walk north on Charing Cross Rd., turn left on Newport St., left on Newport Pl., right on Lisle St. Open daily noon–11:30.

Taffgoods Sandwich Bar. Here you'll find London's cheapest noshes: Bagels with lox and cream cheese cost 90p, salt-beef bagels £1.50. It's possible to eat in, but most order to go. 128 Wardour St., W1, tel. 0171/437–3286. Tube: Piccadilly Circus. Walk NE on Shaftesbury Ave., turn left on Wardour St. Open weekdays 7–4.

TIP FOR MASOCHISTS: The staff at Wong Kei's (41–43 Wardour St., W1, tel. 0171/437–6833) is legendary for its rudeness. They ignore you, then they yell insults, and still people line up around the block. Could the noodle dishes (£3) really be worth it? Go find out.

West End Kitchen. Run by the same genius who brought you the Stockpot chain (see box Beyond Mickey D's, above), West End Kitchen offers hearty, cheap food such as lentil soup (85p), fish and chips, and omelets (£3–£4). Their three-course lunch special goes for £3 (£3.50 on weekends). Gourmets may think this joint totally lacking, but less finicky folk will find its comfort and simplicity charming. 5 Panton St., SW1, tel. 0171/839–4241. Tube: Piccadilly Circus. Walk south on Haymarket, turn left on Panton St. Open daily 7 AM–11:45 PM.

➤ **UNDER £10 • Bar Sol Ona.** You walk through a vibrantly painted hallway and descend into the basement to enter this Spanish tapas joint. Choose from a large variety of tapas in three sizes, priced £3.50 and up. Don't miss happy hour (6 PM–10 PM), with Estrellas beer for £1. 17 Old Compton St., W1, tel. 0171/287–9932. Tube: Leicester Square. Walk north on Charing Cross Rd., turn left on Moor St. (which becomes Old Compton St.). Open daily 6 PM–3 AM (Sun. until 11 PM). AE, V.

Belgo Centraal. Step onto the industrial elevator and descend into deep, deep trendiness. Don't ask why the waiters are dressed like Trappist monks in this Belgian diner—it's just one of those things, much like the exposed brick arches, brushed copper walls, and very stylish furniture. Belgo's specialty is mussels, served on platters (£9) or in pots (£11). At lunchtime try their wild-boar sausage with mash and a beer (£5). Weekdays come early for dinner and play Beat the Clock: Order one of three set meals (chicken, sausages, or mussels and a beer) and pay a price corresponding to the time you order—if it's 6:10 PM, you pay £6.10). The beer menu is even larger than the food menu—with Belgian ales, pilsners, and more for £2.25–£3.25. If you're in the north end, **Belgo Nord** (22 Chalk Farm Rd., NW1, tel. 0171/267–0718) is mellower but serves the same delicious food. 50 Earlham St., WC2, tel. 0171/813–2233. Tube: Covent Garden. Cross Long Acre to Neal St., turn left on Earlham St. Open daily noon–11:30 (Sun. until 10:30). AE, MC, V.

Gaby's Continental Bar. Gaby's menu features cuisine from all over the Continent (and other parts of the planet as well). There's schnitzel (£4), falafel (£2), stir-fried chicken (£5.50), and lamb couscous (£6), plus tons of salads and vegetarian dishes. The restaurant itself has been newly repainted a cheery all-white. *30 Charing Cross Rd., WC2, tel. 0171/836–4233. Tube: Leicester Square. Open Mon.–Sat. 9 AM–midnight, Sun. 11–10.*

Hamine. Patrons of this slick noodle shop run the gamut from homesick Japanese business-men to local cognoscenti. And most are here for one thing: huge, steaming bowls of ramen with meat or vegetables (£4.50–£6.50) guaranteed to leave you stuffed. Note to the uninitiated: Place your order and pay at the counter first, and then take a seat. *84 Brewer St., W1, tel. 0171/287–1318. Tube: Piccadilly Circus. Walk north on Sherwood St., turn left on Brewer St. Open weekdays noon–3 AM, Sat. noon–2 AM, Sun. noon–midnight.*

Harry's Bar. The happy, happy, happy world of Harry's Bar can be confusing at first: It's a bar, yes, but by day it also serves Thai food (£4–£7). Then from 11 PM to 6 AM it morphs into one of Soho's only late-night nosh spots, serving full English breakfasts (£5) and the even fuller Harry's Breakfast Blowout (£7). *19 Kingly St., W1, tel. 0171/434–0309. Tube: Piccadilly Circus. Walk north on Regent St., turn right on Beak St., left on Kingly St. Open Mon.–Sat. 7:30 AM–6 AM. MC, V.*

Italian Graffiti. This fun joint makes inexpensive gourmet pizzas; a large prosciutto-and-mush-room runs £5.50. Graffiti also does a good job with calzones and pasta, particularly spaghetti *puttanesca,* with tomatoes, olives, and onions (£5). If it's even vaguely warm enough, sit at one of their sidewalk tables. *163–165 Wardour St., W1, tel. 0171/439–4668. Tube: Oxford Circus. Walk east on Oxford St., turn right on Wardour St. Open weekdays noon–3 and 5:45–mid-night, Sat. noon–11:30. AE, V.*

La Reash Cous-Cous House. Lebanese and Moroccan fare is what you'll find at La Reash, with couscous (£5.50–£7) an obvious specialty. A bolder option is the platter of *mazah* (£9), a col-lection of yummy small dishes that can easily feed two. In summer, they roll tables out on the sidewalk—fantastic for people-watching. *23–24 Greek St., W1, tel. 0171/439–1063. Tube: Leicester Square or Tottenham Court Road. From Leicester Square, walk north on Charing Cross Rd., turn left on Moor St. (which leads to Greek St.). From Tottenham Court Road, walk south on Charing Cross Rd., turn right on Moor St. Open daily noon–midnight. AE, MC, V.*

It's hard to believe such a thing could be true, but Tokyo Diner has a "no tips accepted" policy.

Tokyo Diner. Inside Tokyo Diner you'll find decently priced, well-prepared Japanese food, such as sushi, teriyaki (£5–£6), and *donburi* (sticky rice flavored with soya, egg, onion, and the meat of your choice; £3.50–£6). The trick is finding the door-way, hidden Japanese-style behind flapping fabric (city coun-cil boors would like to see this replaced with a proper British facade). *2 Newport Pl., WC2, tel. 0171/287–8777. Tube: Leicester Square. Walk north on Charing Cross Rd., turn left on Little Newport St., right on Newport Pl. Open daily noon–midnight.*

Wagamama. A Japanese word meaning "selfishness," Wagamama is the home of positive eat-ing. Don't let the long lines put you off; rest assured that the turnover rate of customers is high at this ramen bar. The menu features a staggering variety of noodles; novice ramen eaters should start with *yaki udon* (pan-fried noodles with shitake mushrooms, eggs, prawns, and chicken; £4.90) or the spicy chili chicken ramen (£5.90). The menu is nearly as entertaining as the waitstaff, who are clad in Paul Smith gear. Slurping is encouraged; apparently the extra oxygen helps the flavor. *10A Lexington St., W1, tel. 0171/292–0990. Tube: Oxford Circus. Walk south on Regent St., turn left on Beak St., right on Lexington St. Open daily noon–11 (Sun. until 10). Other location: 4 Streatham St., WC1, tel. 0171/323–9223. MC, V.*

➤ **SPLURGE • Alastair Little.** Don't be put off by the sparse interior—it's intentional, dar-ling. Chef Little has made quite a name for himself with delicious Asian- and Mediterranean-influenced food, the ultimate in modern British cooking. On a given day you might tuck into sea bass with roast vegetables, basil, and olives, or lamb with rosemary gravy. Set lunches are £12.50 for two courses, or £25 for a decadent three. *49 Frith St., W1, tel. 0171/734–5183. Tube: Leicester Square. Open weekdays noon–3 and 6–11:30, Sat. 6–11:30. AE, MC, V.*

For a bit of river culture, grab a sandwich in Gabriel's Wharf and chill out in South Bank, London's answer to Paris's Left Bank. A number of expensive restaurants have sprung up along the river, but for better value you'll need to wander farther afield into the urban sprawl of Waterloo. **Lower Marsh,** behind Waterloo Station, is dotted with anonymous little cafés.

➢ **UNDER £5** • M. Manze. Eels aren't for everyone, especially not the squeamish, but M Manze has been serving steaming plates of them to happy/daring customers since 1892—making it the oldest remaining eel, pie, and mash shop in the world. A traditional meat pie and mash (£1.80), eels and mash (£2.45), and (ulp!) jellied eels (£2) are all served with a ladle full of "liquor," a spring green, parsley-based sauce. This place gets busy at lunchtime so you'll probably need to share one of the marble tables and long wooden benches—perfect for gleaning eel-eating tips. *87 Tower Bridge Rd., SE1, tel. 0171/407–2985. Tube: London Bridge. Walk SE on St. Thomas St., turn right on Bermondsey St. (which joins Tower Bridge Rd. just before M. Manze). Open Mon. 11–2, Tues.–Thurs. 10:30–2, Fri. 10–2:15, Sat. 10–2:45.*

➢ **UNDER £10** • Côte à Côte. If it's rich French food you're craving, look no further. The restaurant is a bit dark, but the well-presented food is guaranteed to satisfy both wallet and palate. Generous starters are a steal at £1.85; try the mussels steamed in wine and garlic or the avocado, mozzarella, tomato, and basil salad. Delicious entrées like chicken marinated in chili and coconut milk served over pasta or baked aubergines stuffed with tofu and vegetables cost a mere £4.45. *74–76 Battersea Bridge Rd., SW11, tel. 0171/738–0198. Tube: Sloane Square. From station, take Bus 19 or 249 to Battersea Bridge Rd. Open daily noon–3 and 6–midnight. MC, V.*

Waterloo Fire Station. This huge establishment occupies a converted fire station: The old tiles and metal supports remain, but the red engines have been replaced by a huge bar, an open kitchen, and rows of wooden tables. In the restaurant, happy diners chow down on goodies like braised lamb with broccoli and butter-bean mash (£10) or pasta with oyster mushrooms, garlic, and truffles (£7.75) served by a a friendly staff. The Italian-Continental menu changes twice daily, but it's always good. There's a limited bar menu (of equally tasty food) when the full restaurant is closed. *150 Waterloo Rd., SE1, tel. 0171/620–2226. Tube: Waterloo. Walk south on Waterloo Rd. Bar open Mon.–Sat. 11–11, Sun. noon–5. Restaurant open Mon.–Sat. 12:30–2:30 and 6:30–11, Sun. 12:30–3:30. AE, MC, V.*

Cafés

Let's be honest: London is not Paris or Rome, and cafés don't crowd the squares and line the boulevards here. While the Italians and French may swear by their lattes and cappuccinos and gâteaux, Brits prefer to relax over a pints at the corner pub. That said, you'll find Euro- and Seattle-style cafés on the rise in London—perhaps they're just trying to keep up with the influx of caffeine-craving foreigners. At any rate, the city just received its first Starbucks and has grown a few coffee chains of its own: You'll find branches of **Aroma** (*see box* Beyond Mickey D's, *above*), which makes a kick-ass cuppa joe, just about everywhere.

Al's Café Bar. This City café features half a dozen styles of chairs and flatware, Cityfolk in suits, and a funky staff. Fortify yourself with a "super big breakfast" (£6), or go decadent with cherry pie and custard (£2.50) and a serious cappuccino (£1.50). Hearty soups like lobster bisque, scotch vegetable, or carrot and butter-bean (£2.80) come with a hefty hunk of bread—the perfect lunch on a chilly day. *11–13 Exmouth Market, EC1, tel. 0171/837–4821. Tube: Farringdon. Walk right on Cowcross St., turn right on Farringdon Rd., right on Exmouth Market. Open weekdays 7 AM–11 PM, weekends 10–8.*

Bar Italia. In Soho's primo coffee bar, ineffably cool Italian waiters serve what's generally considered the best cappuccino (£1.30) in town. If you're looking for quiet contemplation, head elsewhere—but if you want hip crowds, blaring MTV on a giant-screen television, funky surroundings, and 24-hour access to caffeine, then baby, this is your café. *22 Frith St., W1, tel.*

0171/437–4520. Tube: Leicester Square. Walk north on Charing Cross Rd., turn left on Old Compton St., right on Frith St. Open 24 hrs (closed some weekdays 6 AM–7 AM).

Bliss. Let the tricolour awning decorated with a large chicken lead you to Bliss, just south of the Angel tube station in Islington. Munch on a delicious array of baked goods such as fruit tarts (£1.40), filled croissants (£2.65), and ham or basil and tomato quiche (£1.75) in a brightly painted room peopled with Islingtonians in the know. Surprisingly good coffees (£1–£2) and teas (£1) round out the menu. *428 St. John St., EC1, tel. 0171/837–3720. Tube: Angel. Open weekdays 8–7, weekends 9–6.*

The Coffee Cup. This old standard—reputedly the oldest coffee lounge in London—serves up a full range of coffees as well as pastas (£4.70), sandwiches (£2.30–£2.80), and specials like garlic and herb prawns with chips (£4.70). Locals love the place; you'll have to move fast to score one of the coveted outside tables. *74 Hampstead High St., NW3, tel. 0171/435–7565. Tube: Hampstead. Walk SE on Hampstead High St. Open daily 8 AM–midnight.*

Cyberia. More than just a cybercafé, Cyberia is a way of life. There are 10 PCs with Internet access (£2.50 per half hour, £1.90 students); a good range of hot and cold food like filled baguettes (£2.80) and amazing Irish mussels in garlic sauce (£3.55); a friendly staff not infected by the "cooler-than-thou" virus; and a varied and lively clientele—not all of whom come for the computers. The Cyberians are also the force behind *Cyberia* magazine (£2.20) and Channel Cyberia, the world's first free 24-hour Internet service (http://channel.cyberi-acafe.net). *39 Whitfield St., W1, tel. 0171/209–0982, cyberia@easynet.co.uk. Tube: Goodge Street. Turn left on Tottenham St., left on Whitfield St. Open Mon.–Sat. 11–10, Sun. 11–9.*

Kaffe Opera. The best place to relax after shopping King's Road in Chelsea is this stylish café, which announces its Austrian heritage by hanging a chandelier above the small clutch of tables and chairs. Sandwiches (£1.10–£2.80) and pastries (under £2) fill the menu. *315 King's Rd., SW3, tel. 0171/352–9854. Tube: Sloane Square. Walk SW on King's Rd. Open daily 8 AM–midnight (Fri.–Sat. until 1 AM).*

The Living Room. There's no better place to chill for a few hours in Soho than this newish café, which offers comfy chairs, sofas, and stacks of old books for your lounging pleasure. Cappuccino is £1.20, sandwiches and such are under £4. *3 Bateman St., W1, tel. 0171/437–4827. Tube: Leicester Square. Walk north on Charing Cross Rd., turn left on Old Compton St., right on Greek St., left on Bateman St. Open Mon.–Sat. 10 AM–midnight, Sun. noon–11.*

Maison Bertaux. It's not much to look at, but this decades-old shop is one of Soho's best-loved pâtisseries. Settle at one of the Formica tables and enjoy an éclair, strawberry tart, or gooey, flaky almond croissant (£1.20)—all baked fresh daily on the premises. *28 Greek St., W1, tel. 0171/437–6007. Tube: Leicester Square. Walk north on Charing Cross Rd., turn left on Old Compton St., right on Greek St. Open daily 9–8 (closed Sun. 1–3).*

Maison Bouquillon. Grand gâteaux and exquisite pastries, most around £1.50, are what this Bayswater café does best. The almond croissants (£1.05) are suitably dense, and the strawberry mousse (£1.60) is *the* thing on a hot summer's day. They also serve savory items like sausage rolls (£1.20). *41–45 Moscow Rd., W2, tel. 0171/229–2107. Tube: Bayswater. Walk north on Queensway, quick left on Moscow Rd. Open Mon.–Sat. 8:30 AM–9:30 PM, Sun. 8:30–8:30.*

Marnie's. This airy, friendly place in Notting Hill Gate is regularly packed to the hilt. Fill up on bacon and eggs (£3.15) and fresh coffee (95p) before an arduous day of bargain hunting. Or settle in with a slice of one of their rich, delicious cakes (£1.50). *9 Portobello Rd., W10, tel. 0171/229–8352. Tube: Notting Hill Gate. Walk north on Penbridge Rd., turn left on Portobello Rd. Open Mon.–Sat. 7:45–4:30.*

The Muffin Man. Just off Kensington's tony High Street is this snug little shop—which hasn't changed an iota since opening its doors over 60 years ago. Regulars drop by afternoons for full tea (£4.70) and delicious baked goodies. Best of all, lingering's encouraged. *12 Wright's Ln., W8, tel. 0171/937–6652. Tube: High Street Kensington. Walk west on Kensington High St., turn left on Wright's Ln. Open Mon.–Sat. 8–5:45.*

Pâtisserie Valerie. This cool, dark Soho café has been around since 1926. Most recently it's become a hangout for artsy types, and it's packed day and night. For snacking, there are sandwiches (£1.80–£2.50), luscious desserts like éclairs, berry tarts, and white-chocolate truffle cake, and a stellar selection of handmade chocolates. *44 Old Compton St., W1, tel. 0171/437–3466. Tube: Leicester Square. Walk north on Charing Cross Rd., turn left on Old Compton St. Open weekdays 8–8, Sat. 8–7, Sun. 10–6. Other locations: 215 Brompton Rd., SW3, tel. 0171/589–4993; 66 Portland Pl., W1, tel. 0171/631–0467.*

Primrose Pâtisserie. This Polish café is popular with locals, in part because it's far from the maddening crowds on Camden High Street. Sit in the cozy dining room, or take your food away to eat at nearby Primrose Hill. Sandwiches, small salads, and cakes all go for £1.50, about 50p less if you take them away. *136 Regent's Park Rd., NW1, tel. 0171/722–7848. Tube: Chalk Farm. Open daily 8:30 AM–9:30 PM.*

The World Cafe. Four PowerMac terminals provide Internet access for £2.50 per half hour (£1.90 students) and printing facilities for 10p per page. Japanese-style food items like sushi (from £6) or salmon salad (£3) match the minimalist decor. *394 St. John St., EC1, tel. 0171/833–3222, worldcafe1@smallplanet.co.uk. Tube: Angel. Walk south on Islington High St. (which becomes St. John St.). Open daily 11–9.*

Markets and Specialty Stores

For excellent deals, especially on produce, you can't beat London's **street markets**; once you hear a barrow boy bellowing out the bargains of the day, you'll know you've arrived in London Towne. Street markets are described in detail in Chapter 6, but briefly, here are a few of the best for food: In the East End, the **Old Fruit and Vegetable Market** (Brushfields St.), held Sundays 9–3, is known for its selection of organic produce, as is **Spitalfields Market,** held Fridays and Saturdays. **Berwick Street Market** is one of the best-loved food fairs in London's West End. **Brixton Market** on Electric Avenue features Afro-Caribbean and Latin foods like yams, papayas, and pig trotters. In the vast **Camden Markets,** look for cheese stalls on Inverness Street and organic produce at the Stables (Chalk Farm Rd.).

Much more upscale, though equally frenzied, are the **food halls** in various department stores. All the big ones have 'em: **Harvey Nichols** (*see* Department Stores, in Chapter 6); **Harrods** (*see* Kensington and Knightsbridge, in Chapter 2); **Fortnum & Mason** (*see below*); and **Selfridges** (*see below*). With their elaborate (bordering on grotesque) displays of abundance, they're just as much tourist spectacle as they are source of sustenance.

Carluccio's. At this traditional Italian shop, mouthwatering pasta sauces and ready-to-eat dishes like pizzas (£1.30), calzones (£2), and marinated chicken (£4) are prepared fresh daily. You can also pick up the essentials to make your own affordable Italian feast: dried pasta, mushrooms, fresh veggies, cured meats, and all sorts of herbs. *28A Neal St., WC2, tel. 0171/240–1487. Tube: Covent Garden. Turn right on Long Acre, left on Neal St. Open Mon.–Thurs. 11–7, Fri. 10–7, Sat. 10–6.*

Fortnum & Mason. Wealthy Londoners have flocked to Fortnum & Mason since 1707, shopping for everything from caviar and truffles to Swiss cheese and bacon in an environment of crystal chandeliers and royal red carpets. For decades it has also held the title of "supplier to the royal household," but mum's the word on whether the queen is a corn flakes girl. For exotic splurges, this is indeed the place. Don't leave without a peek at the tea shop. *181 Piccadilly, W1, tel. 0171/734–8040. Tube: Green Park or Piccadilly Circus. From Green Park, walk NE on Piccadilly. From Piccadilly Circus, walk SW on Piccadilly. Open Mon.–Sat. 9:30–6.*

Neal's Yard Wholefood Warehouse. London's original health food emporium has all sorts of seeds, nuts, fruits, and cakes. There's also an impressive selection of British and Irish cheeses at nearby **Neal's Yard Dairy** (17 Shorts Gardens, tel. 0171/379–7646), and fresh loaves of bread at **Neal's Yard Bakery** (6 Neal's Yard, tel. 0171/836–5199). *21–23 Shorts Gardens, WC2, tel. 0171/836–5151. Tube: Covent Garden. Walk right on Long Acre, turn left on Neal St., left on Shorts Gardens. Open weekdays 9–7, Sat. 9–6:30, Sun. 11–5:30.*

Selfridges. The food hall at Selfridges is a very modern, chrome and white-tiled Aladdin's cave piled with food. It's particularly strong in ethnic and international stuff, including beers, cheeses, and ready-to-eat snacks. It's also a good stop for perishable gifts, and a fine place to shop for groceries if you live nearby. *400 Oxford St., W1, tel. 0171/629–1234. Tube: Bond Street. Open Mon.–Sat. 9:30–7 (Thurs. until 8).*

Steve Hatt. If you're a fish fiend then this is the place to come—even if only to admire the array of absolutely fresh creatures in scales and shells. *88 Essex Rd., N1, tel. 0171/226–3963. Tube: Angel. Walk north on Upper St., veer right on Essex Rd. Open Tues.–Sat. 7–5.*

The Tea House. This store takes the traditional British beverage—tea—and stands it on its ear. Of course you can get Earl Grey, but you can also buy funky blends like "Lovers' Tea" (flavored with passion fruit), "Campfire Tea" (flavored with cinnamon and almonds), and strawberry-kiwi tea. They also stock a hundred fancy teapots and kettles. *15A Neal St., WC2, tel. 0171/240–7539. Tube: Covent Garden. Open Mon.–Sat. 10–7, Sun. noon–6.*

Villandry. In this foodie's paradise you'll find French pâté, Continental cheeses, fruit tarts, biscuits, breads, and more. If you must indulge but can't wait, there's a small café in back that serves exquisite lunches. Villandry hopes to move to huge new premises at 19–21 Great Portland Street by January 1997, a move that will give it a tearoom, a dining room, and a larger food section than the hallowed food halls of Harrods. Call ahead to check. *89 Marylebone High St., W1, tel. 0171/487–3816. Tube: Bond Street. Walk west on Oxford St., turn right on James St. (which becomes Mandeville Pl., Thayer St., and Marylebone High St.). Open weekdays 8:30–7, Sat. 9–5.*

Reference Listings

BY CUISINE

AFRO-CARIBBEAN AND AFRICAN

UNDER £5
The Jacaranda Garden
(Brixton)

UNDER £10
Asmara (Brixton)
Calabash (Covent Garden)
La Reash Cous-Cous House
(Soho and Mayfair)

BRITISH

UNDER £5
Alfredo's (The City and
Islington)
Benjys (Earl's Court and South
Kensington)
Chelsea Bun Diner (Chelsea)
Dino's Grill (The East End)
M. Manze (Southbank and
Waterloo)
The New Piccadilly (Soho
and Mayfair)

Norman's (Bayswater and
Notting Hill Gate)
Phoenix Restaurant (Brixton)
The Rock & Sole Plaice
(Covent Garden)
Sydney Street Cafe (Chelsea)
West End Kitchen (Soho and
Mayfair)

UNDER £10
Byron (Hampstead and
Highgate)
The Eagle (The City and
Islington)
The Engineer (Camden Town)
Geales (Bayswater and
Notting Hill Gate)
Harry's Bar (Soho and
Mayfair)
The Lansowne (Camden
Town)
The Quality Chop House (The
City and Islington)

SPLURGE
Alastair Little (Soho and
Mayfair)

CHINESE AND VIETNAMESE

UNDER £5
New World (Soho and Mayfair)
Poons (Soho and Mayfair)

UNDER £10
Thanh Binh (Camden Town)

CONTINENTAL

UNDER £5
Kramps Creperie (Earl's Court
and South Kensington)
Portobello Café (Bayswater
and Notting Hill Gate)

UNDER £10
Ambrosiana Creperie
(Chelsea)
Belgo Centraal (Soho and
Mayfair)
Brahms (Chelsea)
Chapter 11 (Chelsea)
Côte à Côte (South Bank and
Waterloo)

The Eagle (The City and Islington)
Gaby's Continental Bar (Soho and Mayfair)
The Lansowne (Camden Town)
Le Bistroteque (Camden Town)
Luna (Camden Town)
Mars (Covent Garden)
Scandies (Kensington and Knightsbridge)
Waterloo Fire Station (South Bank and Waterloo)

GREEK AND MIDDLE EASTERN

UNDER £5
Al Rawshi (Earl's Court and South Kensington)
Café Sofra (Soho and Mayfair)
Lahore Kebab House (The East End)
Manzara (Bayswater and Notting Hill Gate)

UNDER £10
Daphne's (Camden Town)
La Reash Cous-Cous House (Soho and Mayfair)
Neal's Yard Dining Room (Covent Garden)

INDIAN AND BENGALI

UNDER £5
Anwars (Bloomsbury)
Clifton (The East End)
Diwana Bhel Poori House (Bloomsbury)
Govinda's (Soho and Mayfair)
Lahore Kebab House (The East End)
Ravi Shankar (The City and Islington)

UNDER £10
Chutney's (Bloomsbury)
Curry Inn (Kensington and Knightsbridge)
Khan's (Bayswater and Notting Hill Gate)

ITALIAN

UNDER £5
The New Piccadilly (Soho and Mayfair)
Pizzeria Franco (Brixton)
Pollo (Soho and Mayfair)

UNDER £10
Buona Sera at the Jam (Chelsea)
Italian Graffiti (Soho and Mayfair)
La Bardigiana (Bloomsbury)
Osteria Basilico (Bayswater and Notting Hill Gate)
Pucci Pizza (Chelsea)
Spago (Earl's Court and South Kensington)
Waterloo Fire Station (South Bank and Waterloo)

JAPANESE

UNDER £10
Hamine (Soho and Mayfair)
Tokyo Diner (Soho and Mayfair)
Wagamama (Soho and Mayfair)

JEWISH AND EAST EUROPEAN

UNDER £5
The Bagel Bar (Camden Town)
Brick Lane Beigal Bake (The East End)
Taffgoods Sandwich Bar (Soho and Mayfair)

UNDER £10
Zamoyski's (Hampstead and Highgate)

SPANISH AND PORTUGUESE

UNDER £5
La Barraca (Kensington and Knightsbridge)

UNDER £10
Bar Sol Ona (Soho and Mayfair)
Caravela (Kensington and Knightsbridge)

TEX-MEX

UNDER £10
Texas Lone Star Saloon (Earl's Court and South Kensington)
Viva Zapata (Hampstead and Highgate)

THAI, MALAYSIAN, AND INDONESIAN

UNDER £5
Malaysia Hall Dining Hall (Soho and Mayfair)

UNDER £10
Churchill Thai Kitchen (Bayswater and Notting Hill Gate)
Harry's Bar (Soho and Mayfair)
Thai Taste (Earl's Court and South Kensington)

VEGETARIAN

UNDER £5
Café Vert (Hampstead and Highgate)
Diwana Bhel Poori House (Bloomsbury)
Food for Thought (Covent Garden)
Govinda's (Soho and Mayfair)
Greenhouse (Bloomsbury)
Mildred's (Soho and Mayfair)

UNDER £10
Chutney's (Bloomsbury)
Cranks (Covent Garden)
Neal's Yard Dining Room (Covent Garden)
The Place Below (The City and Islington)

SPECIAL FEATURES

BREAKFAST PLACES

UNDER £5

Alfredo's (The City and Islington)

The Bagel Bar (Camden Town)

Benjy's (Earl's Court and South Kensington)

Brick Lane Beigal Bake (The East End)

Café Vert (Hampstead and Highgate)

Chelsea Bun Diner (Chelsea)

Food for Thought (Covent Garden)

Le Bistroteque (Camden Town)

Norman's (Bayswater and Notting Hill Gate)

Phoenix Restaurant (Brixton)

Portobello Café (Bayswater and Notting Hill Gate)

Sydney Street Cafe (Chelsea)

Taffgoods Sandwich Bar (Soho and Mayfair)

UNDER £10

Harry's Bar (Soho and Mayfair)

OUTDOOR DINING

UNDER £5

Pizzeria Franco (Brixton)

Portobello Café (Bayswater and Notting Hill Gate)

Sydney Street Cafe (Chelsea)

UNDER £10

Churchill Thai Kitchen (Bayswater and Notting Hill Gate)

Cranks (Covent Garden)

Daphne's (Camden Town)

The Engineer (Camden Town)

Italian Graffiti (Soho and Mayfair)

La Reash Cous-Cous House (Soho and Mayfair)

Scandies (Kensington and Knightsbridge)

LATE-NIGHT DINING

UNDER £5

Brick Lane Beigal Bake (The East End)

Clifton (East End)

La Barraca (Kensington and Knightsbridge)

UNDER £10

Asmara (Brixton)

Bar Sol Ona (Soho and Mayfair)

Buona Sera at the Jam (Chelsea)

Caravela (Kensington and Knightsbridge)

Hamine (Soho and Mayfair)

Harry's Bar (Soho and Mayfair)

Pucci Pizza (Chelsea)

Spago (Earl's Court and South Kensington)

Texas Lone Star Saloon (Earl's Court and South Kensington)

PUBS

5

By Jennifer L. Brewer and Sunny Delaney

The English take their drink very seriously, and pubs are where Londoners go to hang out, see and be seen, act out the drama of life, and drink themselves into oblivion. Neighborhood pubs—patronized by local drunks and families alike—make up the largest group of London's 1,000 or so public houses. If you're a student (or not too old to pretend), most colleges have on-campus pubs for socializing between lectures.

Although the atmosphere is rarely inspiring, the clientele certainly is, and you won't find cheaper alcohol unless you buy discount cans at an "off-license" (the British equivalent of a liquor store).

Bartenders don't get tipped in pubs. If you want to show appreciation for exceptional service, buy the bartender a drink; after placing an order say, "and one for yourself."

Once you decide where to drink, the big decision is *what* to drink. Most English pubs are affiliated with particular breweries and are beholden to sell only beers produced by that brewery. Some of the larger chains, identified on the pub's sign, include Bass, Chef and Brewer, Courage, Samuel Smith, Guinness, and Whitbread. In contrast, independently owned pubs, called "free houses," can serve whatever they wish and tend to offer a more extensive selection. Besides cask-conditioned real ales (made without chilling, filtering, or pasteurization) and more commercial beers, there is also a new range of bottled drinks on the market. Alcoholic lemonades, with brand names like Hooch and Two Dogs, have alcohol contents that hover around 5% yet taste like fizzy soda. Other junk booze to watch out for includes Schott's line of alcoholic seltzers, bottled mixed drinks like Moscow Mule (vodka, ginger ale, and lime), Ginzing (gin, ginseng, and lemon-lime soda), and even alcohol-laced sparkling water.

Unless otherwise noted, all pubs listed below—as well as most pubs throughout the city—are open Monday–Saturday 11–11, Sunday noon–10:30. For late-night drinking try wine bars (which charge exorbitant prices to subsidize their expensive after-hours liquor licenses), pubs featuring music or theater, or hope to find a small neighborhood pub that just doesn't give a damn. People also head to restaurants for after-hours drinking since some serve alcohol as late as 2 AM. Of course, the pints are more expensive, and sometimes you must also order food.

BAYSWATER AND NOTTING HILL GATE

If you want to avoid the tourist crowd in Bayswater, wander just a little way west to Notting Hill Gate, where London's fashionable crowd dines in ever-so-trendy restaurants before winding things up with a refined pint.

The Ashes. Flags from all over the globe cover the ceiling of this popular, loud, and smoky pub which caters to international tourists who come for pints and animated conversation. It's a great, friendly place to shoot some pool, or watch the football or cricket games on their big-screen TV. *51 Moscow Rd., off Queensway, W2, tel. 0171/229–0647. Tube: Bayswater.*

The Market Bar. Weird, drippy candles and heavy velvet curtains give this Notting Hill locale an almost clubby feel. A mix of urban trendies, rastas, and punks haunt the bar, which has a selection of cocktails in addition to your basic beer. *240A Portobello Rd., at Lancaster Rd., W11, tel. 0171/229–6472. Tube: Ladbroke Grove. Open Mon.–Thurs. 11–11, Fri.–Sat. 11–midnight, Sun. noon–10:30.*

Uxbridge Arms. The King's College set—young, urbane, and slightly drunk—packs this place on weekends. During the week you'll find a smattering of businessfolk in this happily noisy pub. *13 Uxbridge St., off Hillgate St., W8, tel. 0171/727–7326. Tube: Notting Hill Gate.*

Windsor Castle. Drinkers of every ilk are welcome at this cozy pub with sloping, sawdust-covered floors. On warm summer nights the large courtyard out back is packed with students from King's College and denizens of the nearby Holland Park hostel. *114 Campden Hill Rd., off Notting Hill Gate, W8, tel. 0171/727–8491. Tube: Notting Hill Gate.*

BLOOMSBURY

With its myriad tourist attractions, Bloomsbury might seem a more likely locale for afternoon tea than a nighttime pub crawl. On the other hand, after blitzing the British Museum you'll be parched. Besides, all those University of London students have to drink *somewhere.* Many choose to drink in their own college bars. **University of London Union** (Malet St., WC1, tel. 0171/580–9551) opens daily at noon and stays open "until at least 11." Unfortunately, after 7 PM you'll probably need to show University of London ID—so go early or go elsewhere. **University College London Union** (25 Gordon St., WC1, tel. 0171/387–3611), two blocks north, has a number of bars, though most close over the summer break. Their "security" is less overt, though you may be asked to pay a 15p entrance fee after 5 PM.

The Lamb. Lamb's Conduit Street is peppered with bars and cafés, but The Lamb is the best of the bunch. Bask in the sun (if applicable) at an outdoor table with the relaxed crowd of locals and students. *Lamb's Conduit St., WC1, near Guilford St., tel. 0171/405–0713. Tube: Russell Square. Open Mon.–Sat. 11–11, Sun. noon–4 and 7–10:30.*

Princess Louise. This fine, popular pub has an over-the-top Victorian interior—glazed terracotta, stained and frosted glass, and a glorious painted ceiling. It's not all show, either; the food is a cut above normal pub grub (especially the Thai dishes) and there's a good selection of real ales. *208 High Holborn, WC1, tel. 0171/405–8816. Tube: Holborn. Open weekdays 11–11, Sat. 12:30–3 and 6–11.*

The Rising Sun. Good food, good drinks, and a nice interior—what more could you want? By day it's a quiet hideaway and a great place for lunch—try a lamb or vegetable pie (small £3.45, enormous "standard" £4.45) or a big sandwich (£2.25–£3). At night it's noisy and packed with students sampling the wide range of beers, including lots of real ales. *46 Tottenham Court Rd., W1, tel. 0171/636–6530. Tube: Goodge Street.*

The Valiant Trooper. During the school year, you'll find a professor or two holding court with students in this large and comfortable pub, while a variety of characters spill out into the streets on any sunny afternoon. *18–20 Goodge St., W1, tel. 0171/636–0721. Tube: Goodge Street.*

Water Rats. Also a venue for indie-rock (*see* Clubs, in Chapter 6), this place is very popular with students. Rumor has it Marx and Engels used to drink here on breaks from the British Library Reading Room. A member of the evening staff hasn't seen them though; "Maybe they come in during the day." *328 Gray's Inn Rd., near Euston Rd., W1, tel. 0171/837–7269. Tube: King's Cross. Open daily 11:30 AM–midnight.*

CAMDEN TOWN

Camden's pubs reflect the trendy, boho character of the neighborhood. Unwind with a pint after haggling at the markets or strolling along the canal.

The Good Mixer. Don't be surprised if you spot a celeb or two hanging out after a recording session at a nearby studio. There's a pool table and lots of smoke, but not much space; arrive early on weekends or risk being shut out of this popular pub. *30 Inverness St., off Camden High St., NW1, tel. 0171/916–7929. Tube: Camden Town. Open Mon.–Sat. 11–midnight, Sun. 11–11.*

Harvey Floorbanger's. On weekend nights, the always popular HF's is filled with pre-clubbing twentysomethings throbbing to techno beats. Not everyone's cup of tea, but where else can you see people dancing in a pub? *202 Camden High St., NW1, tel. 0171/284–1513. Tube: Camden Town.*

WKD. WKD is one of Camden's trendiest bars, with a wide range of clientele and music. Truly brave souls may want to try "Cool Runnin's" (£4), a vicious, opaque mix of rum, blue curaçao, and fruit juices—tasty, but deadly! During happy hour (Mon.–Sat. noon–9:30, Sun. noon–7), jugs of cocktails are £5.50 and beers £1.50. After 9 PM, there's live music and a £2–£5 cover; check *Time Out* for live music listings. *18 Kentish Town Rd., NW1, tel. 0171/267–1869. Tube: Camden Town. Open Tues.–Sat. noon–2 AM, Sun. noon–11.*

World's End. After a busy Saturday at the markets, retreat to Camden's largest pub. Built in a former Victorian workhouse, World's End has two bars, three floors, and woefully inadequate toilets. Check out Lt. Colonel Wyldboare-Smyth's insect collection rotting away across from the food counter. This place gets packed on weekends. *174 Camden High St., NW1, tel. 0171/482–1765. Tube: Camden Town.*

CHELSEA

Chelsea's resident wealthy young things love to drink almost as much as they love to shop, and you'll find tons of pubs that strike a careful balance between street hip and yuppie chic. Typically, the farther you get from King's Road, the more mellow the pub.

Ferret & Firkin. The full name is "The Ferret & Firkin in the Balloon up the Creek," and it's a trek south from King's Road. Your reward is cool indie tunes on the jukebox and an alternative crowd (dubbed the Balloonatics) at the bar. Have a pint of Balloonastic (£1.75) or Dogbolter (£2) and watch the world blur. *114 Lots Rd., SW10, tel. 0171/352–6645. Tube: Fulham Broadway.*

"Phoenix My Pint, & I'll Firkin Kill Ya!"

Nearly every neighborhood in London boasts a pub from the & Firken chain. Though some are better than others, all share a few trademarks: Firkin Brewery beers, wooden floors, a friendly staff, and theme decor. The Phoenix & Firkin (5 Windsor Walk, SE5, tel. 0171/701–8282), built on the site of a burnt-out BritRail ticket hall, features railroad memorabilia, while the Pharaoh & Firkin (90 Fulham High St., SW8, tel. 0171/731–0732) is filled with Egyptian tchotchkes like mummies, camels, and a wee sphinx. Most of the Firkin pubs brew their own beer in-house, whereas others are supplied by the brewery in the cavernous Falcon & Firkin (360 Victoria Park Rd., E9, tel. 0181/985–0693), out in Mile End. Firkin pubs tend to attract young crowds, and all have good selections of "own-brews," so give them a firkin try.

Front Page. This classy, intimate pub is currently the *in* spot for Chelsea's *in* crowd. By day, it's more mellow, and perfect for lingering. The menu features delicious "new British"–style dishes (£3–£7). *35 Old Church St., just south of King's Rd., SW3, tel. 0171/352–0648. Tube: Sloane Square.*

Legend has it that an 80-year-old local, Fred, drinks 10 pints a day at Man in the Moon. He's been doing so for 55 years.

Man in the Moon. Let the rich Georgian splendor of this theater pub dazzle you—then join the artsy crowd in the back room for a show (Tues.–Sun. 8:30 PM). *392 King's Rd., at Park Walk, SW3, tel. 0171/352–5075. Tube: Sloane Square.*

Orange Brewery. Many champion the solid, clubby, Victorian-era Orange as the "best pub in London." It makes its own brews: Try SW1 (a bitter) or Pimlico Porter (a dark ale) for £1.80–£2 per pint. Brewery tours are £3, half pint included. *37 Pimlico Rd., off Lower Sloane St., SW1, tel. 0171/730–5984. Tube: Sloane Square.*

Trafalgar. Cavernous and crowded, Trafalgar hooks the Chelsea youth brigade with £3 pitchers (Mon.–Thurs. 6 PM–11 PM), darts, pool, a ski simulator, 11 TVs, and a jukebox (free Sun. from 6 PM). *200 King's Rd., SW3, tel. 0171/352–1076. Tube: Sloane Square.*

The Water Rat. Don't come to this standard-looking pub for the pounding music (house to opera) or outdoor tables with prime views of King's Road. Come for exotic shots (£1 Mon. and Fri. from 1 PM) of Absolut vodka, flavored with red hot chili peppers, passion fruit, mint, marshmallow, and even Mars Bars. *1–3 Milman's St., at King's Rd., SW10, tel. 0171/351–4732. Tube: Sloane Square.*

THE CITY AND ISLINGTON

The City is mainly a daytime drinking area: When the suits leave at the end of the business day, so does the life, such as it is. Regardless, the pubs here are some of the oldest in London—once frequented by the likes of Dr. Samuel Johnson and Charles Dickens. Islington, in contrast, is less stuffy, less wealthy, and more conducive to hanging out.

Black Friar. Located in a 12th-century friary, Black Friar has a large outdoor terrace, but the atmosphere inside is much more inspiring than the speeding traffic on New Bridge Street. Sip a pint in the cozy, stone-walled room whose barrel-vaulted ceiling is decorated with mosaics and maxims like "Industry is all" and "Wisdom is rare." *174 Queen Victoria St., EC4, tel. 0171/236–5650. Tube: Blackfriars. Open weekdays 11–10.*

Cittie of Yorke. Order a pint at what's reputedly the largest bar in London and retire to one of the dozen or so wooden "snugs" that line the walls. The clientele leans toward the white-collar set at lunchtime, but it's the young urban professionals who flock here after work. Their Cellar Bar is cozier and quieter. *22 High Holborn, WC1, tel. 0171/242–7670. Tube: Chancery Lane. Open Mon.–Sat. 11:30–11.*

Mitre. This quiet, relaxed Islington public house plays host to a wide range of locals. By day it's pretty quiet, but at night things pick up considerably. Inside, the mood is set by candles and subdued lighting, or take your pint outside to the beer garden and watch the moon through the rooftops. *130 Upper St., N1, tel. 0171/226–3531. Tube: Angel.*

The Old King Lud. A young, friendly crowd gathers in this woodsy pub on the east end of Fleet Street. They serve 20 cask-conditioned real ales, along with frequently changing guest kegs. *78 Ludgate Circus, EC4, tel. 0171/329–8517. Tube: Blackfriars. Walk north on New Bridge St. Open weekdays 11:30–11, weekends noon–7.*

The Purple Turtle. Over 100 beers from around the world are served up in this purple heaven. Try some viciously strong (8.4%) Merry Down cider (£2.20) or a bottle of Delirium Tremens (£2.60). Paranoia (£2.65) comes in two colors, red (made with beets) and green (made with spinach). A fun, funky crowd and a well-stocked CD jukebox make it all the better. *108 Essex Rd., off Upper St., N1, tel. 0171/704–9020. Tube: Angel. Open daily noon–11.*

Ye Olde Cheshire Cheese. One of the oldest pubs in London (*rebuilt* after the Great Fire of 1666), YOCC has long been a famous haunt of Fleet Street journalists. Charles Dickens and lexicographer Samuel Johnson also both drank here. Though it's an institution, you're still more likely to see suits than tourists. *Wine Office Court, 145 Fleet St., EC4, tel. 0171/353–6170. Tube: Blackfriars. Open weekdays 11:30–11, Sat. noon–11, Sun. noon–5.*

EARL'S COURT AND SOUTH KENSINGTON

Earl's Court and South Kensington may be popular budget-lodging areas, but that's about it. When night falls, the streets are pretty empty—except for wandering bands of jet-lagged tourists looking for a nearby, no-hassle drink.

Admiral Cordington. You'll find an upscale crowd chatting on the outdoor patio of this handsome Victorian relic; note the gas lamps and antique mirrors. Come for a satisfying pub-grub lunch. *17 Mossop St., off Draycott Ave., SW3, tel. 0171/581–0005. Tube: South Kensington.*

Drayton Arms. This Victorian pub may have lost its Elvis impersonator (neighbors complained about the noise), but they've just added a new sound system, so it's still a good time. Try the Caffrey's Irish Ale (£2.05), which takes four minutes to settle. *153 Old Brompton Rd., SW5, tel. 0171/373–0385. Tube: Gloucester Road.*

Hoop and Toy. From the gaslights outside to the beef-and-ale pie on the menu, everything about the Hoop and Toy says "Edwardian!" It's a free house, with more beer to choose from than usual. *34 Thurloe Pl., off Cromwell Pl., SW7, tel. 0171/589–8360. Tube: South Kensington. Open weekdays 7:30 AM–11 PM, Sat. 11–11, Sun. noon–10:30.*

The Prince of Teck. Come here to tip cans of Victoria Bitter ("VB") with Aussie, Kiwi, and South African crowds. Authentic touches include a stuffed male kangaroo, Kevin "Bloody" Wilson on the jukebox, and toilets marked SHEILAS and BRUCES. *161 Earl's Court Rd., SW5, tel. 0171/373–3107. Tube: Earl's Court.*

SOHO AND COVENT GARDEN

Thousands of revelers, both tourists and Brits, crowd the pubs of Soho and Covent Garden every night of the week. On weekends, folks spill out into the streets with pints in hand—bring your mates and join the fun. One caveat: If you're allergic to crowds and noise, go elsewhere. And know that some local pubs levy a cover charge of a pound or so on weekends.

Coach & Horses. Bright orange lights and lots of Naugahyde make this place look like a new Denny's franchise, but the crowds aren't here for the decor. It's an historic hard-drinking place—local character Jeffrey Barnard (a British Bukowski) spent the 1950s pissed at this bar, observing Soho's "Low Life" for *Spectator* magazine. *29 Greek St., off Shaftesbury Ave., W1, tel. 0171/437–5920. Tube: Leicester Square.*

Crown & Anchor. This otherwise standard pub has a noticeably hippie clientele. And no wonder—it's situated in the best part of Covent Garden. After pints, cruise to nearby Neal's Yard Dining Room (*see* Chapter 4). *22 Neal St., WC2, tel. 0171/836–5649. Tube: Covent Garden.*

De Hems. Although it's just steps away from Chinatown, De Hems's theme, if you can't guess, is Dutch; hence the gins and Orangeboom beers in the hands of the youngish, mixed crowd. Suits overrun the pub between 5 and 7. *11 Macclesfield St., off Shaftesbury Ave., W1, tel. 0171/437–2494. Tube: Piccadilly Circus.*

The Dog House. The Dog House has the hippest divey scene in Soho. It's below ground, with weird little rooms, funky furniture, and bright spacey murals on the walls. The music kicks, it's smoky, and it's loud. *187 Wardour St., W1, tel. 0171/434–2118. Tube: Tottenham Court Road. Open weekdays 5:30 PM–11 PM, Sat. 6 PM–11 PM.*

French House. The unofficial Resistance headquarters during World War II, this pub still maintains a distinctly French aura. Predictably, there's an excellent wine selection. *49 Dean St., at Shaftesbury Ave., W1, tel. 0171/437–2799. Tube: Leicester Square.*

The Intrepid Fox. If you're into hard-core punk/thrash/metal, hey, yeah, this is your place. Join the raucous, pierced, tightly packed crowd boozin' on Carlsberg's extrapotent Elephant Ale beneath posters of gods like Metallica. *99 Wardour St., W1, no phone. Tube: Piccadilly Circus. Open Mon.–Sat. noon–11, Sun. 3–10:30.*

Lamb & Flag. "The oldest tavern in Covent Garden" sits in an alley just off Floral Street. With the cobblestone courtyard and wee fluffy lamb on the sign outside, you'd never guess people once boxed bare-knuckle upstairs, prompting the pub's nickname, "Bucket of Blood." *33 Rose St., btw Long Acre and Flora St., WC2, tel. 0171/497–9504. Tube: Covent Garden.*

The Porcupine. This traditional pub offers outdoor tables and easy stumbling distance to the Leicester Square tube station (it's just around the corner). You'll meet tons of international students; drink enough, and you just might join in on the nightly air-jam sessions of Sub-Pop bands. The upstairs bar is a bit more mellow. *48 Charing Cross Rd., WC2, tel. 0171/836–0054. Tube: Leicester Square.*

GAY AND LESBIAN PUBS

London has a great gay scene, but pubs are a bit hard to find, especially if you're looking for something that caters exclusively to lesbians. Browse through free magazines like *The Pink Paper, Thud, Shebang* (lesbian focus), or *Boyz* (gay focus) for current details on pubs that nurture London's sizable community. *Time Out* also lists some pubs in its "Gay" section. A wander around London's **Gay Village** in Soho (the area around Old Compton Street) will lead you to any number of gay-owned or gay-friendly nightspots.

Angel Café Bar. A relaxed atmosphere and friendly staff make this a wonderful place to hang out. Older couples lounge on the comfy sofas and nibble delicious vegetarian food like lasagna (£3) or quiche (£2). Tuesday is women's night, but the crowd is always mixed and friendly. Every Friday there's a DJ and dancing. *65 Graham St., btw Vincent Terr. and City Rd., N1, tel. 0171/608–2656. Tube: Angel. Open Mon.–Sat. noon–midnight, Sun. noon–11:30.*

The Black Cap. This no-holds-barred drag bar features nightly acts. The cover is £2–£3 Tuesday through Saturday, free on Sunday and Monday. There's never a cover at the upstairs bar. *171 Camden High St., NW1, tel. 0171/485–1742. Tube: Camden Town. Open Mon.–Thurs. noon–2 AM, Fri.–Sat. noon–3 AM, Sun. noon–midnight.*

The Box. This supertrendy, girl-friendly Covent Garden spot does duty as café by day and bar by night. Sunday nights feature "Girl Bar," with an all-woman staff and nonstop music. *32–34 Monmouth St., WC2, tel. 0171/240–5828. Tube: Leicester Square. Open Mon.–Sat. 11–11, Sun. noon–6 and 7–10:30.*

The Coleherne. This is an in-your-face male pub for the hard core. Dress code: black leather. *261 Old Brompton Rd., at Coleherne Rd., SW5, tel. 0171/373–9859. Tube: Earl's Court.*

Drill Hall. This gay cultural center and meeting place also has a cozy, popular bar. The folks are friendly, the music is sociable, and the drinks are decently priced. On Monday night it's womyn-only, with happy-hour prices (£1 pints!) 5:30–7:30. *16 Chenies St., WC1, tel. 0171/631–1353. Tube: Goodge Street. Open daily 6 PM–11 PM (Mon. from 5:30).*

Earl's. Although this place draws mostly boys, the attitude is easygoing, upbeat, and comfortable for just about everyone (well, maybe not when the male strippers are at work). *180 Earl's Court Rd., SW5, tel. 0171/835–1826. Tube: Earl's Court. Open Mon.–Sat. 4–midnight, Sun. noon–midnight.*

King William IV. One of the oldest gay pubs in Britain, the popular, noisy King William is patronized by a mixed group—all ages, both sexes. You can drink in the leafy courtyard out back or squeeze into the upstairs lounge. *77 Hampstead High St., NW3, tel. 0171/435–5747. Tube: Hampstead. Open Mon.–Sat. noon–11, Sun noon–10:30.*

AFTER DARK

6

By Jennifer L. Brewer and Sunny Delaney

London has a raging after-hours scene that's been setting global trends for decades.
Rock music, jazz, raves, you name it, London probably did it first and often does it best. The cost, however, can be a bummer: A pint will cost you £2, movie tickets are £4–£9, and clubs usually charge covers of £6 and up, up, up. Student and rush tickets often soften the blow for theater and classical music, and many dance and live-music clubs distribute half-price flyers on street corners. Even so, the fact is that London is an expensive place to play.

First-run movie theaters, jazz joints, dance clubs, and big-name theaters are concentrated around Soho and Covent Garden, but you'll find hip alternative clubs and theaters all over London. A number of publications give detailed rundowns of what's on where and are great resources if you plan to stay in London for more than a few days. The best of the lot by far is the weekly magazine *Time Out* (£1.70), which is absolutely invaluable to travelers and locals for listing and reviewing the ever-evolving night scene in London. If it's happening in London, it's probably listed in *Time Out,* complete with a useful description that will help you wade through the barrage of options. *What's On* (£1.20) is a cheaper but less comprehensive version of the same thing. Alternatives to these relatively mainstream rags include *New Music Express (NME)* (85p) and *Melody Maker* (80p). *The Evening Standard* (30p), available at all newsstands, also has all-purpose entertainment info, especially in the free supplement "Hot Tickets," which comes out every Friday.

As Frank Sinatra said, "London by night is a wondrous sight," but not from the upper deck of a Night Owl bus—it's prime mugging turf.

Pick up the little cards and invites lying in heaps at clothing and record shops for suggestions on where to spend your evening; sometimes these promo cards entitle you to bargain admissions. Student ID cards also come in handy at dance clubs and some music venues, which offer "concession" prices to students with identification as well as to OAPs (old-age pensioners) and UB40s, i.e., the unemployed (it's the form one fills out to go on the dole). And remember: Theaters and cinemas will only sell you reduced-rate and standby tickets if you can show them one of the above IDs.

Pubs (*see* Chapter 5) generally close at 11 PM, which can put a major damper on your evening if you just wanted to enjoy a quiet pint. The tube also closes early (about 12:30 AM), so for late-night fun you'd better figure out London's extensive Night Owl bus system (*see* Getting Around London, in Chapter 1). Night Owl buses operate on fewer routes and less often than daytime buses, but you still won't wait much more than 30 minutes for your double-decker. To avoid getting mugged, never sit alone on the upper deck of a Night Owl bus. Rides with minicab drivers who chirp "Taxi? Taxi?" outside nightclubs should also be avoided, especially by women traveling alone. They are often illegal and uninsured, and they sometimes overcharge for late-night trips, especially if they hear a foreign accent. For more details on the taxi scene, *see* Getting Around London, in Chapter 1.

Dance Clubs

Every night of the week, scores of clubs spin contemporary dance music (jungle, drum and bass, *every* variety of house and techno), old R&B hits, '70s funk and disco, and the occasional indie platter. One-nighters ("theme" nights that take place at particular clubs on the same night every week, or move around from club to club) are very popular but tend to confuse matters with erratic opening and closing times—always check the daily listings in *Time Out* for current info. Some venues that normally stage live music also have dancing with DJs, sometimes after the bands, sometimes before.

The Artsline (tel. 0171/388–2227) is a free events-info service for people with disabilities—ask about anything from wheelchair accessibility to dramatic interpretations for the hearing impaired to "touch exhibits" at museums.

The dress code at most of London's clubs is casual; jeans are often okay, though some places will specify "no trainers" (athletic shoes) or "smart dress" (no blue jeans). Throughout London, clubs typically open by 10 PM and close around 3 AM (when many liquor licenses expire). Though you might have to pay handsomely for the privilege of partying into the wee hours, some "after-hours clubs" *open* at 3 AM and run until after sunrise—perfect for those who can't face the prospect of returning to their schoolkid-infested hostel. A growing movement is the day club, where the fashionably idle can while away those empty hours until the sun sets. The standard cover charge for dance clubs on weekday nights is £5–£7, though you may get a break for arriving early—usually before 11 PM—or for showing a student ID. On weekends, prices can skyrocket up to £15, but some clubs still offer cheaper fun.

There are plenty of trendy, expensive discos—the sort mainly patronized by tourists lured in by the neon and London's rich and beautiful—spread throughout Soho and Covent Garden. Many are around Leicester Square, and all charge covers of £10–£15. If you're looking for nothing more than flashing lights, bass-driven dance music, and snazzy crowds, try the huge **Equinox** (Leicester Sq., WC2, tel. 0171/437–1446), upscale **Stringfellows** (16 Upper St. Martin's Ln., WC2, tel. 0171/240–5534), or the showy **Hippodrome** (Leicester Sq., WC2, tel. 0171/437–4311)—just look for the neon horses over the entrance. If a bouncer refuses you admission into one of these trendy clubs because you're "not a member," it most likely means your 501s and hiking boots just don't cut it. But, don't worry, you'll definitely fit in somewhere else.

The Astoria/LA2. Although normally a live-music venue, The Astoria also hosts a variety of one-nighters both in its main hall and in its Siamese twin LA2. The *verrrry* popular "G.A.Y." alternates between the two halls on Monday, Thursday, and Saturday, playing trashy disco and funk. Friday brings the aptly named "Popscene" at LA2 and "Rockscene" at the Astoria. The Astoria's huge balcony is a good place to chill out and peer down on the dancing masses. *157 Charing Cross Rd., WC2, tel. 0171/434–0403. Tube: Tottenham Court Road. Cover: free–£8.*

Bar Rumba. This place hosts a variety of wildly popular one-nighters every night of the week. Check out "Bubblin Over" (Sunday) for R&B and swing, "Space" (Wednesday) for house, and the "KAT Klub" (Friday) for soul, R&B, and drum and bass. Saturday's "Garage City" is regularly packed to the rafters, so come early or prepare to queue. *36 Shaftesbury Ave., W1, tel. 0171/287–2715. Tube: Piccadilly Circus. Cover: £3–£10.*

Blue Note. Quite possibly the best variety of music in London is trotted out at this club's one-nighters. The hottest night of the week must be Sunday's "Metalheadz," featuring jungle-guru Goldie and his crew. Monday night is the world-beat wonder "Anokha," featuring tabla, bass, and live percussion dubbed over records. "Magic Bus" pulls up on Fridays with a mix of acid jazz, soul, funk, and old-school hip-hop. *1 Hoxton Sq., N1, tel. 0171/729–8440. Tube: Old Street. Walk east on Old St., turn left on Rufus St. Cover: £3–£8.*

Camden Palace. A wide mix of one-nighters draws large dancing crowds throughout the week. Tuesday's "Feet First" features DJs Jonathon and Eko spinning a fun mix of indie, guitar, and rock music, along with a live band that might just be the next big thing. The lively "Peach featuring garage and house music" rears its oh-so-pretty head on Friday until 6 AM. Look for flyers near the Camden Town tube station for discounted admission. *1A Camden High St., NW1, tel. 0171/387–0428. Tube: Camden Town. Cover: £4–£12. Wheelchair access.*

Cross. Inside a set of converted railway arches, Cross is no mere warehouse club—there's a good atmosphere here. Sunday's "Big Picture" is a bright mix of dub, house, jazz, and disco, while Friday's "Glitterati" brings out the beautiful with glamorous fun and house anthems; dress *way* up or stay home. *Goods Way Depot, off York Way, N1, tel. 0171/837–0828. Tube: Kings Cross. Walk north on York Way, turn left on Goods Way. Cover: £3–£15.*

The End. The Shamen's Mr. C set up The End to be a club for clubbers run by clubbers. And he's done a pretty good job—good ventilation and (wonder of wonders) air-conditioning mean you won't sweat to death without really trying. A host of monthlies rotate around Friday and Saturday nights, and Mr. C takes over the decks himself a couple of nights a week. *16A West Central St., WC1, tel. 0171/419–9199. Tube: Tottenham Court Road. Walk west on New Oxford St., turn right on West Central St. Cover: £7–£13.*

The Fridge. Brixton's major dance venue is like a three-ring circus, often with multimedia displays, live performances, and go-go dancers. It hosts some cool reggae and roots-oriented gigs, as well as the legendary "Love Muscle" gay club on Saturdays. *Town Hall Parade, Brixton Hill, SW2, tel. 0171/326–5100. Tube: Brixton. Walk south on Brixton Rd. Cover: £7–£12.*

Gardening Club. All sorts of stylish one-nighters are held in this upbeat, easygoing club. The music is mostly house and techno, with "Scrambled Eggs" attracting students on Thursdays, "The Pinch" offering cheap drinks (£1.20) to a young crowd on Tuesdays, and Sunday's "Queer Nation" attracting a mixed gay crowd. *4 The Piazza, Covent Garden, WC2, tel. 0171/497–3154. Tube: Covent Garden. Cover: £3–£12.*

Heaven. This massive club turns into London's largest lesbian and gay party spot several nights a week. "Garage" (Friday) attracts a mixed gay/straight clientele, "Heaven" (Saturday) brings in a throbbing gay and lesbian crowd, and "Fruit Machine" (Wednesday) is mainly gay men. Heaven's maze of rooms is great for getting lost. *Under The Arches, Villiers St., WC2, tel. 0171/930–2020. Tube: Charing Cross or Embankment. From Charing Cross, walk NW on the Strand, turn left on Villiers St. From Embankment, walk NW on Villiers St. Cover: £3–£8.*

Leisure Lounge. "Jet Set" packs them in on Saturday with happy and hard house. Friday's wonderful "Popstarz" plays indie and Britpop to gays who chose Jarvis of Pulp over Donna Summer as their resident icon. Lace up some Adidas and join the throng—who says you can't dance to Oasis? This cavern gets pretty hot inside, so be warned. *121 Holborn, EC1, tel. 0171/242–1345. Tube: Chancery Lane. Cover: £5–£12.*

Loughborough Hotel. On Saturdays the Loughborough becomes the "Mambo Inn," a long-running and extremely popular one-nighter that's the best of its kind. Totally danceable African and Latin grooves are mixed downstairs, while upstairs it's hip-hop and house. A similar mix of tunes attracts clubbers to "Go Bananas" (Thursday) and "La Salsa" (Friday), while "El Swing" (Monday) features salsa. Many nights feature lambada, samba, or tango classes, so you don't have to feel like a klutz on the dance floor. *Cnr Loughborough and Evandale Rds., SW9, tel. 0171/737–2943. Tube: Brixton. Walk north on Brixton Rd. for ½ mi, turn right on Loughborough Rd. Cover: £2–£6.*

Mars. During Friday's "Kitty Lips," easily the hottest lesbian club in London, lesbians and their gay male pals shake it all over this friendly place to a great mix of modern dance music. Thursdays bring "Speed" with its heavy drum and bass jungle vibe, and Saturday the champagne flows at "Red Moet Society." *12 Sutton Row, W1, tel. 0171/439–4655. Tube: Tottenham Court Road. Walk south on Charing Cross Rd., turn right on Sutton Row. Cover: £6–£10.*

Ministry of Sound. Yes it's global, yes there are now record and clothing labels, but the Ministry of Sound has stopped short of becoming a mere tourist attraction. Remarkably, the Ministers have managed to bring good atmosphere and good grooves to this yawning cavern of a club. Still, expect huge queues (though you'll be glad to have people around in this neighborhood late at night), a snobby staff, and a scads of Italian tourists with cellphones. Fans of house and big beats shouldn't miss "Frisky?" on Fridays. *103 Gaunt St., SE1, tel. 0171/378–6528. Tube: Elephant & Castle. Walk north on Newington Causeway, turn left on Gaunt St. Cover: £12–£15.*

The Office. Wednesday's "Double Six Club" lopes along on a hilarious "easy-listening" vibe, with every boardgame you played in your elementary years spread out on tables. The rest of the week features eclectic one-nighters; Thursday's "Do Me a Favour!" is a good bet for pop, rock, disco, and northern soul. *3–5 Rathbone Pl., W1, tel. 0171/636–1598. Tube: Tottenham Court Road. Walk west on Tottenham Court Rd., turn right on Rathbone Pl. Cover: £3–£6.*

RAW. The music selection runs the gamut at the one-nighters in this subterranean venue. Wednesday's "Erection Section" pumps out club classics and Thursday's "Cabbage Patch" plays a rocky mix, sometimes with live bands. Friday is the fabulous "Ghetto Heaven," a blend of funk, soul, R&B, and boogie classics, while Saturday's "Barcaboodle" pulls in a funky crowd with disco, trip-hop, hip-hop, garage, and house. *112A Great Russell St., WC1, tel. 0171/436–1903. Tube: Tottenham Court Road. Walk north on Tottenham Court Road, turn right on Great Russell St. Cover: £3–£10.*

Turnmills. It hosts all sorts of one-nighters, including Saturday's legendary "Heavenly Social," where music from trance to indie pumps up a high-energy, do-anything crowd, followed by the hugely popular gay rave "Trade" from 3 AM until dawn. Have breakfast afterward in the attached café. *63B Clerkenwell Rd., EC1, tel. 0171/250–3409. Tube: Farringdon. Walk north on Farringdon Rd., turn right on Clerkenwell Rd. Cover: £6–£10.*

Velvet Underground. This intimate venue with velvet couches and bubble pillars features Super DJ Carl Cox spinning space, techno, and a bit of house at "Ultimate" on Thursday. Monday's "World Recession" is a hoot with club classics, garage, house, and £1 drinks. *143 Charing Cross Rd., WC2, tel. 0171/439–4655. Tube: Tottenham Court Road. Cover: £4–£10.*

Wag Club. This Soho club keeps shedding its skin and renewing itself. The one-nighters nowadays lean toward the guitar side of things: Wednesday's "Camouflage" plays indie music and Thursday's "Cigarettes & Alcohol" plays guitar rock from the '60s to the '90s. "Planet Earth's Big Night Out" (Friday) packs the Wag for an '80s revival, while "Blow Up" (Saturday) features a jarring mix of Britpop, R&B, and easy listening. Most nights this place does get groovy—once you get past the goons at the front door. *35 Wardour St., W1, tel. 0171/437–5534. Tube: Piccadilly Circus. Walk NE on Shaftesbury Ave., turn left on Wardour St. Cover: £3–£9.*

One-Night Stands

If none of the other clubs strike your fancy, keep an eye out for these wandering one-nighters:

- *Bambina: Smooch! This superglam gay night attracts a pile of pretty people, so pucker up and get down. Not for the timid.*

- *Club Fantastic: One of the best of the '80s revival throng. Draws in late-twentysomethings who danced with their friends in high school cafeterias under balloons and streamers.*

- *Starsky & Hutch: Not to be missed if you have a '70s-friendly bone in your body. Funk, soul, jazz, and disco keep it smokin'.*

Live Music

On any given night London hosts a stupefying number of shows, but nothing comes cheap: Covers and tickets cost anywhere from £3 to £20, with most falling in the £5–£7 range. On the upside, you generally get what you pay for: London's jazz clubs are first-rate, as are its rock and indie venues. There is also a thriving international music scene, with Caribbean, African, and Latin bands playing to enthusiastic crowds. Britpop continues to thrive, with acts like Blur, Pulp, and Gene drawing ever-larger crowds. (Oasis is so overwhelmingly popular that it has already spawned a tribute band, No Way Sis.) Pick up *Time Out, What's On, Melody Maker,* or *New Music Express (NME)* and face the music.

More established (some might say "over the hill") bands like the Rolling Stones and U2 are usually booked at **Wembley Stadium** (Empire Way, Wembley, Middlesex, tel. 0181/900–1234), an easy walk from the Wembley Park tube station. The **London Arena** (Limeharbour, Isle of Dogs, E14, tel. 0171/538–1212), near the Crossharbour/London Arena Docklands Light Railway station, is attracting a growing number of not-quite-mega acts. Some of pop music's royalty also graces the stage of the **Royal Albert Hall** (*see below*). The **University of London Union** (Malet St., WC1, tel. 0171/580–9551) regularly hosts local bands. Tickets are dirt cheap, but you may have to fake being a University of London student—or the guest of one. Smaller gigs are also held at colleges around town; check bulletin boards or *Time Out* for the latest. Free live music can also be found in pubs (*see* Chapter 5) and at local record stores like HMV and Virgin Megastore (*see* Music, in Chapter 7), which often host in-store performances.

MAJOR VENUES

The Astoria. When it's not being used as a dance club, all sorts of good bands play at this mid-size theater—lots of rock, some indie, a splash of reggae. Come early and snag a seat in the upstairs bar; it overlooks the stage. Siamese sibling LA2 (London Astoria 2) also hosts bands and one-night clubs, so make sure you're in the proper queue. *157 Charing Cross Rd., WC2, tel. 0171/434–0403. Tube: Tottenham Court Road. Wheelchair access.*

Brixton Academy. This Brixton institution is one of the bigger venues for hip indie and established acts. Despite a capacity of 4,000 people, the Academy's atmosphere seems more club-like than crowded, with interesting decor, plenty of bars, and upstairs seating. The sloping floor can be a bit scary, especially when slicked up by a night full of beer, but it provides good views of the stage. *211 Stockwell Rd., SW9, tel. 0171/924–9999. Tube: Brixton. Walk north on Brixton Rd., turn left on Stockwell Rd.*

Forum. This is a favorite venue for bands that are big but not quite ready for Wembley Stadium. The place gets packed with a fine mix of folks, and it's well designed so everyone has a great view. "House of Fun" takes over on Saturday with a DJ spinning disco, new wave, and club classics plus circus acts and trendies galore. *9–17 Highgate Rd., NW5, tel. 0171/284–2200. Tube: Kentish Town. Walk north on Kentish Town Rd., veer left on Highgate Rd.*

Hammersmith Apollo. Formerly called the Odeon, it's still one of London's most famous mainstream venues—so mainstream that it's often used for touring theater productions. *Queen Caroline St., W6, tel. 0171/416–6080. Tube: Hammersmith. Follow signs from station.*

National Kilburn. Way out in Kilburn, the National still manages to attract large crowds to see its biggish performers. *234 Kilburn High Rd., NW6, tel. 0171/625–4444. Tube: Kilburn.*

Shepherds Bush Empire. This award-winning venue lines up an interesting roster of hot new bands and old favorites. The downstairs area has three bars to quench your thirst. *Shepherds Bush Green, W12, tel. 0181/740–7474. Tube: Shepherds Bush. Wheelchair access.*

CLUBS

ROCK, REGGAE, AND WORLD BEAT In addition to having a variety of live acts, many of these clubs host one-nighters to fill their calendars. Always check current listings before heading out unless you want to be surprised by disco denizens when you were expecting a punk band.

Africa Centre. Visiting musicians from Africa and the Caribbean often play here. On other nights, DJs mix it up for a fairly diverse dance crowd. *38 King St., WC2, tel. 0171/836–1973. Tube: Covent Garden. Turn right on James St., right on King St. Cover: £5–£9.*

Borderline. When record companies want to try out new bands, they send 'em to this hip Soho establishment. Who knows, maybe you'll see the next big thing. *Orange Yard, off Manette St., W1, tel. 0171/734–2095. Tube: Tottenham Court Road. Walk south on Charing Cross Rd., turn right on Manette St. Cover: £5–£10.*

Dublin Castle. A great mix of lesser-knowns play nightly at this noisy Camden Town pub. The crowd tends to be enthusiastic—perhaps because of the pub prices for beer. *94 Parkway, NW1, tel. 0171/485–1773. Tube: Camden Town. Walk SW on Parkway. Cover: £4–£5.*

Garage. Clear views of the stage and a killer sound system make this a good place to see live rock and indie acts. The appropriately named **Upstairs at the Garage** shares the building and telephone but hosts different acts for a separate cover every night. Both places get pretty busy no matter what's offered. *20–22 Highbury Corner, N5, tel. 0171/607–1818. Tube: Highbury & Islington. Cover: £4–£9.*

Mean Fiddler. The flagship of the ever-growing Mean Fiddler empire, this club features indie, country, and pop bands, including some big names. The adjacent **Acoustic Room** hosts—you guessed it—acoustic acts for a mere £4–£5; look out for Thursday's "Floor Spot Night" with up-and-coming artists and free admission. *22–28A High St. Harlesden, NW10, tel. 0181/961–5490. Tube: Willesden Junction. Cover: free–£12.*

Monarch. You may not have heard of the bands playing the Monarch—then again, everyone has to start somewhere. A friendly crowd gets down to rock and pop bands most nights. *49 Chalk Farm Rd., NW1, tel. 0171/916–1049. Tube: Chalk Farm. Cover: £5–£8.*

Orange. Small, friendly, and favored by Aussies and Kiwis, Orange hosts nightly bands ranging from pop to folk to indie. Or check out "Thank Funk It's Friday" with grooving funk bands. *3 North End Crescent, W14, tel. 0171/371–4317. Tube: West Kensington. Walk north on North End Rd., veer right on North End Crescent. Cover: £5.*

Powerhaus. This recently moved venue is still small, sweaty, and smoky. The major draws are pub prices for beer, and talented rock, indie, and folk acts. When the Powerhaus rocks, it rocks hard. *240 Seven Sisters Rd., N4, tel. 0171/561–9656. Tube: Finsbury Park. Cover: £6–£12.*

Rock Garden. Though guitar-heavy rock still has a place here, the Garden has changed its lineup to include a more diverse mix of live funk and indie bands, and DJs playing house, garage, soul, and swing. Come during happy hour (weekdays 5–8 PM) for £1–£2 drinks and free snacks; you pay £2 to get in but can stay and see that night's show for free. *6–7 The Piazza, Covent Garden, WC2, tel. 0171/836–4052. Tube: Covent Garden. Cover: £5–£10.*

Underworld. This sprawling nightclub is located under the equally huge World's End pub. The music leans heavily toward the industrial, hard core, and indie side, but anything is possible. For example, Monday nights the club hosts sugar-sweet "Bubblicious," with DJs playing '70s disco, '80s trash, and '90s pop; free candy; and pub-priced pints at the bar. *174 Camden High St., NW1, tel. 0171/482–1932. Tube: Camden Town. Cover: £3–£8.*

Water Rats. The small stage in back is just perfect for the intimate mosh pit fueled by the thrash guitar. Red velvet curtains and candles add a bit of (decaying) elegance. "The Splash Club" brings indie rockers here most nights, often unsigned American bands. *328 Gray's Inn Rd., WC1, tel. 0171/837–7269. Tube: King's Cross. Walk NE on Euston Rd., turn right on Gray's Inn Rd. Cover: £5–£6.*

R&B, FUNK, AND SOUL Many of the rock and pop clubs above also have R&B, funk, or soul acts on certain nights. **Blue Note** (*see* Dance Clubs, *above*) often features live jazz, hip-hop, or rap acts. Camden's **WKD** (*see* Chapter 5) also has a good range of jazz, soul, and R&B.

Ain't Nothing But Blues Bar. The name says it all. Come in and chill out to the nightly live blues in a crowded atmosphere. Most nights there's no cover. *20 Kingly St., W1, tel. 0171/*

287–0514. Tube: Oxford Circus. Walk south on Regent St., turn left on Great Marlborough St., quick right on Kingly St. Cover: free–£5.

Station Tavern. This West London pub is known for excellent blues bands and mellow crowds that pack the place every night of the week. And you can't beat the price—it's free. *41 Bramley Rd., W10, tel. 0171/727–4053. Tube: Latimer Road. No cover.*

Subterania. Dance all night long at this small but outrageous club, which showcases rap, hip-hop, funk, and R&B during the week. On weekends, a variety of one-nighters bring in big crowds and big-name DJs. *12 Acklam Rd., W10, tel. 0181/960–4590. Tube: Ladbroke Grove. Walk north on Ladbroke Grove, turn right on Cambridge Gardens, right on Acklam Rd. Cover: £8–£10.*

Twelve Bar Club. A smattering of rock, a sprinkle of folk, and a heavy dollop of blues are served up at this venue. Pity there aren't really twelve bars here; the queue for drinks can be *long*. *Denmark Place, Denmark St., WC2, tel. 0171/916–6989. Tube: Tottenham Court Road. Walk south on Tottenham Court Rd., turn left on Denmark Pl. Cover: £4–£8.*

JAZZ Jazz is alive and well in London; more and more restaurants are bringing in jazz musicians to entertain their diners. The tasty **Pizza Express** chain features some very good—and "free to diners"—jazz in some of its locations; try the Hampstead (70 Heath St., NW3, tel. 0171/433–1600) or Finchley (820 High Rd., N1, tel. 0181/445–7714) branch. More central locations like Soho (10 Dean St., W1, tel. 0171/437–9595) or "Pizza on the Park" (11 Knightsbridge, SW1, tel. 0171/235–5273) feature higher-profile acts and charge significantly higher prices (up to £20), even to diners.

100 Club. This basement was the site of one of the Sex Pistols' first London gigs. The 100 Club has since evolved into a hip blues and jazz joint, with the occasional pop or indie band tossed in for good measure. Fortunately, it's still a dive. *100 Oxford St., W1, tel. 0171/636–0933. Tube: Tottenham Court Road. Cover: £5–£9.*

606 Club. Pro jazz musicians often come to—and sometimes play at—this basement club following a gig; inexperienced players are often encouraged to join in. It has a nice vibe, although you may have to wait hours for a table on weekends. Make reservations or prepare to stand inside by the bar. One minor drawback: Alcohol can only be served with meals. *90 Lots Rd., SW10, tel. 0171/352–5953. Tube: Fulham Broadway. Walk east on Fulham Rd., turn right on Wandon Rd., left on King's Rd., right on Lots Rd. Cover: £4–£4.50.*

Bull's Head Barnes. This is one of the best jazz pubs in town, even if it is far away in Hammersmith. The pleasant scene—right on the Thames—and big names who jam here regularly make it well worth the trip. Shows start nightly at 8:30. *Barnes Bridge, SW13, tel. 0181/876–5241. Tube: Hammersmith. From station, take Bus 9 to Barnes Bridge. Cover: £3–£8.*

Jazz Café. A fine way to end a day of carousing in Camden Town is an evening at the Jazz Café, though lines can be long and empty seats few and far between. Big-name talents often play here when touring London. Prices lean toward the high end except at Sunday afternoon's "Space," a showcase for up-and-coming acts and DJs—a bargain at £3. *5 Parkway, NW1, tel. 0171/916–6060. Tube: Camden Town. Cover: £3–£16.*

Ronnie Scott's. This legendary Soho club, opened in the early '60s, is the leading venue for jazz in London—if they're the best, they'll play here. Its status is, unfortunately, reflected in the prices, though students can often get considerable discounts (40%–50% off). Book in advance or get in line early. *47 Frith St., W1, tel. 0171/439–0747. Tube: Tottenham Court Road. Walk west on Oxford Circus, turn left on Soho St., cross Soho Sq. to Frith St. Cover: £12–£14. Closed Sun.*

Classical Music, Opera, and Dance

The arts scene in London is rich and varied. A bounty of internationally respected orchestras, opera companies, and ballet troupes make their homes here, including the **London Symphony Orchestra** (the most recorded symphony in the world), the **London Philharmonic Orchestra,** and the world-famous **Royal Ballet.** While it's true that ticket prices to any of these groups' performances can easily reach right into the stratosphere (seats for the Royal Opera top out at £188), that's no reason to retreat to your hotel room with an armload of Hobnob cookies. With some careful planning or a bit of luck, you can fill your evenings with song and dance, rub shoulders with the rich, and still have a few quid left over for a late-night snack. First of all, reserve early. If a program interests you it has probably also captivated hundreds of others, and performances *do* sell out; check *Time Out* and *What's On* for schedules. Tickets for classical concerts, ballet, and opera range anywhere from £2.50 to over £100 for special performances. Most venues offer **standby tickets** to students with valid ID, available an hour or so before curtain (call first to check on availability). In some cases this means whichever seats are left go for the lowest-cost ticket price—so you can get a £45 front-row seat for, say, £6.

In summer your arts options expand exponentially, as gala festivals fill theaters, concert halls, and even parks and squares. Probably the biggest—and most affordable—spectacle for lovers of classical music are the **Proms,** more formally known as the BBC Henry Wood Promenade Concerts, held at the gorgeous Royal Albert Hall (*see* Major Venues, *below*). The series runs for eight weeks from mid-July to mid-September and features a smorgasbord of well-known pieces, as well as a smattering of new works. Tickets are £3–£30; call 0171/589–8212 for more info. The **City of London Festival** (*see* Festivals, in Chapter 1), held the first three weeks in July, features classical performances in venues and squares throughout the city; many are free. The **BOC Covent Garden Festival** (tel. 0171/312–1997), in May and June, showcases opera and the musical arts. The **South Bank Centre** (*see* Major Venues, *below*) hosts the summertime dance festival **Ballroom Blitz** and **Meltdown,** a showcase for contemporary music. During summer you can also enjoy alfresco opera and ballet performances at **Holland Park Theatre** (Kensington High St., W8, tel. 0171/602–7856), a graceful open-air pavilion, and classical concerts at **Kenwood House** (Hampstead Ln., NW3, tel. 0171/973–3427). Many churches offer free (or low-cost) **lunchtime concerts** throughout the year; several are listed below.

MAJOR VENUES Sadly, the historic **Sadler's Wells Theatre** (tel. 0171/713–6060), the city's primary venue for dance, closed its doors in late 1996 for major reconstruction and will not reopen until 1998. In the meantime, performances will most likely be staged at the Royal Theatre on King's Way; call for the latest word.

Barbican Centre. The music hall at this giant arts center (*see* The City, in Chapter 2) is home to the famous **London Symphony Orchestra** and the **English Chamber Orchestra.** Frequent guests include the Royal Philharmonic, City of London Symphonia, and the Philharmonia Orchestra. And if that's not music to your ears, perhaps its eclectic menu of everything from brass bands to smoky jazz acts is. Student standby tickets (£6.50 or £8.50) are available for select performances beginning 1½ hours before curtain. *Silk St., EC2, tel. 0171/638–8891. Tube: Barbican. Admission: £5–£45. Wheelchair access.*

The London Coliseum. For opera and ballet, the Coliseum is a good bet. In 1997 it will become the permanent home of the **English National Ballet** troupe, formerly in residence at the South Bank Centre. It also attracts talented dance companies from around the world. Sharing the stage, so to speak, is the **English National Opera (ENO) Company.** It's well-known for English-language operas and offers lower prices (and less stodgy renditions) than the Royal Opera Company. One drawback: The Coliseum is *huge.* The cheapest upper balcony seats are known jokingly as "the gods"—consider renting a pair of opera glasses (20p) unless you like your art served up with severe eye strain. One hundred balcony seats go on sale the day of the performance at 10 AM for £5. *St. Martin's Ln., WC2, tel. 0171/632–8300. Tube: Leicester Square. Walk NE on Long Acre, quick right on St. Martin's Ln. Admission: £5–£50. Wheelchair access.*

The last night of the Proms at Royal Albert Hall is the capper, a madly jingoistic display of singing, Union Jack waving, and general merriment. Demand for tickets is so high that you must enter a lottery.

Royal Albert Hall. This major-league concert venue really comes into its own during summer when it hosts the **Proms** (*see above*). Otherwise, it's home to the acclaimed **Royal Philharmonic Orchestra.** Looming in the near future for Royal Albert Hall is a £40 million-plus refurbishment. *Kensington Gore, SW7, tel. 0171/589–8212 or 0171/589–3203. Tube: Knightsbridge. Walk west on Kensington Rd. Admission: £3.50–£37.*

Royal Opera House. This is the classiest venue for opera in London; it's hugely popular and very quick to sell out. Sadly, it will interrupt its 1997 season in July by closing for over £78 million worth of renovations and won't reopen until around 2000. Until then, it's home to the **Royal Opera Company** and the **Royal Ballet.** For both opera and ballet, 65 nosebleed seats (£12.50) and cheap standing-room tickets become available at 10 AM on the day of the performance. Tickets in the upper balcony cost about £5 (you can hear the operas just fine from here, but you'll want to rent a pair of opera glasses to see anything). Note for monolingual opera fans: If it's sung in a foreign tongue, the translation appears on a nifty electronic screen above the stage. *Covent Garden, WC2, tel. 0171/304–4000. Tube: Covent Garden. Admission: £5– £188! Wheelchair access.*

St. James's Church. This 17th-century church was the last of Sir Christopher Wren's London churches and his own personal favorite. What better place to enjoy a free lunchtime concert? Performances are at 1:10 PM Wednesday–Friday, year-round. The church hosts frequent evening recitals and, in summer, the **Lufthansa Festival of Baroque Music,** one of the top festivals of early music in the world. *Piccadilly, W1, tel. 0171/734–4511 or 0171/437–5053 for box office. Tube: Piccadilly Circus. Admission: £5–£15.*

St. John's Smith Square. This beautiful baroque church, blessed with excellent acoustics, has rapidly become one of London's leading venues for classical music. Programs vary widely, but renowned chamber orchestras and soloists are frequently featured. The BBC hosts lunchtime concerts Mondays at 1 PM. *Smith Sq., SW1, tel. 0171/222–1061. Tube: Westminster. Walk south on St. Margaret St. (which becomes Old Palace Yard, Abingdon St., and Millbank), turn right on Dean Stanley St. Admission: £5–£25.*

Beyond Ballet

There's a whole world beyond the saccharine ballets of "Swan Lake" and "The Nutcracker Suite"—the world of modern dance. While ballet might be criticized for having become stale and institutionalized, modern dance is highly charged and attuned to its audiences (possibly because many performance spaces that host modern-dance troupes are so darn small). If this piques your interest, London is a great place to broaden your horizons: Michael Clark, Yolanda Snaith, and choreographer Lea Anderson's troupe, the Cholmondeleys (pronounced "Chumleys"), are all examples of homegrown talent who've gone on to international acclaim. Tickets to modern-dance performances run £3–£10, and student discounts are often available; check Time Out for current listings. If you're in town during autumn, don't miss the five-week, citywide festival "Dance Umbrella" (tel. 0181/741–4040), one of the world's premier showcases for emerging dance talent. Some of London's top spots for modern dance are:

CHISENHALE DANCE SPACE. For avant-garde dance by promising new dancers from around the globe, this is the spot. 64–84 Chisenhale Rd., E3, tel. 0181/981–6617. Tube: Bethnal Green.

INSTITUTE OF CONTEMPORARY ARTS (ICA). Often the site of unconventional dance performances. The Mall, SW1, tel. 0171/930–3647. Tube: Piccadilly Circus.

THE PLACE. A dance school by day, a small, cheap, cutting-edge performance space by night. 17 Duke's Rd., WC1, tel. 0171/387–0031. Tube: Euston. Wheelchair access.

St. Martin-in-the-Fields. This attractive church (*see* Trafalgar Square, Major Attractions, in Chapter 2) is a cool venue for classical recitals, both acoustically and atmospherically. Free concerts take place Monday–Wednesday and Friday at 1:05 PM—you won't get the acclaimed Academy of St. Martin-in-the-Fields Orchestra, but it's usually good. Evening gigs (£6–£20) are by candlelight, and performers are usually big-name ensembles. *St. Martin's Pl., Trafalgar Sq., WC2, tel. 0171/839–8362 box office or 0171/930–0089 for recorded info. Tube: Charing Cross. Wheelchair access.*

South Bank Centre. This mammoth arts complex (*see* South Bank, in Chapter 2) is a haven for fans of music, opera, and dance, with three venues to choose from: The largest is the **Royal Festival Hall,** which reigns as one of the finest concert halls in Europe. It's home to the **London Philharmonic Orchestra** (Mar.–July and Sept.–Dec.), the **Philharmonia Orchestra** (May–July and Sept.–Feb.), and usually hosts the **Opera Factory** two times per year. Additionally, it's the site of numerous literary events (*see box* Poet's Corner, *below*). A bit smaller in size is **Queen Elizabeth Hall,** which features visiting modern-dance companies, chamber orchestras, and performances of lesser-known symphonies by the Philharmonic. Finally, the tiny **Purcell Room** hosts performances by up-and-coming chamber groups and soloists, plus the occasional visiting tap-dancing troupe. For many performances, student standbys are available two hours before curtain. The South Bank Centre is also home to two major annual festivals: **Ballroom Blitz,** with free performances and classes in everything from belly dancing to the waltz, as well as **Meltdown,** featuring contemporary music. *South Bank, Belvedere Rd., SE1, tel. 0171/960–4242. Tube: Waterloo. Admission: £2.50–£30. Wheelchair access.*

Wigmore Hall. The Wigmore's Sunday "Coffee Concerts" (11:30 AM), held year-round, are enormously popular with musically inclined Londoners; tickets are £7, plus the cost of your breakfast from the Wigmore Hall café. Otherwise, chamber music, period music, and all sorts of other soothing melodies fill the air of this pleasant, acoustically stellar forum most evenings. *36 Wigmore St., W1, tel. 0171/935–2141. Tube: Bond Street. Walk north on James St., turn right on Wigmore St. Admission: £4–£35. Wheelchair access.*

Theater

London is the theater capital of a country that truly loves the stuff, training would-be actors as if they were actual professionals, to be taken as seriously as bankers and academics. The theater sections in *Time Out* and *What's On* run for pages and pages, with everything from Shakespeare to Mike Leigh to Brecht. Theater in London falls into two basic categories: West End and Fringe. The **West End** is London's equivalent of Broadway, featuring big-budget productions and musicals like *Cats, Les Misérables,* and *Sunset Boulevard*. It's a dubious distinction, but London has even overtaken New York as the launching ground for new Andrew Lloyd Webber–ish "vehicles," so if you must see the latest round of dancing cats, orphans, or silver-screen divas, do it here. **Fringe** theaters present everything from small productions by prominent playwrights—folks like Samuel Beckett, Harold Pinter, Caryl Churchill, David Mamet, and Tom Stoppard—to experimental offerings by young local talent. Fringe performances are sometimes pretentious and obscure, but rarely boring.

London has always been passionate about its theater. When the Puritans tried to ban performances in the 16th century, underground productions simply moved to the new hot-chocolate houses (established specifically to serve the trendy delicacy imported from the Americas) that were springing up everywhere in London Towne.

It shouldn't come as a surprise that this theater-mad city hosts some extravagant summer whoop-de-doos. The **London International Festival of Theatre (LIFT)** (tel. 0171/490–3964), with performances from all genres, is held every other year June–July, with the next scheduled for 1997. Events are staged in theaters around London and even in the great outdoors. British Telecom recently began sponsoring the **BT Streets of London Festival,** also every other year, with free performances by international casts held in locations throughout London. It'll come around next in the summer of 1998.

MAJOR VENUES The Barbican and the Royal National Theatre are major-league houses, but the productions they stage are often fringe in style—partly because they're both state subsidized and housed within larger arts centers.

Barbican Centre. This giant arts complex has two venues for drama: Its **Barbican Theatre** is home to the Royal Shakespeare Company, which stages productions of the Bard's great works on a regular basis. Its smaller, more intimate theater, **The Pit,** is the place for avant-garde and whimsical stuff. Student standby tickets (£6) are sometimes available for performances to either theater; call to check. *Silk St., EC2, tel. 0171/638–8891. Tube: Barbican. Barbican Theatre tickets: £7–£24.50; The Pit tickets: £16–£17. Wheelchair access.*

National Theatre. The National Theater (home of the Royal National Theatre Company) offers three performance venues: the **Olivier Theatre,** the **Lyttleton Theatre,** and the **Cottesloe Theatre.** The Cottesloe is the smallest and usually puts on new works by up-and-coming playwrights. The range at the other two spans everything from cutting-edge stuff to imaginative interpretations of old standbys. "Platforms" (admission £3.50, £2.50 students), a series of talks and lectures by playwrights, directors, and other theater personnel, is also presented here. Student standby tickets (£6.50) are available for select performances; call to inquire. *South Bank, Belvedere Rd., SE1, tel. 0171/928–2252 box office or 0171/633–0880 for recorded info. Tube: Waterloo. Tickets: £10–£24. Wheelchair access.*

WEST END THEATERS The principal West End theaters are on **Shaftesbury Avenue** in Soho, **Haymarket** in St. James's, and around **Covent Garden.** Tickets can run anywhere from £6 to £30, depending on the performance and available seating; book way in advance if you're planning to see a hit show. You can reserve tickets directly through the theater, either in person at the box office, or over the phone using a credit card. Or you can use a 24-hour ticket agency such as **First Call** (tel. 0171/240–7200) or **Ticketmaster** (tel. 0171/379–4444), which will levy a hefty 10%–20% service charge. You'll also see ticket outlets in tube stations and in the West End—yes, they're convenient, but the commissions are a ripoff.

If your day of drama is starting to sound like an enormous, expensive hassle, relax. Many theaters also offer cheap preview performances or matinées—though you're more likely to see understudies at these instead of big stars. Half-price, same-day tickets cost £3–£10 at the **Society of London Theatres (SOLT) kiosk** on Leicester Square. It sells these bargain tickets for a £1–£1.50 service charge Monday–Saturday noon–30 minutes before curtain for matinées, and 2:30–6:30 for evening shows. If you have a student ID you can also score cheap same-day tickets directly from individual theaters' box offices; call or visit to inquire about availability. The Society of London Theatres' **Student Theatreline** (tel. 0171/379–8900) lists which West End theaters are offering student tickets on a given night. The recording is updated daily at 2 PM for weekday performances and on Friday afternoon for weekend shows. Some prominent West End theaters are listed below.

Adelphi Theatre. Home indefinitely to Andrew Lloyd Webber's *Sunset Boulevard. Strand, WC2, tel. 0171/344–0055. Tube: Charing Cross.*

Her Majesty's Theatre. Home indefinitely to *The Phantom of the Opera. Haymarket, SW1, tel. 0171/494–5400. Tube: Piccadilly Circus.*

London Palladium. Opening in 1996 and running through at least the spring of 1997: *Oliver! Argyll St., W1, tel. 0171/494–5020. Tube: Oxford Circus.*

New London Theatre. Now and forever, New London is home to *Cats. Drury Ln., WC2, tel. 0171/405–0072. Tube: Covent Garden.*

Old Vic. In early 1997, look here for a remake of *Wind in the Willows. Waterloo Rd., SE1, tel. 0171/928–7616. Tube: Waterloo.*

Palace Theatre. Here's *Les Misérables,* the world's most popular musical; wouldn't Victor Hugo be proud? *Shaftesbury Ave., W1, tel. 0171/434–0909. Tube: Leicester Square.*

Prince Edward Theatre. *Martin Guerre* opens here in 1996 and promises to run through at least spring of 1997. *Old Compton St., W1, tel. 0171/734–8951. Tube: Leicester Square.*

St. Martin's Theatre. For the last quarter-century, this has been home to that Agatha Christie thriller *The Mousetrap. West St., WC2, tel. 0171/836–1443. Tube: Leicester Square.*

Theatre Royal, Drury Lane. Home indefinitely to *Miss Saigon. Catherine St., WC2, tel. 0171/ 494–5062. Tube: Covent Garden.*

FRINGE THEATERS For the price of one West End blowout you can afford to see three fringe plays—shoestring affairs staged in basements, pubs, or anywhere else they can squeeze in a small stage and an audience. Tickets are usually in the £4 to £10 range, and most offer discounts to students. Fringe theaters generally sell cheap student standbys and standing-room tickets just before show time. In addition to the venues listed below, **Man in the Moon** pub in Chelsea (*see* Chapter 5) stages various theater productions.

The Almeida. This old, successful theater maintains high standards for its contemporary and classical offerings. *Almeida St., N1, tel. 0171/359–4404. Tube: Highbury & Islington.*

Drill Hall Arts Centre. All sorts of cool plays are here for the watching; its forte is excellent gay and lesbian productions. *16 Chenies St., WC1, tel. 0171/637–8270. Tube: Goodge Street.*

Etcetera Theatre. A quaint 50-seater best known for its esoteric one-night productions. *Oxford Arms, 265 Camden High St., NW1, tel. 0171/482–4857. Tube: Camden Town.*

Greenwich Theatre. This 400-seat theater hosts everything from comedies to classics to the experimental. *Crooms Hill, SE10, tel. 0181/858–7755. BritRail: Greenwich. Or take DLR to Island Gardens, then walk under river via Greenwich Foot Tunnel.*

Hen and Chickens Theatre Bar. One of Islington's best theater pubs. *109 St. Paul's Rd., Highbury Corner, N1, tel. 0171/704–2001. Tube: Highbury & Islington.*

King's Head Theatre. This is one of the oldest, best known, and most respected venues for pub theater in London. The ancient, high-ceilinged pub (no cover) is an experience in itself. *115 Upper St., N1, tel. 0171/226–1916. Tube: Highbury & Islington.*

Lyric Studio. Mainly contemporary works, with plenty of literary adaptations that'll appeal to bookworms. *Kings St., W6, tel. 0181/741–2311. Tube: Hammersmith.*

New End Theatre. This intimate theater in Hampstead is known for presenting period works rarely staged in London's bigger venues. The New End also tackles modern politics, both left- and right-wing. *27 New End, NW3, tel. 0171/794–0022. Tube: Hampstead.*

The Young Vic. The nominal offspring of the Old Vic (*see above*), this theater showcases cutting-edge productions and actors. *66 The Cut, SE1, tel. 0171/928–6363. Tube: Waterloo.*

OUTDOOR THEATER Outdoor theater in London is not a completely ridiculous, hideous, and cruel idea; believe it or not, summers can be warm sometimes. Really. The biannual **London International Festival of Theatre** (*see above*) always includes offerings in the great outdoors. Also in 1997 is the gala opening of the meticulously constructed **Shakespeare Globe Playhouse** (*see* The South Bank, Southwark, in Chapter 2). Its premiere season will open in June and run through September. From May through September, **Regent's Park Open-Air Theatre** (Regent's Park Inner Circle, tel. 0171/486–2431; Tube: Baker Street) offers perfor-

Poets' Corner

London does not lack for poets and a look at the "Books and Poetry" section in Time Out will clue you in to a variety of readings and workshops, held in bookstores, university halls, and sometimes pubs. One of the city's premier spots to catch a notable performance by artists, authors, and poets is Voice Box (tel. 0171/921–0906), a small space on Level 5 of the South Bank Centre (see above). Tickets cost £2.50–£7.

mances ranging from Shakespeare to contemporary works, but the emphasis is on Shakespeare. Tickets cost from £6 to £18.50; check *Time Out* for details.

Film

London is home to many small repertory cinemas that specialize in seminal, epochal, and downright groovy flicks. These repertories are much more interesting than the multiscreen complexes around Leicester Square, which screen big-budget–small-plot Hollywood flicks, and they're cheaper, to boot. Even though some charge a nominal membership fee of 50p–£1 per day or year, the tickets are reasonable, and many have the bonus of bars and lounges where you can sit and deconstruct the latest viewing. One of London's loveliest cinemas, Notting Hill's **Electric Cinema** (191 Portobello Rd., W11), has closed again, though hopefully someone will take over the venue and reopen it in the near future; keep your eyes peeled.

If it's a Hollywood blockbuster you're looking for, head straight for **Leicester Square.** Tickets at the spiffy multiscreen venues here cost £6–£10, and student discounts are rare—save for the MGM and Virgin cinemas, which offer students a 40% discount at most shows. There are, of course, cheap weekday matinées at most cinemas—but did you come to London to spend your days indoors watching American films? Also remember that, while British films open fairly quickly in the States, American-made films are released in London long after their debut in the colonies. Almost every London newspaper lists movie schedules in its entertainment section, though the detailed reviews in *Time Out* are most useful.

Londoners aren't known for their love of foreign films, and you'll have to do some digging to find the latest from the Continent. Filling the gap are two highly respected venues: **Institut Français** (17 Queensberry Pl., tel. 0171/838–2144) and **Goethe Institute** (50 Prince's Gate, Exhibition Rd., tel. 0171/411–3400), both in South Kensington. Most shows cost £2–£4.50, with double bills at £7. Some films aren't subtitled, so call ahead if it really matters.

Barbican Cinema. Foreign and arty films are rapidly being supplanted by mainstream stuff in the two cinemas here, which is a real shame. Tickets are £6, £4 for student standbys (when available). Every Monday, movies cost a mere £3. *Silk St., EC2, tel. 0171/638–8891. Tube: Barbican. Wheelchair access.*

Stand-Up in The City

London had a pitifully weak comedy scene until The Comedy Store (Haymarket House, Oxendon St., SW1, tel. 01426/914–433) opened its doors about 10 years ago. Although most London comedians are still understated, dry, and cerebral, today there's also plenty of cussing, physical comedy, and other comic vulgarity that goes over fine with British audiences. Wednesday and Sunday nights, it's wacky improv along the lines of "Whose Line Is It Anyway?" Tickets are £9–£10.

Other popular comedy clubs include Comedy Café (66 Rivington St., EC2, tel. 0171/739–5706), with free admission on Wednesday nights, £1–£8 Thursday–Saturday; Jongleurs (Middle Yard, Camden Lock, Chalk Farm Rd., NW1, tel. 01426/944–346), where you also get bar access Friday and Saturday until 3 AM for your £10 (£7 students) admission; and Canal Café Theatre (The Bridge House, Delamere Terrace, W2, tel. 0171/289–6054), whose very witty "Newsrevue" runs Thursday–Sunday and features up-to-the-minute topical comedy.

Everyman Cinema. Billing itself as "London's oldest repertory," this cozy venue shows an excellent selection of classic, foreign, avant-garde, and almost-new Hollywood titles. Many shows are double (even triple) features at no extra cost: Tickets are £4.50–£5, £3.50 students, and membership costs 60p a year. *Holly Bush Vale, NW3, tel. 0171/435–1525. Tube: Hampstead. Walk south on Heath St., turn right on Hollybush Vale. Wheelchair access.*

ICA Cinema. Housed within the Institute of Contemporary Arts, this cinema shows practically anything arty and/or esoteric. Tickets for the main screen cost £6.50, £5 on Mondays and for students. A £1.50 day membership includes admission to exhibits. The frequently changing films at the small **ICA Cinematheque** make the selection on the big screen look downright mainstream. Tickets cost £5, including day membership. *Nash House, The Mall, SW1, tel. 0171/930–3647. Tube: Charing Cross Road or Piccadilly Circus. From Charing Cross, walk SW on The Mall. From Piccadilly Circus station, walk south on Regent St., turn right on The Mall.*

Minema. This small venue is a film freak's dream. It seats 68 lucky people in broad, comfy chairs with plenty of legroom and prides itself on showing "only the best" international cinema. There's even a chic little café attached. Tickets are £6.50, £4 for students and matinées. *45 Knightsbridge, SW1, tel. 0171/369–1723. Tube: Hyde Park Corner.*

The National Film Theatre hosts the London Film Festival each November, featuring hundreds of flicks from Europe, India, and Australia; see Festivals, in Chapter 1, for more info.

National Film Theatre. The NFT is one of London's best repertory cinemas. Its three cinemas screen more than 2,000 titles each year, including foreign films, documentaries, Hollywood features, and animation. Tickets are £5.50, £4.10 students (40p for day membership). *South Bank Centre, SE1, tel. 0171/928–3232. Tube: Waterloo. Wheelchair access.*

Prince Charles. Come for reasonably recent flicks, as well as artier ones, at rock-bottom prices. Tickets are £2.25, £1.75 for the first show of the day. *7 Leicester Pl., WC2, tel. 0171/437–8181. Tube: Leicester Square. Walk west on Cranbourn St., turn right on Leicester Pl.*

Renoir. A little bit of everything, from Hollywood classics to obscure international fare. Tickets are £6, £4 students. *Brunswick Centre, Brunswick Sq., WC1, tel. 0171/837–8402. Tube: Russell Square. Walk east on Bernard St., turn left on Brunswick Sq.*

Ritzy. This cinema shows small arthouse flicks in addition to big mainstream films on its five screens. The groovy café serves excellent food, and locals patronize the bar whether or not they're attending a film. Tickets are £6; £3 students, Mondays, and shows before 6 PM. *Brixton Oval, Coldharbour Ln., SW2, tel. 0171/737–2121. Tube: Brixton. Walk south on Brixton Rd., turn left on Coldharbour Ln.*

Screen on the Green. Nowadays, this nice but nondescript midsize theater right on Islington Green features mainstream films, but in the frenetic days of the late '70s this place was a stomping punk club, immortalized in the Adam and the Ants song "Fall In." *Islington Green, N1, tel. 0171/226–3520. Tube: Angel. Walk north on Islington High St. (which becomes Upper St.), veer left at Islington Green.*

SHOPPING   7

By Jennifer L. Brewer

Name your poison, because London rivals any place in the known universe when it comes to shopping. Funky street markets, swank department stores, music stores for the most discriminating ears, shoe stores for the least discriminating feet—it's all here. London may not trumpet its fashion sensibility the way other European capitals do, but there's no disputing that fashion slaves worldwide look to this city for the latest trends.

Be warned: Competition doesn't do much to keep prices low, and you can easily empty your wallet before blinking. For what it's worth, the weekly *Time Out* (£1.70) regularly lists bargains in its "Sell Out" section, and many of London's stores have huge, gala sales in January and July. Otherwise, street markets (*see below*) are your best bet. The vibe is better, and they offer plenty of basic items at bargain prices.

Department Stores

In 1870, William Whiteley started a revolution in London shopping by housing different departments—including men's and women's clothing, housewares, books, and even a funeral department—under one roof. Thus, London's first "department store" was born. His 1911 custom-built store **Whiteley's** (Queensway, W2, tel. 0171/229–8844) has since mutated into an upscale shopping *mall,* but if you're in Bayswater, stop by to see the building and poke around the sale racks. If you insist on browsing through the high-priced selections at **Harrods** (*see* Kensington and Knightsbridge, in Chapter 2), get an early start—crowds can be maddening by midday. For a glimpse at how the other half shops, head for **Fortnum & Mason** (*see* Markets and Specialty Stores, in Chapter 4), where you can dreamily contemplate the old-fashioned opulence of its designer salons. At the other end of the price scale is **John Lewis** (278–306 Oxford St., W1, tel. 0171/629–7711), with its "never knowingly undersold" policy.

Harvey Nichols. Whether you worship at the shrine of Calvin, Ralph, or Versace, Harvey Nichols should be your first stop in London. Over 200 designers hang their labels here (often at astronomical prices). The selection of British designers is especially good, and the new "Swim and Gym" department provides spandex for all. A sumptuous food hall, decently priced café, and chic restaurant with nosebleed prices are on the fifth floor. Don't forget to pause and admire the witty, award-winning window displays. *109–125 Knightsbridge, SW1, tel. 0171/235–5000. Tube: Knightsbridge. Open weekdays 10–7, Sat. 10–6, Sun. noon–5.*

Liberty. Arthur Lazenby Liberty opened this shop in 1875 to sell material from the Orient. Soon members of the aesthetic movement—including William Morris, Edward Burne-Jones, and

John Ruskin—were clamoring for its trademark blue-and-white porcelain and brightly colored textiles. To this day, Liberty's atmosphere remains a cross between an Eastern bazaar and a rich aunt's living room: To experience it fully, climb to the top floor and peer down the central stairwell at the treasure trove of Oriental carpets, Liberty textiles, and international arts and crafts. Though prices are high, the sale at the end of June is a must-do. *210–220 Regent St., W1, tel. 0171/734–1234. Tube: Oxford Circus. Open Mon.–Sat. 10–6:30 (Thurs. until 7:30).*

Marks and Spencer. Though the stores look like British Kmarts, Marks and Spencer offers a good range of basics and some of the best bargains on fashionable new clothes in London. Not surprisingly, Labour Party leader Tony Blair (as well as a ton of people who'd look more at home in Harrods) shops for undies here. For the scoop on Marks and Spencer's vast array of edibles, *see* Chapter 4. *458 Oxford St., W1, tel. 0171/935–7954. Tube: Marble Arch. Open Mon.–Sat. 9–7 (Thurs. until 8). Other locations: 47–67 Baker St., W1, tel. 0171/935–4422; 113 Kensington High St., W8, tel. 0171/938–3711; Queensway, W2, tel. 0171/229–9515.*

Selfridges. Founded by American businessman Gordon Selfridge in 1909, Selfridges didn't rise from humble beginnings like many other London shops—it *started* big. Godlike, Selfridge proclaimed, "I want my customers to enjoy the warmth and light, the colors and styles, the feel of fine fabrics." And so it was. Now, nearly a century later, the store has just undergone a £50 million renovation and opened what's touted as the "largest cosmetics and beauty hall in the world." Other bonuses include a splendid food hall, fashionable clothing, friendly staff, and stunning art-nouveau architecture. Prices are ever so slightly lower than those at Harrods and Harvey Nichols. Look for its spinoff **Miss Selfridge** boutiques if you're a chick on the hunt for low-price fashions. *400 Oxford St., W1, tel. 0171/629–1234. Tube: Bond Street. Miss Selfridge: 40 Duke St., W1, tel. 0171/318–3833. Other locations: 75 Brompton Rd., SW3, tel. 0171/225–0833; 42 Kensington High St., W8, tel. 0171/938–4182; 221–223 Oxford St., W1, tel. 0171/434–3541. All locations open Mon.–Sat. 9:30–7 (Thurs. until 8).*

Specialty Stores

CLOTHING

"Let's have a shop!" is a familiar rejoinder in a city whose most famous consumer of clothes, Princess Di, has recently had her *minimum* annual wardrobe expenditure pegged at £82,500 by fashion insiders. Even if you can't keep up with her well-heeled pace, just a few rungs down the ladder you'll find plenty of shops plying classy wardrobe essentials. And don't forget the street markets (*see below*), which are stocked with more affordable treasures.

VAT Refunds

Value Added Tax (VAT) is the European version of sales tax, though in this case it's an extortionate 17.5% of the net price. VAT is always included in the price, so half the time you don't even realize you're being taxed. Fortunately, foreigners are exempt from paying the VAT if any single purchase exceeds £75; at some tourist-oriented shops, you can claim a refund on purchases of £20 or more (be sure to ask). To collect a refund, ask the store for form VAT 407, which you'll submit to British customs when you leave the country. At the airport, look for the "VAT Refund" window in the departure lounge. You can wait in line to receive your refund for a small processing fee (a few pounds), or turn in your form and in about eight weeks you will receive a refund. Customs officials may ask to see the goods, so be sure to have them available.

NEW CLOTHES Clothing boutiques of all shapes and sizes crowd the "Golden Mile" of **Oxford Street**, stretching east and west of the Oxford Circus tube station. You'll also find happy hunting around Covent Garden, Kensington High Street, King's Road in Chelsea, and South Molton Street in Mayfair. For cutting-edge fashion, head to **Petticoat Lane Market** (see Street Markets, below), where a number of aspiring designers have set up shop.

American Retro. Surprise: American Retro sells new, reasonably fashionable men's and women's gear—particularly accessories like belts, bags, and undies. The prices aren't retro either, but most things are cheaper than a single silk hanky at Harvey Nichols. 35 Old Compton St., W1, tel. 0171/734–3477. Tube: Leicester Square. Open Mon.–Sat. 10–7.

The Cavern. The Cavern's owners stockpile various fashion goods in a warehouse, then bring them out again when the styles come back around. Stock is displayed by decade, and though most stuff is "uncirculated," some used items do show up from time to time. 154 Commercial St., E1, tel. 0171/247–1889. Tube: Aldgate East. Open Tues.–Fri. noon–6, Sat. noon–5.

Hyper-Hyper. This indoor market is the place to come for all varieties of hats, outrageous outfit-making accessories, and serious clubbing attire. Its stalls are rented by struggling British designers, so the selection changes constantly and prices tend to be prohibitive—but look around and you'll find some cool bargains. 26–40 Kensington High St., W8, tel. 0171/938–4343. Tube: High Street Kensington. Open Mon.–Sat. 10–6 (Thurs. until 7).

Kensington Market. The indoor stalls here ply everything from silk scarves to studs to records to hair dye. Goths and grebos (motorcycle types) come here for denim and leather; club kids come for outrageous PVC and rubber gear. You'll find quite a few booths offering vintage clothing, shoes, and accessories from the '20s, '50s, and '70s, too. 49–53 Kensington High St., W8, tel. 0171/938–4343. Tube: High Street Kensington. Open Mon.–Sat. 10–6.

Next. This British equivalent of The Gap offers a much wider range of styles, and the shops themselves are pretty classy, too. Men's and women's clothes are reasonably priced and fashionable. There are 15 Next stores in London, found in all the major shopping districts. 327–329 Oxford St., W1, tel. 0171/409–2746. Tube: Bond Street. Open weekdays 10–6:30 (Thurs. until 8), Sat. 10–7, Sun. noon–6.

Red or Dead. This cool seller of threads and shoes began as a stall in Camden Market. Now, people flock to the three stores for the reasonably priced stock of dresses, jeans, jackets, and accessories. Their line of big clunky shoes is a major draw. 33 Neal St., WC2, tel. 0171/379–7571. Tube: Covent Garden. Open Mon.–Sat. 10:30–7, Sun. 12:30–5:30. Other locations: 186 Camden High St., NW1, tel. 0171/482–4423; 36 Kensington High St., W8, tel. 0171/937–3137.

Shelly's Shoes. Shelly's sells outrageous ultramodern shoes—some so cutting edge they look more like art than footwear. Leave those to RuPaul, and dive into the extensive selection of competitively priced Doc Martens and boots. Shelly's has branches are all over the city; the best are listed below. 159 Oxford St., W1, tel. 0171/437–5842. Tube: Oxford Circus. Open Mon.–Sat. 9:30–6:30 (Thurs. until 8). Other locations: 40 Kensington High St., W8, tel. 0171/938–1082; 124B King's Rd., SW3, tel. 0171/581–5537; 266–270 Regent St., W1, tel. 0171/287–0939.

Stock Market. You'll find T-shirts, flannel shirts, and other casual garb aplenty, but the large selection of Doc Martens (£40 and up) is the real reason to come. 245 Camden High St., NW1, tel. 0171/284–2174. Tube: Camden Town. Open weekdays 10–6, weekends 9:30–6:30.

Top Shop/Top Man. Cheap is the word for this fashion megachain, with branches all over London. Smart shoppers avoid Top Shop's own label (the clothes are poorly made) and head for the faux-vintage "souled-out" section. The best selection and the loudest atmosphere are in the flagship store on Oxford Street. 214 Oxford St., W1, tel. 0171/636-7700. Tube: Oxford Circus. Open Mon.–Sat. 10–7 (Thurs. until 8), Sun. noon–6.

SECONDHAND CLOTHING One of the best places to get used clothes in London is **Oxfam,** which runs 40 charity shops citywide. Each one offers the usual thrift-store finds: sturdy duds, household items, used books, and the like. Hipsters favor the shop near Oxford Circus, called

No Logo (*see below*). Otherwise, try the Oxfam branches at 89 Camden High Street, 23 Drury Lane, and 202B Kensington High Street.

If you'd rather browse for used clothes, head to **Camden Lock** in Camden Town or **King's Road** in Chelsea. Both avenues are lined with shops selling almost everything a bona fide clothes horse could want. On weekends, Camden Lock is home to an excellent street market (*see* Street Markets, *below*). Finally, the indoor **Kensington Market** (*see above*) has a bunch of stalls devoted to clothing, shoes, and accessories of the '20s, '50s, and glorious '70s.

Blackout II. Attention, kitsch shoppers: Blackout stocks glam fashions from the 1940s to the 1970s, plus a wide selection of secondhand handbags and shoes. Look in the basement for real bargains (stuff that's out of season or needs repair). *51 Endell St., WC2, tel. 0171/240– 5006. Tube: Covent Garden. Open weekdays 11–7, Sat. 11–6.*

Cornucopia. This is the place to find the vintage dress and accessories you've been searching for. The selection is varied, and prices range from bargain-basement to reasonable. *12 Upper Tachbrook St., SW1, tel. 0171/828-5752. Tube: Pimlico or Victoria. Open Mon.–Sat. 11–6.*

Flip. Here you'll find basic and funky shirts and classy sweaters, plus jeans and old poodle skirts. Downstairs they sometimes have good deals on shoes. *125 Long Acre, WC2, tel. 0171/836–4688. Tube: Covent Garden. Open Mon.–Sat. 10–7 (Thurs. until 8), Sun. noon–6.*

No Logo (Oxfam). Of all the Oxfam shops in London, this is the best for funky castoffs. New stock arrives almost daily: As the sign proclaims, HUBBA HUBBA—WE'VE GOT SOME LOVELY NEW CLOTHES. *26 Ganton St., W1, tel. 0171/437-7338. Tube: Oxford Circus. Open Mon.–Sat. 11–6.*

Salvation Army Charity Shop/Cloud 9. Skip quickly past the ground-floor offerings (sportswear, kid's clothes, old books, etc.) and head upstairs to Cloud 9, where you'll find retro and groovy threads. Students get a 12% discount on all Cloud 9 purchases. *9 Princes St., W1, tel. 0171/ 495–3958. Tube: Oxford Circus. Open weekdays 10:30–5:30, Sat. 11:30–5:30.*

BOOKSTORES

Generations of great authors have scribbled their lives away in London, from Henry Fielding, Charles Dickens, Oscar Wilde, and Virginia Woolf to current champs like Martin Amis, Kazuo Ishiguro, Doris Lessing, and Jeanette Winterson. And London has a plethora of bookstores to deal with its massive literary output. Note that many of these wonderful bastions of literacy hold *free* author signings, readings, workshops, and lectures weekly; check the "Books and Poetry" section of *Time Out* for more info.

GENERAL-INTEREST BOOKS As far as chains go, one of the best is **Waterstone's,** whose main branch is at 121–125 Charing Cross Road (tel. 0171/434–4291). Nearby is **Books Etc.** (120–122 Charing Cross Rd., WC2, tel. 0171/379–6838), another major chain with a friendly and helpful staff, a basement full of bargains, and a logical layout. The award for largest and most chaotic bookstore goes to **Foyles** (119 Charing Cross Rd., WC2, tel. 0171/ 437–5660); if it's in print, they probably have it.

The **Dillons** chain has nearly a dozen outlets in London, including one dealing only in art books (*see below*). However, the best Dillons to visit is the colossal, five-story behemoth in Bloomsbury at 82 Gower Street (tel. 0171/636–1577). At any given time it stocks 250,000–300,000 titles, guaranteed to staunch the reading frenzy of enrollees at the nearby University of London. Browsing at length is encouraged, and there's even a "CyberSt@tion" for net surfing.

SPECIALTY BOOKS **Compendium.** With its potpourri of political tracts, new-age mani- festos, and radical poetry, this alternative bookstore draws a devoted crowd. The store hosts fre- quent readings, and employees are extremely helpful and knowledgeable. *234 Camden High St., NW1, tel. 0171/485-8944. Tube: Camden Town. Open Mon.–Sat. 10–6, Sun. noon–6.*

Dillons Art Bookshop. This first-rate bookshop, part of the Dillons chain (*see above*), tempts academics, art students, and poets with a wide range of works on film, theater, fashion, art, and architecture. *8 Long Acre, WC2, tel. 0171/836-1359. Tube: Covent Garden or Leicester Square. Open Mon.–Sat. 9:30 AM–10 PM (Tues. from 10 AM), Sun. noon–7.*

Forbidden Planet. Horror, sci-fi, and fantasy fans will get sucked into this shop, never to return. The selection includes all those elusive anthologies you can't find elsewhere, trading cards, sci-fi videos, and a massive comics section. *71 New Oxford St., WC1, tel. 0171/836–4179. Tube: Tottenham Court Road. Open Mon.–Sat. 10–6 (Thurs. and Fri. until 7).*

Gay's the Word. The name says it all. This Bloomsbury shop carries London's finest selection of gay and lesbian books (new and used), magazines, and videos. *66 Marchmont St., WC1, tel. 0171/278–7654. Tube: Russell Square. Open Mon.–Sat. 10–6 (Thurs. until 7), Sun. 2–6.*

Murder One. Inside this dingy, unimposing shop lies a treasure trove of British mysteries, true crime stories, and thrillers. If you're a fan of Hitchcock, Christie, and friends, don't miss it. Fantasy and science fiction junkies will get their fix here, too. *71–73 Charing Cross Rd., WC2, tel. 0171/734–3485. Tube: Leicester Square. Open Mon.–Wed. 10–7, Thurs.–Sat. 10–8.*

Silver Moon Women's Bookshop. This friendly, feminist bookshop is London's sisterhood central for literature by and about women. *64–68 Charing Cross Rd., WC2, tel. 0171/836–7906. Tube: Leicester Square. Open Mon.–Sat. 10–6:30 (Thurs. until 8), Sun. noon–6.*

Soma Books. Soma specializes in black literature and in works on the history, art, politics, architecture, cuisine, and landscape of Asian, African, and Caribbean countries. Lose yourself in the latest Dominican fiction, or drool over cookbooks from south India. *38 Kennington Ln., SE11, tel. 0171/735–2101. Tube: Kennington. Open weekdays 9:30–5:30, Sat. 10–4.*

Sportspages. London's only comprehensive sports bookstore has a selection of football fanzines that's to die for (if that's your thing), plus books that will help you unlock the secrets of cricket or improve your performance at croquet. *Caxton Walk, 94–96 Charing Cross Rd., WC2, tel. 0171/240–9604. Tube: Leicester Square. Open Mon.–Sat. 9:30–7.*

Stanford's. Stanford's flagship store stocks over 30,000 travel books covering all sorts of exotic foreign locales, and its selection of atlases, charts, and maps is simply amazing. If you need a map of your hometown or a topographical map of the moon, chances are you'll find it here. *12–14 Long Acre, WC2, tel. 0171/836–1915. Tube: Covent Garden. Open Mon. and Sat. 10–6, Tues.–Fri. 9–7. Other locations: 156 Regent St., W1, tel. 0171/434–4744; 52 Grosvenor Gardens, SW1, tel. 0171/730–1314.*

USED BOOKS London's secondhand and antiquarian bookstores are excellent, though a bit chaotic—if you want that original edition of *Beowulf* pronto, expect to go dig it out yourself. Otherwise, you'll find the staff at most stores incredibly helpful and well informed. In Bloomsbury, you can make an entire day of wandering amid the dozens of secondhand bookstores on **Tottenham Court Road, Charing Cross Road,** and the adjacent **Cecil Court.**

Gloucester Road Bookshop. The fiction titles are especially well chosen in this cozy bookshop. *123 Gloucester Rd., SW7, tel. 0171/370–3503. Tube: Gloucester Road. Open weekdays 8:30 AM–10:30 PM, weekends 10:30–6:30.*

Henry Pordes Books. The musty smell here cues visitors to the great selection of old books—some of the antiquarian variety and some just plain old. Fiction is one of the strongest sections. Prices for paperbacks start at 50p, not including a 10% student discount. *60 Charing Cross Rd., WC2, tel. 0171/836–9031. Tube: Leicester Square. Open Mon.–Sat. 10–7.*

Pleasures of Past Times. Inside proprietor David Drummond's cozy little book kingdom you'll find a wealth of Victorian and Edwardian ephemera. Titles range from the familiar to the obscure. *11 Cecil Ct., WC2, tel. 0171/836–1142. Tube: Charing Cross. Open by appt. only.*

Skoob. This is one of the best and most popular used-book stores in town, and the slightly higher prices reflect it. Most impressive are the humanities, foreign literature, and political science sections. Next door, **Skoob Two** (tel. 0171/405–0030) focuses on a more eclectic assortment of books about the occult, religion, anthropology, and so on. Students get a 10% discount at either store. *15 Sicilian Ave., at Southampton Row, WC1, tel. 0171/404–3063. Tube: Holborn. Open Mon.–Sat. 10:30–6:30.*

MUSIC

From postpunk and rockabilly to hip-hop and rave, London's music scene is first-rate, and plenty of record stores have sprouted up in recent years to meet the growing demand for major and indie music. Multinational chains like HMV and Virgin (*see box, below*) have megastores the size of small villages, and there are tons of tiny, funky, independent shops specializing in rare vinyl, bootleg recordings, dance 12"s, you name it. If you're in no hurry, you can spend an entire day cruising the music shops: Try **Berwick Street** in Soho, **Camden High Street,** and **Hill Gate** at Ladbroke Grove.

Wherever you go, expect to pay £5–£10 for vinyl, £8–£15 for CDs, and around £2 for CD singles. Though prices aren't cheap, that same record or CD sells for at least $20 as an import the second it hits the shelves in the United States. If you've brought your collection with you, know that London's smaller music stores pay top dollar for American CDs and indie records. For the latest buzz in town, check out mags like *Melody Maker, New Music Express, Q, Select,* or *Vox.* They are available at most music shops and newsstands.

Black Market. Twelve-inch import singles take up most of the ground floor, sharing some space with Euro music and listening turntables. Follow the booming music downstairs to the basement, which houses all varieties of techno, rap, and hip-hop. *25 D'Arblay St., W1, tel. 0171/437–0478. Tube: Oxford Circus. Open Mon.–Sat. 11–7.*

Honest Jon's. Here you'll find an amazing selection of reggae, jazz, and funk. Take CDs for a test listen before plunking down your quid. *276 Portobello Rd., W10, tel. 0181/969–9822. Tube: Ladbroke Grove or Notting Hill Gate. Open Mon.–Sat. 10–6, Sun. 11–5.*

Mister CD. There's something from every genre here: country, indie, international, jazz, classical. You may have to sift through a lot of crazy stacks, but this is the cheapest place in town. *Berwick St., W1, no phone. Tube: Oxford Circus. Open daily 10–7.*

Music & Video Exchange. Those in the know give this London minichain top marks for prices (low), selection (plentiful), and staff (friendly and helpful; never snarling, abrupt, or rude). The used CDs are tucked away in glass cases, and you have to crane your neck to read the titles, but the substantial markdowns are worth the trouble. *36–38 Notting Hill Gate, W11, tel. 0171/243–8573. Tube: Notting Hill Gate. Open daily 10–7. Other locations: 95 Berwick St., W1, tel. 0171/434–2939; 229 Camden High St., NW1, tel. 0171/267–1898.*

Reckless Records. You'll find nothing but bargains in these aisles: secondhand 12" dance singles, classical, reggae, even country music, not to mention rock, soul, and jazz. The Islington branch (79 Upper St., N1, tel. 0171/359–0501) has a good collection of rare titles at rare prices. *30 Berwick St., W1, tel. 0171/437–4271. Tube: Oxford Circus. Open daily 10–7.*

Rough Trade. The fine selection of indie music, grunge, and U.S. imports draws lots of young skinheads to this store in the basement of a skateboard shop. Then again, it could also be Rough Trade's fairly impromptu (and free) performances by visiting bands. The original shop (130 Talbot Rd., W11, tel. 0171/229–8541) has a lot more punk junk on the walls, but the selection is the same. *16 Neal's Yard, WC2, tel. 0171/240–0105. Tube: Covent Garden or Tottenham Court Road. Open Mon.–Sat. 10–6:30.*

Selectadisc. This place is all about indie rock, thoughtfully organized and with a good depth of titles—but they've got plenty of jazz, folk, blues, dance, and techno, too. Best of all, vinyl starts at 25p. If you can't find something, ask the helpful staff. *34–35 Berwick St., W1, tel. 0171/734–3297. Tube: Oxford Circus or Tottenham Court Road. Open Mon.–Sat. 9:30–7.*

Stern's African Record Centre. The drum is king at Stern's, the best world-music shop in London. It features an amazing collection of music from Africa and Latin America, and you can listen to selections before making a purchase. *293 Euston Rd., NW1, tel. 0171/387–5550. Tube: Warren Street. Open Mon.–Sat. 10:30–6:30.*

UFO Music. If you're into collecting records, not just buying them, this is your place. They've got old classics in mint condition, plus a wide selection of concert posters, T-shirts, and other memorabilia, on everyone from Elvis to Oasis. *18 Hanway St., W1, tel. 0171/636–1281 or 0171/637–1771. Tube: Tottenham Court Road. Open Mon.–Sat. 10–6:30.*

HOUSEHOLD STUFF

Sure, London's department stores (*see above*) have just about all the furnishings and household items you need under one roof—but you'd need a royal title and trust fund to afford them. If you want funky old stuff, spend your weekends scouring the street markets (*see below*). For cheap, functional, new furniture (the kind that is slapped together in the sweatshops of China or Eastern Europe), check out the shops lining **Holloway Road** or **Walworth Road.** When all else fails, flip to the "Furniture, Secondhand" section in the London Yellow Pages.

Conran Shop. If you're shopping with a rich aunt, or with someone else's credit card, this is the place to go. The stunning collection of household furnishings is presented like fine art. The store itself is located in the historic Michelin Building, which has been lovingly refurbished. *81 Fulham Rd., SW3, tel. 0171/589–7401. Tube: South Kensington. Open Mon. and Thurs.–Fri. 9:30–6, Tues. 10–6, Wed. 9:30–7, Sat. 10–6:30, Sun. noon–5:30.*

Habitat. All the cool furnishings, kitchen stuff, and linens here are by the store's own designers. Though most prices are decent, it would be a major investment to furnish your entire flat here. *196 Tottenham Court Rd., W1, tel. 0171/255–2545. Tube: Goodge Street. Open Mon.– Wed. 10–6, Thurs. 10–8, Fri. 10–6:30, Sat. 9:30–6:30, Sun. noon–6.*

Oxfam Furniture Shop. The charity organization Oxfam devotes its Streatham Hill branch to used furniture and electrical goods, at bargain prices. It's worth the trek south from central London if you're furnishing a flat on a shoestring budget. *23 Streatham High Rd., SW16, tel. 0181/769–1291. BritRail: Streatham Hill. Open Mon.–Sat. 10–5.*

Sound Supermarkets

These behemoths may be lacking in personality and service, but for one-stop shopping they can't be beat. Plus, they typically offer big discounts on CDs during the first week of release.

- *HMV. It's got branches everywhere, but make a special trip to the HMV flagship store for the widest selection. Check the listings in the windows for upcoming autograph sessions and free shows. 150 Oxford St., W1, tel. 0171/631–3423. Tube: Oxford Circus. Open Mon.–Sat. 9:30–7 (Thurs. until 8), Sun. noon–6.*

- *TOWER RECORDS. Tower Records doesn't carry records; go figure. Overlook that and you'll find its specialty departments are some of the best in London. 1 Piccadilly Circus, W1, tel. 0171/439–2500 or 0171/437–1165. Tube: Piccadilly Circus. Open Mon.–Sat. 9 AM–midnight, Sun. noon–6.*

- *VIRGIN MEGASTORE. Richard Branson's pride and joy emerged from a two-year, £10 million refurbishment and is now the second-largest entertainment store in the world with 67,000 square feet of floor space (the Virgin Megastore in New York City is the largest). Come for the world's largest selection of rock and pop music or just to be seduced by the "shopping as entertainment" experience. 14–16 Oxford St., W1, tel. 0171/631–1234. Tube: Tottenham Court Road. Open Mon.–Sat. 9:30–8 (Tues. from 10 AM), Sun. noon–6.*

RJ's Home Shop. This chain sells sturdy new furniture, rugs, and household items from around the world (Americans will be reminded of Pier One Imports). Prices are reasonable. *245–249 Brompton Rd., SW3, tel. 0171/584–7611. Tube: South Kensington. Open Mon.–Sat. 9–7, Sun. noon–6. Other location: 209 Tottenham Court Rd., W1, tel. 0171/ 580–2895.*

Street Markets

You'd be hard pressed to find a better way to shop than in London's street markets, where one person's junk routinely morphs into another person's treasure. And an ever-changing cast of characters—teenage hipsters, pram-pushing mums, Bedouin stallholders, and wide-eyed tourists—makes for excellent people-watching, even when you're down to your last pence. The biggest and best markets are in **Camden** and on **Portobello Road** (*see below*) and draw correspondingly huge crowds. Other, smaller markets are where Londoners have been going for cen-

Ye Odde Shoppes

- *ANYTHING LEFT-HANDED. Lefties of the world unite: Buy yourself a left-handed can opener. 57 Brewer St., W1, tel. 0171/437–3910. Tube: Piccadilly Circus.*

- *GALLERY OF ANTIQUE COSTUMES AND TEXTILES. Although it's expensive, this is a great place to rummage through two floors of pre-1930 costumes, linens, and tapestries. 2 Church St., Marylebone, NW8, tel. 0171/723–9981. Tube: Marylebone.*

- *JUST GAMES. Whether your fancy is backgammon or Pictionary, if you're a player, this is your shop. 71 Brewer St., W1, tel. 0171/734–6124. Tube: Piccadilly Circus.*

- *LUSH. The coolest cosmetics and body-care shop in London sells edible-looking beauty potions, made fresh daily. 123 King's Rd., Chelsea, SW3, tel. 0171/376– 8348. Tube: Sloane Square. Other location: 7 The Piazza, Covent Garden, WC2, tel. 0171/379–5423. Tube: Covent Garden.*

- *THE KITE STORE. Purchase a whimsical kite here and spend a sunny day flying it on Primrose Hill (see Camden Town, in Chapter 2). 48 Neal St., WC2, tel. 0171/836– 1666. Tube: Covent Garden.*

- *MYSTERIES. Here you'll find paraphernalia for the upcoming seance, including Ouija boards, magic oils, and how-to books. 9 Monmouth St., WC2, tel. 0171/240–3688. Tube: Covent Garden.*

- *THE NEW POWER GENERATION. Welcome to the world of the Artist Formerly Known As Prince, chock-full of paraphernalia relating to The Purple One. 21 Chalk Farm Rd., NW1, tel. 0171/267–7951. Tube: Chalk Farm.*

- *THE ZIPPER STORE. For two decades, Zipper has kept fetishists well dressed in leather, rubber, and PVC. Toys and accessories are available, too. 283 Camden High St., NW1, tel. 0171/284–0537. Tube: Camden Town.*

turies to stock the fridge (even before there was such a thing). Most markets even offer food stalls where you can get a cheap and tasty lunch.

Be wary of pickpockets while browsing the markets. Keep cash and other valuables close to your person, as London thieves can be very, very crafty.

Haggling is acceptable in most of the street markets—especially on items without a price tag—but more difficult if you're speaking in an obviously foreign accent. The smartest of hagglers do a little research (i.e., ask around at competing booths) to find out the relative worth of an item, and then bargain from there. One final note: Though street markets are primarily a weekend pastime, some stalls and many shops remain open during the week—without the chatter, commotion, and congestion of claustrophobia-inducing crowds.

WEST AND CENTRAL LONDON

BERWICK STREET Soho's once-thriving Berwick Street produce mart has lost size recently, but it's still a great place to buy a cheap lunch of fruit, bread, and cheese. Stop by around 5 PM—when the merchants are desperate to get rid of their produce—and you'll walk away with incredible deals. Cheapie clothes, used CDs and records, and assorted trinketry can be found on Rupert Street. *Berwick and Rupert Sts., W1. Tube: Leicester Square or Piccadilly Circus. Open Mon.–Sat. 9–6.*

PORTOBELLO ROAD The Portobello Road market is second only to the Camden markets (*see below*) for liveliness and funkiness. You can catch dijeridoo players, rasta cellists, and other performers at the small courtyard near the market's center. The southern end is the most touristy and has tons of Portobello's trademark item: antiques. At the northern end, locals shop for fruit, vegetables, flowers, and secondhand clothes. The whole affair lines Portobello Road for over a mile and can take the entire day to conquer. *Portobello Rd., W10 and W11. Tube: Ladbroke Grove or Notting Hill Gate. Open Sat. 6–4; some clothing and produce stalls also open Mon.–Wed. 9–5, Thurs. 9–1, Fri. 7–4:30.*

ST. MARTIN-IN-THE-FIELDS This small market is chiefly targeted at tourists. Even so, there are some surprisingly cool finds, including ethnic jewelry and art, and some decent clothes. The best stuff is hidden away near Adelaide Street. *St. Martin-in-the-Fields churchyard, off Trafalgar Sq., WC2. Tube: Charing Cross. Open Mon.–Sat. 11–5, Sun. noon–5.*

EAST END

BRICK LANE You can find anything your heart desires at this East End institution, although it's primarily about tacky new clothes and cheap fruit. Best of all, it's rarely glutted with tourists. Listen and learn as the Cockney vegetable sellers twist the English language (and occasionally hurl handfuls of carrots) to hawk their wares. *Brick Ln. and surrounding streets, E1 and E2. Tube: Aldgate East and Shoreditch. Open Sun. 6 AM–2 PM.*

COLUMBIA ROAD For gorgeous flowers and plants, this is the market to hit (arrive around closing time to scoop up bargain bouquets). You'll also find a few shops and stalls devoted to crafts and antiques. Plus, it's conveniently located near the Brick Lane market. *Columbia Rd., near Gosset St., E2. Tube: Old Street or Shoreditch. Open Sun. 8–1.*

PETTICOAT LANE Though not as hip as the Camden Markets (*see below*), Petticoat Lane is almost as mammoth, swallowing Middlesex Street and a host of side streets. It's popular, so arrive early or prepare for heavy crowds. Goods for sale include cheap fashions, old watches, new and used shoes, luggage, household goods, and miscellaneous groovy bric-a-brac. *Middlesex St., E1. Tube: Aldgate East or Liverpool Street. Open Sun. 9–2.*

SPITALFIELDS Spitalfields Market is held inside a huge barnlike warehouse, featuring stalls selling antiques, crafts, and snacks. It's also one of few markets selling organic meat, cheese, and produce (Fridays and Sundays only). Performances of various sorts are held periodically on its small stage. *Commercial St., at Brushfield St., E1. Tube: Liverpool Street. Open weekdays 11–3, Sun. 9–3.*

NORTH LONDON

CAMDEN MARKETS Wait a few moments after stepping off the tube to orient yourself in the crushing mob; after all, Camden markets are the best and busiest in London, unparalleled in atmosphere and selection. The sprawl actually includes five markets, of which **Camden Lock** (Camden Lock Pl., near Chalk Farm Rd.) is indisputably the best. Get your used clothes, bootlegs, incense, crystals, knickknacks, smart drinks, and bongs here. Lots of Londoners come just to hang out, breathe in the scenery, and blow a spliff or two. The lock itself—a pleasant waterway overlooked by cafés and more shops—is just north of the Camden Tube station.

Other Camden markets include **Camden Canal Market** (Chalk Farm Rd.), featuring everything from clothes to old toys; **Camden Market** (Camden High St., near Buck St.), with stalls selling heaps of clothing and unique accessories; the indoor **Electric Market** (Camden High St., near Dewsbury Terr.), best for clubbing garb and used clothes; and the **Stables** (Chalk Farm Rd.), which has organic produce, some antiques, and lots of junk. *NW1. Tube: Camden Town. Camden Lock open weekends 10–6 (indoor stalls open Tues.–Sun. 10–6); Camden Canal Market open weekends 10–6; Camden Market open Thurs.–Sun. 9–5:30; Electric Market open Sun. 9–5:30; Stables open weekends 8–6.*

CAMDEN PASSAGE Not to be confused with the very cool Camden markets, Camden Passage is a narrow alley with antique stores and a two-day-a-week street market. The shops are expensive, but you might find some bargains lurking in the market among the rugs, furniture, jewelry, prints, toys, and other small, oddly shaped items with ancient and obscure applications. *Camden Passage, near Upper St., N1, Tube: Angel. Market open Wed. 7–2, Sat. 9–3:30; shops open Tues.–Sat. 10–5.*

CHAPEL This is where locals from Islington and Pentonville have been coming to buy their fruit, flowers, household items, shampoo, clothing, and other essentials for over a century. It's as untouristy as it gets in central London. *Chapel Market, N1. Tube: Angel. Open Tues.–Sat. 9–3:30 (Thurs. until 1), Sun. 9–1.*

SOUTH OF THE THAMES

BERMONDSEY/NEW CALEDONIAN Some loophole dating back to the 18th century makes it legal to sell furniture and antiques of questionable origin at this Bermondsey Square market. Presumably it's not all hot, and you can't complain about the prices. *Bermondsey Sq., SE1. Tube: Borough or London Bridge. Open Fri. 5 AM–2 PM.*

BRIXTON Rock down to vibrant Electric Avenue for this sprawling Latin and Afro-Caribbean–flavored market. You'll find a scattering of used clothing, exotic produce, good deals on reggae tapes and records, and mounds of more mundane wares like soap, batteries, and shampoo. *Electric Ave., SW9. Tube: Brixton. Open Mon.–Sat. 8–6 (Wed. until 2).*

EAST STREET This market has been popular with south London locals for over 100 years. Crowds make it difficult to walk through, but that's part of East Street's appeal. The cocky shouts of vendors alert you to bargains on everyday items like film, batteries, and cosmetics, as well as cheap hi-fi items. A flower and plant market adds color on Sundays. *East St., SE17. Tube: Elephant & Castle. From station walk ¾ mi south on Walworth Rd.; or take Bus 45, 68, or 171. Open Tues.–Sat. 8–5 (Thurs. until 2), Sun. 8–2.*

OUTDOOR ACTIVITIES 8

By Sunny Delaney

The salaries of professional athletes may not be as preposterously huge in England as they are in the States, but don't believe for one second that the British aren't serious about sports. When things are going well for an English national team, especially at football, there's a definite "feel-good" factor all over the capital. If you feel like joining in as either a spectator or a participant, *Time Out* (£1.70) is a great resource: The "Sport" section lists upcoming events, classes, and sports clubs, along with times, dates, and prices. Also at your disposal is the London **Sportsline** (tel. 0171/222–8000), with information on all things athletic for the price of a local call. Headline events of all sorts take place at **Wembley Complex** (Empire Way, Wembley, Middlesex, tel. 0181/900–1234; Tube: Wembley Park) and **Crystal Palace National Sports Centre** (Ledrington Rd., tel. 0181/778–0131; BritRail: Crystal Palace).

Spectator Sports

CRICKET

Like baseball, cricket is incomprehensible to most of the world outside the game's homeland. Those in England's former colonies also usually know the difference between a batsman and a bowler, but those in the United States have never quite gotten on the ball, so to speak. Still, cricket and baseball are both derived from a sport now known as rounders, so these two sports are distant cousins. Very distant.

Cricket is an extremely complex sport, but even a basic understanding of the rules renders the game enjoyable. It is played by two 11-member teams on a roughly circular, 250- by 225-foot "pitch" surrounded by a rope "boundary." Most of the action, however, takes place on a central rectangle, 66 feet long. The batting team places two batsmen at opposite sides of the rectangle; a *wicket* (two "bails" balanced atop three "stumps" of wood) stands behind each batsman. The object of the batsman is twofold: to guard the wickets and to score runs. The fielding team's "bowler" (pitcher) at one end of the rectangle throws a ball to the batsman at the opposite end, attempting to "bowl" the batsman by knocking the bails off the stumps. The ball is thrown overhand with a straight arm (bent elbows are penalized) and is usually bounced off the pitch, which has been hardened by rollers. The batsman attempts to hit the ball far enough that he and his batting partner can exchange places and score runs. Unlike in

A cricket ball is made of cork covered in red leather with a single seam running around the middle. The same ball is used for an entire inning of cricket and becomes roughed up over the course of play, affecting the way the ball curves. If you see a bowler with red stains on his trousers, he's probably been trying to polish one side of the ball to increase its curve.

165

baseball, there are no foul lines, so the ball may go in any direction. If the ball crosses the boundary on the ground, the batsman scores four runs; if it crosses the boundary without touching the ground, six runs are scored. The batsman's "wicket is taken" (he's out) if the bails are knocked off the stumps while the batsmen are "out of the crease" (changing places) or if his ball is caught on the fly. Once a player's wicket is taken, he is replaced by the next batsman in the order. An "over" (six throws) is bowled from one end of the rectangle; then another bowler takes over from the other end and the fielders rotate accordingly. The batting team remains at bat until 10 wickets have been taken (the end of an "innings") or until they "declare" (decide to stop batting and take the field). A team will declare because to win, they must not only score the most runs but also take all of the opposing side's wickets by the scheduled end of the game. The length of a match varies widely: "Limited over" matches have a set number of overs and are usually one-day events, other county matches last four days, and international "Test matches" last up to five days.

Yes, it can be confusing: two batsmen, hundreds of runs, both teams (usually) wearing white, five-day matches, et cetera. If you're confused, ask another spectator—he or she will probably enjoy sharing some knowledge. But the real fun of cricket lies in the relaxed pace, giving you the opportunity to sit outside and drink pints in the afternoon. If this sounds like your cup of tea, matches are held at **Lord's Cricket Ground** (St. John's Wood Rd., NW8, tel. 0171/289–8979; Tube: St. John's Wood) and **Foster's Oval** (Kennington Oval, SE11, tel. 0171/582–6660; Tube: Oval), the latter generally a friendlier and more laid-back place to witness the *thwack* of willow on leather. Tickets at both venues usually cost £6–£8 (with substantial discounts for students), although prices for the international Test matches can go up to £40.

A recent development, following the 1996 Cricket World Cup, has been the adoption of brightly colored uniforms by the AXA Equity & Law League. Their Sunday matches, held between the different counties of England, have another strangely familiar feature: a white ball. While some purists grumble about the "Americanization" of the sport, and wags see the shift to colored shirts as a marketing ploy to sell team jerseys, the matches are still pure cricket and it's refreshing to see student types and young kids—yes, often dressed in the jerseys—enjoying the matches alongside older viewers. Not so recent is the game of women's cricket, which has been played in England for years and is flourishing. The **Women's Cricket Association** (tel. 0121/440–0567) can clue you in to what's going on in the women's game.

FOOTBALL

Of all sports, football (what Americans call soccer) is the one pursued most passionately by the Brits. It all started in Derby in AD 217 as part of a festival celebrating a victory over Roman troops. Since then more than 140 countries worldwide have fallen in love with the sport, and the Fédération Internationale de Football Association (FIFA), which sponsors the World Cup every four years, boasts more members than the United Nations. Unlike teams in events such as the

W. G. (dis)Grace(d)

W. G. Grace was the greatest cricket player of all time. He played first-class cricket for over 40 years, scoring 54,986 runs, including over 100 centuries (100 runs in one inning). England could use another like him today: Though England invented cricket, its former colonies now excel at the game. A longstanding rivalry exists between England and Australia, culminating in the Test matches. The winner of this series is awarded the "Ashes," a tiny urn containing the remains of a bail symbolically burned to mourn the death of English cricket after a loss to Australia. In recent years Australia has tended to surpass England; hot young spin bowler Shane Warne often stymies the English batsmen. The Aussies will be back in summer 1997 to defend their title.

Super Bowl (whose participants may not even live in the towns they play for), World Cup teams play for their home countries and national fervor runs wild. The United Kingdom comes a bit unglued during these international tournaments, with teams from England, Scotland, Wales, and Northern Ireland all competing for places. England, despite the embarrassment of not qualifying for the 1994 World Cup, has came back strong under the guidance of Terry Venables for a respectable third-place finish (following a heartbreaking penalty shootout) in the Euro 96 tournament. New manager Glenn Hoddle promises to carry on Venables's work, and the outlook is very bright for 1998. For details, check out the **Eurosoccer website** (http://www.eurosoccer.com). It grows and changes over time, but expect to find information on the different European football teams and even screensavers of all the goals scored in Euro 96—including *that* goal by Gazza. Some of England's World Cup qualifiers taking place in 1997 include matches against Italy (February 12), Georgia (April 30), and Poland (May 31).

Most football fans in Britain support their local team first and a major team second. Liverpool and Manchester United are the two favorite major teams, and one of them tends to win the coveted FA (Football Association) Cup Final every year. When it comes to local football, the most popular of London's eight major clubs are probably longtime rivals **Arsenal** (Arsenal Stadium, Avenell Rd., N5, tel. 0171/354–5404) and **Tottenham Hotspur** (White Hart Ln., 748 High St., N17, tel. 0181/365–5050). Other teams in the Premier League are **Chelsea** (Stamford Bridge, Fulham Rd., SW6, tel. 0171/385–5545), **West Ham United** (Boleyn Ground, Green St., E13, tel. 0181/548–2700), and **Wimbledon** (Selhurst Park, Whitehorse Ln., SE25, tel. 0181/771–8841), while First Division squads with big followings include **Crystal Palace** (Selhurst Park, Whitehorse Ln., SE25, tel. 0181/771–8841) and **Queen's Park Rangers** (Rangers Stadium, South Africa Rd., W12, tel. 0181/743–0262). The football season runs from mid-August to May, and most games are held at 3 PM on Saturdays. Big important matches, like the FA Cup Final (May 17 in 1997), are held at London's **Wembley Complex** (*see above*). Tickets, available from each club's box office, run £8–£33, depending on the seats.

POLO

Depending on whom you talk to, polo either originated in Persia in the 6th century and was subsequently "discovered" by British army officers stationed in India, or the soldiers developed the sport themselves. In either case, polo rapidly gained ground with the upper classes and has remained the province of the rich, largely because polo requires a lot of the horses. Players must be able to afford a "string" of steeds so they can switch mounts during each game as horse after horse tires of being slammed into other horses at high speeds.

Prince Charles is an avid polo player, who's often criticized for being more comfortable on a horse than with people. Perhaps that's why he's so fond of Camilla Parker Bowles.

The Guards Polo Club is the choicest of polo grounds, and it's the venue for the **Royal Windsor Cup** in early June. The **Queen's Cup,** the traditional start of the London "season," is usually held shortly afterward; star-spotters can indulge themselves by watching for royals (the queen herself presents the trophy), fading rock stars, and other notables. The club hosts matches most weekends, and quite often "picnic passes" costing £15 per carload of people are available. Tickets for big matches start at £15. *Smith's Lawn, Windsor Great Park, tel. 01784/437–797. BritRail: Windsor & Eton Central.*

RACING

CAR RACING The world-famous **British Formula One Grand Prix** is held every July to sold-out crowds at **Silverstone Circuit** (Silverstone, Northants, tel. 01327/857–271; BritRail: Northampton). Tickets are hard to come by and expensive (£65 and up), so contact the box office as early as possible. During the off-season, Silverstone Circuit hosts local and qualifying races on an irregular basis; flip through *Time Out* for the latest. Another popular racing venue is **Brands Hatch** (Fawkham, Kent, tel. 01474/872–331; Britrail: Swanley).

GREYHOUND RACING Many Londoners love to bet on what they affectionately call "the dogs." Greyhound racing is even shedding its unfashionable skin and becoming vaguely trendy.

You'll find plenty of new-style dog fans at shiny new **Sittingbourne Stadium** (Central Park, Eurolink, Sittingbourne, tel. 01795/475–547). A number of tracks hold weekly races, including **Walthamstow Stadium** (Chingford Rd., E4, tel. 0181/531–4255) and **Catford Stadium** (Ademore Rd., SE26, tel. 0181/690–2261). Spend a Friday evening at **Wimbledon Stadium** (Plough Ln., SW19, tel. 0181/946–8000) and see what Blur's song "Parklife" is all about. Races usually take place in the evening and admission ranges from £1 to £4; check *Time Out* for schedules. And remember, no matter which dog you back, the rabbit always wins.

HORSE RACING While scruffy beer drinkers and quid bettors make up the daily crowd, you couldn't keep the queen herself away from the pomp of the **Royal Meeting at Ascot**, Britain's most prestigious horse race. You'll need to book good seats far in advance for this massive event, held June 17–20 in 1997, although some seats—far away from the Royal Enclosure and winning post—can be bought on the day of the race for £6. There are also Ascot Heath tickets available for a mere £1, but these only admit you to a picnic area in the middle of the race course. You'll be able to see the horses, of course, but that's not why people come to Ascot. The real spectacle is the crowd itself: Enormous headgear is de rigueur, and those who arrive inappropriately dressed (jeans, shorts, tank tops) will be turned away. For more info, contact the **Ascot Racecourse** (Ascot, Berkshire, tel. 01344/22211; BritRail: Ascot).

If you're lucky, you may spy some of the royal family watching from their private stand at the **Royal Windsor Racecourse** (Maidenhead Rd., Windsor, tel. 01753/865–234), best accessed from BritRail's Windsor & Eton Riverside station. Other popular tracks just a short train ride from Waterloo station include **Epsom Racecourse** (Epsom, Surrey, tel. 01372/726–311; BritRail: Epsom), **Kempton Park Racecourse** (Staines Rd. E, Sunbury-on-Thames, tel. 01932/782–292; BritRail: Kempton Park), and **Sandown Park** (Esher, Surrey, tel. 01372/463–072; BritRail: Esher). Admission to the above courses runs £5–£15. One notable exception to these prices is the **Derby,** held every June at Epsom. Tickets for this event start at £5 for distant enclosures and run up steeply to £90 for the "morning dress obligatory" Queen's Stand.

ROWING The **Oxford and Cambridge Boat Race** (tel. 0171/379–3234) takes place on the Thames, southwest of central London between Putney and Mortlake. It will begin at 4 PM on March 29 in 1997. Go early to secure yourself a spot in a pub along the river, or join the crowds on Chiswick or Putney Bridge. Rivalry is fierce between the universities, but most spectators don't really care whether Cambridge (light blue) or Oxford (dark blue) wins—it's just a nice way to spend a Saturday. During the **Henley Royal Regatta** (tel. 01491/572–153), held July 2–6 in 1997, single sculls and two-, four-, and eight-person crews from all over the world race along the Thames. Though it's quite a trek from London to Henley-on-Thames, a day along the towpath watching the rowing—and the people—can be delightful. Take the train from Paddington Station toward Reading (£8.40 return), and change at Twyford to Henley-on-Thames.

RUGBY

Rugby has driven many a mother to an early grave because the players take as much body contact as American football players, but without the benefit of pads or helmets. Legend has it that the game was born when a student of Rugby School picked up a soccer ball in his hands midmatch and ran from one end of the pitch to the other. The game concept hasn't changed much since then: Players move the ball down the field and score goals through some combination of running, passing, and kicking. It's an old sport, steeped in tradition, and rugby's practitioners shun the modern arguments for protection against injury. Perhaps it's this attitude that makes the rowdy spectacle such a satisfying combination of mud, beer, and battle.

It's possible to watch rugby all year round in Britain. The Rugby Union season runs September to May, with games held on Saturday afternoons. Tickets cost £8–£10 depending on the seat. London's principal teams include the **Wasps** (Rangers Stadium, South Africa Rd., W12, tel. 0181/902–4220), the **Harlequins** (Stoop Memorial Ground, Craneford Way, Twickenham, tel. 0181/892–0822), and the **London Irish** (The Avenue, Sunbury-on-Thames, tel. 01932/783–034). Despite having gone professional in 1995, the atmosphere at these matches is still very friendly, and some clubs even welcome spectators into the clubhouse for a postgame party. You'll find a slightly different vibe at a Rugby League match. The professional Rugby League is strongest in the northwest of England, but London is home to the **London Broncos** (The Valley, Floyd Rd., SE7, tel. 0181/776–6670). Tickets for league matches are usually £10, and the season runs February to August.

TENNIS

The world's most prestigious and ballyhooed tennis event is the venerable **Wimbledon** fortnight (June 23–July 6 in 1997), held at the **All England Lawn Tennis & Croquet Club.** Never mind that a Brit hasn't won this Grand Slam tournament since anyone can remember—though Tim Henman *did* make it to the quarter-finals in 1996. Tennis enthusiasts around the world plan their trip to Wimbledon months in advance, so if you're reading this in June, you may be out of luck. A small number of tickets are available each day at the gate, but you have to be willing to camp overnight or arrive very early (5 AM!) to get them. Centre Court, Court 1, and Court 2 tickets allow you to visit several other courts while you wait for play to start on the "higher" courts. Grounds passes (£8, £6 after 5 PM) allow access to all the grounds (with the exception of the higher courts), including the newly redesigned **Lawn Tennis Museum,** which features a history of the game. If you're determined to get in but unwilling to camp, try showing up after 5 PM, when abandoned seats are resold to raise money for charity. Play continues until dusk, so you will still be able to see a few hours of tennis. Or plan ahead and send a stamped, addressed envelope between September and December to All England Lawn Tennis & Croquet Club, Box 98, Church Rd., Wimbledon SW19 5AE. You'll receive an application form for the ticket lottery, which you must return by January 31. Good luck. *Church Rd., Wimbledon, SW19, tel. 0181/944–1066 or 0181/946–2244 for ticket info. Tube: Southfields.*

Another London landmark is the **Queen's Club,** which hosts major and minor competitive and exhibition matches throughout the year such as the **Stella Artois Grass Court Championship** in early June. *Palliser Rd., W14, tel. 0171/385–2366. Tube: Barons Court.*

YANKEE SPORTS

AMERICAN FOOTBALL The beleaguered **World League of American Football** is in a rather sad state, attracting second-stringers and has-beens ("The Refrigerator" was a recent addition) to play in a league with even less prestige than the Canadian Football League. That said, the **London Monarchs** have a dedicated following of fans that attend their Sunday afternoon matches against the likes of the Scottish Claymores and the Rhein Fire. American football certainly won't become a dominant sport, but there's something charming about attending a game where many of the fans have terms like "field goal" explained to them in relation to rugby. *748 High Rd., N17, tel. 0171/396–4525. BritRail: White Hart Lane.*

BASEBALL Baseball is cricket's distant cousin, but it has been played on an organized basis in Britain for nearly a century. Surprised? There's even a **British Baseball League,** and two Premier Division teams—the **Warriors** and the **Wolves**—are based in London. Both teams play dur-

Play Ball!

On any given summer evening you'll find baseball and softball games all over town, especially at Hampstead Heath (much to the chagrin of locals), Regent's Park, and Hyde Park. The British Baseball Federation (66 Belvedere Rd., Hessle, North Humberside, HU13 9JJ, tel. 01482/643–551) can give you the current scoop; send a large, stamped envelope for their magazine or call to be pointed toward the nearest club. Basketball courts are pretty scarce in London, but there are a growing number in neighborhood sports centers (see below) like the London Central YMCA. Check with the English Basketball Association (tel. 0113/236–1166) to join a club or find a court near you.

ing the summer at various fields around town. Check *Time Out* for current games and locations, or contact the **British Baseball Federation** (tel. 01482/643–551).

BASKETBALL The **National Basketball League** (tel. 0121/749–1355) oversees a surprisingly large number of professional and semi-professional basketball teams in England and Wales. Premier-division teams include 1996 champs the London Towers as well as the Leopards—a team that will surely draw crowds since it recently signed a sponsorship deal with Playboy and will be cheered on by the Playboy Kittens. One step down is the men's Division One, with teams like the Brixton Topcats and Hansen's Crystal Palace. The women's Division One also has a London team, the Heat. The season runs September–May; check *Time Out* for current schedules.

Participant Sports

NEIGHBORHOOD SPORTS CENTERS

Almost every neighborhood has at least one gym offering some combination of aerobics classes, weight rooms, trampolines, saunas, solariums, martial arts gyms, swimming pools, squash and badminton courts, and soccer fields. Charges and/or membership fees vary, though they tend to be reasonable. Some centers offer day memberships, and many offer discounts if you arrive with a member. Call in advance to see if they admit nonmembers. To find the nearest center, look in the phone book under "Leisure Centres" or call the **Sportsline** (tel. 0171/ 222–8000). The following are some of London's most popular centers:

Jubilee Hall Leisure Centre. Day use of all facilities in this well-equipped gym is £6.30; exercise and dance classes cost £5.30. *30 The Piazza, WC2, tel. 0171/836–4835. Tube: Covent Garden. Open weekdays 7 AM–10 PM, weekends 10–5.*

London Central YMCA. Membership at this comfortable and popular gym is only available on a weekly (£30) or longer basis, but it gains you access to a pool, over 100 fitness classes a week, and a full gym. *112 Great Russell St., WC1, tel. 0171/637–8131. Tube: Covent Garden. Open weekdays 7 AM–10:30 PM, weekends 10–9.*

Queen Mother Sports Centre. Fees for activities vary: Nonmembers pay £2.05 to swim, £4 for aerobics, and £4.85 to play squash for 30 minutes. *223 Vauxhall Bridge Rd., SW1, tel. 0171/ 630–5522. Tube: Victoria. Open weekdays 6 AM–10 PM, weekends 8–5:30.*

BOATING

If you're feeling inspired by the exertions of the crews at the Henley Royal Regatta or the Oxford and Cambridge Boat Race, you can try your hand at the oars in a few places in London. A vigorous afternoon can be had rowing about the large and scenic lake at Regent's Park. **Regent's Park Boating Lake** (tel. 0171/486–4759) rents rowboats that hold up to four adults for £6 per hour plus a £5 deposit. **Hyde Park** (tel. 0171/298–2100) offers pedalos (pedalboats), canoes, and rowboats for those wishing to splash along the Serpentine for £6 per hour. Boats are available at both parks daily 9–7 March through October.

CYCLING

Lots of people bike in London, but frankly, the traffic-congested streets make for a perilous and carcinogenic ride. Hard-core bikers tie bandannas over their mouths to filter out the crud from passing traffic or invest in specially designed gas masks available at bike shops. Biking *is* great in London's parks, but those intending to brave the roads should invest in a good map that points out the less offensive routes through the city. **London Cycling Campaign** (228 Great Guildford Business Centre, 30 Great Guildford St., SE1, tel. 0171/928–7220) does its best to make London a more bike-friendly place. Send for a copy of their *Cyclists' Route Map* (£5.70 including postage), or look for it at bike shops. If you're planning on heading out into the countryside, consider joining **Cyclists' Touring Club** (69 Meadrow, Godalming, Surrey GU7

3HS, tel. 01483/417–217), the largest cycling organization in Britain. Annual membership is £25; in return they'll send you info on organized bike journeys throughout the country.

Bikepark. It has everything a cyclist could need, including a repair and sale shop, bike storage (£1.50 for 12 hrs, £5 a week), changing facilities, and bicycle rentals. Basic mountain bikes go for £10 for the first day, £5 the second day, and £3 each subsequent day, with a £200 deposit. Luckily, they accept MasterCard and Visa. *14½ Stukeley St., WC2, tel. 0171/430–0083. Tube: Covent Garden. Open weekdays 7:30 AM–8:30 PM, Sat. 8:30–6:30.*

London Bicycle Tour Company. Weather permitting, this South Bank biking outfit offers three-hour bike tours of various London neighborhoods weekends at 2 PM. You can also go it alone: Traditional, mountain, or hybrid bikes cost £29.50 per week or £10 per day (£5 each subsequent day), including a helmet, maps, and route advice. A deposit is required. *1A Gabriel's Wharf, SE1, tel. 0171/928–6838. Tube: Blackfriars. Open Apr.–Oct. daily 10–6, Nov.–Mar. by appointment.*

Mountain Bike and Ski. Mountain bike rentals cost £7 per day or £13 for the whole weekend, not including insurance (£1 per day) and the refundable £50 deposit. This central London shop also has a good selection of bikes and bike-related accessories for sale. *18 Gillingham St., SW1, tel. 0171/834–8933. Tube: Victoria.*

HORSEBACK RIDING

Hankering to stretch someone else's legs on a woodsy trek? Whether you're still learning how to stay upright in the saddle, or you want lessons in dressage and jumping, several stables can set you up with a steed and, if you're willing to pay, an instructor. You can rent a horse from **Belmont Riding Centre** (The Ridgeway, N20, tel. 0181/906–1255), open weekdays 9–6, weekends 9–5, and ride through Totteridge Common's 150 acres in a group for £15 per hour or £21 per hour for private lessons. **Wimbledon Village Stables** (24 High St., SW19, tel. 0181/946–8579) charges £19 per hour during the week, £25 on weekends, for a chance to ride in a group across the scenic Wimbledon Common and Richmond Park. The stables are open Tuesday–Sunday 9–5. **Hyde Park Stables** (63 Bathurst Mews, W2, tel. 0171/723–2813), open Tuesday–Saturday 10–4:30 and Sunday 9–4:30, rents horses for £25 per hour. Telephone reservations with a credit card are required, and no galloping is allowed in the area. And, yes, you will find only English saddles here.

SWIMMING

Many of the city's neighborhood sports centers (*see above*) have indoor pools, so swimmers need not bend to the whims of London's weather. Many of these pools are open to the public regularly throughout the week. Remember that many pools require swimming caps and protec-

---

Windsurfing on the Thames

With its miles of river frontage, the Docklands area is becoming a very popular place for all things aquatic. Pick up the free "Watersports in London Docklands" brochure at the London Docklands Visitor Centre for more info. Watersport centers such as DOCKLANDS WATERSPORTS CLUB (Gate 14, King George V Dock, Woolwich Manor Way, E16, tel. 0171/511–7000), LEA VALLEY WATERSPORTS CENTRE (Greaves Pumping Station, North Circular Rd., E4, tel. 0181/531–1129), and SURREY DOCKS WATERSPORT CENTRE (Greenland Dock, Rope St., Rotherhithe, SE16, tel. 0171/237–4009) offer rentals and lessons for activities like sailing, rowing, canoeing, and windsurfing. Prices vary, but all rentals include tuition and the necessary wetsuits.

tive eyewear, and many do not provide towels. On the plus side, weight rooms, saunas, and whirlpools are often available for use by both guests and nonmembers.

It's a bargain (£1.20) to swim at **University of London Union** (Malet St., WC1, tel. 0171/580–9551), where students and nonstudents alike can swim weekdays 8:30–7 and Saturday 9–5. The most serious laps in town are swum in the Olympic-size pool at **Crystal Palace National Sports Centre** (Ledrington Rd., Upper Norwood, SW19, tel. 0181/778–0131; BritRail: Crystal Palace). At the other extreme, some London pools feature fantabulous setups with slides, cascading waterfalls, wave-making machines, and bizarre floating art objects. A few of the coolest include **Britannia Leisure Centre** (40 Hyde Rd., N1, tel. 0171/729–4485) and the **Elephant & Castle Leisure Centre** (22 Elephant & Castle, SE1, tel. 0171/582–5505).

Hampstead Heath. Choose from three swimming ponds and an outdoor pool. The men-only Highgate Pond (Millfield Ln., tel. 0181/340–4044) and the women-only Kenwood Pond (Millfield Ln., tel. 0181/348–1033) are on the eastern edge of the heath, an uphill slog from the Gospel Oak BritRail station. If you prefer mixed bathing, try the Parliament Hill Lido (0171/485–3873), an outdoor pool just across the street from Gospel Oak, or the Hampstead Mixed Bathing Pond (East Heath Rd., no phone), near the Hampstead tube station. *Hampstead Heath. Admission to ponds free. Admission to Lido: £2, £1 students; free before 10 AM. Segregated ponds open daily 7 AM–1 hr before sunset. Mixed pond open summer, daily 7–7. Lido open summer 7–9:30 and 10–7, winter 7:30 AM–10 AM.*

The Oasis. A spot of water amid the parched concrete of central London, these indoor and outdoor pools get very crowded on hot days. *32 Endell St., WC2, tel. 0171/831–1804. Tube: Covent Garden or Holborn. Admission: £2.50. Open weekdays 7:30 AM–8 PM, weekends 9:30–5.*

Serpentine Lido. This Hyde Park oasis is quite popular in summer, even if a couple of famous people have sunk to its murky depths and never come up again, including Percy Bysshe Shelley's first wife, Harriet Westbrook. Now lifeguards prevent such mishaps from reoccurring. *Hyde Park, south side of the Serpentine, W2, tel. 0171/298–2100. Tube: Knightsbridge. Admission: £2.75. Open late June–Aug., daily 10–5.*

Tooting Bec Lido. This is one of England's largest and oldest pools, a popular haunt on weekends for Londoners of all stripes. *Tooting Bec Rd., SW17, tel. 0181/871–7198. Tube: Tooting Bec. Admission: £2.20 weekdays, £2.70 weekends; free for guests with disabilities. Open late May–late Sept., daily 10–8 (last admission 7:30).*

TENNIS

There are public tennis courts all over London, many administered by neighborhoods or boroughs. Ask at local council halls about ones nearby, as they're often located at neighborhood sports centers (*see above*). Policies and prices vary wildly, though courts generally cost £3–£5 per hour. Sometimes reservations are accepted, sometimes they're required, and sometimes they're not accepted at all. Central London's larger parks, including Battersea Park, Holland Park, Clissold Park, and Hampstead Heath, also have courts. **Regent's Park Tennis Centre** (York Bridge, NW1, tel. 0171/486–4216) rents courts for £2–£5.50 per hour and rackets for £2 per hour plus a £10 deposit. If you're strapped for a partner, check out the **Tennis Network** (195 Battersea Church Rd., London SW11 3ND), which hooks up players by skill level and geographic area if you send them an SASE. Another good resource is the **Lawn Tennis Association Trust** (Queen's Club, W14, tel. 0171/381–7000); their pamphlet "Where to Play Tennis in London" lists dozens of courts and gives the lowdown on reservation requirements and fees.

TRIPS FROM LONDON 9

By Dino Asvaintra and Paula Turnbull

At some point during your stay in London, the realization will hit you like a soggy sausage: As far as countries go, England is extremely compact, and absolutely nothing is very far from the Big City. Moreover, the train and bus networks—though uncomfortably expensive—are extensive, efficient, and easy to figure out. By train from London, it takes a mere 60 minutes to reach Oxford, Brighton, and Cambridge, 75 minutes to reach Bath, and 90 minutes for Cambridge. Only Stratford takes a bit of planning, as there is no direct train from London (there are, however, plenty of buses). While you could tackle any two of the above on a frenzied day trip, consider staying for a day or two. Heavy summer crowds make it difficult to cover the sights in a relaxed manner. And, more to the point, you'll have the time to explore a very different England, one blessed with quiet country pubs, fluffy sheep, and neatly trimmed farms. No matter where you go, lodging reservations are a good idea June–September, when foreigners (like us) saturate the English countryside.

Oxford

Home of the world's first English-language university, Oxford today is bustling and crowded, a vast conurbation expanding ever-outward from the university at its center. Once upon a time, cattle herders led their flocks over this shallow junction of the Thames and Cherwell rivers. These days, however, the horde of buses and foot traffic in the city center are more comparable to those in Piccadilly Circus. Contrary to the way it looks in movies, Oxford is not nearly as small and idyllic as Cambridge, England's other ivory tower. Blame the heavy industry on Oxford's outskirts, particularly the large Rover car factory. Even so, street performers and flying troops of bone-rattlers (those shaky bicycles associated with English academics) make Oxford an engaging city. You'll also find that the food and nightlife rank far above those of quiet Cambridge.

Oxford University is where Lord Shelley was unceremoniously expelled only a few months after arriving, where swashbuckler T. E. Lawrence navigated treacherous underground canals, and where Hugh Grant perfected his "nervous Englishman" look.

Oxford and Cambridge are the nation's most prestigious universities, and the rivalry between the two is intense. You can safely expect an endless stream of comparisons while visiting Oxford's colleges and local pubs. To simplify outrageously, Oxford is better known for the arts, Cambridge for the sciences. Of course, the enormous number of graduates from both schools who occupy positions of power in Britain points to the fact that what students actually study is largely irrelevant. Both Oxford and Cambridge are *names,* and thanks to their legendary old-boy

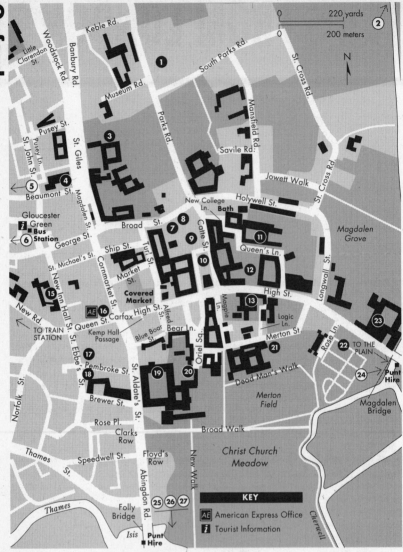

Keble Rd.

Museum Rd.

South Parks Rd.

St. Cross Rd.

0   220 yards

0   200 meters

N

Little Clarendon St.

Woodstock Rd.

Banbury Rd.

Pusey St.

St. Giles

St. John St.

Pusey Ln.

Beaumont St.

St. Cross Rd.

Savile Rd.

Mansfield Rd.

Parks Rd.

Jowett Walk

Magdalen Grove

Gloucester Green Bus Station

George St.

Magdalen St.

Broad St.

New College Ln.

Bath

Holywell St.

St. Michael's St.

Ship St.

Turl St.

Market St.

Cornmarket St.

New Inn Hall St.

Catte St.

Queen's Ln.

High St.

Longwall St.

New Rd.

Covered Market

Carfax

Queen St.

St. Ebbe's St.

Kemp Hall Passage

High St.

Alfred St.

Blue Boar St.

Bear Ln.

Oriel Sq.

Logic Ln.

Merton St.

Rose Ln.

TO THE PLAIN

Punt Hire

TO TRAIN STATION

Pembroke St.

Brewer St.

Norfolk St.

St. Aldate's St.

Dead Man's Walk

Merton Field

Magdalen Bridge

Rose Pl.

Clarks Row

Speedwell St.

Floyd's Row

Broad Walk

Christ Church Meadow

Cherwell

Thames

Thames St.

Abingdon Rd.

New Walk

Folly Bridge

Isis

Punt Hire

KEY

AE   American Express Office

i   Tourist Information

---

networks, a degree from either, in any field, can translate into a lucrative career. But as in every other college town, Oxford student life is a perennial cycle of classes, drinking, more drinking, and frantic bouts of studying.

BASICS

AMERICAN EXPRESS This office provides the usual services for cardholders. Noncard-holders pay a £2 commission for currency exchange. *4 Queen St., OX1 1EJ, tel. 01865/792–066. Open weekdays 9–5:30 (Wed. from 9:30), Sat. 9–5, Sun. 11–3.*

DISCOUNT TRAVEL AGENCIES **STA Travel** (36 George St., tel. 01865/792–800), the biggest of Oxford's budget-travel centers, sells ISIC cards, InterRail passes, and bargain air-fares. When its office gets too busy, stop by **Campus Travel** (105 St. Aldate's, tel. 01865/242–067) or **YHA Adventure Shop** (9–10 St. Clement's St., tel. 01865/247–948), which offers cheaper transportation fares to those with a hostel card.

MAIL The busy very **main post office** (102–104 St. Aldate's St., OX1 1ZZ, tel. 01865/779–286) changes money for a 1% commission and handles poste restante.

VISITOR INFORMATION Oxford's **tourist office** seems more interested in selling merchan-dise than in offering helpful guidance. Nearly every map and leaflet costs something. *The Old School, Gloucester Green, tel. 01865/726–871. Open Mon.–Sat. 9:30–5, Sun. 10–3:30.*

COMING AND GOING

BY TRAIN BritRail runs frequent trains from London's Paddington to **Oxford Station** (1 hr, £12.80 day return, £16.60 open return). The train is convenient, but buses are cheaper. *Bot-ley Rd., tel. 01865/722–333.*

BY BUS All long-distance buses stop at **Gloucester Green Station,** about two blocks from the train depot. Bus company offices here have info and timetables. **National Express** (tel. 0990/808–080) has direct service from Oxford to Birmingham, Bristol, Cambridge, and Nottingham. Two bus companies provide frequent service to Oxford from London's Victoria Coach Station. The 90-minute journey costs £8.50 return (£6.50 students). **Oxford City Link** (tel. 01865/785-400) runs buses from London every 20 minutes, as well as express buses from Oxford to Heathrow (£9 single) and Gatwick (£16 single) airports. **Oxford Tube** (tel. 01865/772–250) runs buses from London every 10 minutes in peak time (at least every hour through the night) and a Heathrow Tube service that leaves for the airport every 30 minutes during the day (£5 single). If you're looking to go to Stratford, **Midland Red** (01788/535–555) runs three buses a day (£6 day return).

War and Peace in Oxford

Throughout Oxford's history, tensions between the city and the university have often erupted into violence. The most famous and bloodiest event, the St. Scholastica's Day Riots, which took place in 1355, began with a tavern brawl between scholars and a local pub owner. Over the next three days, colleges were sacked and six students were killed. In the end the university gained the upper hand because it had royal backing. Despite several attempts on the part of townies to regain control, the university ran things around Oxford until the 19th century. Tension still exists today, but the sparring tends to be limited to the occasional sarcastic comment or verbal fisticuffs.

GETTING AROUND

The town of Oxford and its 40 colleges are inextricably intertwined. The center of it all is **Carfax,** where Cornmarket, St. Aldate's, High, and Queen streets meet, people congregate, and baby strollers battle for space with buses. Beyond Carfax, streets can be hard to identify in the jumbled city center, even with a fairly detailed map; invest in an *Oxford A–Z* map (£1.75) if you want to avoid frustration. With so much to see and do, and so much of it spread over a large area, it's wise to make good use of buses; they're fast, frequent, and fairly cheap.

BY BUS Two main companies, **Oxford Bus Co.** (tel. 01865/785-400) and **Thames Transit** (tel. 01865/727–000 or 01865/727–002), vie for business on similar routes. Oxford's red double-decker buses and green "Nipper" minibuses run about every 7 minutes weekdays and summer Saturdays and at 30-minute intervals at other times. Thames Transit's tan-and-blue minibuses run less frequently but are about 5p–15p less expensive. Just about any bus marked CITY CENTER will take you to within a ¼ mile of Carfax. Most buses to the suburbs also depart from within two blocks of there. Thames Transit offers a **City Hopper** pass good for one day of unlimited travel within Oxford for £1.40 or an **Explorer** pass (£4.50) for wider journeys including Blenheim Palace. Free route maps are available at the bus station.

BY BICYCLE Oxford's flat terrain and extensive network of cycle paths make for great cycling. The free *Cycling in Oxford: A Comprehensive Guide* includes detailed maps of all bicycle paths as well as info on local cycling organizations. Be extremely careful about leaving your expensive mountain bike locked in the town center—thousands are stolen each year in broad daylight. If you haven't brought your own wheels, rent some from **Pennyfarthing** (5 George St., tel. 01865/249–368) for £5 per day or £12 per week.

WHERE TO SLEEP

Finding budget accommodations in Oxford reminds one of the plight of single thirtysomethings on the New York dating scene: There are some good ones out there, but they're usually taken. With two hostels now open, prospects are improving; however, try to book ahead whenever possible. Peak season lasts from May to August, and arriving unprepared could lead to heartache and serious wallet damage.

Brown's Guest House. Brown's is heartily recommended by the hostel staff, who often send overflow backpackers here for the comfortable beds, plush rooms, and yummy breakfasts. Try to get a room that doesn't face noisy Iffley Road. Singles are £25, doubles £36 (£44 with bath). *281 Iffley Rd., tel. 01865/246–822. From Carfax, take Oxford Bus 40 or 42 or Thames Transit Bus 3 toward Rose Hill and alight at Addison Crescent. 9 rooms, 2 with bath.*

Falcon Private Hotel. This hotel really is a home away from home and definitely worth the splurge. The staff is friendly and the attractive rooms have luxuries such as satellite TV and hair dryers. Singles are £26, doubles £45, triples £66. *88–90 Abingdon Rd., tel. 01865/ 722–995. From Carfax, walk south on Abingdon Rd. or take Bus 30, 31, or 32A. 11 rooms, all with bath. MC, V.*

Mrs. O'Neil. This is one of Oxford's true lodging bargains. The rooms are immaculate, but there are only two of 'em (one single, one double), so make reservations right now. Bed-and-breakfast costs £12 per person. *15 Southmoor Rd., tel. 01865/511–205. From Carfax, walk north on Cornmarket St., turn left on Beaumont St., right on Walton St., left on Southmoor Rd. 2 rooms, none with bath.*

Newton House. A number of bargain B&Bs lurk past Folly Bridge far from the city center, and Newton House is the best of them. Because of its larger size—15 spotless rooms with TVs and plenty of light—it's likely to have vacancies even in summer. Doubles cost £37 (£47 with bath), a bit more in high season. *82–84 Abingdon Rd., tel. 01865/240–561. From Carfax, walk south on Abingdon Rd. or take Bus 30, 31, 32, or 32A. 15 rooms, 5 with bath. AE, MC, V.*

HOSTELS **Oxford Backpackers Hostel.** This newly opened hostel is the godsend that budget visitors to Oxford have been waiting for. The central location, friendly staff, and 24-hour access make a perfect base for exploring the colleges, pubs, and nightlife (the hostel even organizes a pub crawl on Tuesdays!). A dorm bed costs £9. *9A Hythe Bridge St., tel. 01865/721–761, fax 08165/721–761. From bus station, turn left on Worcester St., right on Hythe Bridge St. 92 beds. Kitchen, pool table. MC, V.*

Oxford YHA. Clean, comfortable, and expertly managed, Oxford's hostel is a model of efficiency with great kitchen facilities, a pool table, and lots of info. Beds fill quickly year-round in this brick Victorian about a mile outside the town center; reserve ahead and check in before 5 PM. Dorm beds cost £8.80. *32 Jack Straw's Ln., OX3 0DW, tel. 01865/62997, fax 01865/69402. From Carfax, take Bus 72 or 73; Bus 73 also runs from the rail station weekdays after 7 PM and on Sunday. 116 beds. Flexible midnight curfew. Closed Christmas–mid-Jan. Wheelchair access. MC, V.*

CAMPING Oxford YHA (*see above*) has a few campsites available for £4.55 per person. At **Oxford Camping International** (426 Abingdon Rd., tel. 01865/246–551) you'll be vying with motor homes, but hey, it's clean, green, cheap, and open year-round. Tent sites cost £5.30 for two people. To reach the campground take Bus 30, 31, 32, or 32A from Carfax.

FOOD

Oxford has great food, with all ethnicities and price ranges represented. If you're strapped, head to supermarkets like **J. Sainsbury** (Westgate Shopping Centre, tel. 01865/722–179) and **Tesco** (159 Cowley Rd., tel. 01865/244–470), both of which are closed on Sunday. At the **Covered Market,** on Market Street half a block east of Cornmarket Street, greengrocers, butchers, and bakers set up shop Monday–Saturday among the market's clothing and souvenir stands. For delicious hummus, breads, cheeses, and desserts, visit **Gluttons Delicatessen** (110 Walton St., tel. 01865/53748). **Heroes** (8 Ship St., tel. 01865/723–459) serves sandwiches on fresh-baked bread and Italian-style subs for £2–£3.

Attas Brasserie. The central location of this casually elegant brasserie makes it the perfect place for a delicious lunch or dinner, or simply a refreshing drink. The set two-course menu (£7 lunch, £9 dinner) is composed of delights such as sole with cheese and grape sauce. *9A High St., tel. 01865/203–900. Open Mon.–Sat. noon–3 and 6–11, Sun. noon–11. AE, MC, V.*

Café MOMA. This spacious joint is hidden beneath the Museum of Modern Art. By noon it's jumping with the local art crowd, but things quiet down around 3 PM. Chow down on a large salad (£2.50), or try the vegan "Nutroast," a baked loaf of ground nuts and onions (£3.90). *30 Pembroke St., tel. 01865/722–733. From Carfax, walk west on Queen St., turn left on St. Ebbe's St., left on Pembroke St. Open Tues.–Sat. 9–5 (Thurs. until 9), Sun. 11–5.*

Chang Mai Kitchen. Oxford's best Thai food is served up in a ramshackle Tudor building less than a block from Carfax. Despite the classy wooden-beam surroundings, most dishes cost only £5–£6. Splurges like the fish in coconut sauce go for £6.50. *Kemp Hall Passage, 130A High St., tel. 01865/202–233. From Carfax, walk east on High St., turn right on tiny Kemp Hall Passage. Open Mon.–Sat. noon–2:30 and 6–11. AE, MC, V.*

Georgina's Coffee Shop. Toulouse-Lautrec posters line the walls in this hip café hidden within the hectic confines of the Covered Market. Strong coffee complements bagels, pastries, and lunch specials like mozzarella and tomato salad with ciabatta bread (£4). *Covered Market, above Beaton's Deli, tel. 01865/249–527. Open Mon.–Sat. 9–5.*

The Nosebag. This popular upstairs café has been around for more than 25 years. The ever-changing lunch menu features a soup du jour (£2.10), stuffed potatoes (£3), a cold dish (£4.55), a vegetarian dish (£5), and a hot dish (£5.25). Dinners (heftier versions of lunch) cost about £6. Long lines form for both meals. *6–8 St. Michael's St., tel. 01865/721–033. From Carfax, walk north on Cornmarket St., turn left on St. Michael's St. Open Mon. 9:30–5:30, Tues.–Thurs. 9:30 AM–10 PM, Fri.–Sat. 9:30 AM–10:30 PM, Sun. 9:30–9.*

Pizza Express. You'd never know you were in a chain restaurant from the looks of this place. The light, airy building dates back to the year 1200, when it opened as the Golden Cross Inn. Come for a basic pizza margherita (£3.70) or the fancier Cajun pizza (£7.20) topped with prawns, mozzarella, tomato, and Tabasco. Or you can enjoy a glass of wine (£2.40) at the downstairs bar. *Golden Cross, tel. 01865/790–442. From Carfax, walk north on Cornmarket St., quick right on Golden Cross. Open daily 11:30 AM–midnight.*

WORTH SEEING

Before publicly embarrassing yourself, you should know Oxford University isn't one big campus. The 29 undergraduate colleges, six graduate colleges, four permanent halls, and All Souls College (*see below*) collectively compose "the university." They're all scattered around town, each with its own dormitories and lecture halls. Many colleges charge a small admission fee to people who want to wander around or take a tour, but there's no harm in trying to pass yourself off as a student by walking determinedly into the colleges. Aside from what we list below, check out the beautiful gardens at **Merton College** (Merton St., tel. 01865/276–310) and **St. John's College** (St. Giles, tel. 01865/277–300). And definitely don't miss the Bodleian Library, Britain's second-largest, and the adjacent Radcliffe Camera, designed by James Gibbs (*see Museums and Libraries, below*). For a look at rare and historical keyboards, woodwind, brass, and percussion instruments, visit the **Bate Collection of Musical Instruments** (St. Aldates, tel. 01865/276–139), free and open weekdays 2–5. Unless you're interested in a silly Disneyesque experience, skip **The Oxford Story** and save the steep admission price (£4.50).

Not all of Oxford's colleges are as well-off as they look. With ailing endowments and shrinking government funding, colleges like Pembroke, St. Edmund's, and St. Peter's can use every penny they get.

BOTANIC GARDEN In *Brideshead Revisited*, Sebastian Flyte tells Charles Ryder, "There's a beautiful arch there and more different kinds of ivy than I knew existed. I don't know where I should be without the Botanical Gardens." Few gardens are more beautiful or feature a greater diversity of plants than this 300-year-old complex of greenhouses (called "glasshouses" in England). On a cold day, saunter past the rows of rare tropical plants. *High St., across from Magdalen College, tel. 01865/276–920. Admission: £1 June–Sept.; free Oct.–May. Gardens open daily 9–4:30 (until 5 in summer); greenhouses open daily 2–4. Wheelchair access.*

CARFAX TOWER As the last remnant of St. Martin's Church (erected in 1032), Carfax Tower minds the corner all by itself now, marking the passage of time with little mechanical figures that dance every 15 minutes. After the 14th-century St. Scholastica's Day Riots, Edward III ordered the tower lowered to its current 74 feet to prevent townies from showering gownies with rocks, bottles, and flaming arrows. Climb up the tower via the dank stairwell for a good view of the town center. *Admission: £1.20. Open Apr.–Oct., daily 10–6.*

THE COLLEGES Oxford University has been a major player in British history for the past 830 years. The establishment of several monasteries in the early 12th century attracted scholarly clerics, and before long they organized themselves into a *studium generale,* offering a curriculum along the same lines as the University of Paris. The turning point for the university came in 1167 when the French expelled all English students from Paris following the assassination of Thomas à Becket, the Archbishop of Canterbury. Thereafter, Oxford multiplied its faculty and student body, gaining immense power and prestige along the way. Oxford University Press was born in 1477, and until 1948 the university had two representatives in Parliament (talk about privilege). Women, however, weren't granted full student status until 1959.

Most colleges will grudgingly allow visitors to snoop around on weekday afternoons between 2 and 5 PM (except during finals, from late May to mid-June). Be sure to vacate the grounds by 9 PM: The gates shut at 9:05 on the dot, and some unfortunates have been known to get locked in by accident. Student-run **Oxford Student Tours** arranges guided walks (£3) on summer afternoons. To catch a tour, look for the guys in funny hats and bow ties hanging around the tourist office. For more info, contact Oxford University General Information (tel. 01865/270–000). The well-respected **Spires and Shires** (tel. 01865/251–785 or 01865/726–871) also runs 90-minute guided walks (£3) from Broad Street outside the Trinity College gates.

➤ **ALL SOULS** • Possibly the most beautiful college in Oxford, All Souls was founded in 1438 by the Archbishop of Canterbury for spiritual and legal studies. Until the 20th century, All Souls was the only college in Oxford dedicated exclusively to graduate research. The academic program is something of an enigma, but the fellows of All Souls are the best of the brightest; those invited are given academic carte blanche during their seven-year tenure. Today the **North Quad** is a whimsical 18th-century interpretation of Gothic spires and pinnacles, featuring Christopher Wren's sundial and John Hawksmoor's famous twin towers. Sadly, the college doesn't make itself very amenable to tourists; All Souls seems to close "for repairs" every time a light bulb blows out. *High St., tel. 01865/279–379. Open weekdays 2–4.*

➤ **CHRIST CHURCH** • Founded by Cardinal Wolsey in 1525, Christ Church is never referred to as "Christ Church College." Goodness gracious, no—members call it "the House." In fact, everything seems to have a special name here at the House, which many regard as Oxford's snobbiest college. Professors, called "dons" elsewhere in Oxford, are referred to here as "students." The 6¼-ton bell in the clock tower over the entrance is named **Great Tom**, and the quad over which Great Tom presides is (big surprise) **Tom Quad**. Every night at 9:05, Great Tom rings 101 times, once for each of the original students (not professors); afterward, the college's gates are locked shut. Near the **Memorial Garden** is Christ Church's 800-year-old **cathedral,** one of the smallest and most ornate in the country. The cathedral's stained glass is exquisite: Some dates back to the 14th century, while other pieces are 19th-century work by Edward Burne-Jones and William Morris.

A handful of literary giants did time at Christ Church, including W. H. Auden, Jeremy Bentham, John Locke, and Charles Dodgson (Lewis Carroll).

If you have time, take a stroll through the quiet, tree-lined paths of **Christ Church Meadow** alongside the Thames. When school is in session, college "eights" practice their rowing on the Isis (what they call this section of the Thames). Early Italian paintings and drawings dominate the collection at the **Christ Church Picture Gallery** (admission: £1, 50p students). There are also several Dutch paintings and Inigo Jones drawings. The gallery is small, however, and the collection at the **Ashmolean** (*see below*) is better, larger, and free. *St. Aldate's St., tel. 01865/276–150. Admission: £3, £2 students. Open mid-Apr.–Aug., Mon.–Sat. 9:30–5:30, Sun. 12:45–5:30; Sept.–mid-Apr., Mon.–Sat. 9:30–4:30, Sun. 12:45–4:30.*

➤ **MAGDALEN COLLEGE** • Magdalen (pronounced "maudlin") opened its doors to undergrads in 1458 and boasts Oscar Wilde, C. S. Lewis, Peter Brook, and (best of all) Dudley Moore as alumni. The quadrangle is a quiet area enclosed by ancient vaulted cloisters covered with wisteria; beyond it lies a deer park, gardens, and the Cherwell River. At the foot of **Magdalen Bridge,** you can rent punts (*see* Outdoor Activities, *below*). **Magdalen Tower,** one of Oxford's most recognizable landmarks, presides over the college grounds. *High St., tel. 01865/276–000. From Carfax, walk east on High St. Admission: £2, £1 students. Open weekdays 2–6, weekends noon–6.*

Wildness reigns on May Day, when Oxford celebrates the coming of warm weather. At 6 AM the little boys in the Magdalen College choir sing from Magdalen Tower, and the pubs open at 7 AM.

➤ **NEW COLLEGE** • The first college built after the bloody St. Scholastica's Day Riot, New College (officially called St. Mary College of Winchester in Oxenford) incorporated a new design feature—the first enclosed quad—to protect students in the event of another town-versus-gown flare-up. The extra caution proved unnecessary, but founder William of Wykeham (Bishop of Winchester and a wealthy, wealthy man) probably didn't feel like taking chances, on account of the shortage of well-educated people after the Black Death outbreak of 1349. Most of the college and its **chapel** were completed in 1386, with further major additions completed in the 17th century. *Queen's Ln., tel. 01865/279–555. From Carfax, walk north on Cornmarket St., turn right on Broad St., right on Catte St., left on New College Ln. Admission: £1. Open daily 2–5 (from 11 AM during school vacations).*

➤ **UNIVERSITY COLLEGE** • To its embarrassment, University is best known for expelling Percy Bysshe Shelley in 1811 because he wrote and distributed a little pamphlet called "The Necessity of Atheism." After he drowned in Italy, the college had second thoughts and erected a monument to him in the **Front Quad.** This is also where young Bill Clinton dodged the draft and networked like a whirling dervish while on a Rhodes Scholarship. But back to the college: The original foundation dates from 1249, the extant evidence of any college in Oxford (although Merton claims to be 85 years older). University is not open to the public unless the students decide to organize tours; call for the latest word. *High St., tel. 01865/276–602.*

MUSEUMS AND LIBRARIES Not only do Oxford's museums house some tremendous collections, but almost all of them are free. The exceptions to the rule are the **Museum of Modern Art** (30 Pembroke St., tel. 01865/722–733), which badly needs the £2.50 (£1.50 students) admission fee, and **Christ Church Picture Gallery** (Oriel Sq., tel. 01865/276–172), which doesn't need the £1 (50p students) fee but takes it anyway. MOMA does offer free admission Wednesday 10–1 and Thursday 6–9 PM. All university libraries, with the exception of the Bodleian Library, are off-limits to the general public.

➤ **ASHMOLEAN MUSEUM OF ART AND ARCHAEOLOGY** • The Ashmolean, opened in 1683, is Britain's oldest public museum and boasts artifacts and masterworks ranging from drawings by Michelangelo and paintings by Pissarro to Bronze Age tools and weapons. The Egyptian coffins, Byzantine frescoes, and Islamic pottery downstairs deserve a look, but don't miss the drawings and Rodin sculptures in the upstairs galleries. The prize for Most Bizarre Objet d'Intérêt definitely goes to Oliver Cromwell's death mask. *Beaumont St., at St. Giles, tel. 01865/278–000. From Carfax, walk north on Cornmarket St., turn left on Beaumont St. Admission free. Open Tues.–Sat. 10–4, Sun. 2–4. Wheelchair access.*

➤ **THE BODLEIAN LIBRARY AND RADCLIFFE CAMERA** • "Camera" means room in Latin, and the Radcliffe is one hell of a reading room. So, too, is the library, which owns a copy of every book printed in Britain since printing began—about 5.5 million books, give or take a few. The Bodleian is notoriously stingy about who gets to look at the certain books, and it takes a full day to retrieve any requested title. Students can't get inside without a signed letter from their university specifically requesting library access, and even then one may have to haggle. A guided tour (£3) is your surest bet; they start at the Divinity School across the street weekdays at 10:30, 11:30, 2, and 3, and Saturday at 10:30 and 11:30. The library's courtyard and the adjacent fan-vaulted divinity school lobby are always open and well worth a peek. Also take a look inside Duke Humfrey's library (1488), which is rather like a small church. *Catte St., tel. 01865/277–165. From Carfax, walk east on High St., turn left on Catte St. Open weekdays 9–5, Sat. 9–12:30.*

➤ **MUSEUM OF THE HISTORY OF SCIENCE** • While it's hardly the Smithsonian, you get to see the blackboard Einstein once used and some impressive Islamic and European astrolabes. *Broad St., tel. 01865/277–280. From Carfax, walk north on Cornmarket St., turn right on Broad St. Admission free. Open weekdays noon–4.*

Crews and Booze

Perhaps to relieve the tension of impending finals, Oxford students get their blood pumping for four days every May during the Eights Week rowing competition. Boats containing eight rowers (plus coxswain) set off on the Thames in a single-file line with the aim of "bumping" a boat in front of their own without being bumped. In short, it's bumper cars on water. Teams who bump on each of the four days win blades, which are oars inscribed with the names of their team members. Tradition also dictates that the first team of the first division—"The Head of the River"—burn one of their own boats in celebration. The feisty '95 winners, Pembroke College, created an even bigger spectacle by burning a defeated opponent's boat instead. Hey, this sounds rowdier than college football. Of course, Eights Week is really just an excuse to drink a lot (Pimm's is the beverage of choice) and cruise the crews.

➢ **PITT RIVERS MUSEUM** • In the same building as the University Museum (*see below*), the Pitt harbors all sorts of things: masks, hanging sailboats, wooden clothing—fun for flea market enthusiasts or attic addicts. It also hosts special exhibitions of cultural significance, such as the display of Japanese crafts (through Sept. 1997). *Parks Rd., tel. 01865/270–927 or 01865/270–949. From Carfax, walk north on Cornmarket St., turn right on Broad St., left on Parks Rd. Admission free. Open Mon.–Sat. 1–4:30.*

➢ **SHELDONIAN THEATRE** • Christopher Wren's marble-covered Sheldonian Theatre, built in 1669, was intended as an appropriately sober venue to confer degrees upon graduates. With its painted ceiling, heavy columns, and enormous pipe organ, it does indeed feel like the sort of place everyone should pass through before graduating into "the real world." The cupola provides a decent, if frustrating, glass-enclosed view of central Oxford—it's worth a visit. The theater hosts concerts, too, on Saturday evenings. Visitors should call ahead, as the theater often closes for events. *Broad St., tel. 01865/277–299. Admission: 50p. Open Mon.–Sat. 10–12:30 and 2–4:30 (until 3:30 in winter).*

➢ **UNIVERSITY MUSEUM** • One of the greatest natural history museums in the world sits just 20 minutes north of the town center in a massive Victorian Gothic building. There are hundreds of exhibits on just about every facet of nature, but the local dinosaur finds attract the most attention. The collection also includes the head and left foot of a dodo, a large, flightless bird that has been extinct since the mid-17th century. Lewis Carroll (Charles Dodgson) was familiar with the museum's display and cast himself in the role of the Dodo in *Alice's Adventures in Wonderland*. The building itself, designed by Benjamin Woodward, is also worth a gander. *Parks Rd., tel. 01865/272–950. Admission free. Open Mon.–Sat. noon–5.*

AFTER DARK

Once the sun goes down, drinkers, clubbers, theater goers, and lovers of classical music are set. Otherwise, the main after-dark pursuits are hanging out around Carfax near the kabob vans—pretty dismal. *What's On In Oxford* is an invaluable guide to clubbing around town, while *This Month in Oxford* covers other events. Both are available free at the tourist office.

PUBS Most pubs in Oxford stay open through the afternoon for post-tutorial pints. All pubs listed below are open Monday–Saturday 11–11, Sunday noon–10:30.

The Head of the River. This is the biggest "activity" pub in Oxford, complete with barbecues, snooker playoffs, bucking bronco contests, and even bungee jumping on summer Saturday nights. The cement "beer garden" outside allows drinkers to hang by the riverside and get sloshed before taking out a rowboat. *Abingdon Rd., at Folly Bridge, tel. 01865/721–600. From Carfax, walk south on St. Aldate's St. to Folly Bridge.*

The King's Arms. A loud crowd of students makes this one of the best traditional pubs in the center of town. Tweedy professor types mix with students, townies, tourists, gays, straights— what have you. The "K. A.," as the locals affectionately call it, also serves vegetarian dishes. *40 Holywell St., at Parks Rd., tel. 01865/242–369. From Carfax, walk north on Cornmarket St., turn right on Broad St. (which becomes Holywell St.).*

The Bear (Alfred St. and Bear Ln.) is a magnificent 13th-century pub with walls covered by thousands of ties. You get a free pint if you donate your school, regiment, sporting, or dress tie—assuming they haven't yet got one.

The Philanderer and Firkin. This trendy but characterless pub often offers student drink specials and live music with no cover charge. *56 Walton St., next to Phoenix Cinema, tel. 01865/54502.*

Turf Tavern. If you can find this tiny 13th-century pub tucked away in a narrow alley, you may never want to leave (which would explain some of the ancient professors lurking in the dark corners). In warm weather, sit on the patio; in winter, try the mulled wine—cinnamon-spiced and guaranteed to lift even the most discouraged traveler's spirits. The pub's distinctive style is featured in the *Inspector Morse* television series. *4 Bath Pl., tel. 01865/243–235. From Carfax, walk* *north on Cornmarket, turn right on Broad St., right on Catte St., left on New College Ln., walk under Hertford's Bridge of Sighs, and take the first quick left.*

CLUBS **Freud.** Freud (or FREVD as the sign says) is housed in a 19th-century church that retains its stained-glass windows. Don't ask what the holy builders would think of the enormous selection of cocktails. Live jazz or classical music starts at 11 PM most nights. *Walton St., at Great Clarendon St., tel. 01865/311–171. Cover: £1–£3.*

Old Fire Station. This is the ultimate one-stop spot, with a restaurant, theater, bar, and art museum all under one roof. Come Friday or Saturday for live jazz and blues. *40 George St., tel. 01865/794–494. Cover: £4–£6.*

Zodiac. Members of Britpop bands Radiohead, Supergrass, and Ride are among the shareholders of this hip music venue. Local and big-name bands are featured along with DJs and club nights. *190 Cowley Rd., tel. 08165/726–336. Cover: £3–£5.*

THEATER AND MUSIC Home to the accomplished Oxford Stage Company, the **Oxford Playhouse** (Beaumont St., tel. 01865/798–600) frequently hosts first-rate entertainment ranging from Shakespearean drama and Restoration comedy to contemporary dance and musicals. Tickets run £5–£14. **Apollo Theatre** (George St., tel 01865/244–544) has a varied program of plays, comedy, opera, ballet, and pop concerts. Tickets range £4–£20. In the summer, plays are often performed in the gardens of some colleges; check with the tourist office for venues and ticket prices.

OUTDOOR ACTIVITIES

PUNTING AND ROWING One of the great Oxford experiences, punting involves propelling a long, flat boat along the Thames River using a 15-foot pole to push off the riverbed; beginners will probably spin around in circles before getting the hang of it. If you find it easier to punt from the front, do so, even if, technically speaking, you're supposed to push from the rear. One piece of advice: If your pole gets stuck, LET GO—you can use the smaller paddle to go back and retrieve it. You do not want to end up treading water in the slimy Thames. You can, of course, also get a normal rowboat for the same rate. The friendly **Magdalen Bridge Boathouse** (High St., tel. 01865/202–643) rents punts and rowboats for £7 per hour with a £20 deposit. It also offers chauffered punts if you're feeling lazy. Punts and rowboats cost £6 per hour with a £20 deposit at **Riverside Boating Co.** (beneath Folly Bridge), though the owner has been known to raise prices during high-demand periods. Both close for bad weather and boat races.

Stratford-upon-Avon

To go, or not to go, that is the question. Whether 'tis nobler in the wallet to suffer the slings and arrows of outrageous prices, or to take arms against a sea of tourists and by opposing end them. To die: of claustrophobia. No more; and by patience we say you'll end the headache and the thousand natural shocks that visitors are heir to: 'tis a resolution devoutly to be wished. To visit: to enjoy. To enjoy? Perhaps to go to the theater. Ay, there's the rub; for in that theater what plays may come, when we have shuffled off the mortifying crowds, must give us peace.

Stratford is suffocatingly overcrowded—a tourist trap, even—and its soul has been sucked dry by mercenary hucksters looking to make a few quid off Shakespeare's good name. If you're really that keen on saying you've "done" Stratford, you won't mind the crowds or the lack of cafés, movie theaters, and other forms of cultural life beyond the theater. And while the **Royal Shakespeare Company (RSC)** stages frequent productions in Stratford, equally prestigious productions run in London—minus the hype. That said, the RSC is the best thing going for Stratford, and we unabashedly recommend it.

Stratford is just fine during winter—the crowds thin out, the streets become walkable, and the RSC continues its first-rate program of drama. Even so, don't come expecting to find a sprawl-

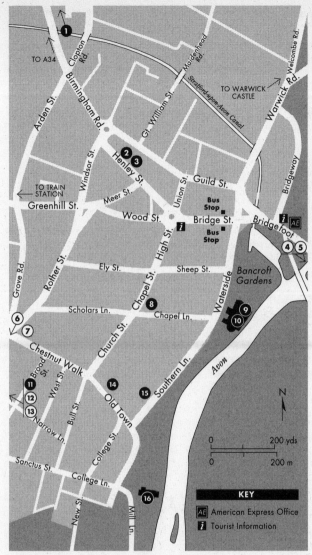

Sights ●

Anne Hathaway's Cottage, **11**

Hall's Croft, **14**

Holy Trinity Church, **16**

Mary Arden's House, **1**

New Place (Nash's House), **8**

The Other Place Theatre, **15**

Royal Shakespeare Theatre, **9**

Shakespeare Birthplace, **3**

Shakespeare Centre and Library, **2**

Swan Theatre, **10**

Lodging ○

Elms Camp, **5**

The Garth House, **13**

Newlands, **12**

Penhurst, **6**

Stratford YHA, **4**

Willowdale Hotel, **7**

KEY

AE American Express Office

i Tourist Information

ing Elizabethan town: Apart from a few heavily restored thatched cottages, the streets of modern-day Stratford are lined with high-fashion clothing stores and the ubiquitous McDonald's. The Shakespearean sights have a certain Old World appeal, but even these have been repeatedly reconstructed and restored. To make matters worse, there's no direct train service from London, which means you'll probably end up on one of three daily buses.

BASICS

AMERICAN EXPRESS Located inside the tourist office, AmEx changes money, issues traveler's checks, and holds client mail. *Bridgefoot, CV37 6GW, tel. 01789/415–856. Open Mon.–Sat. 9–6, Sun. 11–5.*

VISITOR INFORMATION The **tourist office**'s multilingual staff and piles of pamphlets may look helpful, but much of the info is geared toward wealthier tourists. Come mainly to book a room. *Bridgefoot, tel. 01789/293–127. Open Mon.–Sat. 9–6, Sun. 11–5.*

Guide Friday (14 Rother St., tel. 01789/294–466), a bus-tour company, also has tourist info and free flyers, and the lines are much shorter than at the tourist office. On the downside, they're also trying to sell something: a double-decker bus tour (£7) that stops at all five of Stratford's major sights. Since the price doesn't include admission to the sights and most are within walking distance, it's not really worth it unless you're lazy. Take the pamphlets and run.

COMING AND GOING

BY TRAIN While there are no direct trains from London, there is direct BritRail service from Birmingham (£3.20 return). Otherwise, from London's Paddington, take the train to Leamington Spa and change to the Stratford Line (3 hrs, £20 return). Stratford's **train station** (Alcester Rd., tel. 01203/555–211) is closed on Sundays October–May, so you'll have to take the bus.

BY BUS Buses stop on Bridge Street at Waterside, either directly in front of the McDonald's or across the street. National Express sends buses from London three times a day (£13 return, £15.50 on Friday and Saturday and in July). Buy tickets at the **National Express desk** (tel. 01879/262–718) inside Stratford's tourist office; it's closed Sunday. **Stratford Blue** (tel. 01788/535–555) runs a bus service to Oxford for £3.50 single, £6 return.

GETTING AROUND

Stratford Blue buses cover the main sights around Stratford: Bus X16 runs to Warwick (£2.75 return) and Kenilworth, Bus X20 runs hourly to Birmingham, and Bus 18 runs to the YHA hostel. If you really want to go wild, rent a bike from the hostel (summers only) and wheel around town; it's the best way to avoid the congested sidewalks, though the roads aren't much better.

WHERE TO SLEEP

Since nearly every tourist over the age of 40 is magnetically drawn to Stratford, there's no shortage of B&Bs. The hard part is finding a cheap one. No matter what, reserve space *at least* a few days in advance. Stratford has three concentrated pockets of B&Bs: on **Grove Road** near the train station; around **Evesham Road,** the southern extension of Grove Road; and on **Shipston Road,** across the River Avon from the center of town.

Shakespeare's birthday is traditionally assigned to April 23, 1564. More than 400 years later, it's one of the worst days to look for cheap lodging in Stratford.

The Garth House. Unlike most other B&B proprietors, Louise Thomas actually caters to backpackers. The double with bath is especially quiet. Doubles cost £28–£30. *9A Broad Walk, tel. 01789/298–035. From the rail station, walk toward town, turn right on Grove Rd. (which becomes Evesham Pl.), left on Broad Walk. 3 rooms, 1 with bath. Closed weekdays Oct.–Mar.*

Newlands. This unpretentious B&B is wonderfully quiet, and the rooms are surprisingly large. Proprietor Sue Boston is a sweetheart who loves to give advice on the best plays to see in Stratford. Rooms cost £19–£21 per person. *7 Broad Walk, tel. 01789/298–449. Follow directions to the Garth House (see above). 4 rooms, 3 with bath. MC, V.*

Penshurst. If you searched the whole of Stratford, you wouldn't find a better place to stay than this pretty, centrally located B&B. The owner is an absolute treasure, and there are flexible breakfast hours to suit early birds and lazy slobs alike. The rooms are named after Stratford's historical streets, and each contains a book on the history of the corresponding street. Singles start at £15; doubles run £14–£20 per person. *34 Evesham Pl., tel. 01789/295–322. From rail station, walk toward town, turn right on Grove Rd. (which becomes Evesham Pl.). 8 rooms, 2 with bath. Wheelchair access.*

Willowdale Hotel. If you're traveling in a group, the incongruous family room–style sleeping arrangements in this B&B will suit you just fine. The very basic rooms are filled with assortment of beds and, though the decor needs attention, there's a cute garden available to residents. Prices range from £14 to £18 per person and include a decent breakfast. *192 Evesham Rd., tel. 01789/205–416. From rail station, walk toward town, turn right on Grove Rd. (which becomes Evesham Pl. and Evesham Rd.). 5 rooms, none with bath.*

HOSTELS **Stratford YHA.** If you have the time, you should definitely walk the 2 miles to the village of Alveston, where this hostel is located—you'll pass some beautiful Tudor homes that aren't on the bus route. It's one of the few hostels in Britain with cafeteria-style meals for lunch and dinner, so if you only want a pot of tea, you can buy it separately without paying for a full meal. Clean rooms and helpful management make the price (beds £12.20, £9.05 under 18), which includes breakfast, seem not so bad. Definitely reserve ahead. *Hemmingford House, Alveston, Warwickshire CV37 7RG, tel. 01789/297–093, fax 01789/205–513. Take Bus 18 from Stratford (£1.55 return). 154 beds. Midnight curfew. Closed mid-Dec.–early Jan.*

CAMPING **Elms Camp.** It's a great alternative to the local lodging scene and closer to Stratford than the hostel. The nearby village of Tiddington has a pub and market. Sites are £2.50 per person (or £3.50 single). As always in Stratford, reserve in advance. *Tiddington Rd., Tiddington, tel. 01789/292–312. Take Bus 18 from Stratford to Tiddington, then follow signs. 50 sites. Check-in by 9 PM. Laundry, shop, showers. Closed Nov.–Mar.*

FOOD

Finding a reasonably priced, tasty meal in Stratford is nearly impossible. Pubs and greasy fast-food stands will cheaply plug the hole in your stomach, but if you want a full dinner, you'll be eating alongside other tourists and paying heavily inflated prices. Try your luck on **Sheep Street,** one block south of the train station. Nearby **Marco Italian Deli** (20 Church St., tel. 01789/292–889) sells sandwiches for under £2 during the day. **Greenhill Street,** near the train station, is slightly removed from touristy ground zero and has some reasonable places.

The Garrick Inn. A "traditional" English establishment crammed with tourists, the Garrick Inn, built in 1595, still has the cramped feel of an Elizabethan pub. Surprisingly, the food isn't expensive: Chicken-and-mushroom pie (£4.50) and scampi with chips and peas (£4.65) are bargains by Stratford standards. There are good brews on tap, too. *25 High St., tel. 01789/ 292–186. Open Mon.–Sat. 11–11, Sun. noon–10:30.*

Vintner Cafe and Wine Bar. An eclectic group of families, twentysomethings, and Europeans crowd one of Stratford's few cool places. Huge candles stuck in wine bottles dominate the small tables, leaving little room for the plates of ravioli (£7) or the vegetarian dish of the day (£5.50–£6). *5 Sheep St., tel. 01789/297–259. Open daily 10:30 AM–11 PM (Sun. until 10:30).*

Wholefood Café. The antiseptic interior lacks character, but an encouraging mix of locals and visitors gives this vegetarian and whole-food restaurant some life. The soup (£2), quiche (£4), and stuffed potatoes (£2.25) won't do you wrong. The adjacent **Stratford Health Foods** (tel. 01789/292–353), open daily, sells bulk groceries and food to go. *Greenhill St., tel. 01789/ 415–741. Open Mon.–Sat. 9–4:30 (Tues. from 9:30).*

WORTH SEEING

The Shakespeare Birthplace Trust sells a convenient **all-inclusive ticket** (£9, £7.50 students) to the five major sights listed below, not including **Holy Trinity.** If you want to skip Anne Hathaway's Cottage and Mary Arden's House, buy the **three-in-one** ticket (£6, £5 students). For those actually interested in the work of the writer, the **Shakespeare Library** (Henley St., tel. 01789/204–016) has original Shakespeare folios and displays on the Bard's life. Surprisingly, admission to the library is free.

ANNE HATHAWAY'S COTTAGE Anne Hathaway lived in this thatched cottage in nearby Shottery prior to her marriage to William Shakespeare on November 27, 1582. At the time, Will was only 18 years old, and his betrothed, 26; count backward from the birth of their child Susanna on May 26, 1583, and the phrase "shotgun wedding" comes to mind. The Tudor furniture pales in comparison with the lovely apple orchard outside. From Stratford it's a 15-minute walk west through open fields; follow the signs from Evesham Place or hop a frequent bus from Bridge Street. Tel. 01789/292–100. Admission: £2.40. Open Mar. 20–Oct. 19, Mon.–Sat. 9–5:30, Sun. 9:30–5:30; Oct. 20–Mar. 19, Mon.–Sat. 9:30–4, Sun. 10–4.

At the end of the day, the best way to be alone in Stratford is to stroll along the River Avon.

HALL'S CROFT This sight has a tenuous connection at best to the Bard's dramatic life. It was the home of his daughter, Susanna, and her husband, Dr. John Hall. Of the 17th-century antiques on display, Dr. Hall's medical instruments are certainly the coolest. Old Town, tel. 01789/292–107. Admission: £2. Open Mar. 20–Oct. 19, Mon.–Sat. 9:30–5, Sun. 10–5; Oct. 20–Mar. 19, Mon.–Sat. 10-4, Sun. 10:30–4.

HOLY TRINITY CHURCH The remains of Shakespeare lie buried underneath the altar of this traditional Gothic church—not in Westminster Abbey's Poets' Corner, as many think. Will's wife and family rest in peace next to him; above hovers a bust made immediately after his death in 1616 by Gheerart Jansen. It's believed to be one of only two likenesses created in Shakespeare's time. Trinity St., at College Ln., tel. 01789/266–316. Admission: 50p, 30p students. Open Apr.–Oct., Mon.–Sat. 8:30–6, Sun. 2–5; Nov.–Mar., Mon.–Sat. 8:30–4, Sun. 2–5.

MARY ARDEN'S HOUSE Mary Arden probably didn't live here, and the "home" of Shakespeare's mother is definitely boring. The mostly undecorated Tudor farmhouse has been expanded, however, to include the slightly more interesting **Glebe Farm,** where falconers display their art with live birds, all day, every day. To reach the house and farm, take the train from Stratford to Wilmcote (5 min, £1.20 return) and follow the signs from the station. Wilmcote, tel. 01789/293–455. Admission: £3.30. Open Mar. 20–Oct. 19, Mon.–Sat. 9:30–5, Sun. 10–5; Oct. 20–Mar. 19, Mon.–Sat. 10–4, Sun. 10:30–4.

NEW PLACE (NASH'S HOUSE) Shakespeare bought the place in 1597 for £60 (big money at the time) and died here in 1616 at the age of 52. It's called Nash's House after the man who married Shakespeare's granddaughter. Inside, a small museum features artifacts from prehistoric Stratford; the attached garden is much more interesting. Chapel St., at Chapel Ln., tel. 01789/292–325. Admission: £2. Open Mar. 20–Oct. 19, Mon.–Sat. 9:30–5, Sun. 10–5; Oct. 20–Mar. 19, Mon.–Sat. 10-4, Sun. 10:30–4.

SHAKESPEARE'S BIRTHPLACE The birthplace of the Bard has become a sick shrine of vicious, camera-snapping tourists trying to elbow their way in and capture that Kodak moment. This small, heavily restored home is usually too crowded to allow for a casual stroll—which is frustrating since the biographical material is actually interesting. **Shakespeare Centre,** adjacent to the house, contains exhibits based on recent Stratford productions of Shakespeare plays. Henley St., tel. 01789/204–016. Admission: £3.30. Open Mar. 20–Oct. 19, Mon.–Sat. 9–5:30, Sun. 9:30–5:30; Oct. 20–Mar. 19, Mon.–Sat. 9:30–4, Sun. 10–4.

Throw back a pint or two at the Dirty Duck (Waterside, tel. 01789/297–312), Stratford's thespian hangout. Everybody from Olivier to Gielgud to Branagh has drunk here, and nearly all have left signed photographs on the wall to prove it.

AFTER DARK

Stratford's nightlife is the Royal Shakespeare Company, which presents nightly performances on two main stages, the **Royal Shakespeare Theatre** and the **Swan Theatre.** In any given week there are five or six different plays (not all of them written by Shakespeare)—except during the company's annual hiatus, which is expected to be during October and November in 1997. Down the road, a third stage, the **Other Place,** runs smaller, more modern productions during high season. If you don't mind standing during a performance, you can buy tickets for as little as £4.50; balcony tickets start at £8.50. If the show hasn't sold out, students can buy discount tickets at 7:15 PM for about £11, £14 on Saturday. Or, to be safe, you can get up early and catch one of the 20 or so tickets held for day-of-performance sales; be there when the box office opens at 9 AM.

The RSC conducts **backstage tours** (tel. 01789/296–655) year-round; tickets cost £4 (£3 students). Try to book in advance, as groups fill the tours quickly. Otherwise, meet at the stage door following the evening's entertainment for a 30-minute **post-performance tour** (£3). *Southern Ln., tel. 01789/269–191 for recorded info or 01789/295–623 for box office. Performances usually held Mon.–Sat. at 7:30 PM; additional matinées Thurs. and Sat. at 1:30 PM.*

Cambridge

Even the most jaded dropout won't be able to resist the lure of Cambridge's stone walls, massive libraries, and robed fellows strutting about town. Cambridge is best known for producing some of the world's finest scientists (Stephen Hawking, author of *A Brief History of Time,* today occupies the same faculty chair Isaac Newton once held), although the register of literary alumni includes John Milton and Virginia Woolf, among others. Like many other English universities, Cambridge is composed of a number of smaller colleges, around 35 of them. Some of the colleges date back to the 13th and 14th centuries, and nearly all of them have fine examples of architecture from every succeeding age. But for all the grandeur of ancient academia, Cambridge has plenty of life left: You're just as likely to see death-rockers as gray-bearded deans putting down a pint or two in the town's pubs these days.

Since the student area is not concentrated on one campus, the center of town, Market Hill, also serves as the focal point for the university's social and cultural scene. Unfortunately Cambridge isn't all open doors for tourists, even for visiting students. University students eat most meals in their respective colleges, and many activities, bars, and facilities are accessible only to them. For those expecting immediate acceptance into the Cambridge family, coming here cold may prove disappointing. If you happen to know any students at Cambridge, even barely, make an effort to contact them. Having a friend here will open all sorts of doors and improve your visit immeasurably. Even though reasonably collegiate-looking visitors can wander through the colleges without getting tossed, the budding Byrons and Newtons who call Cambridge home have to deal with hundreds of tourist intruders on a daily basis and are understandably impatient.

Don't let this difficulty keep you from coming: Cambridge is beautiful. A narrow, shallow river flows through town, green lawns stretch to infinity, and it's relatively untouched by encroaching industry (unlike that plaguing Oxford). At the first promise of sunshine, many students head to the Botanic Gardens or the banks of the River Cam. Others cruise the streets of Cambridge on bikes, maneuvering between the tourists swarming the tea shops. Occasionally, just occasionally, some studying gets done.

BASICS

AMERICAN EXPRESS The office offers the usual AmEx services. *25 Sidney St., CB2 3HP, tel. 01223/351–636. Open weekdays 9–5:30 (Wed. from 9:30), Sat. 9–5.*

May Balls

The May Balls are all-night parties put on by colleges for their students and graduates during May Week (actually a misnomer, as it applies to the first two weeks in June), a series of postexam celebrations. Tickets, available to students only, cost an arm and a leg, but big-name performers, fairground rides, and well-dressed party goers create an electric atmosphere. The morning after a ball, tipsy, bedraggled "survivors" can often be seen returning home in their soiled finery.

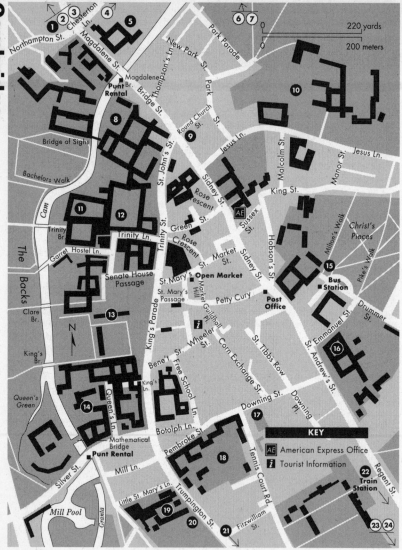

Cambridge

Northampton St. · Chesterton Ln. · Magdalene St. · Magdalene Br. · Punt Rental · Bridge St. · Thompson's Ln. · New Park St. · Park Parade · Park St.

220 yards · 200 meters

Bridge of Sighs · Bachelors Walk · Round Church St. · Jesus Ln. · Jesus Ln. · Malcolm St. · Manor St. · Christ's Pieces

The Cam · Trinity Br. · Garret Hostel Ln. · Trinity Ln. · Trinity St. · Green St. · Rose Crescent · Sidney St. · King St. · Milian's Walk · Sussex St. · AE · Hobson's St. · Pike's Walk

The Backs · Clare Br. · Senate House Passage · St. Mary's Passage · St. Mary's · Open Market · Market Hill · Guildhall · St. Market St. · Sidney St. · Petty Cury · Post Office · Bus Station · Drummer St.

King's Br. · King's Parade · Bene't St. · Free School Ln. · Wheeler St. · Corn Exchange St. · St. Tibbs Row · St. Andrew's St. · St. Emmanuel St.

Queen's Green · Queen's Ln. · King's Ln. · Mathematical Bridge · Punt Rental · Mill Ln. · Botolph Ln. · Pembroke St. · Downing St. · Downing Pl.

Mill Pool · Silver St. · Granta · Little St. Mary's Ln. · Trumpington St. · Tennis Court Rd. · Fitzwilliam St. · Regent St. · Train Station

KEY

AE American Express Office
ℹ Tourist Information

Sights ●

Christ's College, **15**
Downing College, **22**
Emmanuel College, **16**
Fitzwilliam College, **20**
Girton College, **1**
Jesus College, **10**
King's College, **13**
Magdalene College, **5**

Pembroke College, **18**
Peterhouse College, **19**
Queens' College, **14**
Round Church, **9**
St. John's College, **8**
Trinity College, **12**
University Botanic Garden, **21**
University Museum of Archaeology and Anthropology, **17**
Wren Library, **11**

Lodging ○

Aaron Guest House, **6**
Antoni's B&B, **2**
Belle Vue House, **4**
Benson House, **3**
Cambridge YHA, **24**
Carpenter's Arms, **7**
YMCA, **23**

DISCOUNT TRAVEL AGENCIES **STA** books discount airfares and issues ISIC cards for £5, a photo, and proof of student status. *38 Sidney St., tel. 01223/366–966, fax 01223/315– 083. Open weekdays 9–5:30 (Thurs. from 10), Sat. 10–4.*

MAIL The **main post office** cashes checks, processes film, and even has a photo booth. *9– 11 St. Andrew's St., CD2 3HP, tel. 01223/323–325. Open weekdays 9–5:30, Sat. 9–7.*

VISITOR INFORMATION **Cambridge Tourist Information Centre** is cluttered with flyers, posters, and leaflets; also check out the fine map/info booklet "Cambridge & Mid Anglia Tourist Guide" (£2). Two-hour guided walking tours of the city and colleges leave the office daily. Although each tour is different, they are all highly informative—if a bit pricey (£5). The office will book lodging for a 10% deposit and, if you're strapped for cash on a Sunday, will give you change in pounds for a purchase made with a traveler's check. *Wheeler St., behind Guildhall, tel. 01223/322–640. Open Apr.–Oct., weekdays 9–6 (Wed. from 9:30), Sat. 9–5, Sun. 10:30–3:30; Nov.–Mar., weekdays 9–5:30 (Wed. from 9:30), Sat. 9–5.*

COMING AND GOING

BY TRAIN Two trains per hour leave from London (1 hr, £12.30 return), and there's regular service to nearby towns like Ely (20 min, £3.40 return) and King's Lynn (1 hr, £8.60 return). There are a few **luggage lockers** (large £2.50, medium £1.50, small £1), but their availability depends on security measures. To reach town from the station, catch a Cityrail Link bus or walk (30 min); head down Station Road, turn right on Hills Road (which keeps changing names), and continue straight ahead until you reach the city center. *Station Rd., tel. 01223/311–999.*

BY BUS One advantage of taking the bus to Cambridge is the location of **Drummer Street** station, near where St. Andrew's Street becomes Sidney Street. The cramped coach office is hectic, but it does have a good supply of timetables and a helpful staff. **National Express** (tel. 01223/460–711) buses run between London (2 hrs, £9 return) and other cities regularly. **Cambus** (tel. 01223/423–554) services many East Anglian cities, as does **Cambridge Coach Services** (tel. 01223/236–333), which also offers a service to Oxford. Buy tickets on board, as drivers often give special return fares the office doesn't offer. *End of Drummer St., tel. 01223/355–554. Office open Mon.–Sat. 8:15–5:30.*

GETTING AROUND

It's much easier to get around on foot than by car in Cambridge: Much of the city center is off-limits to cars during the day, and traffic on the streets that are open is so bad that the university forbids its students to drive cars within 12 miles of the town. Visitors will also get a better sense of the city by walking or cycling—or punting on the River Cam. The layout of the streets is a bit confusing; streets frequently change names and are diverted by the colleges. But thanks to the flat terrain and ubiquitous cycling lanes, two-wheelers are the most popular and efficient way of negotiating the city and its environs. **Geoff's Bike Hire** (65 Devonshire Rd., tel. 01223/365–629) rents wobbly steeds for £6 a day (with a 10% discount if you're staying at the adjacent YHA hostel). A few other cycle-hire shops are scattered through town, including **Mike's Bikes** (28 Mill Rd., tel. 01223/312–591) and **University Cycles** (9 Victoria Ave., tel. 01223/355–517). If you need to get to nearby **Stansted International Airport** (tel. 01279/ 662–379), trains and Cambridge Coach Services Bus 71 and 75 leave hourly and cost about £7 single.

WHERE TO SLEEP

Inexpensive, central lodging is hard to come by in Cambridge. You'd think the university dorms would throw their doors open to student visitors, but no, it doesn't work that way. Though the colleges' rental policies vary, generally those that *do* have rooms rent them only to large groups. Closest to the colleges are the B&Bs on **Chesterton Road** and **Huntingdon Road.** Alternatively, the accommodations on **Tenison Road** and **Devonshire Road** are closer to the train station; walk down Station Road, hang the first right on Tenison Road, and walk a block or two. Another option is the **YMCA** (Gonville Pl., on Parker's Piece, tel. 01223/356–998), which occasionally rents singles (£19). Availability varies dramatically, as the Y's policy gives preference to locals and large groups over individual travelers. The tourist office's "Where to Stay In and Around Cambridge" booklet (50p) may be worth investing in.

Aaron Guest House. The views of the River Cam and Jesus Green give the Aaron the feel of an English country house that just happens to host a mix of international tourists and visiting professors. Singles are a whopping £22, doubles £35. The four-person family room is a steal at £52. *71 Chesterton Rd., tel. 01223/314–723. Take Bus 3 or 5 from train station or walk from bus station across Jesus Green. 5 rooms, none with bath.*

Antoni's Bed & Breakfast. This friendly B&B is so centrally located and such a bargain it seems too good to be true; fortunately, it's not. The proprietor is helpful and the rooms are clean and comfortable. Singles range from £13 to £20, doubles from £26 to £40. *4 Huntingdon Rd., tel. 01223/357–444. From bus station, turn right on Emmanuel St., right on St. Andrew's St. (which becomes Sidney St., Bridge St., Magdalene St., and Huntingdon Rd.). 15 rooms, 10 with bath.*

Belle Vue House. Spacious rooms with color TVs and a good location make this B&B a deal. The lone single is £17 and the two doubles go for £34. Call ahead to reserve a room. *33 Chesterton Rd., tel. 01223/351–859. Follow directions to Aaron Guest House (see above). 3 rooms, none with bath.*

Benson House. Situated opposite Fitzwilliam and New Hall colleges, Benson House is a mere 10-minute walk from the town center. With a cheery staff and tasteful decor, this has to be one of the best budget places to stay in Cambridge. Singles start at £12; doubles cost £35. *24 Huntingdon Rd., tel. 01223/311–594. Follow directions to Antoni's B&B (see above). 10 rooms, 8 with bath.*

HOSTELS **Cambridge YHA.** The main hostel in Cambridge is a mere three blocks from the train station. Clean beds, powerful showers, and a mellow international crowd make up for the claustrophobia-inducing bedrooms, but *book ahead,* as this place fills early. At the very least, phone the moment you arrive; they'll hold a bed until 6 PM if you call in advance. Beds are £9.70 (£6.55 under 18). *97 Tenison Rd., CB1 2DN, tel. 01223/354–601, fax 01223/312–780. From train station, walk west on Station Rd., turn right on Tenison Rd. 102 beds. Lockout 10–2. Reception open 24 hrs. Kitchen, laundry, luggage storage. MC, V.*

Carpenter's Arms Backpackers' Accommodations. If cost is your number one concern, this hostel certainly fits the bill. You'll find a motley crew of characters staying here (some less savory than others), though the owners are quite friendly. Dorm beds in coed rooms are £6–£8. *182–186 Victoria Rd., tel. 01223/351–814. From bus station, walk down Drummer St., turn left on Emmanuel Rd. (which becomes Short St. and Victoria Ave.), left on Chesterton Rd., right on Albert St., left on Victoria Rd.*

CAMPING **Camping and Caravaning Club Ltd.** Buses don't go often enough to this modern, sprawling campground—complete with a playground and 70 RV hookups—3 miles south of Cambridge, to make it convenient. If you don't mind the trek, sites cost £4.50–£5 per person. *Cabbage Moore, Cambridge Rd., Great Shelford, tel. 01223/841–185. From Drummer St., take Bus 102 or 103 to Great Shelford (£1.80 return). 120 sites. Laundry, showers, toilets. Closed Nov.–late Mar.*

Toad Acre Caravan Park. This well-equipped campsite is frequented by mobile homes, but the grassy strip to the side is peaceful for tent campers, especially when the apple trees are in bloom. Sites are £4.50–£5.50 per person. *Mills Ln., Longstanton, tel. 01954/780–939. From Drummer St., take Bus 155 or 157 (£1.40 return) to Longstanton. 48 sites. Laundry, showers.*

FOOD

Although the students generally eat within their colleges, there are plenty of cafés and restaurants vying to tempt your tastebuds. Cambridge's many parks, gardens, and commons are also ideal spots for a picnic on a clear day. **Peppercorns** (48 Hills Rd., near the train station, tel.

01223/369–583) is a good place to pick up big sandwiches (£1.50) and a variety of enticing sweets (45p–95p). In the middle of town, **Market Hill** has an open market Monday–Saturday with a colorful selection of fruits and vegetables. **Cambridge Health Food** (5 Bridge St., tel. 01223/350–433) is the best spot in town to pick up muesli and other whole-food supplies.

7A Jesus Lane. Scarf down gourmet pizzas (many under £5) in the snazzy former dining room of one of Cambridge's most uptight eating clubs—still a popular place for college students to chat over a long meal. *7A Jesus Ln., tel. 01223/324–033. Open daily noon–midnight.*

Cambridge Curry Centre. With attractive decor and Indian music playing softly, this place has the feel of an elegant restaurant—but with reasonable prices. If you're tired of bland English food, try the spicy chicken jalfrazi (£7). The traditional curry (£3–£4) and tandoori (about £6) dishes are also delicious. Take-out orders get a 10% discount. *45–47 Castle St., tel. 01223/302–687. Open daily noon–2:30 and 6–midnight. AE, MC, V.*

Clown's. If you like a smoky ambience, strong coffees (90p–£1.60), and an attractive, young clientele, you'll enjoy this coffee bar displaying clown memorabilia on the walls. Clown's serves sandwiches (£2.10) and quiches (£2), too, but tends to run out of food around 9 PM. *52 King St., tel. 01223/355–711. From bus station, walk across Christ's Pieces Park to King St. Open daily 9 AM–midnight (Sat. from 8:30 AM).*

Rainbow. This basement vegetarian and whole-food establishment feels like a friend's living room, with about 10 tables. All dishes are prepared fresh each day, and the restaurant specializes in vegan and gluten-free food. They serve an excellent three-course lunch with soup, main course, and dessert for £7. A three-course dinner costs £10. *9 King's Parade, across from King's College, tel. 01223/321–551. Open daily 9–9.*

WORTH SEEING

Because of the city's relatively compact size, the main sights are all accessible on foot. For some striking architecture, saunter past the colleges clustered on the west bank of the River Cam, starting perhaps with King's College Chapel and Christopher Wren's library in Trinity College (*see below*). Other colleges worth seeing include **St. John's, Emmanuel, Magdalene, Downing, Jesus,** and **Christ's.** The list is hard to whittle down, but you'd be insane to attempt to see each of the 35 colleges that make up Cambridge University, especially if you've just come from, or are heading to, Oxford. When you've had your fill of academia, stop by the **Round Church** (cnr of St. John's and Bridge Sts.), built in the early 12th century. It is the oldest of the four remaining round churches in England and now houses the **Cambridge Brass Rubbing Centre,** where you can make rubbings of medieval church brasses in gold, silver, or bronze wax (£2–£15, depending on size).

THE COLLEGES Unlike most American universities, Cambridge University has no exact center but is spread over many residential colleges scattered around town. There are only a few large lecture classes, and students spend most of their scholastic careers attending weekly tutorials in the offices of "fellows," an upscale term for graduate students. And yes, students are required to wear black gowns when attending tutorials. The rest of their time is spent keeping up with the massive reading lists. Bear in mind many colleges close to visitors during final exams, from the fourth week of May until mid-June. The rest of the year, colleges often change their opening hours and close to the public unexpectedly, so call ahead.

The nonstudent residents of Cambridge don't always appreciate the way the university is considered synonymous with the town. This town-versus-gown rivalry is as old as the school itself. Much of the friction dates back to the English Civil War, when the university sided with the Royalists while the town's citizens were fiercely loyal to Cromwell (who, incidentally, attended Cambridge's Sidney Sussex College briefly in 1617). The university shares another endless antagonistic tradition with Oxford University: Both rank among the best universities in the world, with Cambridge leading the way in the sciences. To the outside world, the differences can seem quite cosmetic, and Brits not privileged enough to attend either often meld the two names to come up with "Ox-Bridge," a useful adjective.

➤ **KING'S COLLEGE** • King Henry VI founded King's College in 1441 and five years later began constructing its greatest monument, **King's College Chapel.** Calling it a chapel seems a bit insulting; it feels more like a cathedral. Completed in 1536, the 289-foot-long Gothic structure features the world's longest expanse of fan-vaulted ceiling (the spider-web-style branches supporting the arches). Peter Paul Rubens's *Adoration of the Magi* hangs behind the altar. During the summer there are public recitals—look for a schedule inside—and on Christmas Eve a festival of carols is broadcast worldwide. *King's College, tel. 01223/331– 100. Admission to chapel: £2.50, £1.50 students. Open Mon.–Sat. 9:30–4:30, Sun. 10–5.*

➤ **QUEENS' COLLEGE** • Queens' College—founded in 1448 by Margaret of Anjou, wife of Henry VI, and later built up by Elizabeth of Woodville, wife of Edward IV—is a mess of architectural styles. The unspoiled Renaissance cloister court lies beside some ugly, recently constructed buildings funded by Sir John Cripps, owner of the worldwide patent for Velcro. Legend has it that the so-called **Mathematical Bridge** that crosses the Cam to connect both sides of the college was designed and built without screws or fastenings by Sir Isaac Newton. Not true. A local carpenter named James Essex designed the bridge in 1750, more than 20 years after Newton's death. The current bridge is a modern copy, supported by bolts and screws. The college allows visitors to stroll through quietly while term is in session, daily 10–12:45 and 1:45–4:30. *Queens' College, tel. 01223/335–511. Admission: 80p.*

➤ **TRINITY COLLEGE** • The largest and richest of Cambridge's colleges, Trinity counts among its graduates Lord Byron and Isaac Newton. Trinity is also the third-largest landowner in Britain—after the Crown and Church, of course. It's possible to walk from Cambridge to Oxford and London to Dover entirely on Trinity-owned land. The college's impressive **Wren Library,** designed entirely by Christopher Wren down to the bookshelves and reading desks,

Punting on the Cam

To punt means to maneuver a flat, wooden, gondola-like boat through the shallow, vermin-infested River Cam by the "backs" of the colleges. (You get a better view of the ivy-covered walls from the water than from the front.) Mastery of this sport lies in one's ability to control a 15-foot pole, which you use to propel the punt. To avoid the humiliation and failure of losing your pole to the muddy river floor in full view of people watching along the banks, consider punting at night. The Granta Inn Punt Hire (tel. 01223/301–845) rents punts until 10 PM. Get a bottle of wine, some food, and a small group of people, and you'll find yourself saying things like, "It doesn't get any better than this." One piece of advice: If your pole gets stuck, LET GO. You can use the smaller paddle to go back and retrieve it.

The lazier at heart may prefer chauffeured punting. Cambridge students wearing Venetian-type straw hats will punt you along the Cam and even give a fairly informative spiel on the colleges. Each chauffeur rents his or her punt independently from Scudamore's Boatyard, so there's no organization to contact; just go down to the dock and wait for the first available boat. Prices are negotiable, though £4 a head is the usual rate. If you choose to get your own punt, hourly rentals are £4–£8; all companies require a deposit of £30. One "dock" for rentals or tours is between two local pubs, the Anchor (see below) and the Mill, at the end of Mill Lane near the Silver Street Bridge; another is near the Magdalene Street Bridge.

contains an astonishing display of valuable books, including one of Shakespeare's first folios and Newton's pocket book. *Trinity College, tel. 01223/338–400. Admission: £1.50. Open daily 10–6; closed during exams. Wren Library, tel. 01223/338–488. Open during school year, weekdays noon–2, Sat. 10–2; during vacations, weekdays noon–2; closed during exams.*

➤ **OTHER COLLEGES** • The granddaddy of them all, **Peterhouse College,** features structures dating from the 13th century, when a disgruntled monk from Oxford's Merton College decided to begin a little school of his own. **Emmanuel College,** known as Emma College by the faithful, has a beautiful layout—the chapel and colonnades are by Christopher Wren—and a magnificent duck pond. **St. John's College** (admission: £1.50, 75p students) features the famous Bridge of Sighs, spanning the Cam, built in 1831, and modeled on the original in Venice. **Christ's College,** which educated Milton and Darwin, houses some of Cambridge's best neoclassical architecture, as well as some of the worst architecture; in particular, a notoriously ugly, recently completed dorm dubbed "the Typewriter" because of its sloping, gridded design. The adventurous traveler may want to trek 2 miles north to **Girton College,** the first women's college in Cambridge. Set outside the city center to keep male and female students apart, Girton suffered much ridicule from the Cambridge community at first, before graduating enough distinguished alumnae—Virginia Woolf, among them—to earn respect. Take the bus directly from Drummer Street or walk north up Sidney Street, which changes names several times, eventually becoming Huntingdon Road.

The huge rivalry between Oxford and Cambridge comes to a head at two annual sporting events: the boat race, where their rowing eights race one another down the Thames near Putney, and the rugby match, played before a sell-out crowd at Twickenham in London.

MUSEUMS AND GARDENS **The Fitzwilliam Museum.** The permanent collection of this first-rate museum features antiquities from ancient Greece and Egypt in the Lower Galleries as well as works by Picasso, Degas, Monet, Renoir, Cezanne, Seurat, Brueghel, Constable, Gainsborough, and more in the Upper Galleries. Temporary exhibits range from the fascinating to the truly snooze-worthy, so call ahead to see what's on. *Trumpington St., tel. 01223/332–900. Admission free. Lower Galleries (antiquities and manuscripts) open Tues.–Fri. 10–2; Upper Galleries (painting and sculpture) open Tues.–Fri. 2–5; both galleries open Sat. 10–5 and Sun. 2:15–5. Wheelchair access with advance notice.*

The University Botanic Garden. This is the perfect place to break the musty monotony of cobblestone or to kill time while waiting for a train. Among its many delights are a glass igloo, a limestone rock garden, and flowers, flowers, flowers. *Cory Lodge, Bateman St., tel. 01223/336–265. From train station, turn right on Hills Rd., left on Bateman St. Admission: £1.50; free Wed., and weekdays Nov.–Feb. Open daily 10–4 or 6, depending on the weather.*

The University Museum of Archaeology and Anthropology (UMAA). Cambridge University pioneered the study of social anthropology, and the UMAA traces conceptual progress in the field over the last 100 years. The Anthropology Gallery houses an interesting collection of totem poles, masks, costumes, and other culturally significant artifacts. This is one of Cambridge's most engrossing museums and it's absolutely free. *Downing St., near Corn Exchange St., tel. 01223/333–516. Open during summer, weekdays 10:30–5 (Anthropology gallery closed 1–2), Sat. 10–12:30; call for winter hours.*

AFTER DARK

Lord only knows what goes on behind the walls of the colleges late at night, and you'll never know unless you make friends quickly. Still, there's plenty of culture happening outside the college gates: Great rock bands come through Cambridge regularly, so pick up a copy of *Varsity* (20p) at a newsstand for current listings. Art movies are cheap and abundant, and student theater is excellent. If you have a chance to see a student drama production at the ADC Theatre, go. Many famous thespians, including Emma Thompson, Stephen Fry, and Hugh Laurie, have gotten their start on a small Cambridge stage. In the summer Cambridge gets festival fever, beginning with the **Cambridge Beer Festival** in May, the **Midsummer Fair** in June, and the **Film**

Festival, **Fringe Festival** and **Cambridge Folk Festival** in July. Plays are also staged in the gardens of some of the colleges during the month of June.

PUBS **The Anchor.** Right along the Cam near the punt rental, this four-story, all-wood pub is filled with locals day and night. The outdoor deck is inviting if and when the sun comes out. *Silver St., tel. 01223/353–554.*

The Eagle (Bene't St.) is a traditional pub with a colorful past. It was frequented by scientists Watson and Crick, who announced their discovery of DNA in a back room. British and Allied airmen used the Eagle during World War II, and the ceiling still bears names and squadron numbers written in candle smoke.

Baron of Beef. This small, traditional pub enjoys a good mix of punters (no boating pun intended) and a cheery atmosphere. Real ale is served here along with a no-nonsense attitude to drinking; do not, on pain of death, ask for a piña colada! *19 Bridge St., tel. 01223/576–720.*

Henry's. This café-bar is a great place to unwind with a delectable cocktail (£2.50 on Monday and Tuesday nights). The atmosphere is mellow in the afternoon and early evenings, though later it throngs with a lively crowd, which spills out onto the adjoining riverside courtyard on hot summer nights. *Quayside, tel. 01223/324–649.*

The Maypole. The Maypole is *the* place in Cambridge to overhear pretentious conversation. Thespians hang out here when they're not working on the latest reinterpretation of a Beckett play. Don't leave without trying one of its award-winning cocktails. *Park St., near Jesus College, tel. 01223/352–999.*

MUSIC Look for flyers posted around town to determine what the big show is this week, or pick up a copy of the locally published *Varsity* to see who's playing. You'll find everything from jazz and classical to *Melody Maker's* flavor-of-the-month band playing at the **Corn Exchange** (cnr Wheeler St. and Corn Exchange, tel. 01223/357–851). Tickets usually cost around £10. the **Junction** (Clifton Rd., near train station, tel. 01223/412–600) is home to local indie bands, hip-hop, house, jazz, and just about everything else six nights a week. Tickets range from £5 for small gigs to £12 for big-name bands.

THEATER AND FILM The **Amateur Dramatic Club (ADC)** presents two different student-produced plays per week and late-night arty flicks. The university drama productions here tend to be much better than their American counterparts. Ticket prices range from £3 to £7. *Park St., near Jesus Ln. and Bridge St., tel. 01223/359–547 or 01223/352–001 for box office.*

Grantchester: Getting There Is All the Fun

Need a small challenge? Demonstrate your boating skill by punting 2 miles up the River Granta from Cambridge to Grantchester, a village favored by locals for a retreat from the academic maelstrom. You can reach Grantchester a number of ways: a 45-minute walk, a 15-minute bike ride, or the killer punt—not an easy task for beginners. It's hard to find the walking trail to begin the journey, but once you start along the River Granta just ask folks along the way. Keep in mind, though, that directions may be somewhat ambiguous (e.g., "Turn left when you see the horses"). Film critic Roger Ebert told one Berkeley Guides writer that he gives the walk a thumbs up.

The town of Grantchester is only one "bend" long, and its three pubs are mainly frequented by punting heroes who've come up from Cambridge for the day. Mind you, if it's raining, don't bother: The thrill of visiting Grantchester is in getting here and spending a lovely day outdoors.

Arts Cinema (Market Passage, tel. 01223/504–444 or 01223/572-929), affiliated with the ADC, usually shows three different American and European art flicks a day; late-night shows are scheduled about four days a week. Seats are £4 from 5:30 PM to 11 PM, £3 at all other times.

Canterbury

While Chaucer's *Canterbury Tales,* the ultimate chronicle of church hypocrisy and gender politics in medieval England, tells us more than enough about pilgrims on their way to visit Canterbury Cathedral, it says nothing about the city itself (Chaucer died before his characters could get there). In Chaucer's day, horse-backed hundreds made their way from London across harsh terrain in bad English weather to visit the shrine of martyr St. Thomas à Becket, who was killed by knights of Henry II in 1170. The stupendous cathedral in which the deed was done—and the surrounding town with its curving streets and tightly packed Tudor-style buildings—keeps the tourists flooding in by the busload. While Canterbury is encircled by a Roman wall, it's the city's medieval aspect that prevails—which is quite a feat considering that Canterbury was heavily damaged in the Blitz of 1941.

Modern Canterbury pilgrims are more concerned with cheap lodging and picture-perfect moments than spiritual enlightenment. On the plus side, B&Bs are generally of high quality and competitively priced, and the presence of local University of Kent students prevents the city from becoming a complete Disneyland. Every April, Chaucer fans follow in the footsteps of his characters on a pilgrimage from London's Southwark Cathedral to Canterbury. Their arrival is enthusiastically met by the **Chaucer Festival** (tel. 01227/470–379), which sends the city into the throes of a large and raucous medieval fair. If you're not in a jousting mood, come back in October when a calmer air falls on the city as it plays host to a renowned **arts festival.**

BASICS

BUREAUX DE CHANGE Avoid changing money at the hostel, the tourist office, or the post office if you can help it: They all have bad rates and even worse commissions. Banks—where you get a vastly better rate if you change traveler's checks rather than cash—are scattered along High Street and all its aliases. **American Express** (29 High St., tel. 01227/784–865) probably offers the best rates in town for traveler's checks.

MAIL Canterbury's largest **post office** (28 High St., CT1 2BA, tel. 01227/822–000) is often distressingly crowded. If you're in a hurry, try the one at the corner of Church and Lower Bridge streets. Both offices are open weekdays 9–5:30, Saturday 9–12:30.

VISITOR INFORMATION The **Tourist Information Centre** offers free lodging guides and a Book-a-Bed-Ahead office. Wherever you stay, the 10% deposit charged for booking rooms is applied toward your bill. The office also sells a number of good hiking and biking maps and stocks "What, Where, When," a free guide to current events. *34 St. Margaret's St., tel. 01227/766–567. From Canterbury East, turn right and follow city wall, turn left on Watling St., right on St. Margaret's St. Open Mon.–Sat. 9:30–5.*

COMING AND GOING

BY TRAIN **Canterbury East** station is a major stop between London and the ferry-hovercraft port in Dover. Trains leave London's Victoria Station every 30 minutes on weekdays and hourly on weekends (1½ hrs, £14.70 single, £15.40 five-day return). The journey to Dover takes about 30 minutes and costs £4 single, £4.30 return. *Station Rd. E, off Castle St., tel. 01732/770–111. Ticket window open Mon.–Sat. 6:10 AM–8 PM, Sun. 6:45 AM–9 PM.*

The **Canterbury West** station serves coastal resort towns like Margate (£6.90 return) and Broadstairs (£4.60 return), as well as London's Charing Cross station. The South Eastern lines pass through some of the best scenery in Kent. *Station Rd. W, off St. Dunstan's St., tel. 01732/770–111. Ticket window open Mon.–Sat. 6:15 AM–7:10 PM, Sun. 9:15–4:30.*

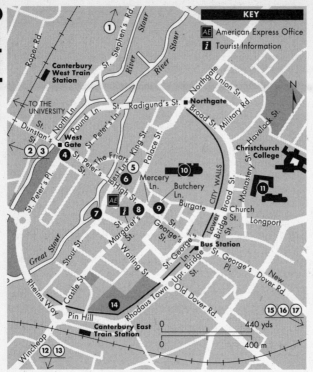

KEY

AE	American Express Office
i	Tourist Information

Sights ●

Canterbury Cathedral, **10**

Canterbury Heritage Museum, **7**

Canterbury Tales Exhibition, **8**

Dane John Monument, **14**

Roman Museum, **9**

Royal Museum Art Gallery, **6**

St. Augustine's Abbey, **11**

West Gate Museum, **4**

Lodging ○

Alverstone House, **15**

Canterbury YHA, **16**

Clare Ellen Guest House, **12**

Courteney Guest House, **2**

Dar Anne, **3**

Kingsbridge, **5**

Let's Stay!, **17**

St. Stephen's, **1**

Wincheap Guest House, **13**

BY BUS The main bus station's entrance is on the corner of St. George's Lane and St. George's Place, near the shopping district on High Street. **National Express** coaches leave about every two hours for London's Victoria Coach Station (£10.50 single). Buy a reserved ticket for high-traffic periods and destinations. It's especially hard on Fridays to get a seat on a bus to Dover (£3.10 single, £3.75 return) because of the mass exodus to France for the weekend. *Tel. 01227/766–151. Open Mon.–Sat. 8:15–5:30.*

GETTING AROUND

Canterbury is encircled by a medieval city wall and is so small that you can walk almost anywhere in less than 20 minutes. The main road that bisects the city center changes names several times: It's St. Peter's Street in the west, High Street in the center, St. George's Street in the east, and New Dover Road even *farther* east. Walk northwest on this main road for 2½ miles or take Bus 604 to reach the University of Kent. **Stagecoach/East Kent and MiniLink** (tel. 01227/766–151) runs buses around Canterbury and environs. Stagecoach/East Kent buses leave from the main bus station while MiniLink buses depart from the Gravel Walk just across St. George's Lane. Fares range from 38p to £1.15.

WHERE TO SLEEP

Abundant B&Bs line New Dover, London, and Whitstable roads. During the summer, Canterbury is a popular destination and most B&Bs are tiny, so try to reserve ahead. The majority of Canterbury's B&Bs observe a strict no-smoking policy, so smokers should always inquire ahead. If you're willing to spend a bit more for a little luxury and private bath, **St. Stephen's Guest House** (100 St. Stephen's Rd., tel. 01227/767–644) charges £20–£22 per head, while **Clare**

Ellen Guest House (9 Victoria Rd., tel. 01227/760–205) charges £20–£24 per head. Both are about a 10-minute walk from town.

Alverstone House. The pink rooms in this pretty brick house are nicely laid out, with flower-patterned bedspreads and spanking clean sheets. Doubles, triples, and quads are £15 per person. *38 New Dover Rd., tel. 01227/766–360. From bus station, turn right onto St. George's Pl. and continue straight for ¾ mi. 5 rooms, all with shower.*

Courtney Guest House. This immaculate house has large, bright rooms and a pleasant solarium-library where you can catch up on your Chaucer. Doubles with bath cost £36 (the double without bath is £30), and the large room that sleeps up to five costs £15–£19 per person. *4 London Rd., tel. 01227/769–668. From Canterbury West, turn right on St. Dunstan's St., left on London Rd. 5 rooms, 4 with bath.*

Dar Anne. Theresa and Dennis Morey love students, and their place is always filled with young people. Theresa is a vegan, so herbivores don't get that sidelong look when they ask for no sausage with their breakfast. The facilities are excellent (all rooms have TVs), and the house is only a short walk from the city center. Students pay £12 for singles, £22–£24 for doubles; everyone else pays a few pounds more. *65 London Rd., tel. 01227/760–907. Follow directions to Courtney Guest House (see above). 3 rooms, none with bath.*

Kingsbridge. For £14–£18 per person you can't beat the incredibly central location of this large B&B. You can practically touch the Cathedral from most of its south-facing rooms. As a bonus, the downstairs breakfast room becomes a popular Italian restaurant by night. Unlike most Canterbury B&Bs, this is a haven for smokers. *15 Best Ln., tel. 01227/766–415. From tourist office, turn left on High St., right on Best Ln. 12 rooms, 8 with bath.*

Wincheap Guest House. This simple, red-carpeted B&B is run by a friendly proprietor, who keeps the place clean and will even do laundry for you. It's on a busy road, but just around the corner from Canterbury East station and a five-minute walk to town. The lone single is £12, while doubles cost £28–£35 depending on the season. *94 Wincheap, tel. 01227/762–309. From Canterbury East, turn left on Station Rd. E, left on Wincheap. 7 rooms, none with bath.*

HOSTELS **Canterbury YHA.** This place is often full, so try to book a week or two in advance. However, if you do arrive without reservations, don't despair: The proprietors will always refer you to another cheap bed. Dorm beds cost £9.10 (£6.15 under 18). *54 New Dover Rd., Kent CT1 3DT, tel. 01227/462–911, fax 01227/470–752. From bus station, turn right on St. George's Pl. and continue straight for 1 mi. From Canterbury East, turn right on Station Rd. E, veer right on Rhodaus Town (which becomes Upper Bridge St.), then right on St. George's Pl. 72 beds (91 in summer). Curfew 11 PM, lockout 10–1. Laundry, luggage storage. AE, MC, V.*

Let's Stay! Hostel and B&B. Mrs. Connolly started taking travelers into her tiny home five years ago when she found a backpacker crying on her fence because the hostel was full. Since then, she and her husband have been housing travelers cheaply in two dorm-like bedrooms. Beds cost £9, including a full English breakfast. In summer you can crash in the huge garden under their big tent or camp with your own equipment for £5. If you're lucky, Mrs. Connolly's son, John, will lead you on a pub tour. Unfortunately, reservations are not accepted. *26 New Dover Rd., tel. 01227/463–628. Follow directions to YHA. 8 beds. Curfew 11 PM.*

CAMPING **The Camping and Caravanning Club Site.** A huge number of sites guarantees little privacy. Of course, if you want to meet people, that should be no problem—a lot of characters hang out at the shop. The campground is in a rural area 1½ miles out of town and just ¼ mile from a main road. Two-person tent spaces cost £11–£11.70. *Bekesbourne Ln., tel. 01227/463–216. From Canterbury East, turn right on Rhodaus Town, right on Church St., right on Longport (which becomes St. Martin's Hill), continue for 1½ mi, then right on Bekesbourne Ln. 210 sites. Hot showers, laundry. Closed late Oct.–late Mar.*

FOOD

Canterbury's cheaper restaurants are found mostly along the smaller lanes and alleys off High Street. Self-caterers can find a variety of ethnic and vegetarian foods near the North Gate at

Canterbury Wholefoods (10 The Borough, tel. 01227/464–625), which also sells scrumptious filled rolls for just 95p.

August Moon. With its enormous menu and low prices, August Moon packs in the university crowd. For an even cheaper meal, request self-service from the take-out counter and then bring your food to the seating area across from the bar. Dim sum (£2.50), Kung Po Chili Chicken (£3.20), or the Vegetarian Feast for two (only £5.90) are just a few of the tantalizing options. *49A St. Peter's St., tel. 01227/786–268. Open daily 11 AM–midnight.*

Beaus Creperie. This bright creperie, adorned with assorted fake plants of dubious legality, serves a variety of crepes and interesting starters like prawns with peaches and rye (£2.95). Crepes start at £2.35 for a basic cheese and go up to £5.15 for those loaded with goodies. Specialty crepes like the Crepe Indonesia (chicken curry) cost £5.75. *59 Palace St., tel. 01227/464–285. Open weekdays 10–10, weekends 9:30 AM–10 PM.*

Fungus Mungus. With its psilocybin-inspired decoration, this groovy eatery may make you think that your name is Alice and your best friend is a rabbit. The mushroom theme continues in dishes like tasty garlic mushrooms on toast (£3.25). Main dishes cost £5.95 and feature pastas, spinach and ricotta pancakes, and Caribbean curry. *34 St. Peter's St., across from West Gate, tel. 01227/463–175. Open daily 10 AM–midnight.*

Simple Simon's. Housed in a 14th-century building, this restaurant faithfully maintains the atmosphere of a medieval hall—including an open fire. Although they serve a full range of game, poultry, steaks, and fish, they specialize in pies. The lamb and apricot pie (£5.25) and Chaucerberry pie (£6.50) are favored by the locals, while the vegetable pie (£5) is a hit with vegetarian students. After finishing your meal, you can quaff a pint (£1.70) downstairs in their ever-popular ale house. The main restaurant serves dinner only (7 PM–10 PM), but lunch is served in the downstairs bar from 11 to 3. *Radigund Hall, 3 Church Ln., off St. Radigund's St., tel. 01227/762–355. Bar open daily 11–11.*

WORTH SEEING

Canterbury's small size makes it easy to see everything in one day. To avoid the crowds, get an early start, and remember that most attractions are less crowded an hour or so before closing time. For a fine view of Canterbury, climb up Pin Hill to **Dane John Monument,** a short walk from Canterbury East station. The **Royal Museum & Art Gallery** (High St., above library, tel. 01227/452–747), open Monday–Saturday 10–5, hosts temporary exhibits ranging from interesting to embarrassing—but at least it's free. For a good overview, consider the 90-minute walking tours offered from the tourist office daily at 11 AM and 2 PM (£2.40, £1.70 students).

CANTERBURY CATHEDRAL As you come through the main entrance, built to commemorate Henry V's 1415 victory at Agincourt, the view across and up the cathedral is dizzying with row upon row of towering pointed arches. The cathedral, as it exists today, is the product of several periods of architecture. The oldest part of the church is the Norman crypt, built by Archbishop LanFranc between 1070 and 1077 over the ruins of St. Augustine's church, destroyed by fire in 1067. This construction was hasty and resulted in a structure that was too small, so

Heads Up!

Chaucer isn't the only literary ghost haunting Canterbury; Joseph Conrad is buried in Canterbury Cemetery, and the head of Sir Thomas More (author of "Utopia") lies in St. Dunstan's church on Dunstan Road. After his execution, More's body was buried within the Tower of London while his head was displayed on Tower Bridge. The head was recovered by his daughter, who had a friend knock it down from its spike while she waited below in a boat to catch it and steal it away to Canterbury.

it was replaced by a larger building in 1130. Immediately after Thomas à Becket's canonization in 1173, a new Gothic-style choir was installed. Archbishops have traditionally been enthroned at **Trinity Chapel,** east of the choir area, on St. Augustine's chair behind the altar. Inside the chapel are the tombs of Henry IV and his wife, Joan of Navarre, and an effigy of Edward the Black Prince, the warrior son of Edward II. Beneath the chapel is the crypt where Thomas à Becket was first buried and where Henry II completed his penance for the murder. Becket's tomb was later destroyed during Henry VIII's smash-and-grab attempts to weaken the church while securing some of its treasures for himself.

The northwest transept is the site of Becket's murder. Becket, a dissident priest who disagreed with King Henry II's meddling in the church's business, was murdered in 1170 by four of Henry's knights seeking the king's favor. Becket's assassins probably entered by the door from the cloisters, which contain amazing vaults decorated with the paintings of almost 1,000 heraldic shields. A marker indicates where Becket fell more than 800 years ago. Don't miss the 13th-century stained-glass windows that illustrate Becket's miracles. By 1173, Becket had been canonized St. Thomas of Canterbury, although this did little to appease the French king (who took the murder of Becket, formerly under his protection, as a personal affront). It was only a matter of time before the pressure on Henry II, who felt enormous remorse at the death of his old friend, became too great, and he relinquished a great deal of power to the church. Subsequently, Canterbury Cathedral was made the hub of English Catholicism and is now the center of the Anglican Church. If the cathedral seems too daunting to explore alone, guided tours (£2.80, £1.80 students) leave from the pulpit Monday–Saturday at 10:30, noon, 2, and 3. *Sun St., at St. Margaret's St., tel. 01227/762–862. Admission: £2, £1 students; free Sun. Open Mon.–Sat. 9–7 (Oct.–Easter until 5), Sun. 12:30–2:30 and 4:30–5:30.*

CANTERBURY HERITAGE MUSEUM Medieval Canterbury was filled with impoverished clergymen, many of whom fell ill as a result of poor living conditions. To cope with this growing problem, the lord mayor ordered a poor priests' hospital built specifically for the purpose of treating sick clergymen. Usually the help they received in this drafty building actually worsened their condition. This one-time hospital is now the site of the popular Canterbury Heritage Museum, which exhibits a collection of artifacts left by pilgrims at Canterbury. *Stour St., tel. 01227/452–747. From tourist office, turn right down Hawks Ln. Admission: £1.70, £1.10 students. Open Mon.–Sat. 10:30–5 (June–Oct., also Sun. 1:30–5).*

Canterbury's Norman Castle (Castle and Gas streets), built for William the Conqueror in 1175, is now a crumbling mass of gray bricks neighbored by a parking lot.

THE CANTERBURY TALES Canterbury's attempt to re-create a historically accurate, multisensory version of Chaucer's stories has resulted in the Canterbury Tales—perfect for children but insulting to anyone with a more mature intellect. Radio-controlled headphones guide you from room to room, where excerpts from Chaucer's *Canterbury Tales* are illustrated by moving, plywood cutouts. The stories are funny, but it's less expensive (and more fulfilling) to read the book. *St. Margaret's St., tel. 01227/454–888. Admission: £4.75, £4 students. Open Mar.–June and Sept.–Oct., daily 9:30–5:30; July–Aug., daily 9–6; Nov.–Feb., daily 10–4:30.*

ROMAN MUSEUM Before Canterbury became a religious and tourist mecca, it was actually quite a substantial Roman settlement. Through the use of paintings, reconstructed scenes, and archaeological fragments of everyday items, this small museum attempts to give insight into life in Roman Canterbury. The museum culminates around the actual foundation of an excavated Roman house. Though the display is unremarkable, it is interesting to see how much farther down the Roman town was than today's city. *Butchery Ln., tel. 01227/785–575. From tourist office, turn right on High St., left on Butchery Ln. Admission: £1.70, £1.10 students. Open Mon.–Sat. 10–5 (June–Oct., also Sun. 1:30–5).*

ST. AUGUSTINE'S ABBEY In 596, Pope Gregory I bought Augustine, then a monk, a one-way ticket from Rome to England in an attempt to convert the Saxons. Ethelbert, King of Kent, allowed Augustine and his 40 followers to build a church outside the city walls. Ethelbert's wife, Bertha, was the daughter of a Frankish king and already a Christian, so she went to the new church daily through the **Queningate.** Eventually Ethelbert converted, and Augustine established Canterbury Cathedral. Enough stones and walls remain in the grassy ruins to evoke the former whole—a cloister, church, and refectory. *Cnr of Lower Chantry Ln. and Longport Rd., tel. 01227/767–345. Admission: £1.50, £1.10 students. Open Apr.–Sept., daily 10–6; Oct.–Mar., Tues.–Sun. 10–4.*

WEST GATE MUSEUM Inside West Gate (the medieval, double-towered city gate at the end of St. Peter's Street) lurks the tiny **West Gate Museum,** which has exhibits on Canterbury's historical defenses, its Roman walls, and examples of the chains and manacles used on the prisoners who were once detained here. Even if you're bored by museums, come for the great views from the battlements on top of the tower. *West Gate, St. Peter's St., no phone. Admission: 70p, 45p students. Open Mon.–Sat. 11–12:30 and 1:30–3:30.*

AFTER DARK

According to the Church of England, gluttony is a deadly sin but beer drinking is not, and many pub owners have set up shop in the shadows of the cathedral. When you go pub crawling, try to avoid lingering on the streets after 11 PM; the sometimes less-than-tolerant Canterbury police seem to enjoy getting in a little harassment before the end of their shift. Most pubs in Canterbury are open Monday–Saturday 11–11, Sunday noon–10:30.

PUBS **The Cherry Tree.** This cozy pub is a favorite of students and young people for its mellow atmosphere. Entertainment consists of a TV, jukebox, pinball machines, and, of course, pints (£2). *10 White Horse Ln., tel. 01227/451–266. From West Gate, walk down St. Peter's St. to Royal Museum; turn right on first narrow alley, which is White Horse Ln.*

Cubaa. This modern, jazzy place attracts a diverse crowd. All day long you can order from a delectable menu that includes orange-and-onion salad (£3.50) and lime chicken with rice (£4.50). During happy hour (6–8), down bottled beers for £1.20 while waiting for the nightly DJs, who get the place hopping with acid jazz, Latin funk, and the latest drum and bass. If you want to take a chill pill, escape to the back garden or do some net surfing in the budding Internet café upstairs. *59 Northgate, tel. 01227/458–857. Open daily noon–midnight.*

The Flying Horse. This updated, 16th-century pub may be one of the friendliest places in town. Amazingly, it attracts the young university crowd as well as old-timers who may bend your ear about the glory days of big bands and dance halls. Pints cost £1.60–£1.90. *1 Dover St., at Upper Bridge St., tel. 01227/463–803.*

University of Kent Bars. Each of the four colleges—Darwin, Keynes, Eliot, and Rutherford—has its own bar, and each has its own unique crowd. **Woody's** is the most fun with its sociable, young, and hip crowd. *From Canterbury, take Bus 604 about 2½ mi up St. Dunstan's St. to university entrance, turn left at road just before the second bus stop, enter courtyard (keeping to the left), and ask someone where Woody's is. All bars open daily 5 PM–11 PM.*

CLUBS **The Penny Theatre.** This place is highly regarded by hipsters as both a venue for live music and an after-hours club with an eclectic range of theme nights. Wednesday is jazz night, while Friday's "Pulse" features indie rock. *30–31 Northgate, tel. 01227/470–512. Cover: £2–£3. Open daily 7 PM–2 AM.*

THEATER AND CINEMA The **Marlowe Theatre** (The Friars, off St. Peter's St., tel. 01227/787–787) stages first-rate London shows as well as crappy pop bands and cheesy British slapstick plays. Before spending £4–£24 on a ticket, pick up a copy of the seasonal brochure to gauge what's on. Amateur drama and performance art get top billing at the University of Kent's **Gulbenkian Theatre** (University Rd., tel. 01227/769–075), where tickets cost £3–£9. **Cinema 3,** which shares the same box office as the Gulbenkian, shows avant-garde oldies and some independent flicks for £3.50 (£2.50 students).

OUTDOOR ACTIVITIES

BIKING If you're interested in mountain biking, pick up an Ordnance Survey map of the area from the tourist office; it shows altitude contours in the **North Downs.** The **Canterbury Cycle**

Mart (19 Lower Bridge St., tel. 01227/761–488) rents mountain bikes for £10 per half-day, £15 per day, and £50 per week. A credit-card number or £100 cash deposit is required.

HIKING About 3 miles northwest of Canterbury, the little-used **Forest of Blean** is the remnant of a much larger ancient forest of the same name. The hiking trails are quiet, and the forest is renowned for its bird life. The Ordnance Survey Map, available at the tourist office, gives details of various hikes. Many trails start at Rough Common, which can be reached by Bus 602 from Canterbury. Alternatively, you can walk a portion of the **North Downs Way.** From Canterbury, you could walk these public footpaths southeast to Dover or even over 100 miles westward into Surrey.

Brighton

The back-to-back palatial hotels along Brighton's waterfront attest to its status as England's premier 19th-century beach resort. And despite the thin layer of seaside grit covering the entire town, Brighton remains England's premier beach resort, even if the modern clientele is far removed from the ritzy trendsetters who once frequented these shores. While the **Lanes,** the old shopping quarter where lords and ladies once browsed for finery, still retain some prestige, they've since been supplanted by the younger, more colorful **North Laine,** a veritable potpourri of cafés, shops, street musicians, and honest-to-goodness atmosphere.

Brighton has its short list of worthwhile monuments and sights, but it's the town's active youth culture that makes it so popular. It's the liberal hole in the conservative belt of the South and home to Britain's largest, most vibrant gay community outside London. With two universities and countless English-language schools, Brighton manages to sustain the feel of a large international city.

Most Americans don't respond well to the magnetic draw Brighton exerts on British and other Euro-youth, which perhaps is due to the town's reputation as a sleazy entertainment mecca. It certainly has its share of problems, among them polluted water and a rising petty crime rate. However, the town has recently agreed to participate in an expensive, long-term water-improvement project, and you'd be hard-pressed to find a rumble between mods and rockers these days. If you can somehow avoid Brighton's usual seaside tourist trappings, you'll find that it's a fine place to blow off steam before heading off to another quaint, medieval town.

In ages past, a walk along Brighton's pebbly beach and the Palace Pier ended with tea and aristocratic banter. These days, it ends up at the Pleasure Dome, a tacky amusement center with video games and burger stands.

BASICS

The **Tourist Information Centre,** across the street from the town hall, is swamped during peak months. They don't answer the phone at all if too many people are waiting to be helped, so you're better off just coming in for accommodation bookings (£1 fee), maps, and pamphlets. *10 Bartholomew Sq., tel. 01273/323–755. From train station, take Brighton Bus Lines Bus 27, get off at North St., and follow the TOWN HALL signs. Open July–Aug., daily 9–6; June and Sept., weekdays 9–5, Sat. 10–6, Sun. 10–4; Oct.–May, weekdays 9–5, weekends 10–4.*

For information on gay events or referrals to queer resources, contact **Gay Switchboard** (tel. 01273/690–825) or the University of Sussex's **Gay, Lesbian, and Bisexual Society** (GLB) (tel. 01273/673–395). **American Express** (82 North St., tel. 01273/321–242) provides the usual services for cardholders. The money-changing offices in the train station are a rip-off, so head to one of the banks along North Street; **Lloyd's Bank** (171 North St., tel. 01273/324–971) has good rates for traveler's checks. The **post office** (51 Ship St., BN1 1BA, tel. 01273/573–208) is open Saturday 9–7.

COMING AND GOING

Trains leave Brighton's main **rail station** (top of Queen's Rd., tel. 01273/206–755) about twice hourly for London (£12.30, £20 return). The rail station is a 15-minute walk up Queen's Road from the clock tower. National Express Bus 64 leaves for London every 1½–2 hours from the **bus station** (Pool Valley, tel. 01273/674–881) near the waterfront on the southern edge of Old Steine. **Stagecoach** (tel. 0345/581–457) buses serve the surrounding area and are good for short hops to places like Rye.

GETTING AROUND

Brighton's four main roads—Queen's Road, North Street, West Street, and Western Road—converge at the clock tower and roughly divide the city center into four quadrants. The southwest quadrant is dominated by Churchill Square, a central bus depot for local routes. The southeast quadrant, bounded by Palace Pier and the waterfront, is considered to be the heart of old Brighton and is where you will find the Lanes and the Royal Pavilion. North of North Street is the area known as North Laine. Brighton is large and hilly, so walking may be a little draining. Two bus companies, **Brighton and Hove** (tel. 01273/886–200) and **Brighton Borough Transport** (tel. 01273/606–141), serve the area frequently and efficiently. Free maps detailing each company's routes are available at the tourist office (*see above*). Local fares are 60p.

WHERE TO SLEEP

The cheapest places are on the east side of town on Madeira Place, Charlotte Street, and Upper Rock Gardens, a short walk east of the Royal Pavilion. As usual, you should always ask to see your room before paying for it. The tourist office has a free list of approved lodgings. In May, hotels fill up for conventions, and reservations are a fine idea.

Almara Guest Hotel. It's not luxurious, but it is clean, simple, and close to both the water and the center of town. The attentive owner charges £16 for a single, while doubles start at £30, including a full English breakfast. The showers are said to have the best water pressure this side of the Atlantic. *11 Madeira Pl., tel. 01273/603–186. From Palace Pier, walk east along Marine Parade, turn left on Madeira Pl. 9 rooms, none with bath.*

Alvia Hotel. Here you get a full breakfast with your lovely, sunny room. Some of the rooms have dark-wood, four-poster beds, and most have showers. This place is far better than the others nearby, and not more expensive. Singles £18, doubles £32–£40. *36 Upper Rock Gardens, tel. 01273/682–939, fax 01273/607–711. From Palace Pier, walk east on Marine Parade, turn left on Upper Rock Gardens. 12 rooms, 10 with bath. AE, MC, V.*

Chester Court. This small, immaculate hotel is near the seafront and nicer than most of the other hotels on Charlotte Street. Singles cost £18–£20, doubles £38–£40. *7 Charlotte St., tel. 01273/621–750. From Palace Pier, walk east on Marine Parade, turn left on Charlotte St. 11 rooms, 6 with shower. Wheelchair access.*

Queen's Park Guest House. This bright Victorian house is sparsely decorated, but the building itself is beautiful. It's also on a busy road near Queen's Park (ask for a room away from the street). Take a cab from the station (about £4) or Bus 81 from Churchill Square instead of lugging your gear up the hill. All rooms cost £15–£17 per person, including breakfast. *20 Queen's Park Rd., tel. 01273/685–230. 8 rooms, none with bath.*

HOSTELS **Brighton Backpackers Hostel.** This fun, funky, independent hostel is a great place to hang out and meet adventurers from around the world. It's also right next to the Lanes and a half-block from the waterfront. Dorm beds cost £9 per night or £40 per week. Around the corner is their new complex with 12 large rooms, each containing a double bed, bunk bed, and bath. These rooms cost £25 for two people, £33 for three people, and £40 for four people. The reception desk in the hostel handles booking for both complexes. *75–76 Middle St., tel. 01273/777–717. From Brighton station, walk straight down Queen's Rd. to seafront, turn left, then left again on Middle St. 50 beds. Bar, key deposit (£5), kitchen, laundry, luggage storage, sheet rental (£1), TV room.*

Friese Green. Although identical in price (beds £9 per night, £40 per week), quality, and clientele to the Backpackers Hostel just down the road, this house is more spacious. Film fanatics may want to stay here for the sheer fact that it was in this very house that Mr. William Friese Green invented the art of cinematography. The owner also runs overnight excursions around the Isle of Wight in his 40-foot sailboat for about £30. *20 Middle St., tel. 01273/747–551. Follow directions to Brighton Backpackers Hostel (see above). 50 beds. Bar, kitchen, TV room.*

Patcham Place YHA. The local YHA hostel is clean but more than 3 miles from town on London Road. The large open space in front of the building is ideal for picnicking or just hanging out. Beds cost £9.10. *London Rd., Sussex BN1 8YD, tel. 01273/556–196, fax 01273/509–366. From Preston Park rail station, turn left on road at bottom of hill and walk 1½ mi. 84 beds. Curfew 11 PM, lockout 10–1. Key deposit (£1), luggage storage.*

FOOD

Brighton has a host of terrific restaurants and cafés, though stay away from overpriced restaurants near clusters of hotels and B&Bs. Reasonable semi-upscale restaurants can be found along the Lanes, off North Street. Head to North Laine for cheaper cafés and a funkier atmosphere. If you really want to save money, stock up at **Sainsbury's** (1 London Rd.) or **Safeway** (9 St. James's St.), just up the street from the Pavilion. The best traditional cream tea (£2.70) is served in the Lanes at the **Mock Turtle** (4 Pool Valley, no phone).

Food for Friends. This pleasant, whole-foods restaurant right off the Lanes serves up organic and tasty versions of international favorites. The rotating menu features chimichangas, falafel, Chinese stir-fry, and Sussex shepherdess pie, all for £3.35–£3.95. *17A–18 Prince Albert St., tel. 01273/736–236. From the clock tower, walk down North St., turn right on Ship St., veer left on Prince Albert St. Open Mon.–Sat. 8–10:30, Sun. 9–10:30.*

Gardner's Cafe. Amid a bargain-shopper's fantasyland, this tiny North Laine café specializes in "cheese melts"—assorted sautéed vegetables topped with melted cheese in a pita (£3.20). Work by local artists is splattered on the walls, as are flyers advertising various goings-on in Brighton and Hove. *50 Gardner St., tel. 01273/670–743. From clock tower, walk down North St., turn left on Bond St. (which becomes Gardner St.). Open Mon.–Sat. 9–7, Sun. 10–7.*

Piccolo. This is a hungry traveler's dream—the hefty portions of pasta (£5) are fresh and flavorful and the pizzas are cheap (£3–£5). Ask about a student discount at lunch. *56 Ship St., in the Lanes, tel. 01273/203–701. Open daily noon–midnight.*

Shapla Tandoori. The fact that everything on the menu is £2–£3 cheaper if you eat before 10:30 PM is a testament to the mass of late-night clubbers who come here to chow down before some serious bump and grind. The food is good and the portions adequate, although you'll have to ask them to spice it up if you like your Indian genuine. Before 10:30, curries are a deal at £2.40–£4. *120 St. James's St., tel. 01273/677–387. From Churchill Sq., walk west on Western Rd. to St. James's St. Open daily noon–1:30 and 6–midnight.*

WORTH SEEING

Every year, usually from the first weekend of May and throughout the month, Brighton breaks out with a huge festival celebrating every imaginable artistic form, and the whole town buzzes with excitement. At other times of the year the least expensive escape from the beachfront jungle is an afternoon in one of the town's many parks. From downtown, hike uphill to **Queen's Park** or stroll westward into Hove, the town that borders Brighton, through the grassy area along the coastal road, **Kingsway**.

BRIGHTON MUSEUM AND ART GALLERY This free museum is housed in a wing of Brighton's main library. Contained within its various galleries are exhibits of armor, art deco glass, archaeological finds, fashion, and costume. Be sure to listen to the huge ceramic cat at the entrance say "Meow, thank you, meow" when you donate a few quid into it. *Church St., at Marlborough Pl., tel. 01273/713–287. Around cnr from Pavilion. Admission free. Open Mon.–Tues. and Thurs.–Sat. 10–5:30, Sun. 2–5.*

THE LANES This narrow maze of lanes, or "twittens," was originally the quarter where the local fishermen lived. The houses were eventually masked with Georgian and Victorian facades, transforming the Lanes into *the* shopping area for the well heeled. Today, a healthy wallet is still useful to bring along on your visit as the Lanes are cluttered with jewelry, antiques, and collectibles shops. Even if you're not in a buying mood, take a walk down claustrophobia-inducing Meeting House Lane. **North Laine** can't compare in quaintness or age but draws the young and hip with a multitude of friendly cafés and trendy stores selling records, art, and clothing. Both the Lanes and North Laine are best accessed from North Street.

PALACE AND WEST PIERS The **West Pier,** once a marvel of high Victorian architecture, is closed due to storm damage: There's a 200-foot gap in the pier's approach. **Palace Pier,** with the requisite amusement rides, arcade, and slot machines, was featured in a number of films, notably *Mona Lisa* and *Quadrophenia.* At night the pier sparkles like an airport runway and a seedier crowd emerges, but it's still reasonably safe. *Old Steine, at Grand Junction Rd., tel. 01273/609–361. From station, head south on Queen's Rd. (which becomes West St.), turn left at the ocean. Open daily 9 AM–midnight.*

PRESTON MANOR This Edwardian manor is the former home of the Prestons, once Brighton's leading aristocratic family, who had fabulous taste (despite a weakness for dog portraits). Check out the Flemish leather wallpaper in the small salon behind the living room, and definitely have a look at the kitchen, the oldest part of the house. Also look out for evidence of the upstairs-downstairs relationship between the masters of the house and their servants. *Preston Dr., off Preston Rd., tel. 01273/713–239. From Marlborough Pl. (behind the Pavilion), take Bus 5 or 5A to Preston Manor. Admission: £2.85, £2.35 students. Open Mon. 1–5, Tues.–Sat. 10–5, Sun. 2–5.*

ROYAL PAVILION In 1786 the Prince Regent (later King George IV) commissioned architect Henry Holland to build a simple seaside villa for his mistress, Mrs. Fitzherbert (whom he was later forbidden to see by his mother). Shortly afterward another architect, John Nash, was given license to rebuild the villa into something a bit more grandiose. By the time Nash was through with it in 1822, Brighton found itself with a palace that looked less like a royal retreat and more like the Taj Mahal—note the extravagant Indian architecture and Chinese interior decor. For a real dose of decadence, check out the **Banqueting Room** with its 1-ton bronze dragon and glass orb chandelier, or the ornately furnished **Music Room.** All this and more was completed at no small expense—the royal family nearly went bankrupt over construction costs. During the summer, deck chairs are spread out on the lawn for musical performances. *Cnr North St. and Old Steine, tel. 01273/603–005. From station, walk down Queen's Rd., turn left on Church St., and look for the domes. Admission: £4, £3 students. Open June–Sept., daily 10–6; Oct.–May, daily 10–5.*

ST. BARTHOLOMEW'S CHURCH Supposedly built to the exact dimensions of Noah's Ark (upside down?) as described in the Bible, St. Bart's was initially laughed at for being too tall and lacking certain churchly attributes like aisles or chancels. It was called a "barn," a "cheese warehouse," and a "monster excrescence," but its height and kaleidoscopic rose window are what make a visit here an experience. *Ann St., tel. 01273/620–941. From Brighton Station, take underpass down Trafalgar St., turn left on York Pl. (which becomes London Rd.), left on Ann St. Admission free. Open Tues.–Sun. 11:30–3:30.*

AFTER DARK

The backbone of Brighton's famed nightlife is, unquestionably, the clubs; even Londoners come to Brighton for the experience. What the clubs lack in inventiveness is made up for by good DJs spinning some of the latest tunes and throbbing crowds of people of all sexual orientations out for a good time. For the best information on Brighton's nocturnal diversions, peruse the posters and flyers in the windows of stores in North Laine, or pick up *BASH Listings* (50p) or *Punter* (70p) at newsstands. Expect to pay £5–£6 to get into the larger, trendier clubs. Smaller clubs charge £3–£4 and some give discounts to students.

PUBS **Smuggler's Pub** (Ship St., tel. 01273/775–030) is a popular student pub with an upstairs dance club (The Reform) and a downstairs jazz club (The Jazz Place). **Leek and Win-**

kle (39 Ditchling Rd., tel. 01273/698–276) plays good music and has a beer garden that's popular with students. **Squid and Starfish** (78 Middle St., tel. 01273/727–114) is a hip pre-club watering hole across from Casablanca (*see below*).

CLUBS Beachfront **Zap** (King's Rd. Arches, tel. 01273/821–588) and the **Event** (West St., tel. 01273/732–627) are Brighton's largest and most mainstream clubs and draw kids from all over Britain with the latest dance music and most expensive speakers. **Revenge** (32–34 Old Steine, tel. 01273/606–064) is the best gay club, while the **Lift** (Queen's Rd., tel. 01273/776–961) hosts a lesbian night regularly. The **Royal Escape** (10 Marine Parade, tel. 01273/606–906) is in a cool building with an outdoor terrace and draws a trendy university crowd. **Casablanca** (Middle St., tel. 01273/321–817) is a velvety subterranean den featuring live acid jazz and Latin funk. The **Beachcomber** (Kings Rd. Arches, tel. 01273/202–807) draws a funkier crowd for its weekly "Soul Kitchen."

Bath

Bath's history has been shaped by its hot springs, which pour out of the earth at a steady 116°F. In the 1st century AD, the Romans dedicated the township to the goddess Sul Minerva, named it Aquae Sulis (Waters of Sul), and constructed an intricate series of baths and pools around the hot springs. Centuries later, Bath became synonymous with elegance, engendering a social scene second only to London's. The Royals have always shown a preference for the town: Queen Elizabeth I brought a certain prestige to the baths with her visit in 1574, while Queen Anne's visits to the waters in 1702 and 1703 established the "Bath season." In subsequent years, architect John Wood (1704–1754) gave Bath its distinctive, harmonious look; using the yellowish "Bath stone" cut from nearby quarries, he created a city of crescents, terraces, and Palladian mansions that curve through the city like scalloped paper cutouts.

Jane Austen's novel 'Persuasion,' much of which is set in Bath, is useful for an insight into the town's history and high-society past.

Sadly, you can no longer bathe in the springs, although you can drink the horrible-tasting water if you so desire. The museums, parks, and architecture make a visit worthwhile. Bath is on every tourist's itinerary, from little old ladies to mangy backpackers. Remember that lodging is expensive and you'll hear lots of American accents.

BASICS

The very efficient **Tourist Information Centre** (Abbey Chambers, 11 Bath St., tel. 01225/462–831), open Monday–Saturday 9:30–5 (June–September until 7), gets miserably crowded in summer. Come early to book a room (£2.50 fee), as the bargains go fast. **American Express** (5 Bridge St., tel. 01225/444–747) offers regular cardholder services and cashes all brands of traveler's checks free of charge (for cash transactions there's a £2 commission). **Lockers** are available for £1–£3 on Platform 1 of the station, which closes in the wee hours but reopens about 5 or 6 AM—just in time to retrieve your things and catch an early train. Lockers outside the bus station are accessible 24 hours. The main **post office** (New Bond St., BA1 1AA, tel. 01225/445–358) is open Saturday until 1 PM in addition to its standard weekday hours.

COMING AND GOING

Great Western (tel. 0117/929–4255) makes the 75-minute trip from London's Paddington Station to **Bath Spa Station** for £17.50–£35 return. **National Express** sends nine coaches daily to and from London for £18 return. Buy National Express tickets at Bath's **bus station** (Manvers St., across from train station, tel. 01225/464–446). Two other bus companies offer cheaper service to and from London's Marble Arch to Bath. **Turner's** (0117/955–5333) runs one bus per day (with additional service on Friday and Sunday) for £6.50 single, £12.50 return, as does **Bakers Dolphin** (tel. 01934/616–000) for £8.45 single, £14 return. Tickets for both can be purchased by phone with a credit card at least a day in advance or from the driver.

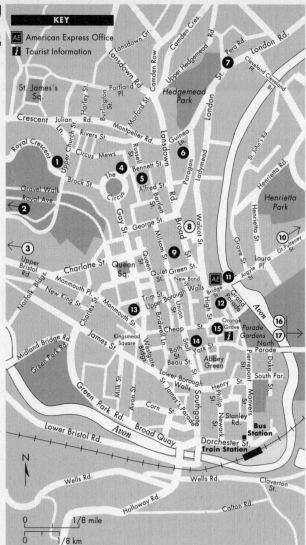

KEY

AE American Express Office

i Tourist Information

Sights ●

Bath Abbey, **15**

Building of Bath Museum, **6**

Museum of Costume, **5**

Museum of East Asian Art, **4**

Pulteny Bridge, **11**

Roman Baths and Pump Room, **14**

Royal Crescent (No. 1), **1**

Royal Photographic Society Gallery, **9**

Royal Victoria Park, **2**

Theatre Royal, **13**

Victoria Art Gallery, **12**

Lodging ○

Bathurst Guest House, **7**

Bathwick Hill YHA, **10**

The Limes, **16**

Membland and The Garden, **17**

Woodville House, **3**

YMCA, **8**

The bus station, which is within striking distance of all Bath's attractions, also dispatches **Badgerline** buses to neighboring towns. If you plan to make day trips from Bath, purchase a **Day Rambler** pass (£4.60) good for unlimited travel on regional Badgerline buses. The blocks surrounding the depot contain bus stops for local routes that fan throughout the city and into the suburbs. Call the **Avon County Council Traveline** (tel. 0117/557–013) for a comprehensive listing of local bus times throughout the county.

WHERE TO SLEEP

Seek bargains in Bath and ye shall find them so long as you don't mind a short bridge-crossing into town. Reasonably priced B&Bs are clustered along Pulteney Road in the east and along Charlotte Street and Upper Bristol Road in the west. The tourist office has a bulky accommodations brochure, but the hostel's list of cheap B&Bs is better. In summer it's wise to book at least two weeks in advance.

Bathurst Guest House. This typical Georgian house is an easy seven-minute walk north of the city center. All rooms are nonsmoking and tastefully decorated—one double even has a four-poster bed. Rooms cost £17–£20 per person depending on the season. *11 Walcot Parade, tel. 01225/421-884. From stations, walk to Bath Abbey, then ½ mi up High St. (which becomes Walcot/London Sts.), turn left on Walcot Parade. 6 rooms, 2 with bath.*

The Garden and Membland. Peter and Katey Moore, the young proprietors, make you feel like family in either of their two guest houses. Rooms are £17.50–£19 per head, though you can negotiate a 10% discount for longer stays. If you arrive in the evening, they may pick you up at the train station. Check in at the Garden; they'll direct you to Membland. *7 Pulteney Gardens, tel. 01225/337-642. From stations, walk up Manvers St., turn right on North Parade, cross bridge, turn right on Pulteney Rd. 9 rooms, all with shower.*

The Limes. Mrs. Ellis only lets out two rooms because her kids and grandkids often come to stay. The guest rooms are large and decorated with white chenille bedspreads and some fine antiques. Pulteney Road is busy, but street noise is not a problem. Rooms cost £13 per person. *1 Pulteney Rd., tel. 01225/311-044. Follow directions to the Garden (see above). 2 rooms, none with bath.*

Woodville House. Tom and Anne Toalster's classic Bath house, right next to Victoria Park and the Royal Crescent, is the best deal around. Laze around in sunny rooms with views and comfy beds. Rooms cost £14 per head (£20 if you're alone, though they don't take in solo travelers during summer). *4 Marlborough Ln., tel. 01225/319-335. From stations, walk to Bath Abbey, turn left on Cheap St., right on Monmouth St. (which becomes Upper Bristol Rd.), right on Marlborough Ln. 3 rooms, none with bath. TV lounge.*

HOSTELS **Bathwick Hill YHA.** This Italianate building has a mellow atmosphere, and the staff has lots of info on what's going on in Bath. The hostel is open year-round, and reservations are essential in summer. Beds are £8.25 (£5.55 under 18). You'll definitely want to take a bus up the steep hill. *Bathwick Hill, Avon BA2 6JZ, tel. 01225/465-674, fax 01225/482-947. From stations, take Badgerline Bus 18 (50p single) directly to hostel. 121 beds. Reception open 7:15 AM–11 PM. Kitchen, laundry.*

YMCA. It's closer to the center of town than the YHA hostel, but the atmosphere is less lively. It's clean but pretty spartan. A dorm bed costs £10, singles £12.50, doubles £23, all with breakfast. *Broad Street Pl., tel. 01225/460-471. From stations, walk up Manvers St. to Bath Abbey, walk north on High St., turn left on Broad St. (look for YMCA sign leading down alley to right). 86 rooms, 40 dorm beds. Key deposit (£5), laundry. Closed Christmas–early Jan.*

CAMPING **Newton Mill Touring Centre.** This is the closest campground, 3 miles west of Bath. Sites cost £3.70 per person or £10 for two persons, tent, and car (a bit less in winter). *Newton St., Loe, tel. 01225/333-909. From the bus station, take Bus 5 to Twerton (ask driver), then walk through playground and down footpath. Bar, laundry, restaurant, showers.*

FOOD

You'll find plenty of burger stands and other cheap restaurants around the Theatre Royal, Sawclose, and Kingsmead Square. If you'd rather create your own gustatory masterpiece, there's a **Waitrose** supermarket in the Podium shopping center on High Street and a cheaper **Somerfield** market in the Southgate Shopping Centre behind the bus station. Enhance your meal with some fresh produce, meat, cheese, and pastries from the **Guildhall Market** on High Street.

Café Retro. The decor in this mellow and mirrored café-restaurant tends toward art nouveau but is pared down by simple tables and old wooden chairs. The food is good and reasonably priced with main courses like "Smokie Fish Pie" and asparagus-and-smoked-ham crepes for £4.30–£4.50. *18 York St., near tourist office, tel. 01225/339-347. Open Mon.–Sat. 10–6 and 6:30–10, Sun. 10–6.*

The Canary Restaurant. Crook your pinkie here amid the strains of 18th-century chamber music. Winner of several recent Tea Council Awards, the Canary sits on a quiet street lined with flowers. Eggs Benedic—their spelling—costs £3.50, pasta and vegetarian dishes £5.25–£5.75, Somerset or Irish rabbit (each made from an 18th-century recipe) £4. *3 Queen St., near Upper Borough Walls, tel. 01225/424–846. Open Mon. 8:30–7, Tues.–Sat. 8:30–10, Sun. 11–7.*

The Crystal Palace. This "very English" pub is a fine place to enjoy a wide range of sandwiches (£2.45–£2.65), especially in its garden patio on a sunny day. Other dishes include an open-face prawn sandwich (£4) and three kinds of ploughman's lunches (£3.75–£4.30). *Abbey Green, tel. 01225/423–944. From entrance to Roman Baths, turn left and walk less than a min. Open Mon.–Sat. 11–11, Sun. 11–10:30.*

You can probably live quite happily without ever sampling the famous "Bath bun," a teatime treat that's degenerated into a tourist attraction. If you do feel compelled to try one, Scoffs (20 Kingsmead Sq.) sells them for £1 in an unpretentious atmosphere.

Fodder's. Gourmet sandwiches are the specialty at this small take-away in the city center. Choose from prawns in garlic or mayo (£2.50), pâté de campagne (£2.10), vegetarian fillings, deli meats, and condiments like garlic-olive pâté. *9 Cheap St., near High St., tel. 01225/462–165. Open Mon.–Sat. 9:30–4 (also Jun.–Aug., Sun. noon–3:30).*

Tilley's Bistro. With the land of haute cuisine just across a narrow body of water, it's troubling that good French restaurants like Tilley's haven't infiltrated the English food scene. For £5–£7 you can order entrées such as sliced pork tenderloins in a Dijon-mustard cream sauce, as well as vegetarian and vegan dishes. For lunch try a set two- or three-course meal for £5.50 or £6.60, respectively. *3 North Parade Passage, btw Abbey Green and North Parade Bridge, tel. 01225/484–200. Open Mon.–Sat. noon–3 and 6:30–11, Sun. 6:30–11.*

WORTH SEEING

Bath's city center is easily navigable by foot, and a free, comprehensive walking tour is a great way to learn about the city's highlights. Tours leave daily from the Roman Baths entrance (*see below*) in the Abbey Churchyard at 10:30 AM and 2:30 PM; confirm times at the tourist office.

The Square, the Circle, and the Crescent

Bath wouldn't be Bath without its distinctive 18th-century Georgian architecture, most of which was conceived by John Wood the Elder, an architect obsessed. Wood saw Bath as a mythical city destined for greatness along the lines of Winchester and Glastonbury. He nurtured the myth that Bath was founded by Prince Bladud (ostensibly with the help of an errant pig rooting in the ground for acorns; Wood later used stone acorns as a motif). Wood sought an architectural style that would do justice to his great concept and found it in the Palladian style, made popular in Britain by Inigo Jones.

Influenced by nearby ancient stone circles as well as round Roman temples, Wood broke loose from convention in his design for Bath's outstanding Circus, a full circle of houses broken only three times for intersecting streets. After the death of Wood the Elder, John Wood the Younger carried out his father's plans for the Royal Crescent, an obtuse crescent of 30 interconnected houses overlooking Victoria Park—the first row houses in Britain. Stop in at No. 1 Royal Crescent for a look at one of these Georgian homes decked out in period style. Tel. 01225/428–126. Admission: £3.50, £2.50 students. Open Mar.–Dec. 11, Tues.–Sun. 10:30–4.

BATH ABBEY In one form or another, Bath Abbey has been around for 1,200 years; what started as a Norman church eventually evolved into this 15th-century Gothic construction. Stained-glass windows at the eastern end portray Christ's biography, though the abbey is better known for its spindly, fan-vaulted ceiling—don't forget to look up. If you don't mind the £2 admission (£1 students), explore the subterranean **Heritage Vaults,** open Monday–Saturday 10–4, and see some slightly cheesy exhibits on the abbey's history. In summer also check for flyers advertising organ recitals in the abbey. *High St., tel. 01225/422–462. Admission free. Open Mon.–Sat. 9–6 (in winter until 4:30), Sun. 1–2:30 and 4:30–5:30.*

BUILDING OF BATH MUSEUM If "Norm" makes you think of *This Old House* instead of *Cheers,* you'll dig the architectural displays at the Building of Bath Museum. If not, the small print and paucity of big pictures make it a bit of a struggle. Check out the huge model of Bath. *The Countess of Huntingdon's Chapel, The Paragon, off Broad St., tel. 01225/333–895. Admission: £3, £1.50 students. Open Mar.–mid-Nov., Tues.–Sun. 10:30–5.*

MUSEUM OF EAST ASIAN ART Cultivated Bath makes the perfect setting for this amazing museum, which showcases a private collection of East Asian art spanning over 7,000 years, from 5,000 BC to the 20th century. Since the museum is small, only one-third of the over 1,500 pieces of jade, gold, silver, wood, bronze, ceramics, and silk (many of which are very rare) that compose the entire collection can be displayed. The emphasis is on Chinese art, but works from Southeast Asia, Tibet, Japan, and Korea are also exhibited. *12 Bennet St., off The Circus, tel. 01223/464–640. Admission: £3, £2 students. Open Mon.–Sat. 10–6 (Nov.–Mar. until 5), Sun. 10–5 (Nov.–Mar. from noon).*

ROMAN BATHS AND MUSEUM OF COSTUME The Romans built their luxurious baths here between the 1st and 5th centuries AD, at a site where springs already bubbled from the earth. The bath network is well preserved, and the smell of sulfur, the looming Roman statuary, and the murky green pools make it easy to imagine what it was like being a Roman bather. You can't swim here, but you can sample some vile-tasting mineral water at the overpriced **Pump Room** above the Roman Baths. Be forewarned: This is one of the most popular attractions in England, and the large crowds can be a bit of a turn-off. If you have some extra time, buy a combined admission ticket and visit the **Museum of Costume** (Bennett St., tel. 01225/ 477–000), one of the most prestigious and extensive collections of historical costumes in Britain, which covers more than 400 years of fashion. It's housed in the Assembly Rooms, a series of elegant chambers built in 1771. *Abbey Churchyard, tel. 01225/477–000. Admission: £5.60. Combined ticket with Museum of Costume: £7.50. Open daily 9–6 (Aug., also 8 PM–10 PM).*

ROYAL PHOTOGRAPHIC SOCIETY GALLERY This is one of the largest independent galleries devoted entirely to photography and home to the oldest photographic society in the world. The constantly rotating exhibits feature works by up-and-coming and renowned photographers as well as stock from the society's massive collection of everything from heliogravures to holograms. The society is particularly well endowed in its collection of 19th-century photographs from around the world—call it a perk of colonialism. *Octagon Galleries, Milsom St., tel. 01225/462–841. Admission £2.50, £1.75 students. Open daily 9:30–5:30.*

CHEAP THRILLS

If Bath's pricey atmosphere has you feeling penniless, enrich yourself with some very fine art at the free **Victoria Art Gallery** (Bridge St., tel. 01225/464–111, ext. 2772). The gallery has a permanent collection of over 6,500 drawings, prints, and paintings from traditional masters to modern artists. Downstairs the gallery hosts temporary exhibits ranging from Picasso and Dalí to Sir Matthew Smith, a little-known but highly emotive artist, often dubbed the most "French" of all British painters. If the sun is shining, take a walk through the large open spaces of **Royal Victoria Park,** south of Royal Crescent. In the east of the park, the beautiful botanical gardens house a vast array of flowers, trees, and plants from around the world, some of which were planted in the early 19th century. In the summer, free concerts are performed throughout the park; for more information check at the tourist office.

AFTER DARK

Bath's nightlife is lively, if somewhat yup-scale, which explains the £2–£6 cover many pubs charge for live music; for serious out-of-your-head clubbing you may want to catch the next train to Bristol.

PUBS AND CLUBS A handful of pubs and clubs have a more relaxed and down-to-earth feel, making them favorites of Bath University students. The **Bell** (103 Walcot St., tel. 01225/460-426) is the most casual and progressive pub in town. It also has an Internet café and back patio. The **Hub** (The Paragon, up from Broad St., tel. 01225/446–288) and the **Loft** (off Queen Sq., next to Theatre Royal, tel. 01225/466–467) are cool and casual places to hear live bands. The **Garrick's Head** (St. John's Sq., next to Theatre Royal, tel. 01225/448–819), which almost never charges cover, has two bars: The Green Room (it's painted red) is Bath's gay bar, and the Nash Room next door is not. **Moles** (14 George St., tel. 01225/333–448) is an exclusive, pricey, private club that attracts good bands; either phone in advance to get on the guest list or chat up members in line so they'll let you in on their cards. For something sweaty, unglamorous, and raging, head to the **Swamp** (8–9 North Parade, tel. 01225/420–330) and let it all hang out.

THEATER For highbrow theatrics, catch a show (or two) at the old and illustrious **Theatre Royal** (Sawclose, tel. 01225/448–844), which has comedy and plays starring renowned British actors like Derek Jacobi, Simon Callow, and Pauline Collins. Tickets range from £7 to £20 and the box office is open Monday–Saturday 10–8; standby tickets (£4.50) are available at 10 AM on the day of the performance.

OUTDOOR ACTIVITIES

Though Bath feels like a mini-metropolis, its surrounding area is green and lined with paths for walking and biking. Ask at the tourist office for pamphlets about the 80-mile **Avon Cycleway,** which takes you through a string of rural villages, or the **Bristol and Bath Railway Path,** a 12-mile route along an old railway line with great views and scenery. Bikes can be rented at the **Avon Valley Cyclery** (Arch 37, rear of train station, tel. 01225/461–880) for £8.50 per day, £40 per week; mountain bikes are an expensive £17.50 a day, £84.50 a week. If you want to use your own two feet, pick up a copy of the pamphlet "Country Walks Within 5 Miles of Bath Abbey" from either the tourist office or the youth hostel to get *detailed* descriptions of the best local strolls. A great, easy day hike is to follow the River Avon north from Cleveland Bridge and watch as the line between culture and countryside becomes progressively fuzzier. Rowboats and punts on the River Avon cost £5 per person and can be rented at the **Bath Boating Station** (Forrester Rd., tel. 01225/466–407); pick up a voucher at the tourist office for a £1.50 discount.

Index

Notes

TELL US WHAT YOU THINK

We're always trying to improve our books and would really appreciate any feedback on how to make them more useful. Thanks for taking a few minutes to fill out this survey. We'd also like to know about your latest find, a new scam, a budget deal, whatever . . . Please print your name and address clearly and send the completed survey to: The Berkeley Guides, 515 Eshelman Hall, U.C. Berkeley, CA 94720.

1. Your name _____

2. Your address _____

_____ Zip _____

3. You are: Female   Male

4. Your age: under 17   17–22   23–30   31–40   41–55   over 55

5. If you're a student: Name of school _____ City & state _____

6. If you're employed: Occupation _____

7. Your yearly income: under $20,000 $21,000–$30,000 $31,000–$45,000
$46,000–$60,000 $61,000–$100,000   over $100,000

8. Which of the following do you own? (Circle all that apply.)

Computer   CD-ROM Drive   Modem

9. What speed (bps) is your modem?

2400   4800   9600   14.4   19.2   28.8

10. Which on-line service(s) do you subscribe to apart from commercial services like AOL?

_____

11. Do you have access to the World Wide Web? If so, is it through a university or a private service provider? _____

12. If you have a CD-ROM drive or plan to have one, would you purchase a Berkeley Guide CD-ROM? _____

13. Which Berkeley Guide(s) did you buy? _____

14. Where did you buy the book and when?   City _____ Month/Year _____

15. Why did you choose The Berkeley Guides? (Circle all that apply.)

Budget focus	Design
Outdoor emphasis	Attitude
Off-the-beaten-track emphasis	Writing style
Resources for gays and lesbians	Organization
Resources for people with disabilities	More maps
Resources for women	Accuracy
	Price

Other _____

16. How did you hear about The Berkeley Guides? (Circle all that apply.)

Recommended by friend/acquaintance   Bookstore display   TV

Article in magazine/newspaper (which one?) _____

Ad in magazine/newspaper (which one?) _____

Radio program (which one?) _____

Other _____

17. Which other guides, if any, have you used before? (Circle all that apply.)

Fodor's   Let's Go   Rough Guides

Frommer's   Birnbaum   Lonely Planet

Other _____

18. When did you travel with this book?   Month/Year _____

19. Where did you travel? _____

20. What was the purpose of your trip?

Vacation   Business   Volunteer

Study abroad   Work

21. About how much did you spend per day during your trip?

$0–$20 $31–$45 $61–$75   over $100

$21–$30 $46–$60 $76–$100

22. After you arrived, how did you get around? (Circle all that apply.)

Rental car   Personal car   Plane   Bus

Train   Hiking   Bike   Hitching

23. Which features/sections did you use most? (Circle all that apply.)

Book Basics   City/region Basics   Coming and Going

Hitching   Getting Around   Where to Sleep

Camping   Roughing It   Food

Worth Seeing   Cheap Thrills   Festivals

Shopping   After Dark   Outdoor Activities

24. The information was (circle one):   V = very accurate   U = usually accurate

     S = sometimes accurate   R = rarely accurate

Introductions	V U S R	Worth Seeing	V U S R
Basics	V U S R	After Dark	V U S R
Coming and Going	V U S R	Outdoor Activities	V U S R
Where to Sleep	V U S R	Maps	V U S R
Food	V U S R		

25. I would _____ would not _____ buy another Berkeley Guide.

26. Which of the following destinations are you planning to visit in the next five years?

The Americas
Chicago
Washington, D.C.
New Orleans
Los Angeles
Boston
Austin
The Midwest
The South
The Southwest
New England
The Pacific Northwest
Hawaii
Canada
South America

Europe
Spain
Portugal
Greece
Russia
Scandinavia
Berlin
Prague
Rome

Australia/Asia
Australia
New Zealand
Vietnam
Philippines
Indonesia
Thailand
Singapore
Malaysia
Cambodia
India/Nepal

Middle East/Africa
Turkey
Israel
Egypt
Africa